The Gift of Story

The Gift of Story

Narrating Hope
in a Postmodern World

Edited by

Emily Griesinger
Mark Eaton

Baylor University Press
Waco, Texas

Cover Design: Cynthia Dunne, Blue Farm Graphics

The editors wish to thank the publishers for permission to reprint or adapt material from the following publications: Mark Eaton, "Inventing Hope: The Question of Belief in White Noise and Mao II," *Approaches to Teaching Don DeLillo's "White Noise,"* eds. John N. Duvall and Tim Engles (New York: MLA, 2006); Susan Gallagher, *Truth and Reconciliation: The Confessional Mode in South African Literature* (Portsmouth, NH: Heinemann, 2002); Emily Griesinger, "Harry Potter and the 'Deeper Magic': Narrating Hope in Children's Literature," *Christianity and Literature* 51iii (Spring 2002): 455–80, and "Why Read Harry Potter?: J. K. Rowling and the Christian Debate," *Christian Scholar's Review* 32iii (Spring 2003): 297–316; Robert K. Johnston, *Useless Beauty: Ecclesiastes Through the Lens of Contemporary Film* (Grand Rapids: Baker, 2004); and Carole Lambert, *Is God Man's Friend? Theodicy and Friendship in Elie Wiesel's Novels* (New York: Peter Lang, 2005).

Library of Congress Cataloging-in-Publication Data

The gift of story : narrating hope in a postmodern world / edited by Emily Griesinger, Mark A. Eaton.
      p. cm.
   Includes bibliographical references and index.
   ISBN 1-932792-47-3 (pbk. : alk. paper)
   1. Literature, Modern--20th century--History and criticism. 2. Religion and literature. 3. Performing arts--Religious aspects. I. Griesinger, Emily, 1954-
II. Eaton, Mark A., 1965-

PN771.G54 2006
809'.933820904--dc22

                              2005035024

Contents

Acknowledgments

The editors wish to thank our colleagues in the Department of English at Azusa Pacific University (APU) for all their help putting on the Western Regional Conference on Christianity and Literature in 2002 and for their encouragement in seeing this project through to completion. In particular, we want to thank our chair, Jim Hedges, for his support from first to last. Best wishes, too, on his retirement. Thanks also to David Weeks, Dean of the College of Liberal Arts and Sciences at APU, for his support of both the conference and the book, and to Susan Ney, Interim Dean of the College of Liberal Arts and Sciences at APU, for help with printing costs. We are grateful to APU reference librarians Liz Leahy, Doane Wylie, Tom Jacobs, and members of the Haggard School of Theology faculty, especially Jacquelyn Winston, who helped us locate several citations as we completed the manuscript. We would be remiss if we did not also acknowledge the essential contribution and support of Carey Newman, whose vision for this project helped us strengthen it considerably. Finally, we could not have persevered without the loving support of our families. Emily thanks her husband, Don Griesinger, Professor Emeritus at Claremont Graduate University, for reading the manuscript and making excellent editorial suggestions and for his constant encouragement from start to finish. Mark thanks his wife, Victoria, and two sons, Andrew and Elliot, just for being there every step of the way.

Preface

The idea for this book began after the Western Regional Conference on Christianity and Literature hosted by Azusa Pacific University in March 2002. As co-chairs for this conference, we posed the theme which is echoed in the title of this book, "The Gift of Story: Narrating Hope in a Postmodern World." Our conference had been announced in the summer of 2001. If anything, the events of September 11 confirmed the relevance of our theme. What role, if any, might film and literature play in awakening and sustaining hope in the midst of such tragedy and loss? The conference, which drew over one hundred participants from across the United States, stimulated lively discussion among scholars and creative artists in literature and film and prompted our decision to publish a collection of original essays, solicited specifically for this volume, which would continue this important conversation.

The issue is perhaps best summarized by Andrew Delbanco, who argues in his book *The Real American Dream: A Meditation on Hope* that people today have lost confidence in any transcendent vision of the future, any common project or dream, whether it be commitment to Christianity, with its communal ethic of loving one's neighbor, or commitment to citizenship in a "sacred" republic. Postmodern rejection of transcendent vision as well as the suspicion of metanarratives have enormous implications for hope, or its opposite, despair. "[H]uman beings need to organize the inchoate sensations amid which we pass our days—pain, desire, pleasure, fear—into a story," Delbanco observes. "When that story leads somewhere and helps us navigate through life to its inevitable terminus in death, it gives us hope" (1). Metanarratives are navigational stories that lead somewhere. They ground human experience in some larger framework, some idea or purpose that makes sense of our lives. Without metanarratives or grand stories, we lose hope for understanding the past, making sense of the present, and imagining and working towards a better future.

The problem with metanarratives, critics insist, is their potential for exploiting, suppressing, or even erasing groups of people, races, or cultures who do not want to "navigate" in the direction of those telling the story, groups who will not be "led" to this somewhere but fight for the right to go elsewhere. Should we abandon metanarratives because they have the potential for "totalizing violence," as Jean-François Lyotard urges, or is it possible to rethink their content and develop critical guidelines for their use? Postmodern suspicion of metanarratives, if taken seriously, poses an undeniable challenge to Christianity, as addressed in the introduction. The essayists in this volume agree with Delbanco that human beings fundamentally need framing narratives, if for no other reason than because we desire answers to fundamental questions: Who am I? Why am I here? Given life's difficulties—evil, suffering, death—how shall I respond, act, live? Should I be joyful or sad, happy or resigned, hopeful or despairing?

In their analysis of the Ridley Scott science-fiction film *Blade Runner*, J. Richard Middleton and Brian J. Walsh call attention to our desperate need to inhabit a meaningful story while fewer and fewer stories merit our trust. "Not only can no story or tradition be regarded as absolute, but postmodern people have come to experience themselves more and more as storyless" (77–78). One of the distinctions between humans and the "replicants" pursued by the "blade runner" is that replicants are constructed. They have no story, and they do not like it. Without a grand story that answers basic questions—Where did I come from? Where am I going? Why should I be good?—humans suffer unbearable anomie like the replicants in the movie, with the same potential for violence and brutality. While calling into question the truth claims of all grand narratives, the postmodern metanarrative, according to these authors, "does not itself have the resources to enable us to live with integrity and hope in a postmodern world" (78).

Middleton and Walsh are not alone in their assessment. A brief sampling of scholarly books published since 1990 suggests increasing concern from all quarters that, despite economic prosperity and advances in technology and medicine, and notwithstanding the spread of liberal democracy across the globe, we have somehow lost our way. Along with Delbanco's *The Real American Dream*, three recent books come to mind:

Richard Rorty's *Philosophy and Social Hope* (1999), Richard Dawkins's *A Devil's Chaplain: Reflections on Hope, Lies, Science, and Love* (2003), and Tzvetán Todorov's *Hope and Memory: Lessons from the Twentieth Century* (2003). Works from a Christian perspective published during this period include Josef Pieper's *Faith, Hope, Love* (1997), David Bruce Hegeman's *Plowing in Hope: Toward a Biblical Theology of Culture* (1999), Glenn Tinder's *The Fabric of Hope: An Essay* (2001), John Polkinghorne's *The God of Hope and the End of the World* (2002), and most recently, Mirâslôv Volf and William Katerberg's edited collection, *The Future of Hope: Christian Tradition amid Modernity and Postmodernity* (2004). Most significant from a Christian standpoint is the work of the German theologian Jürgen Moltmann, whose *Theology of Hope: On the Grounds and the Implications of a Christian Eschatology* (1967) refocuses the eschatological content of the biblical narrative from end-time catastrophe to a culturally engaged theology of hope, thus opening the way for Christian scholars to analyze and critique the expression of hope in postmodern culture, drama, art, music, film, and literature.

Along with many creative writers, filmmakers, and literary critics, we fear that "incredulity towards metanarratives"—Lyotard's famous phrase—means not just the rejection of any larger story but the rejection or impoverishment of all stories. Situated within a Christian framework, the essayists in this volume view story itself, which encompasses all narrative arts, both literary and cinematic, as a creative gift from God that can enrich and inform life and infuse readers with God's own sense of creativity and purpose. Our aim is not so much to theorize about hope, narrativity or story, but to read some of the stories that have emerged against the background of postmodernism, assessing the degree to which these stories do and do not narrate hope. The introduction provides a framework for what follows by tracing the loss of confidence in any larger story and the ensuing loss of hope from the Enlightenment through the disillusionment and betrayals of the twentieth century— two world wars, the Holocaust, Vietnam—and now global terrorism. Of particular importance in this chapter is the articulation of a Christian theology of hope and suggestions for ways Christians might employ such a theology to read and critique contemporary literature and film. While individual essays may be read on their own apart from the introduction, this opening essay also addresses some of the challenges Christian scholars face when attempting to bear witness to the claims of their faith in a secular postmodern culture.

Christians believe that their lives are part of a profoundly hopeful story of God's engagement with his beloved creation, a story where even grief and pain will find redemptive purpose and meaning. Many of the novels and films critiqued here do not see life in this way but reflect the postmodern ethos of despair. Certainly, nonbelievers, doubters, and seekers experience hope just as confirmed believers experience doubt, suffering, and sadness. Readers can expect darkness as well as light. The degree to which each text narrates hope is the connecting thread. Views of the future that end in cosmic collapse, which is the position of some modern physicists, along with continuing concerns about global pollution, poverty, and now global terrorism, all point to the fragility and/or futility of life on this planet. Despair not hope would seem to be the only appropriate response. By contrast, the essayists in this volume read postmodern culture more hopefully, in light of God's creative and redemptive purposes. The "kingdom of God" is revealed in ways large and small, even in the tiniest mustard seed, a brief glimmer of trust, forgiveness, hope, or love. Christians engaging postmodern culture must have "eyes to see" and "ears to hear" the kingdom however it comes, whether in a novel that tells the truth about the human condition apart from God or a film that discerns the coming of God, however disguised, into the ordinary circumstances of life. We invite you—poets, novelists, filmmakers, literary critics, scholars, and people of faith, Christian and non-Christian—to enjoy and celebrate the gift of story. Whether you wholly agree with the views expressed here or not, we challenge you through these essays to think more deeply about the necessity and possibility of narrating hope in a culture of increasing cynicism, pessimism, and despair.

Emily Griesinger
Mark Eaton
Azusa Pacific University

Introduction

Narrating Hope in a Postmodern World

Emily Griesinger

The contemporary movement of postmodernism is well known for its rejection of grand narratives. That rejection was first proclaimed in the late 1970s by Jean-François Lyotard in *The Postmodern Condition* and has gained widespread acceptance among philosophers and cultural critics, who generally see the loss as positive. Grand narratives say too much, it is argued, and say it too conclusively. Far too often the result is oppression, fanaticism, and tyranny. And yet, as Andrew Delbanco points out in his book *The Real American Dream*, "[T]he sapping of symbolic power from transcendent ideas such as God and nation cannot, in the end, be replenished by intensified local commitments—because the most urgent problems of our time are not local problems" (115). "Meta" or "grand" narratives supply "a collective vision of a better future," meeting the otherwise "unquenchable human need to feel connected to something larger than the insular self" (94). At the same time, grand narratives undeniably can (and often do) impose their grand vision in a totalizing, violent manner, exploiting, marginalizing, or eliminating

1

peoples, races, and cultures who disagree. But does their potential for abuse mean they must be abandoned completely, or can we rethink their content and develop critical guidelines for their use? Alternatively, a model that privileges local as opposed to universal narratives seems equally problematic. Clashing local stories are tearing the world apart in places like Rwanda and Kosovo, Israel and Iraq. However we get there, survival in a postmodern world would seem to require a vision that unites rather than divides, as Zygmunt Bauman insists in his treatise on postmodern morality: "Contemporary humanity speaks in many voices and we know now that it will do so for a very long time to come. The central issue of our times is how to reforge that polyphony into harmony and prevent it from degenerating into cacophony" (*Life in Fragments* 284).

Since the Christian faith is anchored in a grand narrative, the postmodern critique raises difficult issues for Christian scholars. J. Richard Middleton and Brian J. Walsh address some of these in their book *Truth Is Stranger Than It Used to Be*. Arguing for thee "inbuilt ethical thrust" and "antitotalizing potential" of the biblical narrative—its "radical sensitivity to suffering" and the fact that the story is "root[ed] in God's overarching creational intent" (87)—these authors acknowledge, nevertheless, the inherent problems of this grandest of all grand narratives. The main problem (which applies to all metanarratives) is that those who articulate and try to live out the claims of the narrative are "inevitably finite, fallible (indeed fallen) human beings" (83). The postmodern critique follows from this certainty: "namely that the biblical story has, in fact, often been used ideologically to oppress and exclude those regarded as infidels or heretics. In the hands of some Christians and communities, the biblical metanarrative has indeed been wielded as a weapon, legitimating prejudice and perpetuating violence against those perceived as the enemy, those on the outside of God's purposes" (84). But we must be clear:, this same story has also brought emancipation from wrongful oppression, uniting people in the cause of justice, healing, and hope. We cannot resolve the tensions between biblical faith and the postmodern critique of grand narratives in this essay, and the purpose of our essayists is not to challenge or defend the biblical story. Rather our goal is to bring some of the issues raised by this debate into conversation with literature and the arts. In particular, we wish to explore the nature and importance of hope in contemporary literature and film. We share the conviction that narratives, perhaps, and especially the grand story of God's intent to redeem fallen creation, have the potential to sustain and enable hope, even in a secular, postmodern age.

The relation between postmodern suspicion of grand narratives and the crisis of hope that grips us is of major importance to the critical conversation engaged by this volume. My aim in this chapter is to situate the material that follows within the cultural context of postmodernism and to consider how readers might engage the current crisis with a Christian theology of hope. The first part of this essay traces the growing disillusionment with the Enlightenment "grand narrative," which Christians would argue invested unwarranted confidence in creaturely goodness while marginalizing or denying the participation of the Creator. Similarities but also significant differences exist between Christianity's critique of the Enlightenment and the hostility toward Enlightenment thinking advocated by many postmodernists. The main differences are anthropological, beliefs about human nature; and theological, beliefs about God, his existence, and his purposes for creation.

The second part looks at the Christian grand narrative, which was largely deconstructed during the Enlightenment and which continues to be marginalized or maligned by many postmodernists, for example, by Terry Eagleton, who describes Christianity as just another form of "organized violence" (176) and Richard Dawkins, who believes all religion, especially Christianity, is a "mental virus" (141). Drawing on the work of Jürgen Moltmann and other theologians working in the area of Christian hope, I will argue that despite notable abuses that have occurred "in the name of the Lord," if rightly understood, the Christian metanarrative is neither oppressive nor violent nor the product of mental illness, but a credible account of a loving God who is radically and fundamentally the God of peace, justice, and hope.

Finally, in the last part I will offer a Christian perspective on literature and film that embraces rather than rejects the Christian metanarrative and allows for the possibility that even in postmodern culture, God is working to restore hope and move human beings towards his creative and redemptive ends.

It is important to acknowledge from the outset that the perspective offered here is not intended as the definitive Christian perspective. My approach is not unaffected, in other words, by my own historical and geographical situation. In his book *The Fall of Interpretation*, James K. A. Smith encourages a hermeneutics of "here" and "now" that recognizes the finitude of the human condition (91). Thus I stand "here," in this place, seeing things from this perspective; I stand here "now," at this time in my own personal history and in the history of the world. As far as the Christian metanarrative is concerned, I should add that I grew up in the Bible Belt and fully embraced, and in most respects still embrace, a Protestant, evangelical telling of the Christian story. My understanding of that story is based on the biblical narrative, to be sure, but is also colored by the ways the Scripture has been interpreted and mediated by fallible human beings within the evangelical community. It is also affected by my professional training and the scholarly communities of which I am a part. So, while I read the modern/postmodern debate and the story of Christian hope through the lens of particular interpretive traditions, this interpretation is not meant to exclude others. Since we are limited and finite in how and what we know, our interpretations cannot be closed or "total," and we must read and live with a lot of questions unanswered. Obviously, the essayists in this volume will approach the Christian metanarrative from their own "here" and "now," and may disagree with my perspective, with that of my co-editor, Mark Eaton, or with each other. Our aim has not been to fit all perspectives into a single, monologic frame but to respect different voices in ways that enable dialogue and conversation.

Hope for the Future: The Enlightenment Project

The Enlightenment grand narrative begins in the sixteenth century and peaks in the mid-twentieth century, the point at which literary historians place the beginning of the postmodern era. While it is tempting to summarize this story as the coopting of the biblical narrative by secular humanists, the substitution of progress for providence, the picture is a good deal more complicated. Christianity prepared the way, ironically, for secularization. It was the good soil in which the seeds of secular humanism took root and grew. This theory is maintained, anyway, by several sociologists including Max Weber, Peter Berger, and most recently Rodney Stark. Weber's thesis is developed at length in his well-known study *The Protestant Ethic and the Spirit of Capitalism*. For Weber, the Protestant work ethic motivated westerners to view their labor as a "calling" from God, and in this way fueled the industrial revolution and free market capitalism, both significant contributors to the Enlightenment project. In *The Sacred Canopy*, Peter Berger makes a slightly different point, blaming the Protestant Reformation for blowing a hole, as it were, in the "sacred canopy" that covered western civilization for over sixteen hundred years.

> The Catholic lives in a world in which the sacred is mediated to him through a variety of channels—the sacraments of the church, the intercession of the saints, the recurring eruption of the "supernatural" in miracles—a vast continuity of being between the seen

and the unseen. Protestantism abolished most of these mediations. It broke the continuity, cut the umbilical cord between heaven and earth, and thereby threw man back upon himself in a historically unprecedented manner. (112)

In this way Protestantism unintentionally emptied the sky of angels, Berger suggests, literally leaving space for astronomers and astronauts. If this interpretation is correct, then one has to agree with Weber that Christianity contributed as much as science to the "disenchantment of the world" ("Science as a Vocation" 155). In his treatise on the sociology of religion, Stark argues that the rise of science was, in fact, a natural extension of medieval Christian doctrine: "Christianity depicted God as a rational, responsive, dependable, and omnipotent being and the universe as his personal creation, thus having a rational, lawful, stable structure, awaiting human comprehension" (*Glory of God* 147). If we have lost sight of this fact, Stark says, it is only because during the Enlightenment secular humanists and militant atheists succeeded in claiming credit for the rise of science themselves (123). This provocative thesis, which is gaining ground among historians, substantially debunks the idea that modern science and Christianity are fundamentally opposed. On the contrary, Stark argues, the flowering of science occurred in tandem with the flowering of Christianity.

Whether one agrees with Stark that secular humanism stole the credit for science from medieval theology, clearly both humanists and atheists became dominant players and, some would argue, stole the show as the drama unfolded. What appears to have happened during this pivotal period (and I would argue continues to this day) is the collision of three grand narratives: scientific rationalism, liberal politics, and Christianity. Scientific rationalism promised that human suffering could be alleviated through the domination of nature. Liberal politics argued that the benefits of science and reason should be made available to all, regardless of class, race, or gender. But the church, which could (and should) have had something to say about the moral dimensions of such projects, remained silent, having sold its soul, as many believed, to a corrupt monarchy. The bloodbath that accompanied the French Revolution was the first indication that reason alone was insufficient to enable the hopes generated by the Enlightenment. The king and queen were beheaded and thousands went to the guillotine during what was aptly described as a Reign of Terror. Sadly, this pattern would be repeated— glorious dreams followed by terror. From the Enlightenment until now, the story of human hope traces a narrative arc of rising expectations followed by, at best, partial fulfillment. This pattern leads some to the utopian conclusion that we have arrived. When that conclusion proves not to be the case, it leads to the dystopian undermining of any and all conclusions, whether derived from philosophy, science, or theology.

As Josef Pieper points out in his classic analysis *Faith, Hope, Love*, both attitudes are dangerous. The former leads to presumption, "a perverse anticipation of the fulfillment of hope"; the latter leads to despair, "a perverse anticipation of the non-fulfillment of hope." From the beginning, the Enlightenment narrative was indeed vulnerable to what Augustine said would kill the soul, both presumption, or false hope, and despair (*Sermon* 87:10:413). According to Pieper, both these "sins" will eventually "destroy the pilgrim character of human existence," transforming the "not yet" of genuine hope into the "already" of presumption or the "not ever" of despair (113). This dynamic is clearly at work in the Romantic movement, whose case against the Enlightenment predated postmodernism by at least 150 years. After witnessing the Reign of Terror, the Romantics, especially Wordsworth, despaired of all political solutions. Whereas reason "kept humanity firmly anchored to the realities of this world," the Romantics believed the imagination "liberated humanity from bondage to the material order, enabling it to discern transcendent spiritual truths" (McGrath, *Brief History of Heaven* 5). Thus, William Blake extols the salvific power of "Poetic Genius" and asserts that redemption comes through the agency of the human imagination, which plays a crucial role in recovering the biblical "lost Eden" and establishing the "New Jerusalem" depicted in the Book of Revelation (2). Blake's engraving of a little man at the base of a ladder suggests the grandeur or foolishness of Romantic dreams. The rungs of the ladder appear to end at the moon. The man begins to climb, the cry of all humanity on his lips: "I want! I want!" (261).

It would be a mistake, however, to read into the Romantic movement a return to Christian notions of a divine Creator, much less the Christian doctrine of creation which asserts that human beings are fallen creatures, that neither human reason nor imagination are entirely dependable in the pursuit of truth. As the century wore one, rationalist undermining of Christianity proceeded virtually unchallenged by Victorian Christians, who seemed to agree with Matthew Arnold that the "Sea of Faith" had finally ebbed, "retreating, to the breath / Of the night wind, down the vast edges drear / And naked shingles of the world" ("Dover Beach," lines 21–28). In what appears now to have been the "Golden Age of Atheism" (McGrath, *Twilight of Atheism* 18), secular humanism demythologized the Christian belief in six-day creation, the virgin birth, the miracles, the resurrection, and the historicity of Jesus. Thomas Huxley coined the term "agnosticism" and Thomas Hardy wrote poems about "purblind Doomsters" who rule the universe, amoral forces of destiny and chance, strewing joy, but mostly pain, along the human pilgrimage ("Hap," lines 13–14). Not all the Victorians were this gloomy. Francis Thompson found solace and hope in the arms of the "hound of heaven," and Gerard Manley Hopkins saw the world "charged with the grandeur of God." But for the most part, among intellectuals anyway, agnosticism and atheism prevailed.

Meanwhile, the Enlightenment narrative of scientific and technological progress literally steamed ahead. The automobile, the telephone, the airplane, the electric light bulb—who will argue that these inventions have not improved human society and, for the most part, bettered the human race? The celebration of human reason fostered by the Enlightenment can hardly be responsible for the "crimes against humanity" that lay ahead. If anything, optimism for the future was never higher than at the dawn of the twentieth century. So, what went wrong? There are many explanations, none of which can be fully developed here. What seems to be clear in retrospect is that the world was not ready, had not thought through nor adequately prepared for the challenge of rapid industrialization. Walking the streets of Manchester, a great factory town in England at the time, Friedrich Engels concluded that Darwin was right. Human existence is not a pilgrimage but a "war of all against all" where "the stronger tramples the weaker underfoot" and "the vast majority succumb to the most abject poverty" (31). The workers found a champion in the German philosopher and political economist Karl Marx (1818–1883), who, together with Engels, wrote and published *The Communist Manifesto* in 1848. Marx's critique of religion had enormous influence on the rejection of the Christian metanarrative in the twentieth century. With his famous dictum that "religion is the opiate of the people," Marx rejects the Christian understanding that God created man and seeks to redeem what has gone wrong with his creation, including the sinful exploitation of one class by another. For Marx, Christianity is a drug sold by the ruling bourgeoisie to keep the proletariat unaware of socialist solutions to their suffering.

With the proclamation of a communist paradise, Marxism substitutes the collective for the individual, but otherwise, follows the progressive-redemptive path of the Enlightenment. From a Christian perspective, Marx coopted the Church's neglected teachings on social justice and care for the poor and led thousands of compassionate, well-meaning intellectuals to embrace an atheistic alternative to

Christianity. As it turned out, the dream of communism was impossible to achieve even by military force. As Bulgarian philosopher and literary theorist Tzvetân Todorov observes in his book *Hope and Memory*, the central lesson to be learned from the failure of Marxism is that Marxist hopes, like the hopes of the French Revolution, were grounded on an overly optimistic view of human nature. When human nature did not cooperate—people did not love, share, or willingly redistribute their goods—the answer was military coercion. What is totalitarianism, Todorov asks, if not a form of human presumption that "promises happiness for all—but only when all who are not worthy of it (enemy classes, inferior races) have been wiped out" (312). Arguing that totalitarian doctrines "belong, as do all doctrines of salvation, to the field of religion," Todorov concludes that it was no coincidence that "this Godless religion prospered in a period marked by the decline of Christianity" (19).

Ironically, the rise of totalitarianism becomes postmodernism's justification for rejecting all grand narratives, including the Christian grand narrative, whose declining influence, according to Todorov, contributed to totalitarianism's rise. Society has paid an exceedingly high price to dismantle the totalitarian nightmares of the twentieth century, Communism under Lenin, Stalin, and Mao; Fascism under Hitler. Eight and a half million soldiers lost their lives in the Great War of 1914–1918, an additional six million were maimed for life, and ten million civilians died in a battle that would "make the world safer for democracy." This, too, was a false hope. Thirty-five million more would die in the Second World War between 1939 and 1945, including the annihilation of six million Jews in Nazi Germany, as well as several hundred thousand deaths during the Allied bombings of Japan at Hiroshima and Nagasaki. The horrors of atomic and nuclear warfare, the "killing fields" of Cambodia, the present threat of chemical and biological weapons of mass destruction, have all contributed to the current crisis of hope. "Our modern gods have failed us," as one theologian puts it, "and in this twilight we are left without a sun and with no prospects for new illumination. Having been confidently marching toward the Garden to recapture paradise, we found the gates barred by flaming swords— World Wars, genocide, apartheid . . . (so many swords)" (Smith, "Determined Hope" 201). Some of those atrocities were committed, ironically, in the name of freedom, and more recently, we have discovered the further irony that even the freedoms fought for during these wars are now "of great benefit to terrorists" (Todorov xi). The tragedy of 9/11 was masterminded not by a totalitarian government or state but by a few alienated if coordinated individuals, which raises the possibility that similar individuals, working with anthrax or nuclear weapons, could do, if one can imagine it, even worse damage.

Postmodernists are suspicious, and rightly so, of madmen and saviors, the dictators of the last century, and the master narratives they lived by and sought to impose on the world. However, rejection of all meta-narratives will not do either. Certainly it does not satisfy the longings of the human heart for some larger truth, some shared hope for humanity that transcends mere optimism and resists despair. One answer has been to embrace a pluralism of smaller, local narratives produced in a variety of historical and cultural contexts. On the positive side, this increases the validity and importance of story. Incredulity toward metanarratives does not have to mean the end of story but opens the door to a proliferation of stories. But which stories and which storytellers can we trust? Since none of the smaller stories has universal legitimation, what happens when stories collide, as they did at the World Trade Center on September 11, 2001? Without the common beliefs and shared hope provided by an overarching story, how do people determine, for example, if the story of radical Islamic fundamentalism is more or less worthy of belief and support than the story of liberal democracy? In the aftermath of 9/11 and with the threat of terrorism worldwide, we can afford neither naive optimism nor pessimism in answering such questions.

What is needed, according to Christopher Lasch, is "a more vigorous form of hope," one that "trusts life without denying its tragic character." We can fully appreciate such hope "only now that the other kind, better described as optimism, has fully revealed itself as a higher form of wishful thinking" (530). Yet, even this wisdom sounds hollow when one considers the end of the story. Scientists concede that the Enlightenment's final chapter will be written on a much larger canvas by cosmic forces beyond human control, either a massive explosion or entropy heat death. "Whatever hopes there might be of human progress within history," John Polkinghorne admits, "they can amount to no more than a stay of execution of a sentence of inevitable futility." Not only the human species, but the whole of carbon-based life will eventually prove only to have been "a transient episode in cosmic history" (*God of Hope* 11). Science itself poses the most formidable challenge to the hope of the Enlightenment, suggesting that even the best technology and a liberal and just political system will not save us. If science is right, the world will not end in the attainment of some evolutionary "omega point," but in "the whimper of cold decay or the bang of fiery collapse" (12). German theologian Christopher Schwobel underscores the importance of such an unhappy ending: "[W]hat comes last, that which concludes the history of the cosmos, seems to throw light (or shadow) on everything that comes before it. . . . If the story of our universe will end, as science teaches us to understand, with a final scenario of utter futility, this calls the meaning of the whole story into question" (109). Is this the last word? Is the universe an entirely closed system, as science proposes, or is there a new dawn ahead, wholly infused with God's glory, a future where, in the words of Saint Julian, "all things shall be well"?

After Modernity: What Dare We Hope?

Postmodernism is not without warrant in its critique of the Enlightenment and its distrust of grand narrative. We no longer expect salvation to come from enlightened politics, economics, or science. Can the human future be made different from the human past without the coercion, bloodshed, and violence that accompanied the previous century's utopian dreams? More to the point of this volume, given the vulnerability of all grand narratives to the corrupting influences of wealth, status, and power, how might Christian scholars contend with the far-reaching claims of their own grand narrative, which has too often been wrongly invoked to support corruption and abuse of power? There are at least three options. We can admit that the story is too grand and deconstruct, mute, or deny its most offending features. What could be more offensive in an age of diversity and religious pluralism than a story that makes monotheistic claims about one true God? As Stark has shown, differences between those who believe in "One True God" have fueled some of the most brutal conflicts in history. "[E]ven minor variations in doctrine unleash the dogs of war and 'justify' mass butchery" (*One True God* 115). This problem is serious for all monotheistic faiths, including Judaism, Christianity, and Islam. The only way to protect against brutal conflict, according to Stark, is to insist on "norms of civility" in a free market of religions governed by "mutual respect among faiths" and "public moderation of particularism" (222). Absent such civility, a second option is to declare all faith private, to be shared only within the confines of one's own faith community. Given the real dangers of intolerance and oppression when church and state get together, or when, lacking civility, religion comes out too aggressively in the public square, this option holds a certain appeal. A third possibility is to rethink and begin to rearticulate the radical claims of the biblical story in a way that takes up the challenge of modern pluralism, as Berger puts it, "to hold convictions without either dissolving them in utter relativity or encasing them in the false absolutes of fanaticism" (*A Far Glory* 46).

Instead of rejecting redemptive metanarratives, William Katerberg proposes we both articulate and deconstruct them. "The hope that must be retrieved from [this] dilemma comes in recognizing that, in our narratives, interpretations, living, and politics, we must refuse to *give up* metanarratives and refuse to accept them as *given*" (13). He calls for Christians to be self-critical in retelling, interpreting, and living out their metanarrative, always open to the need for revision and change. "In Christian terms, we might say that this sensibility recognizes both the unity and universality of God's Truth and the abiding provisionality of the *truths* of God's finite and sinful creatures." Katerberg admits this is a "messy way of living, storytelling, and interpreting," but what choice do we have? "In that mess, among the 'wheat' and the 'tares,' lies the 'sin' that we fear and hate, and the redemption that we need and desire" (13). This open and provisional attitude characterizes the work of a number of theologians, who in the last fifty years have devoted increasing attention to the doctrine of Christian hope.

While it is not my task to analyze or even summarize their work, I do want to examine briefly certain developments that pertain directly to the themes of this book. For Christians, the question "what dare we hope?" is primarily about eschatology, that branch of theology concerned with the end of the biblical story. Eschatology studies the last things, the return of Jesus Christ to earth, the *parousia*, and the consummation of Christ's eternal kingdom, the *eschaton*, depicted in the Book of Revelation as the "new heaven and the new earth" (McKim 93, 201). The enormously successful Left Behind series by Jerry B. Jenkins and Tim LaHaye, which has sold well over 50 million copies (Noll 6), attests to the fascination of "apocalyptic" eschatology, especially among conservative evangelical Christians. German theologian Jürgen Moltmann warns against this narrow understanding, which too often leads to "theological dogmatism" and "apocalyptic arm-twist[ing]" (*Coming of God* xi). What Moltmann offers instead is a revolutionary refocusing that aligns eschatology more broadly with the doctrine of Christian hope. Following Karl Barth, Moltmann argues that eschatology, if rightly understood, is not only about the end but encompasses the entire biblical narrative from Genesis to Revelation: "Eschatology is the medium of Christian faith as such, the key in which everything in it is set, the glow that suffuses everything here in the dawn of an expected day. . . . From first to last, and not merely in the epilogue, Christianity is eschatology, is

hope, forward looking and forward moving, and therefore also revolutionizing and transforming the present" (*Theology of Hope* 16).

Moltmann's theology of hope offers a starting point for rethinking
the Christian metanarrative, in particular, those features that might sustain and enable hope in a postmodern world. Drawing on the insights of
Ernst Bloch's *Principle of Hope*, a Marxist analysis, but recasting these
insights in a Christian framework, Moltmann urges that any philosophy
of hope that claims to be Christian and not merely utopian speculation
must have its foundation in Christology:

> By [C]hristology we do not mean: did the earthly Jesus express
> prophecies of this kind? We mean: is the Christian hope based on
> Christ's coming, his surrender to death on the cross, and his resur-
> rection from the dead? The fact that Christ came into this world
> and appeared in Jesus, the crucified and risen One, is the eschato-
> logical presupposition of the whole Christian faith. But to say this
> is to assert nothing less than that with the coming of Christ the
> new, eternal *aeon* has dawned in the midst of this old *aeon* which is
> a passing away: "The night is far gone, the day is at hand . . ."
> (Romans 13:12). The "lordship" of the risen Christ is still disputed
> here and now, for "we do not yet see everything in subjection to
> him" (Hebrews 2:8); so life in the community of Christ must also
> be called participation in Christ's struggle. (*Coming of God* 194)

His theology does not deny the need for political and economic liberation, social justice, or ecological healing—all features of modern liberal agendas today—but grounds such hopes solely on the promises and
faithfulness of God. He does not advocate hope for some ever-receding
future horizon, some pie-in-the-sky paradise. No. With the coming of
Christ, the future is already here. Biblical *shalom* and the kingdom of
God are moral and political ideals that human beings infused by the
power of Christ can address in this world. "Life out of this hope then
means already acting here and today in accordance with that world of
justice and righteousness and peace, contrary to appearances, and contrary to all historical chances of success" (*Coming of God* 234). In sum,
Moltmann's theology of hope is for "combatants, not onlookers"; it will
have no appeal to " 'rapturists' fleeing from the world, who tell the world
'goodbye' and want to go to heaven," but is aimed specifically at "resistance fighters, struggling against the godless powers on this earth"
(*Coming of God* 146, 153).

In bringing eschatology from the margins to the center and refocusing its content from end-time catastrophe to a culturally engaged theology of hope, Moltmann opens the way for Christian scholars to consider

the cultural expression of hope in the arts, music, poetry, drama, fiction, and film. His work stresses the role of hope in Christian cultural analysis: "If it is hope that maintains and upholds faith and keeps it moving on, if it is hope that draws the believer into the life of love, then it will also be hope that is the mobilizing and driving force of faith's thinking, of its knowledge of, and reflections on, human nature, history, and society" (*Theology of Hope* 33). Commenting on this passage, Alister McGrath urges Christians to rediscover their own doctrine of hope and realize its importance to a world "longing for hope, and seeking hope outside the Christian tradition. . . . Only by rediscovering its own theology of hope can the [C]hurch hope to gain a hearing in a secular culture" (*Christian Theology* 565).

The essays in this volume contribute to this activity by critically examining the longing for hope expressed in postmodern literature from a Christian perspective. Before moving to these essays, it will be useful to draw together, however briefly, several orienting motifs of a Christian theology of hope, in particular, as these have developed under Moltmann, but also in the work of other theologians, including Alister McGrath, Glenn Tinder, Mirâslôv Volf, John Sanders, and John Polkinghorne. We can identify at least the following themes common to their understanding of the Christian metanarrative.

First, God created the world with a purpose and plan. The goal or *telos* of God's plan is to develop a people who love and trust him in such a way that they collaborate in his "divine project" to redeem and bless all peoples and renew the earth (Sanders 12ff.). The horizon of Christian hope is the completion of the project, the achievement of shalom, the word used throughout the Old Testament; or the consummation of the kingdom of God referred to in the gospels. Second, from the beginning, God's purpose has been contested. Desiring a relationship of volitional love, God gives his creatures the freedom to resist or rebel against the demands of shalom. Despite God's efforts to work with his creatures, such resistance and rebellion, which the Bible calls "sin," continues to hinder God's purpose and plan. Third, God never gives up. Working relentlessly through the power of love, he still seeks a people through whom he can bless and redeem the world. To that end, God speaks words of encouragement and direction to his chosen people through the Mosaic law and later through prophets, priests, and kings. He speaks ultimately and definitively through the life and ministry of Jesus Christ, the Incarnate Word. Christian hope is a "crucified hope," meaning that God's love is so great that he took on human flesh, suffered, and died on a cross to break the power of sin and death (Moltmann, *Experiment*

Hope 141). In the crucifixion and resurrection of Jesus, Christians see the extent of God's determination to complete the divine project and his ability to overcome every evil with good. Fourth, and finally, while God's promised future "breaks into" the present in a new and unique way in Jesus Christ, the project is still contested today, the world does not yet experience shalom, and the kingdom is not yet fully come. While Christians are challenged to extend the kingdom and shalom, they know that humanity apart from God is inadequate to the task.

Christian hope for redemption, therefore, is grounded in God's love for his creation, his empowering presence in those who put their trust in him, and his commitment, whatever the cost, to overcome evil with good. Obviously, one cannot do justice to the riches of such a grand narrative in a single paragraph. Nor can its vision be fully grasped and articulated by those to whom it has been entrusted. Despite their glorious efforts, even gifted writers like Dante, Milton, and Bunyan are "vessels of clay" who must be content to see it all "in a dim mirror" (1 Cor 13:12). The Christian journey toward the promised end requires humility. We do not know and cannot see everything. We must walk by faith not sight. Hopefully, this reality opens a door for dialogue with those who see the world differently. While believing that their grand narrative is objectively true—that is, not a figment of personal or corporate imagination—thoughtful Christians, many of whom embrace the postmodern critique of modernity, recognize that cultural forces and human subjectivity color all interpretations of truth, including the truth of the Bible as they understand it. Though we see through a glass imperfectly now, clarification of all truth claims comes only at the end when we see God "face to face" (I Cor 13:12). McGrath refers to this as "eschatological verification" (*Foundations* 135). With these caveats in mind, let us return to our question, "After modernity, what dare we hope?" How might Christians respond to the collapse of the Enlightenment dream? To the extent that modernity has failed, how is that failure explained or at least illuminated by the insights of Christian theology?

We have argued that the Enlightenment project failed at least partly because of flawed anthropology and a bankrupt theology. When we consider these failures from a Christian perspective, several important insights emerge. To begin with, the concept of God's kingdom as shalom, and the idea that God is determined to bring the whole creation to its divinely intended telos redirects the human pilgrimage. We are kept from modern presumption by realizing the scope of eternal salvation for all humanity is larger than either hopes of individual fulfillment in this life or hopes of transforming the social order. We are kept from despair by the knowledge that we are not asked to achieve the kingdom on our own, unaided by the presence and power of God himself. This truth was explicitly rejected by the secular humanism that came to dominate the Enlightenment, as noted by Stanley Grenz and John R. Franke in their major work on the subject, *Beyond Foundationalism*:

> [T]he revival of the humanistic impulse led thinkers to divorce the biblical idea of history as a linear movement encompassing both "the beginning" and "the end" from its theological moorage. . . . In the modern era, the anthropocentric shift reached its zenith. "Man" deposed the biblical God as the subject of the historical narrative. . . . What formerly had been the account of God bringing creation to its telos became the story of the rise and advance of "civilization." (260)

A Christian theology of hope recovers the profound truth that "history is not our story—it is not the story of Man or the tale of the progress of humankind" (261). Rather, history is the story of God's divine telos unfolding. "[T]he grand culmination of history arrives only because God who stands at the end of the human story is already in grace ordering the cosmic story toward its intended goal" (261–62).

However, the Christian doctrine of redemption asserts that human beings are flawed characters in God's story, characters who frequently say no to God's purposes and seek to destroy rather than build up the kingdom. This is a disabling condition requiring God's own intervention. Humanity cannot be saved through its own efforts. To paraphrase the Apostle Paul, the good that we wish we would do, we do not do; the evil we wish we would not do, we keep doing (Rom 7:15-19). While God stands at the end and will ultimately achieve his purposes for creation, the story does not roll along inevitably toward a happy ending, as in the modern myth of progress. Out of concern for our sinful condition and in a radical move to get the project back on track, God takes on human flesh in the incarnation of Jesus, who "humbled himself and became obedient to the point of death" (Phil 2:8). This means that thoughtful Christians ought not to be surprised by the failures of the Enlightenment project in its various manifestations over the last four hundred years. To return to Blake's man on the ladder, both Enlightenment science and Romantic imagination are entirely too optimistic about what is and is not possible apart from God. The little man on the ladder seems unaware of his "creatureliness," as Pieper says. He wants what he wants when he wants it, with no limits and no accountability. It seems abundantly clear by now that the human future will not be made better than the human past through our creaturely reason or creaturely imagination alone. On this Christian and secular postmodernists can agree.

Another important theological insight is that God's promised future "breaks in" to the present in many ways, including works of science and the creative imagination. These breakthroughs will occur despite the fact that both human reason and the imagination are fallen and, therefore, insufficient apart from God to bring about the kingdom. To say that reason and the imagination are fallen does not mean God does not use them, even in their fallen state, to move creation towards its divinely intended end. God calls all of humanity to collaborate in the divine project. All discoveries of scientific truth answer to this call insofar as they reveal God's glory and work towards God's kingdom and shalom. Works of literature and film can similarly anticipate God's promised future, pointing the way to Christ and the shalom of God. Therefore, Christians are more likely to resist the position of some postmodernists, for example, that human reason and the human imagination are nothing but political weapons, inherently incapable of discovering or revealing truth. Christian postmodernists are wary of the excesses of rationalism and the reductive materialism of modern science, to be sure, but to "chasten rationality" (Grenz and Franke 22–24) does not require the rejection of reason itself, as some deconstructionists seem to imply. Christians maintain that human reason and the human imagination are gifts of a rational and creative God, and as such are best employed not toward just any selfish scientific or creative end but toward the fulfillment of God's redemptive goal for creation.

Modernity also challenges the belief that God is relational and chooses to establish his kingdom through the power of sacrificial love. Throughout the modern period, starting with the "unmoved mover" of Enlightenment Deism, belief in a God who was intimately involved with his creation and who desired a personal relationship with human beings gave way to a God who was dead (the Nietzschean view), or a projection of human desire (the Freudian and Feuerbachian view), or the opiate of the people (the Marxist view). Both the New Testament and the Communist Manifesto express the hope that someday human beings will be able to love and take care of the needs of others as they would love and take care of themselves. They differ radically about how this condition will be achieved. Unlike Soviet and other totalitarian attempts to impose a communist ideology through domination and fear, Jesus talks about leaders who practice a relational ethic of love, washing feet, binding up wounds, and selling all they have and giving to the poor. Moreover, in contradiction to the Marxist critique, the kingdom of God as shalom functions as a "norm that judges every human arrangement that is less than just and peaceful for all humans" (J. Jones 707). Thus it is not true that Christianity, properly understood, keeps victims of oppression anesthetized to their own suffering, as Marx alleged. Nevertheless, the Marxist critique of religion provides a much needed wake-up call to live out the good news of the gospel in ways that challenge and resist the status quo. Rightly understood and practiced, Christianity is not an opiate but a yeast, a position echoed by Moltmann:

> That is why faith, wherever it develops into hope, causes not rest but unrest, not patience but impatience. It does not calm the unquiet heart, but is itself this unquiet heart in man. Those who hope in Christ can no longer put up with reality as it is, but begin to suffer under it, to contradict it. Peace with God means conflict with the world, for the goad of the promised future stabs inexorably into the flesh of every unfulfilled present. (*Theology of Hope* 21)

A final insight rediscovered by a Christian theology of hope is the belief that "all will be well," as St. Julian has said, because all will end well. T. S. Eliot's famous line from *The Four Quartets* expresses the paradox of endings that turn into beginnings: "We shall not cease from exploration / And the end of all our exploring / Will be to arrive where we started / And know the place for the first time" ("Little Gidding," lines 239–42). In one of his darker moments, Blaise Pascal could see only death: "The last act is tragic, however happy all the rest of the play is: at the last a little earth is thrown upon our head, and that is the end, forever" (qtd. in Coles 125). Most postmodernists—Richard Rorty and Terry Eagleton are two exceptions—are similarly pessimistic, prompting the perceptive comment by Richard Bauckham and Trevor Hart that tragedy is the most appropriate literary genre for hope's story in a postmodern world (44). Moreover, the postmodern "eschewal of story" is itself the "tragic narrative denouement, a dark and despairing final scene in which dashed hopes, failed plans and unfulfilled promises litter the stage like corpses" (44). Overshadowing this dark ending are even darker scenarios predicted by modern science outlined in the previous section. Christians resist such pessimism through their faith in the resurrected Christ: "Wherever life is perceived and lived in community and fellowship with [the risen] Christ, a new beginning is discovered hidden in every end. . . . In God's creative future, the end will become the beginning, and the true creation is still to come and is ahead of us" (Moltmann, *Coming of God* xi).

Pressing the point further, Christianity insists that flesh and blood cannot inherit the kingdom of God, that what is perishable must put on the imperishable, what is mortal must be transformed into immortality. Even the heavens and the earth will undergo this process before the end, as described in the Book of Revelation: "Then I saw a new heaven and a new earth; for the first heaven and the first earth had passed away" (21:1). Christian hope transcends fear of personal death or the death of the universe through galactic expansion or collapse. "[A]lthough the human species, life, the earth, the sun, and the universe will end," writes William Stoeger, "that end is not ultimate but somehow leads to a fuller, transformed reality, to which the natural sciences provide no access, and to which our human experience gives us only obscure, but nevertheless real, intimations and indications" ("Scientific Accounts" 20). It is this openness to transcendence that modernism—Darwin, Marx, Freud—challenges and seeks to remove. For Christians, the loss of transcendence drains the meaning and purpose of life from the universe, undermining any sense of destiny or higher purpose, reducing all of life to what "dies and decays" (Stoeger, "Cultural Cosmology" 67). This is the spiritual vacuum into which Christianity must speak if it is to engage postmodern culture: "Only by allowing our imaginations to be blown wide open by a transcendence which blows the future itself wide open can we begin, however partially and tentatively, to envisage a *telos*, an end or purpose, which may legitimately furnish us with an object of hope" (Bauckham and Hart 51).

In restoring a transcendent vision of the future and redirecting the human pilgrimage to the path of true hope, Christian theology charts a course between modern presumption and postmodern despair. The world is not getting better and better but neither are its faults beyond redemption. This is not to suggest that Christianity was not involved historically with the Enlightenment project—I have already noted its paradoxical role in secularization and the rise of modern science—nor should anyone draw the conclusion that Christians agree about the validity of the postmodern critique. In his book *Postmodernity*, David Lyon concedes that "foundations" that claim universal legitimacy are no longer viable. Furthermore, solutions to the postmodern crisis of hope cannot be found in the totalizing metanarratives of modernity. The challenge is to formulate a Christian response that recognizes both the achievement and the problems of modernity while avoiding the relativism and nihilism that seem inevitable given the postmodern critique of reason and its rejection of metanarrative. Lyon argues for a "complex interaction between the premodern, modern, and postmodern" that recognizes modernity itself as "the product of both authentic expressions of Judeo-Christian culture, *and* would-be autonomous human reason" (109). Overly confident that the future was in human hands, "modern arrogance denied the divine and diverted all hope to human resources," says Lyon, but "today, the human is being displaced, decentered, and the grip on the future seems once more up for grabs." The time may be auspicious, in other words, to reclaim the wisdom of biblical Christianity— "Jesus' call to love one's neighbor, and an ethic of responsibility"—with the caveat that we not simply proclaim but live out that wisdom in today's globalizing, consumer-driven, fragmented world (110).

Where a Christian literary and cultural aesthetic is concerned, the most problematic view of the future is one that sees radical discontinuity between the present order and the world to come, God's "new heaven and new earth." According to this view, which is similar to the catastrophic scenarios predicted by modern physicists, all human works will be destroyed, along with the physical creation itself. In his book on the eschatology of work, Mirâslôv Volf takes another view, arguing that the world will not end in apocalyptic destruction but eschatological transformation. The products of human creativity will be "cleansed from impurity, perfected, and transfigured" to "form the 'building materials' from which (after they are transfigured) 'the glorified world' will be made" (*Work in the Spirit* 91). Works of creative beauty, moments of joy in nature, acts of kindness and justice for the poor, healings and miracles are all anticipations of God's future kingdom breaking through here and now. The proleptic expectation of eschatological transformation invests human work, including that of literary artists and critics, with ultimate significance. "Through it human beings contribute in their modest and broken way to God's new creation" (92). The contributors to this volume take courage from this perspective. Perhaps our task can be understood as providing glimpses of God at work through contemporary literature and film, glimpses of God's redemptive love penetrating the darkness of life as we know it, narrating hope in a postmodern world.

Narrating Hope: The Gift of Story

The demise of secular hope poses a challenge for Christian thinkers seeking to engage contemporary culture. The essayists in this collection take seriously the dynamics at work in postmodernism—attitudes and beliefs about God, ourselves, and others that strongly contribute to the crisis of hope lamented by Delbanco and others. Views of the future that end in annihilation and despair, along with present threats of terrorism, global pollution, and global poverty, all point to the ephemerality and futility of life on this planet. In contrast, the authors in this volume read postmodern literature hopefully, in light of God's creative and redemptive purposes as we best understand them. God's promised future "breaks in" to the present in ways large and small; in postmodern literature it may be only a "grain of wheat" or a "tiny mustard seed," some "leavening" impulse barely discerned, a small flash or brief glimmer of trust, forgiveness, hope, or love. That future is foreshadowed, anticipated, and prefigured in art that tells the truth about the human condition apart from God, conveys transcendent yearning for God, or discerns the coming of God in the small and often tragic circumstances of life. The work of Christian literary criticism is to recognize and call attention to God's promised future "breaking in," the "now but not yet" kingdom of God unfolding. The ways of the kingdom are disclosed to artists and critics who have eyes to see and ears to hear.

Our essayists are on the side of hope, but Christian hope is not naive. It recognizes pain, suffering, and evil. According to Glenn Tinder, [H]ope is the capacity for carrying on one's life in the confidence that it will finally be seen as a story fashioned by an omnipotent and merciful God" (61), a story where even pain and suffering find redemptive purpose and meaning. Many of the novels and films critiqued in this volume do not see life in this way but reflect the crisis of hope brought on by increasing secularism and the failures of modernity. "Much modernist/postmodernist literature and art," writes Robert Jenson, "is directly and thematically either lamentation about, or defiant proclamation of hopelessness" (23).

So the reader should be prepared for considerable darkness as well as flashes of light. The degree to which each text narrates hope is the connecting thread. Drawing on Andrew Greeley's sociological study, *Religion as Poetry*, Daniel Johnson argues that story and storytelling are essential to hope and vice versa:

> It is only by means of narrative that hope is experienced in the first place, . . . for the experience of hope has a narrative structure built right into it. When people hope, they lay a story arc over a certain span of history, one that identifies the limitations of the present, offers a vision of how those limitations may be overcome in the future, and furnishes grounds for expecting that that future will be realized. (31)

Bauckham and Hart agree:

> The quest for meaning, truth, goodness and beauty is closely bound up with hope as an activity of the imagination in which we seek to transcend the boundaries of the present, to go beyond the given, outwards and forwards, in search of something more, something better, than the given affords us. . . . Hope is, in this sense, an activity of imaginative faith. (52–53)

My purpose is not to provide an extensive critical analysis of hope, covering all its philosophical, theological, social, economic, and political dimensions, and its narrative possibilities in literature and film. Instead, I offer a broad definition of hope as the belief, however tenuous, that the longings of the human heart will one day be fulfilled (Griesinger 208). While this definition is not unique to a Christian perspective, it accommodates several important Christian insights. First, it acknowledges that within every human heart are longings, some placed there by human invention and imagination, and some by the Creator. The longings of our hearts draw us forward into the unknown future. They are the stuff dreams are made of, evoking our passions, directing our gaze, focusing and giving meaning to our actions. Augustine grounds the heart's deepest longings in the divine in the famous phrase, "Thou has formed us for Thyself, and our hearts are restless till they find rest in Thee" (*Confessions*, bk. 1, par. 1). Second, hope is subject to major uncertainty. In the wake of modernism's collapsed dreams and in the presence of postmodernism's "incredulity toward metanarratives," belief in God is problematic, not easily produced, and, if present, may be riddled with doubt. Christians hold to the promise that God is responsive to the prayer, "I believe; help my unbelief!" (Mark 9:24). This yearning leads to a third point. Belief, faith, and hope are matters of degree. We may have a little or a lot. Nowhere does this seem more evident than in trying times. When the situation becomes critical or when hope is long deferred, we become discouraged and are tempted to give up, or we are motivated to resist and overcome. Jesus chided his disciples for their "little faith," but also taught that even a little faith—as small as a mustard seed—could accomplish great things. By his compassion, Jesus demonstrated that the God of grace hears the cries of those burdened by postmodern despair. Finally, the imagination enables us to envision possibilities and sustain hope, even when fulfillment seems far off. From a Christian perspective, story and storytelling are gifts that can nourish our imaginations, fortify our confidence, and help us resist evil and despair. Stories that narrate hope, moreover, offer a welcome antidote to the widespread cynicism and gloom prevalent in postmodern society today.

These insights provide the organizing framework for this book. The essays in section 1, "The Postmodern Condition," reflect on the implications and contradictions of postmodernism's fragmented and relativistic understanding of the world. Postmodern fiction by Don DeLillo, personal narratives by Gloria Anzaldúa, bell hooks, and Roberta Bondi, and several contemporary films, including *American Beauty, The Sixth Sense, Twelve Monkeys*, and *Memento*, are analyzed, revealing an "unslaked craving for transcendence" (114), Delbanco's term, the ongoing tensions between belief and unbelief, and the role of story in clarifying our way. Section 2, "The Valley of Despair," addresses hope's nemesis, despair. How does one believe again after facing the horrors and finality of death, whether it is the horror of the Holocaust, the death of a loved one, betrayal by a friend, or the collapse of a dream? Featured in this section are critical analyses of the fiction of Doris Betts, Amy Tan, Hugh Cook, Jurek Becker, and Elie Wiesel. Section 3, "Resisting the Night," considers hope's prophetic vision. Stories that envision God's promised future also critique the present that falls short of that vision and seek to motivate change. Included in this section are thoughtful discussions of the fiction of John Okada and James Baldwin, as well as confessional narratives drawn from South Africa's attempt, through the Truth and Reconciliation Commission, to move beyond the injustice and shame of apartheid.

Section 4, "Adversity and Grace," deals with the complex relationship between hope, suffering, and perseverance, looking at the transforming power of grace in hard times. Featured in this section are analyses of illness narratives (pathographies) by Reynolds Price and Oliver Sacks, as well as critical analyses of fiction by Kathleen Norris, Isak Dinesen, and two contemporary films, David Lynch's *The Straight Story* and Terry Gilliam's *The Fisher King*. Section 5, "Imagination and Hope," concludes the book by examining the way story engages the imagination and extends its capacity to envision and sustain hope. Even in postmodern, post-Christian culture, authors like the ones discussed here, J. R. R. Tolkien and C. S. Lewis, draw readers and viewers toward the kingdom and shalom, while others, like J. K. Rowling and Bernard MacLaverty, provide "unfocused gleams of divine truth."

Whether we like it or not, we live in a postmodern world where, as Peter Berger reminds us, transcendence has been reduced to a rumor. "We must begin in the situation in which we find ourselves," writes Berger, "but we must not submit to it as to an irresistible tyranny. If the signals of transcendence have become rumors in our time, then we can set out to explore these rumors—and perhaps to follow them up to their source" (*Rumor* 180). Stories of hope are like these rumors—gestures of human longing for something better, higher, richer than present reality affords. Such stories invite critical reflection. Delbanco asserts that human beings write and tell stories "to hold back the melancholy suspicion that [they] live in a world without meaning" (23). We contend that stories may do more. The best stories may lead us beyond the trials and sufferings of this life, directing our gaze upward and forward to the unfolding of God's kingdom. Despite current trends that suspect or undermine the viability of narrative, the essays in this volume celebrate the gift of story. Our aim is to engage contemporary stories in literature and film, not trailing the Zeitgeist and "bearing its train," as Moltmann says, but shining the light of Christ before it, "enkindling and enabling hope" (*Experiment Hope* 46).

Section One

The Postmodern Condition

Thinking about hope would be unnecessary if we possessed it.
—*Glenn Tinder*

The essays in section 1 engage literary texts, both print and film, that reflect on the implications and contradictions of the postmodern ethos. Postmodernism is many things: a kaleidoscopic portrait of a world in change, an information revolution, a knowledge revolution, a cultural revolution. Zygmunt Bauman defines postmodernism as a change of mood or intellectual climate characterized by "exhilarating freedom to pursue anything and the mind-boggling uncertainty as to what is worth pursuing and in the name of what one should pursue it" (*Intimations* vii). In this section we attempt to capture both the freedom and uncertainty of telling, living, and interpreting stories in such a world. No longer a predictable *scene* where the play is staged and directed "towards some concrete ending, even if we do not know in advance what it is," writes Bauman, this world is *obscene*—"a lot of noise and bustle without plot, scenario, director—and direction" (151–52). Authors, characters, and readers are on their own, it would seem, to find their way in an ever-shifting moral and spiritual landscape where belief, if present at all, is precarious, and stories of faith are often highly subjective, idiosyncratic, eclectic, exotic, and sometimes just bizarre. The challenge of acting, reading, and living in such a place is the focus of the four essays in this section.

The first essay, Mark Eaton's "Inventing Hope: The Question of Belief in Don DeLillo's Novels," opens with a question posed by one of the characters in DeLillo's *Mao II*: "When the Old God leaves the world, what happens to all the unexpended faith?" (7). The question of what has happened to faith since the proverbial death of God is a pivotal one in *White Noise* (1985), *Mao II* (1991), and *Underworld* (1997). In these novels belief is attenuated by doubt. DeLillo delineates the various religious dispensations that actually proliferated rather than disappeared in the late twentieth century, including evangelical Christianity, Islam, Buddhism, and New Age religions. By describing the many permutations of belief and melancholy unbelief in his novels, DeLillo takes an inventory of the current religious scene. Infusing his fictional worlds with radiance and intimations of transcendence, he reveals the interpenetration of the sacred and profane in contemporary culture. Above all, DeLillo captures something essential yet paradoxical about belief: where there is belief, there is likely to be some measure, large or small, of doubt. In postmodernism, this dialectic between belief and unbelief has, if anything, intensified. Thus, DeLillo's characters often appear to be spiritually homeless, even as they desperately try to hold onto some hope in the face of death or natural disasters. Having lost faith in the promises of traditional Christianity, the characters in *White Noise*, *Mao II*, and *Underworld* redirect their hopes into all sorts of religious and metaphysical systems, everything from "transmigration of souls" to "Sufi dervishes" and "trance-walking." These systems illustrate Delbanco's keen observation that lost faith leaves in its wake an "unquenched spiritual longing" (51). Out of some "persistent sense of large-scale ruin," one character in *White Noise* remarks, "we keep inventing hope" (146–47). Clearly, DeLillo is attuned to the basic human need for some higher purpose in life, some reason to hope for a better future at a time when the world offers plenty of reasons to despair. According to Eaton, DeLillo's characters cling to belief as a means of "inventing hope" in the midst of seeming chaos and confusion. Eaton ends his essay on a cautionary note, warning of the dangers of misdirected belief, or more precisely, "the danger of allowing one's beliefs to motivate violent acts," a warning that in the wake of 9/11 takes on new significance. Yet, if we "listen closely . . . beneath all the white noise," Eaton is optimistic enough to believe "we may hear the still small voice of hope."

Postmodern resistance to traditional religion is examined from a slightly different perspective in Anne-Marie Bowery's "Voices from Within: Gloria Anzaldúa, bell hooks, and Roberta Bondi." One of the dangers of redemptive metanarratives, according to William Katerberg, is their tendency to "assimilate" or "annihilate" individual peoples, groups, and cultures. "Even if they acknowledge diversity," writes Katerberg, "they still set that diversity in a larger context which explains and 'masters' it, and thus marginalizes or erases it" (6). Against grand narratives that deny and exclude, Anzaldúa, hooks, and Bondi find a venue that respects and includes the smaller, personal stories of marginalized women. In their autobiographical accounts of racism, sexism, and even religious exclusion, these authors demonstrate how suspicion of metanarrative need not result in the end of story but, more hopefully, in the proliferation of stories, each produced within and reflective of its own historical and cultural context. Bowery takes up postmodernism's willingness not just to entertain but to celebrate a diversity of voices, to hear and tell stories that have been repressed, knowingly and unknowingly, by the privileged and the powerful. Anzaldúa's intensely poetic *Borderlands/La Frontera*, bell hooks's *Wounds of Passion*, and Bondi's *Memories of God*, are autobiographical accounts, local and personal stories that express the urgent concerns of contemporary feminism. Although they write from radically different cultural spaces in terms of race, class, religion, and sexual orientation, Bowery identifies thematic similarities in their stories, ways of thinking, doing, and believing that resist cultural constraints, which for them (and many women) have been obstacles to intellectual and spiritual growth. While these authors do not always share a Christian perspective on life, they each use autobiographical reflection to transform worn-out faith in ways that encourage hope in a culturally diverse postmodern world. But Bowery also notes that postmodern sensitivities toward pluralism, together with the distrust of metanarratives, lead to localization and fragmentation in philosophy and theology, and create serious difficulties when competing philosophical or theological views collide, as they did when the Episcopal Church recently ordained an openly gay priest as bishop, and more lethally when terrorists crashed airplanes into the World Trade Center on 9/11. How can deep philosophical and theological differences be resolved apart from appeal to a grander story, a path postmoderns resist? Poignant personal narratives like the ones discussed in this essay are resulting in a flurry of activity in these fields to provide new paradigms that better accommodate postmodern concerns. Whether a Christian "theology of hope" can be part of this conversation will depend on our willingness to take seriously the pain and suffering of those who, like Anzaldúa, hooks, and Bondi, feel they have for too long been silenced, oppressed, or ignored.

The stories we have examined thus far belong to the literary genres of fiction and nonfiction, respectively. Obviously story encompasses all narrative arts. Chapters 3 and 4 broaden our discussion of postmodernism to include popular culture and film. In the first of these essays, "Time for Hope: *The Sixth Sense, American Beauty, Memento,* and *Twelve Monkeys,*" D. Brent Laytham situates hope in the "provident past" and "redemptive future" of the Christian grand narrative, noting the closing off of both ends of this spectrum in contemporary culture. Postmodernity celebrates the demise of metanarratives that once focused our hopes—the triumph of communism; the rise of democracy; and the end of poverty, disease, and war. According to Laytham, belief in progress was our culture's richest eschatological vision, and short of some replacement, loss of this belief leaves nothing but death as the organizing telos of human life. Laytham analyzes four contemporary movies, each ending with death or some image of an afterlife. The first two, *The Sixth Sense* and *American Beauty*, are viewed as fundamentally hopeful movies where cinematic technique interacts with plot to produce a narrated past that funds present and future hope. *The Sixth Sense* uses a cathartic plot and the doubling of its lead actors to suggest that, yes, there is still time for hope, at least for the living. *American Beauty* combines flashback narration with other cinematic techniques to turn a horrible ending—middle-aged loser murdered by mistake—into a hopeful one. Both movies recognize that time presses but does not preclude hope. *Memento* and *Twelve Monkeys*, however, suggest otherwise.

The complicated and confusing temporal structure of *Twelve Monkeys* builds a sense of inexorable doom. The reverse chronology of *Memento* creates a sense of causal inevitability. Both films imply there is no time for hope. Laytham's essay heightens the tension between belief and unbelief by suggesting that believing a lie can initiate a causal chain that spirals to destruction, allowing little time to reverse course. The parable of the ten virgins comes to mind. Five of them took insufficient oil for their lamps to last the night. None of the five were given time to go back and replenish their oil. All five missed out on the long-awaited coming of the bridegroom. Viewers are left wondering, how late is too late? Furthermore, if it is not too late, with the psalmist we might ask,

"Where does our help come from?" In a noisy, fragmented, postmodern world, can the psalmist's hopeful answer—"from the Lord, the Maker of heaven and earth" (Ps 121).

Chapter 4 concludes this section on the postmodern condition with Robert K. Johnston's splendid essay "Beyond Futility: *American Beauty* and the Book of Ecclesiastes." Johnston examines the contradictory messages of the film *American Beauty* in light of the Book of Ecclesiastes. Readers continue to be fascinated by Ecclesiastes, even while interpreters struggle to understand the book's contradictory trajectories of despair and joy, pessimism and hope. Must not the one cancel out the other, or can both perspectives be true, given the incongruities of life? Johnston explores life's hope, given its futility, by allowing the movie *American Beauty* to provide new perspectives on the paradoxes of Ecclesiastes. In keeping with postmodernism's critique of modernity, *American Beauty* portrays the bankruptcy of the American dream. The artificially bred "American Beauties" are but a veneer, masking the fact that the family in the movie—Lester, Carolyn, and Jane Burnham—are the walking dead. Recognition of their spiritual malaise, their death-in-life, is key to finding life, although this comes about paradoxically in and through death. As the movie ends, viewers hear Lester say he has nothing but "gratitude for every single moment of my stupid little life." Ricky similarly discovers life to be a gift, not a production, as he watches in wonder as a plastic bag, suspended in the air, dances in the wind. Life refuses to yield to our attempts to produce meaning. Yet, by accepting life's uselessness, Johnston concludes, we are positioned to see its grandeur. By recognizing life's seeming hopelessness, we can find revealed to us life's hopefulness. "It is significant," Johnston notes, "that the transcendent vision of life in both Ecclesiastes and *American Beauty* comes without reference to . . . traditional religion. . . . Just as money, fame, wisdom, and pleasure can be a means of shutting out God's transforming presence, so, too, can the certainty of our creeds and dogmas." What Lester and Ricky seek is not the certainty of belief but a glimpse of the beauty upon which their hopes can be placed. There is a striking resonance between the Book of Ecclesiastes and the postmodern mood that may, in the way good poetry can, direct some of us whose hope has failed toward transcendence and meaning for our "stupid little lives." By "reversing the hermeneutical flow," Johnston allows *American Beauty* to read Ecclesiastes, demonstrating how a postmodern story can illuminate an ancient biblical text, and how a conversation of mutual discovery between theology and the arts might proceed in a postmodern world.

Chapter 1

Inventing Hope

The Question of Belief in Don DeLillo's Novels

Mark Eaton

Out of some persistent sense of large-scale ruin, we keep inventing hope.
—*Don DeLillo,* White Noise

"When the Old God leaves the world," one character muses in Don DeLillo's *Mao II* (1991), "what happens to all the unexpended faith?" (7). Posing the question in this way, the character seems to imply retrenchment or at least a transmutation of faith since the proverbial death of God. Belief in the Old God, he suggests, has been lost, redirected, changed. Yet the widespread assumption that religious belief has diminished due to a gradual process of secularization has proved to be quite mistaken, for although belief has clearly faced a formidable adversary in secularism, it has stubbornly refused to go away. On the contrary, the United States remains arguably the most religious nation on earth, and we are currently witnessing a remarkable resurgence of belief in many parts of the world. If DeLillo's character voices here what religion scholars have dubbed the "secularization thesis"—the now discredited notion that the world has been undergoing widespread secularization since the Enlightenment—he still poses an important question about how faith has been shaped by undeniably secularizing forces that, while they failed to stamp out religious belief altogether, nonetheless altered the context in which beliefs are held, if not their actual content.

DeLillo's novels are indeed preoccupied—even obsessed—with what we might call the "question of belief." And the question of belief seems like just the right phrase, too, for belief in DeLillo's fiction is always attenuated by doubt. Whether his characters are challenging a positivist belief in the reality of the natural world or trying to hold onto their belief in some supernatural realm, belief in anything seems precarious at best, provisional or untenable at worst. Above all, DeLillo has managed to capture in his fiction something essential yet paradoxical about belief: where there is belief, there is likely to be some measure, however small, of doubt.

Thus, belief and doubt come to seem less like opposites than two sides of the same coin, mutually constitutive of each other in a kind of cognitive dialectic. Although DeLillo arguably underestimates the persistence of belief in the Old God, as demonstrated in the quotation above, his novels still provide a largely accurate picture of the many dispensations of belief that actually proliferated rather than disappeared in the late twentieth century. What happened to all the unexpended faith, in other words, is that it was redirected into new forms of religiosity or else displaced onto otherwise secular apprehensions of reality, such that the materialistic scientific worldview is infused with a nagging doubt about the adequacy of that worldview to explain all phenomena. In DeLillo's remarkable novel *White Noise* (1985), the range of beliefs includes not only evangelical Christianity but also Eastern religions like Islam and Buddhism, as well as "a flood of unorthodox spiritualities" frequently grouped under the rubric of New Age religions (McClure 142). After first examining the representations of religious and other beliefs in *White Noise*, I will return to the question of belief in *Mao II*, as well as in DeLillo's later novel *Underworld* (1997). Together these novels develop a searching exploration of the permutations of unexpended faith. DeLillo has created a body of work that not only inventories the range of beliefs in the current religious scene but also reveals the uncanny interpenetration of the sacred and the profane in contemporary culture. Throughout these novels, DeLillo maps out the contours of "a new religious America" marked by an unprecedented range of spiritual options. And "nowhere," Diana Eck has observed, "is the sheer range of religious faith as wide as it is today in the United States" (4–5).

Besides registering the range of religious traditions, DeLillo's novels also represent the ways in which beliefs are influenced by the consumerist ethos of postmodern culture as well as by other faiths. Conversely, the author expertly shows how secular individuals still inevitably search for alternative means of spiritual fulfillment or find traces or "rumors" of the supernatural, as Peter Berger has said, everywhere they look. Critics have often noted the ways in which DeLillo's fine-tuned fictional worlds disclose a "sense of transcendence that lies just beyond" even the most mundane aspects of everyday life, or what the author himself once described as "a kind of radiance in dailiness." "Sometimes this radiance can be almost frightening," DeLillo once remarked. "Other times it can be almost holy or sacred" (qtd. in DeCurtis 63). This sense of a residual radiance or transcendence in everyday life is a surprising outcome of the larger historical transformations that have affected both belief and religion in the late twentieth and early twenty-first centuries. DeLillo's interest in the possibility of transcendence is inseparable from his diagnosis of a rampant fear of death in contemporary culture, which is exacerbated by the loss of faith in an afterlife. Hence, to explore the question of belief in DeLillo's work necessarily involves one in larger questions of eschatology. Secular approaches to DeLillo's novels tend to miss his point about the diffusion of unexpended faith into all sorts of religious and metaphysical systems. His novels provide a kind of case study of how religious belief not only persists but indeed has expanded in our supposedly secular postmodern era. By approaching these novels from the perspective of religious studies, we can gain a deeper understanding of the vicissitudes of belief in Don DeLillo's America.

Postmodern Melancholia

Doubt is as old as faith, of course, and yet the nature of doubt has changed since the advent of modernity. Once viewed as the opposite of belief and punishable by death, unbelief has become in the modern era an inescapable shadow of belief itself. That shadow may be light or dark on a gray-scale continuum, but it indicates the ever-present possibility of ineffable despair. As the philosopher Charles Taylor eloquently writes, a postmodern melancholia of unbelief arises,

> in a world where the guarantee of meaning has gone, where all the traditional sources, theological, metaphysical, historical, can be cast in doubt. It therefore has a new shape: not the sense of rejection and exile from an unchallengeable cosmos of significance, but rather the intimation of what may be a definitive emptiness, the

final dawning of the end of the last illusion of significance. It hurts, one might say, in a new way." (*Varieties* 39–40)

Painful as it may be to contemplate, the notion that there is nothing more than what we can see here and now has emerged not only as a distinct possibility, but as a bedrock assumption of the ascendant materialist worldview.

In the modern context, agnosticism became a viable if not the dominant intellectual position, and the notion of transcendence in turn has lost credibility. "As Christianity came under pressure from Enlightenment rationality," Andrew Delbanco argues similarly, "the idea of transcendence . . . detached itself from any coherent symbology," leaving many people with a "lurking suspicion that all our getting and spending amounts to nothing more than fidgeting while we wait for death" (5, 3). Certainly "many people appear to have become completely indifferent to religious and philosophical questions," yet even with the ascendancy of science, "there has been no wholesale rejection of the possibility of belief" (M. Taylor 4; Roof 48). On the contrary, faith remains absolutely central to many people's lives and is clearly on the rise throughout much of the world. There is no question that the so-called secularization thesis—the view that Enlightenment rationalism would ultimately supersede religion altogether—has been decisively challenged by historians of religion, who point to the spread of evangelical Christianity in particular as evidence for the resilience and vitality of belief despite the challenges of modernity and postmodernity (Berger; Jenkins).

DeLillo's novels grapple with big questions like the existence of God, the meaning of life, and what happens after death. His interest in such questions, one suspects, has more than a little to do with his Catholic upbringing. With its heavy emphasis on eschatology, Catholicism is an obvious subtext to Jack Gladney's obsession with death and the afterlife. "I think there is a sense of last things in my work that probably comes from a Catholic childhood," DeLillo admits. "For a Catholic, nothing is too important to discuss or think about, because he's raised with the idea that he will die any minute now and that if he doesn't live his life in a certain way this death is simply an introduction to an eternity of pain" (qtd. in Duvall 9). DeLillo's characters tend to struggle on their own with such questions, however, without the benefit of older certainties, much less catechisms. This disadvantage helps account for the comic pessimism that is a hallmark of DeLillo's style. Elsewhere he talks about the origins of that style: "There's a sensibility, a sense of humor, . . . a sort of dark approach to things that's part New

York, and maybe part growing up Catholic" (qtd. in Remnick 45). The combination of foreboding and humor helps explain DeLillo's ability to make even his protagonist's fear of death, if not of eternal damnation, extremely funny. Having abandoned any traditional belief in the after-life, for instance, Jack finds himself terrified of death: "I woke in the grip of a death sweat. Defenseless against my own racking fears. A pause at the center of my being" (*White Noise* 47). Cut off from any religious community or tradition of faith, DeLillo's characters are terrified of what may happen when they have shuffled off their mortal coils. If Hamlet worried about what dreams may come in the sleep of death, however, at least he could envision the afterlife as a nightmare. For Jack Gladney, death may well be simply oblivion.

Fear of death in DeLillo's characters is often accompanied by either a total lack of belief or a wildly indiscriminate belief that in its very superficiality resembles unbelief. Jack's German teacher, for instance, is another lapsed Catholic who turned away from God and religion after his mother's untimely death: "I collapsed totally, lost my faith in God. I was inconsolable, withdrew completely into myself" (*White Noise* 55). Such solipsism ultimately leaves him feeling unfulfilled, however, and he turns, of all places, to weather reports on TV for solace. Here at least are predictions of the weather delivered with such "self-assurance and skill" that they become a substitute religion. "I realized weather was some-thing I'd been looking for all my life," he says with the enthusiasm of a recent convert. "It brought me a sense of peace and security I'd never experienced" (55). The man's comment reveals not only that meteorol-ogy has replaced religion, but that all religions are subject to the demand for therapeutic self-fulfillment: if they do not meet the need for "peace and security," the adherent will simply turn elsewhere.

No one embodies the consumerist, therapeutic approach to religion more fully, however, than Jack's colleague Murray Siskind, who appar-ently espouses the Buddhist belief that death is merely "a waiting period" or "transitional state between death and rebirth" (37). Death is a time, Murray assures Jack's wife Babette (Bee), when "the soul restores itself to some of the divinity lost at birth." Death is, therefore, not unlike the supermarket where Bee and Murray meet in one memorable scene: "This place recharges us spiritually. Look how bright. It's full of psychic data" (37). Like the supermarket, death appears to Murray to be a mere formality, a way of changing channels. Metempsychosis appeals to him in part because he has rejected the Judeo-Christian afterlife, a tradition much closer to his roots than Buddhism. How reincarnation is any eas-ier to swallow for someone who is otherwise a materialist is beside the point. Murray is the kind of person for whom, when it comes to religion, the more exotic and outlandish it is, the better. And indeed Murray feels that all theories of the afterlife are more or less interchangeable so long as they provide some comfort in the here and now: "[O]nce we stop denying death, we can proceed calmly to die and then go on to experience uterine rebirth or Judeo-Christian afterlife or out-of-body experience or a trip on a UFO or whatever we wish to call it" (38). Murray's anything-goes approach to religion exemplifies a universalism that is quite prevalent nowadays. Babette also seeks to assuage her own fear of death through familiarizing herself with various religious traditions, first consulting a "Sikh holy man in Iron City" and then reading up on "the occult" to see what it has to offer (192). Ultimately, Babette takes part in an experimental clinical trial for the drug Dylar because she is promised that it "could eliminate the fear of death" (251).

This obsession with death, or more accurately with what happens to us when we die, becomes more eschatological after the airborne toxic event spreads panic throughout the town of Blacksmith and beyond. During the environmental disaster at the heart of the novel, Christian millennialism comes to the fore as the Gladney family encounters a "rangy man with sparse hair" in a suit and tie and running shoes shouting, "God's kingdom is coming" (135). Like countless millennial prophets before him, the man sees signs of the second coming in current events. Despite his own doubts about what happens after death, Jack cannot help but think that the notion of Armageddon is a bit hard to swallow: "I wondered about his eerie self-assurance, his freedom from doubt" (137). "Is this the point of Armageddon?" Jack wonders. "No ambiguity, no more doubt? . . . I did not feel Armageddon in my bones but I worried about all those people who did, who were ready for it, wishing hard, making phone calls and bank withdrawals" (137). In an age of modern science, when industrial accidents are real and "airborne toxic events" can occur without warning, it takes a kind of fanaticism to see any cosmic forces at work in what are clearly man-made perils. In another version of millennialism, Jack's older son Heinrich becomes "practically giddy . . . with some kind of end-of-the-world elation" (123). Indeed, the black billowing cloud threatening Blacksmith attains a kind of sublimity despite its toxicity: "Our fear was accompanied by a sense of awe that bordered on the religious" (127). Facing the prospect of death by industrial rather than natural disaster, or "death made in the laboratory," one felt that the cloud itself was a "cosmic force" (127). So the fear of death and the sense of helplessness before technological or cosmic forces leave DeLillo's characters grasping for whatever religious or other belief systems have to offer. It is no wonder that a family of black Jehovah's Witnesses handing out tracts at the shelter for evacuees "seemed to have no trouble finding willing recipients and listeners" (132). Similarly, the toxic event unleashes a frenzy of speculation about what caused it and what side effects exposure to the chemical will cause, yet such speculation often makes no pretense of being factual or even plausible: "People spun tales, others listened spellbound. . . . We were no closer to believing or disbelieving a given story than we had been earlier. But there was a greater appreciation . . . [for] our own ability to manufacture awe" (153).

This willingness to believe almost anything—amounting to a kind of group hysteria—also helps explain why DeLillo's characters are susceptible to charismatic leaders and cults. As John Duvall points out, "DeLillo has long been fascinated with crowds and people's collective urge to be part of something larger than themselves, to surrender to a power that would help explain the felt alienation of their lives and to protect them from a recognition of their own mortality" (15). DeLillo clearly understands our human need for some higher purpose in life, some reason to hope for a better future, at a time when the world offers plenty of reasons to despair. That's why his characters desperately cling to belief as a means of "inventing hope" in the midst of the seeming chaos and confusion of our postmodern era. His novels highlight some of the bizarre, but surely understandable, strategies people use to create meaning, or as Delbanco aptly puts it, "to hold back the melancholy suspicion that we live in a world without meaning" (3).

Shopping for Faith

Today we live in a world where the dialectic between belief and unbelief has, if anything, intensified. Over the last fifty years, a profound reshaping of religion has occurred, although not a weakening or turning away from belief, as many secular intellectuals have assumed. One critic speaks of a fundamental shift "from a world in which beliefs held believers to one in which believers hold beliefs" (Roof 42). This formulation captures a move away from traditional religion toward a more eclectic spirituality on the part of many believers. However, an equally significant shift has occurred, I am arguing, in the very nature of belief. Doubt has curiously emerged as an aspect of faith, such that believers are attuned to the resonance of unbelief, while nonbelievers in turn "combine skepticism with varying degrees of faith, or openness to faith" (48). As doubt and skepticism have become much less stigmatized—and even as outright atheism has become something of a default position among intellectuals and the "unchurched" in America, so, too, has belief itself been altered—shaded, we might say—by the dominant ideology of pluralism.

In order to better understand DeLillo's analysis of belief, we first need to consider the changing nature of belief in these pluralistic, postmodern times. Polls continue to show a high percentage of people who profess to believe in God. *The New York Times* reported in 1997 that 96% of Americans say they believe in God; 90% think there is a heaven; and 87% consider themselves Christians (Mizruchi ix). While only 40% of adults say they attend religious services regularly, 69% say they belong to a church or synagogue, and 90% claim that they pray to God or some higher being (Gallup and Lindsey 2–3). At the very least, these figures suggest that the U.S. is much more religious than one might think. Such figures may, however, paint a somewhat misleading picture of the current state of religion by exaggerating the orthodoxy of belief and by occluding the prevailing secularism of American culture. For whatever the polls say about widespread belief in God, the ways in which people think of their belief relative to other beliefs and to the larger culture are evolving. "Many people remain convinced of God's existence," Robert Wuthnow has observed, "but realize increasingly that the reality of their world is secular" (10). And belief in God does not necessarily result in regular church attendance, either, for today "a wider range of people express religious beliefs that move outside Christian orthodoxy" (C. Taylor, *Varieties* 107). Belief is thus detached from traditional religious communities, as are spiritual disciplines like prayer. According to Wade Clark Roof, "[T]he current religious situation in the United States is characterized not so much by a loss of faith as a qualitative shift from unquestioned belief to a more open, questing mood" (9). "Inherited forms of religion persist and still influence people," he continues, but the heterogeneity of religious practices signals "a shift in the center of religious energy" (7).

Since the 1960s and 1970s, in particular, many baby boomers have sought out alternatives to what they disparagingly called "organized religion," often by rejecting the churches of their parents in favor of a more personalized spirituality. Ironically, in doing so they have conformed to a patently consumerist approach to faith, as suggested by the authors of one study, *Shopping for Faith: American Religion in the New Millennium*: "Today's diverse religious landscape . . . can be compared to a busy marketplace where competition thrives and seekers shop" (Cimino and Lattin 5). In this competitive, free-market environment, traditional Christian denominations are contracting, whereas newer types of churches, many of them associated with evangelical Pentecostalism, are flourishing. Indeed, "evangelical Christianity is the fastest-growing form of religious life" in the U.S. today (C. Taylor, *Varieties* 38). Islam and Buddhism have also grown considerably, to the point where Muslims now equal Presbyterians (Mizruchi ix). While the majority of Americans identify themselves as Christian, the diversity of religions in the United States is surely one of the signs of the times. In emphasizing that diversity, DeLillo arguably understates the clear Christian majority in the United States. Even though a plurality of Americans are Christians, the majority faith is nonetheless influenced by the multifaith context in which it now finds itself.

With his finger on the spiritual pulse of contemporary American culture, DeLillo brilliantly delineates "the increasingly complex hybridity of religious forms" (Mizruchi ix), as well as the diversity of beliefs. The varieties of religious experience are everywhere evident in *White Noise*. The waxing and waning of traditional, mainline denominations; the proliferation of New Age spiritualities; the emergence of a kind of apocalyptic environmentalism; the rise of religious fundamentalisms; the popularization of quasireligious practices like yoga; even the more insidious and sometimes deadly practices of cults: all these phenomena and more fall under DeLillo's purview. "These new spiritualities, like the more traditional forms," John McClure has written, "are often inflected with the rhetoric and values of consumer capitalism, but they tend, at the same time, to appeal to people dissatisfied with secular strategies of fulfillment" (142). There are almost as many beliefs as there are believers, and consumerism, if not a religion in itself, infects virtually all of them. In *White Noise*, Murray Siskind advises Jack Gladney to sample the variety of religions and "pick one you like" (286). "Read up on reincarnation, transmigration, hyperspace, the resurrection of the dead and so on," urges Murray. "Some gorgeous systems have evolved from these beliefs." Knowing that Murray is a nonpracticing Jew and a pop culture professor in the Department of American Environments, Jack demands to know, "Do you believe in any of these things?" Murray simply dodges the question: "Millions of people have believed them for thousands of years" (286). Not one to practice what he preaches, the closest Murray comes to a religious experience is at a tourist site known as the most photographed barn in America: "Being here is a kind of spiritual surrender," he tells Jack. "A religious experience in a way, like all tourism" (12). Another professor in the novel, the New York transplant Alfonse Stompanato, stays on the cutting edge of intellectual trends by making popular culture itself his only religion: "When he talked about popular culture, he exercised the closed logic of a religious zealot, one who kills for his beliefs" (65). I will have more to say below about how *Mao II* explores the dangers of religious fundamentalism, but for now let me suggest only that the specter of fundamentalist zeal arises whenever anyone latches onto a particular religion and embraces it so exclusively, so wholeheartedly as to become irrational or worse: one who kills for his beliefs.

Certainly most characters in *White Noise* are almost comically innocuous in their beliefs, however. DeLillo's characters are for the most part what religious scholars call "seekers." They exemplify a relatively new paradigm of seeking out religious experiences not in traditional churches but in various world religions or even in quasireligions. Wuthnow is helpful on this point: "[A] profound change in our spiritual practices has indeed taken place during the last half century," in which a "traditional spirituality of inhabiting sacred places has given way to a new spirituality of seeking" (3). Following Murray's advice to sample the world's religions and "pick one you like," many characters in *White Noise* are engaged in a freewheeling quest for spiritual guidance. Jack's ex-wife Janet, for instance, lives in a commune or "ashram" on the outskirts of the former copper-smelting town of Tubb, Montana, now called "Dharamsalapur," and goes by the name "Mother Devi." Tweedy Browner, Bee's mother, is described as having "a sense of Protestant disrepair about her" (86). The phrase *Protestant disrepair*, tossed off here with DeLillo's usual aplomb, in fact indexes an important religious trend in America: the shrinking of mainline denominations amidst an increasingly commercialized field of religious institutions. In his book *Selling God* (1994), R. Laurence Moore writes that the "sheer diversity" of religions means that churches now "have to sell" themselves, "not only in the competitive church market but also in a general market of other cultural commodities" (10-11). In the same vein, Donald E. Miller points out that "so-called mainline denominations are clearly losing their market share. In the past several decades denominations such as the Methodists, Presbyterians, and Episcopalians have lost between 20 and 40 percent of their members" (4). Janet Savory, a baby boomer herself, abandons Protestantism for a cultlike rural commune in Tubb, Montana, a move that in its own exaggerated, heightened way replicates the movement away from mainline churches by so many people in the 1960s and 1970s. Jack's colleague Murray Siskind and virtually all of Jack's other sometime spouses together exemplify the typical eclecticism of aging baby boomers who view the whole array of world religions as a kind of spiritual playground. As a scholar of popular culture, Murray perhaps takes his cue from icons such as Elvis Presley, who, as he points out, strongly believed in UFOs and read *The Tibetan Book of the Dead*, a "guide to dying and being reborn" (72). It is no small irony that Elvis, a dabbler in metempsychosis, lives on in so many "Elvis sightings," not to mention in the afterlife of images.

Jack's first and fourth wife Babette takes a similarly eclectic, but arguably more fitness-oriented approach to self-fulfillment through lifestyle changes, exercise programs, and even psychopharmacology. Her role in the Blacksmith community is that of a kind of self-help guru; she gives lectures at a local Congregational Church on yoga, Sufi dervishes, and correct posture. Babette's grab-bag approach derives from the permissive ethos of most New Age adherents: "Nothing is foreign, nothing too remote to apply" (27). Babette's disciples flock to her classes, listening with rapt attention as she lectures incessantly about "yoga, kendo, trance-walking," and other New Age fads. For his part, Jack marvels "at their acceptance and trust, the sweetness of their belief. Nothing is too doubtful to be of use to them. . . . It is the end of skepticism" (27). Such sentimental belief has a nostalgic quality, as if by disavowing incredulity about anything, one might make up for the loss of certainty that made traditional belief systems impervious to doubt. Unmoored from its traditional grounding in a coherent religious framework, belief goes soft. Indeed, there is some indication that some people prefer soft belief to anything that makes a stronger claim on one's convictions. When Jack discusses the possibility of Heinrich visiting his mother, Janet, a.k.a. Mother Devi, he instructs her not to try to indoctrinate him into the beliefs of her ashram. "Let him ride horses, fish for trout," Jack says. "But I don't want him getting involved in something personal and intense, like religion" (273). Concerned that she takes her beliefs so seriously to have dropped out of society for them, Jack wants to protect their child from such strong faith. The sentiment clearly echoes the trend towards privatized, pluralistic religion: keep your beliefs to yourself, American culture increasingly demands, and you'll fit right in.

Perhaps the very superficiality of beliefs that are merely tried on like so many outfits means that one's commitment to them can be a little slack, and one's belief in them not overly skeptical. Babette's unquestioning acceptance of tabloids, for example, is worth exploring in some detail for the ways in which an age-old belief in paranormal phenomena has been displaced into the realm of kitsch. Sitting in a makeshift shelter with "a small and brightly colored stack of supermarket tabloids" (142), Babette relates one preposterous tale after another to a group of people who seem to have no problem believing "documented cases of life after death," or the "transmigration of souls," or even "personalized resurrection through stream-of-consciousness computer techniques" (144). The pseudojournalistic discourse of the tabloids—hyperbolic, surreal, eschatological—does not seem ridiculous; instead it is accepted with a sort of "passive belief . . . [as] a set of statements no less real than our daily quota of observable household fact" (144–45). DeLillo mocks how easily Babette and her listeners swallow these outrageous tales, to be sure, but he also forces us to ponder their extraordinary appeal to some 20 million readers per week. We can surely relate to the scene in which Jack, standing in the checkout line at the local supermarket, is ineluctably drawn to the glossy covers with their sensationalistic headlines: "Everything we need that is not food or love is here in the tabloid racks. The tales of the supernatural and the extraterrestrial. The miracle vitamins, the cures for cancer, the remedies for obesity. The cults of the famous and the dead" (326). Indeed, the author once told an interviewer that the tabloids "ask profoundly important questions about death, the afterlife, God . . . in an almost Pop Art atmosphere" (qtd. in Osteen 179). In this sense, DeLillo's critique of American culture is deliberately embedded in that culture: he realizes his own susceptibility to cooptation, his own fascination with the very cultural forces he deplores. Such credulity towards alien abductions or metempsychosis is easy to ridicule, but the popularity of these publications should give us pause. In its undisguised sensationalism and blatant prevarication, tabloid journalism sheds light on the fringes of faith in America today.

The effects of consumerism on religion are pronounced in *White Noise*: the suburban world of DeLillo's novel is suffused with advertising jingles, screaming headlines, and TV sound bites—the "white noise" of American mass culture. Consumerism is viewed as a religion almost. Jack Gladney finds moments of transcendence not in traditional religion but in shopping: the grocery store provides him with a "sense of well-being" and even a "fullness of being that is not known to people who need less, expect less" (20). Similarly, when a cash machine confirms that his actual bank balance corresponds (roughly) with his checkbook, "Waves of relief and gratitude flow through him" (46). "The system had blessed my life," Jack says matter-of-factly. "I felt its support and approval" (46). In the exquisite shopping spree at the Mid Village Mall, Jack notes the spiritual fulfillment he gets from shopping: "I filled myself out, found new aspects of myself, located a person I'd forgotten existed" (84). Consumerism may assuage Jack's desire simply to buy stuff, and surely we recognize the strange emotional uplift of a shopping spree, but shopping is no panacea for deeper anxieties about his marriage, profession, and imminent death. The significance of consumerism as both a kind of substitute religion and a powerful influence on religions themselves is surely one of the signal contributions of DeLillo's analysis of belief.

The Sublime and the Miraculous

Another contribution DeLillo makes to the question of belief in *White Noise* moves away from the realm of cultural critique and more into the areas of religious studies and, yes, theology itself. Here I have in mind the ways in which DeLillo incorporates elements of mysticism and the miraculous into a world otherwise denuded of the sacred. But DeLillo understands the feeling of what I earlier called "postmodern melancholia" all too well. His characters are, spiritually speaking, left to their own devices, and they struggle to find meaning, to worry about life's ultimate purpose, to wonder about possible supernatural forces at work in the world. With no connection whatever to a viable tradition or community of faith, Jack Gladney understandably latches onto whatever shards of spiritual significance he can find, whether in the quotidian of family life, the plethora of consumer goods, or man-made disasters. Jack likens the thick black, billowy cloud—euphemistically labeled by experts an "air-borne toxic event"—to the sublime: "Our fear was accompanied by a sense of awe that bordered on the religious. It is surely possible to be awed by the thing that threatens your life, to see it as a cosmic force, so much larger than yourself, more powerful, created by elemental and willful rhythms" (127). DeLillo no doubt refers here to the elaboration of the sublime as a corollary to the fear of death in Enlightenment philosophers like Immanuel Kant and Edmund Burke. "Whatever therefore is terrible, with regard to sight," Burke declared in his *On the Sublime and Beautiful* (1794), "is sublime too, whether this cause of terror be endued with greatness of dimensions or not. . . . Astonishment . . . is the effect of the sublime in its highest degree; the inferior effects are admiration, reverence, and respect." In the Romantic era, the sublime became increasingly linked to religion, since it is the power and aura of God which invokes those emotions associated with it: terror, wonder, amazement, and awe. In the black, billowing cloud, DeLillo has found the perfect postmodern embodiment of the sublime, and while its industrial source and chemical toxicity make the cloud as far from a deity as you can get, DeLillo nonetheless means to suggest that Jack's awe bordered on the religious.

We have seen, then, that the characters in *White Noise* discover intimations of the sacred in the most unexpected places, whether in the most mundane, or in this case, the most spectacular events of the day.

Our perception of natural or technological phenomena is always in question; one thinks here of the hilarious discussion between Jack Gladney and his son about about whether it is really raining or it is just a figment of their imaginations. Because nearly everything in the novel is open to interpretation, moreover, DeLillo simultaneously captures the epistemological crisis at the heart of our postmodern condition and "a sense of something extraordinary hovering just beyond our touch and just beyond our vision" (DeCurtis 63). Given the post-Enlightenment "disenchantment of the world" (Weber, "Science as a Vocation" 155), we might say that Jack's world is reenchanted such that a bag of groceries offers a sense of well-being (20); a family dinner gives off "extrasensory flashes and floating nuances of being" (34); his daughter's "ecstatic chant" of a car name, Toyota Celica, strikes him "with the impact of a moment of splendid transcendence" (155); his younger son Wilder's seven-hour bout of crying evokes "a mingled reverence and wonder" in the rest of the family (79); and finally, the simple act of watching his children sleep makes Jack feel oddly "devout, part of a spiritual system" (154). Family life becomes, in this novel, a repository of spiritual intimations. It has, the narrator says, a "colloquial density that makes family life the one medium of sense knowledge in which an astonishment of heart is routinely contained" (117). But the novel goes beyond merely hinting at the sacred qualities of domestic life to suggest that outmoded, primitive forms of religious belief unexpectedly reappear in the postmodern era. Among the various forms of idol worship, none is more recognizably archaic than when his twelve-year-old, prematurely balding son Heinrich is described as a "primitive clay figurine, some household idol of obscure and cultic derivation" (242).

DeLillo clearly engages in what McClure calls "a post-secular project of resacralization" (144), but the author's take on the transcendent is by no means unambiguous. In a bizarre scene near the end of *White Noise*, for instance, Wilder performs what amounts to a miracle by riding his tricycle across an expressway in rush-hour traffic and emerging unscathed at the other end. What to make of this miracle is not at all clear; indeed, DeLillo goes out of his way to emphasize its utter incomprehensibility:

> The women could only look, empty-mouthed, each with an arm in
> the air, a plea for the scene to reverse, the boy to pedal backwards
> on his faded blue and yellow toy like a cartoon figure on morning
> TV. The drivers could not quite comprehend. In their knotted pos-
> ture, belted in, they knew this picture did not belong to the

hurtling consciousness of the highway, the broad-ribboned modernist stream. . . . What did it mean, this little rotary blur?
(322–23)

On one hand, the scene is deliberately cinematic, the suburban
equivalent of Sergei Eisenstein's famous Odessa steps sequence in
Battleship Potemkin (1925), or rather an ironic update on countless
chase scenes in which the hero improbably dodges adversaries, bullets,
and oncoming vehicles with hardly a scratch. The bystanders who watch
Wilder set out across the freeway can only hope "for the scene to reverse,
the boy to pedal backwards . . . like a cartoon figure on morning TV"
(322). On the other hand, DeLillo's language applies a religious frame of
reference for Wilder's wild ride. He is "mystically charged" (322)—as if
guardian angels are escorting him to safety. As such, DeLillo's suburban
landscape is paradoxically both secularized and imbued with spiritual
significance, the transcendent, a sense of the miraculous.

DeLillo's analysis of belief and doubt in *White Noise* culminates in
another bizarre scene in the penultimate chapter, when Jack Gladney,
bleeding profusely from a bullet wound, seeks help in "a three story
building that might have been a Pentecostal church, a day-care center,
world headquarters for some movement of regimented youth" (315).
Instead, it "appeared to be a clinic" run by Catholic nuns (316). What
follows is a curious philosophical discussion about belief, the upshot of
which, as Jack is astounded to learn, is that the nuns themselves do not
believe in heaven. When Jack protests that nuns, of all people, have to
keep the faith, one sister knowingly observes that "nonbelievers need the
believers. They are desperate to have someone believe" (318). "As belief
shrinks from the world," she claims, "people find it more necessary than
ever that *someone* believe. . . . Those who have abandoned belief must
still believe in us" (318–19). Jack's unbelief, in other words, is belied by
his certainty that someone else believes. This is a variation on the dialectic of belief and unbelief. If even the most devout believers find themselves experiencing serious doubt, the converse is also true: nonbelievers
need to believe that there are believers. Ultimately, Jack solves the problem of his own unbelief by resolving to believe everything: "White noise
everywhere. . . . I believed everything" (310). In his book *American
Magic and Dread* (2000), Mark Osteen astutely glosses this scene:
"DeLillo is suggesting that the impulse to believe, a faith in the bare
potential for sacredness or transcendence, will always endure. Tabloids,
TV, supermarkets, toxic clouds—like it or not, these are the sites where
spirits live and the shapes that spirits take" (188).

Fundamentalism and Terror

Conspiracy theory and espionage were, at best, tangential to the domestic drama of *White Noise* (Jack's ex-wife is now married to a CIA agent, for instance); yet DeLillo has never strayed far from these twin aspects of the Cold War. In subsequent novels he returns to them as a way of analyzing the question of belief in the context of not only the continuing appeal of cults but the alarming growth of fundamentalist movements throughout the world. *Mao II*, a political thriller that opens at a large gathering of Moonies in a football stadium, elaborates and deepens DeLillo's treatment of cults and other mass religious movements, touching on the contentious politics of belief: the damage it sometimes causes in people's lives, as well as the violence it often engenders in many parts of the world. The last section, "Beirut," speaks to the spectacular rise in Islamic fundamentalism over the last several decades. Similarly, while cults were always on the periphery of *White Noise*, here they take center stage. The details of the opening scene reinforce my contention that belief can still be virulent in our otherwise cynical, noncommittal age. "Here they come," the novel begins, "marching into American sunlight" (3). A mass wedding is staged at Yankee stadium, where 6,500 couples are to be married by the Reverend Moon, "a man of chunky build who saw Jesus on a mountainside . . . and now he is here, in American light, come to lead them to the end of human history" (6). Moon is the Master of ceremonies, the charismatic leader of a cult:

> The blessed couples move their lips in unison, matching the echo of his amplified voice. There is stark awareness in their faces, a near pain of rapt adoration. He is Lord of the Second Advent. . . . His voice leads them out past love and joy, past the beauty of their mission, out past miracles and surrendered self. . . . He leads them out past religion and history. (15)

The novel reveals that the appeal of cults may derive in part from an implicit promise to remove followers from the weighty cares of the real world.

Belief becomes so all-consuming that it compels followers to give up their personal desires, their families, their very identities. The main character, Karen Janney, is marrying a man named Kim Jo Pak, whom she has only recently met. Her parents, Rodge and Maureen, watch anxiously from the stands, peering through a pair of binoculars and trying in vain to spot their estranged daughter. Looking out on the sea of faces, Rodge muses, "They are a nation . . . founded on the principle of easy belief. A unit fueled by credulousness" (7). In one of DeLillo's trademark narrative devices, the point of view shifts between the parents and Karen herself, or rather the limited omniscient narrator is focalized now through Rodge and now through what he calls Karen's "mindstream." This dizzying shift in perspective forces readers to consider the scene from various viewpoints: that of the parents and the Moonie partici- pants alike. DeLillo's humor and irony are evident in the self-pity of the parents, whose only daughter has joined a cult, marrying without their consent a Korean guy they have never met who knows only "about eight words of English" (5). Mass religious cults like the Moonies do tend to prey on the most vulnerable people in our society and draw them in through the promise of spiritual certainty and a sense of belonging to some larger purpose. Though Karen is middle-class and seems fairly well-adjusted, she gets caught up in the movement enough to marry a complete stranger, and then leads a group of disciples around the coun- try to collect money for the church. She is the kind of character who cannot live without the security of an "absolute being" who provides, in her view, "a way out of weakness and confusion" (163). In DeLillo's novel *The Names* (1982), one character chides his wife: "You need things to be committed to. You need belief" (128). Karen is likewise described as someone who needs to believe in something or someone, not the Old God, in this case, but in the Reverend Moon himself: "She believed deeply in Master and still thought of herself as a seeker, ready to receive what was vast and true" (78). Like so many of her fellow seekers, Karen has not been fulfilled by traditional religious institutions: "She began to think she was inadequate to the strict plain shapes of churchly faith" (78). Again, DeLillo presents his characters as seekers engaged in an almost haphazard spiritual journey that leads them away from organized religion into less traditional, albeit sometimes highly organized, faiths. Even if they do not find exactly what they are looking for, these charac- ters latch onto the latest fads in obsessive and frequently self-destructive ways. They may not even wholly believe in the religions they follow, but their commitment, once made, is unquestionably wholehearted.

Belief, then, is something of a problem for many of DeLillo's char- acters, who are "driven by homeless spiritual impulses and mesmerized by new religious movements" (McClure 142). Those who are highly skeptical of God-talk still sympathize with the human impulse to believe. They ridicule Karen's personal belief in the Reverend Moon as a deity—"Karen thinks God is here. Like walkin' and talkin'" (69)—yet they admit to feeling dissatisfied with their own disbelief or lack of faith. "I don't like not believing," the photojournalist Brita says at one point.

"I'm not at peace with it. I take comfort when others believe. . . . I need these people to believe for me. I cling to believers. Many, everywhere. Without them, the planet goes cold" (69). I can think of no better illustration of this coldness than a poignant scene near the end of *Underworld* (1997). Sister Edgar, another nun, experiences a crisis of faith when a young homeless girl she had been trying to help is brutally raped and murdered. She had seen in the girl "a radiant grace" and "even a source of personal hope, a goad to the old rugged faith" (811), but after Esmeralda is killed, Sister Edgar is well on her way to a loss of faith:

> She believes she is falling into crisis, beginning to think it is possible that all creation is a spurt of blank matter that chances to make an emerald here, a dead start there, with random waste between. The serenity of immense design is missing from her life, authorship and moral form. . . .
>
> It is not a question of disbelief. There is another kind of belief, a second force, insecure, untrusting, a faith that is spring fed by the things we fear in the night, and she thinks she is succumbing. (817)

"The things we fear in the night": this is DeLillo's shorthand for the dark forces of inhumanity and violence at work in our world. Without question, people do inhumane things; the evidence is on every front page. Instead of succumbing to evil and giving up hope, why not try to keep a modicum of faith in human beings—in our capacity for civility, empathy, and love? Sister Edgar's loss of faith in the face of an ever-present evil is a very old and familiar story—more familiar by now, I suspect, than stories about individuals who maintain, against all odds, their belief in human goodness or in God. Regardless of whether one sustains or loses faith, however, I think it is fair to say that DeLillo represents the dialectic between belief and unbelief as a signal feature of a kind of spiritual malaise.

That spiritual malaise has surely worsened during the first part of this century, and for good reason. I'd like to end with a coda of sorts on the dangers of misdirected belief, or more precisely, on the danger of allowing one's beliefs to motivate violent acts. Certain passages in DeLillo's 1991 novel *Mao II* now seem astonishingly prescient in the wake of September 11, 2001. The novel contains a running debate about the architecturally iconic World Trade Center towers, and at one point Brita complains about the sheer size of the buildings with the inadvertently prophetic comment: "the size is deadly" (40). Later she comes across a painting "showing the World Trade Center at precisely

the same angle she saw it from her window and in the same dark spirit
. . . two black latex slabs that consumed available space" (165). Then, in
a development that is in no way connected to these musings on the twin
towers, there are ominous rumblings of a rising Islamic jihad in the
Middle East. In the final section of the book, Brita is on assignment in
Beirut covering a terrorist organization. The leader, a young militant
named Rasheed, explains to her that Muslims resent a "Western presence" in the Middle East because it is "a threat to self-respect" (235).
"Terror makes the new future possible," Rasheed sneers. "We do history
in the morning and change it after lunch" (235). Taken as a whole, *Mao
II* dares to imagine a rather bleak future in which individuals either live
outside history, as Karen does ("He leads them out past religion and history," 15)—or make up history as they go along, as Rasheed threatens to
do ("He is saying we make and change history minute by minute," 235).
These are the extremes, perhaps, of what happens when belief is perverted to serve corrupt ends.

The cover of *Underworld* features a remarkable photograph of the
World Trade Center, which, like the painting Karen Janney describes,
shows the twin towers in a "dark spirit" as massive concrete "slabs"
reaching up to the clouds. After 9/11, of course, that cover photograph
took on added, if unintended, significance. In the foreground, a church
facade is visible through dense fog; the cross is perched right in between
those two giant skyscrapers that no longer exist. In the wake of the most
vicious terrorist attack on United States soil, this picture struck me as an
uncanny gloss on how religion can be an astonishingly destructive force
as well as an undeniable force for good. Looking closely at the photograph, I suddenly noticed a bird soaring off to one side of the twin towers. I like to think of that bird as a dove, the universal symbol of peace,
in part because the last word of *Underworld* is, in fact, "Peace" (818), a
hopeful word that for obvious reasons resonates more deeply now than it
did when the book was first published. I am emboldened by this gesture
to imagine that, in spite of the seemingly insurmountable problems of
our postmodern world, if we listen closely, we may hear the still small
voice of hope beneath all the white noise.

Chapter 2

Voices from Within
Gloria Anzaldúa, bell hooks, and Roberta Bondi

Anne-Marie Bowery

The poignant expression of personal experience in feminist writing has a long history. One need only think of the strong narrative persona in Virginia's Woolf's *A Room of One's Own*, or recall Simone de Beauvoir's detailed exploration of how one becomes a woman in *The Second Sex*, or read Hazel Barnes's autobiography, *The Story I Tell Myself*, to recognize how a strong personal voice can interplay with the sociopolitical and philosophical dimensions of a feminist text. Notwithstanding the presence of these compelling works and the fact that a common theme in feminist scholarship in years past has been to make women's experience visible, many contemporary feminist writers have struggled to create a space between the theoretical and the personal dimensions of their work (Alcoff 43). For example, Susan Bernstein notes that "Despite its current popularity, not all feminists embrace or tolerate the confessional mode" (123), and Woolf herself believes that "it is fatal for a woman . . . in any way to speak consciously as a woman" (108). She views writing "as an art, not a mode of self-expression" (83). Similarly, many contemporary feminists side with Linda Bell, who argues, "An uncritical use of [personal] experience will lead only to ideals that continue to reflect unexamined and unacceptable assumptions of our society" (195). However, rather than abandon the use of personal experience altogether, Joan Scott suggests working with it, analyzing its operations and redefining its meaning. "This entails focusing on processes of identity production, insisting on the discursive nature of 'experience' and on the politics of its construction." (37). Arguing for a properly reconstructed phenomenology, Linda Alcoff warns against any privileged perspective that loses awareness of the nuances and subtle power that come from listening to marginalized voices (40).

Simply put, we must not lose the personal for the sake of the political and theoretical. The loss would be great. Personal confessional narratives offer enormous resources for finding personal meaning, even in human suffering. They can help us overcome deep pessimism about the human condition, offering healing and hope in the midst of cultural despair. While rejecting grand narratives as instruments of domination, postmodernism embraces the pluralism of smaller stories, each produced within its own unique historical and cultural context, and celebrates a diversity of voices, particularly those long silenced by the privileged and the powerful. Recent years have seen the rise of confessional literature that gives voice to the life experience of individuals from underappreciated groups, alerting sensitive readers to the painful struggle of the poor, the disenfranchised, and the marginalized to tell their stories and be heard. Hope, it seems, is forged in the crucible of this struggle. In this essay, I analyze the stories of three contemporary feminist writers, juxtaposing the confessional narratives of Gloria Anzaldúa's intensely poetic *Borderlands/La Frontera*, bell hooks's *Wounds of Passion: A Writing Life*, and Roberta Bondi's *Memories of God: Theological Reflections on a Life*. These writers employ autobiographical reflection to transform the spiritual resources of their varied cultural and religious backgrounds and to expel the ghosts of oppressive societal traditions that haunt them. Anzaldúa, hooks, and Bondi may be unfamiliar to some readers, so I will begin by briefly introducing them, noting in particular the diversity of their cultural and religious backgrounds.

Gloria Anzaldúa describes herself as a "Chicana *tejana* lesbian-feminist poet and fiction writer" (205). She has taught at a number of universities, including the University of Texas, San Francisco State University, and Vermont College. Throughout *Borderlands/La Frontera*, she vividly recalls her childhood experiences growing up on the Texas-

Mexico border. Her anger, fear, and courage provide the human background for her historically grounded cultural critique, linguistic analysis, and poetical reflection. Monika Kaup says of Anzaldúa's text: "*Borderlands/La Frontera* is a book about the culture of the Chicana-mestiza, straddling one national border and multiple racial and sexual borders. In this sense, it is a paradigmatic text that recreates the world of 'women of color' in writing while avoiding a totalizing identity" (101). A black feminist cultural theorist, bell hooks, grew up in Kentucky in the racially segregated South, receiving both her undergraduate degrees at prestigious institutions in California (Stanford and UC Santa Cruz). She has taught at Yale, Oberlin City College and Southwestern University in Georgetown, Texas. Throughout her extensive oeuvre, hooks weaves personal experience into a feminist critique of culture. In *Wounds of Passion*, she acknowledges that writing "against a cultural backdrop where black females have been reluctant to explore in autobiographical work the full range of our emotional universe . . . was both daring and difficult" (xxi). Nonetheless, she "write[s] intimately about the pleasure and the pain [in order] to document the psychological and philosophical foundations of one woman's writing life" (xxiii). By contrast, Roberta Bondi is a white feminist theologian who teaches at Candler Theological Seminary at Emory University. As the subtitle *Theological Reflections on a Life* suggests, Bondi uses theological conceptions to reflect on her life, but the converse is just as true. Her engaging narrative voice recounts personal stories to illustrate Christian theological concepts like the crucifixion, the resurrection, and the communion of saints. She draws upon childhood memories and family stories to illustrate how destructive a patriarchal understanding of theology can be. "In the sixties liberalism of theological education there was a hierarchy of truth. There, theology was an esoteric discipline that did not like stories . . . this was because serious theology concerned itself only with what theologians assumed was universally true. It did not waste its time addressing the personal" (9). Bondi overcomes this hesitancy. In her deft hands, the personal and the theological are intertwined.

My purpose in placing these texts in conversation with each other is to illustrate the aesthetic range of expression and insightful reflection available to feminist readers, writers, and teachers. Clearly, these writers occupy three radically different cultural spaces; each voice is shaped by race, class, nationality, geographic location, sexual orientation, and religion. While maintaining the distinctiveness of these diverse spaces, I locate three important thematic similarities within their boundaries that demonstrate how discovery of voice can be used to gain self-understanding. First, each author describes a passionate relationship with words and literature that develops in childhood. Second, each recognizes the enormous power of education both as a means of cultural domination and as a means of personal liberation. Finally, each woman embraces the dynamic power of spiritual experience in her life's work. Though these writers differ in terms of race, culture, class, sexual orientation, and beliefs about God, their stories resist the prejudices and injustices of patriarchal society and serve as prophetic models of hope.

Lovers of Literature: Becoming a Writer

A dramatic presentation of childhood memories and stories plays an important part in all three books. One striking similarity emerges: the authors each come to love literature, poetry, and words. Words resonate palpably as each recounts her formative experience. This primal relationship with words and with themselves as storytellers culminates in a desire to become a writer. Identification of the self through an engagement with literature provides both emotional solace and intellectual stimulation, but it also provides a path to self-discovery and liberation from their personal demons. In her book *Getting Personal*, Nancy Miller observes that "autobiography provides texts for reading that engender the coming to writing in others. Perhaps the essence of autobiography as a genre—or rather one of its most valuable effects—is to enable this process" (135). Anzaldúa, hooks, and Bondi experience the liberating effects of literature, and all three offer readers intimate accounts of their own personal odysseys. Anzaldúa recalls her early experience with stories. "Nudge a Mexican," she writes, "and she or he will break out with a story" (65). This story of the storyteller begins: "[W]hen I was seven, eight, nine, fifteen, sixteen years old, I would read in bed with a flashlight under the covers, hiding my self-imposed insomnia from my mother. I preferred the world of the imagination to the death of sleep. My sister Hilda, who slept in the same bed with me, would threaten to tell my mother unless I told her a story." Over the years, she continues, "I learned to give her installments, building up the suspense . . . [I]t must have been then that I decided to put stories on paper" (65). In reading this passage, one cannot help but be reminded of Scheherzade's midnight narratives to her husband.

Later in life, Anzaldúa recalls the shock and joyous surprise when she learned that a Chicano person had actually published a book: "In the 1960's, I read my first Chicano novel. It was *City of Night* by John

Rechy, a gay Texan, son of a Scottish father and a Mexican mother. For days I walked around in stunned amazement that a Chicano could write and could get published" (59). She recalls a similar experience with poetry: "[W]hen I saw poetry written in Tex-Mex for the first time, a feeling of pure joy flashed through me. I felt like we really existed as a people" (60). Anzaldúa's deeply emotional relationship with language grows throughout her life, until eventually, she becomes a writer. "[W]riting is my whole life, it is my obsession. This vampire which is my talent does not suffer other suitors. Daily I court it, offer my neck to its teeth. This is the sacrifice that the act of creation requires, a blood sacrifice. For only through the body, through the pulling of flesh, can the human soul be transformed" (75). She achieves a powerful voice through writing, both for herself and for her Chicana experience. Anzaldúa's sense of voice involves more than finding the courage to express previously repressed desires and preferences. It also involves claiming a space for her diverse ethnic background and for her culturally suspect lesbian desires. She explains that her "self" includes all these voices; "I will no longer be made to feel ashamed of existing. I will have my voice: Indian, Spanish, white. I will have my serpent's tongue—my woman's voice, my sexual voice, my poet's voice. I will overcome the tradition of silence" (59). Viewed in this way, Anzaldúa's "own voice" moves beyond a private expression of emotion and into a larger domain of cultural critique.

Like Anzaldúa, hooks knew from a very early age that she wanted to be a writer. She mentions this early self-identification continually in *Wounds of Passion* and reinforces this point in many other books and interviews. Throughout *Wounds of Passion*, hooks writes of her youthful self from the third-person perspective. "Her dream was to be a poet. Her earliest understanding of what that might mean all came from Emily Dickinson, her secret mentor and friend" (4). For hooks, literature offered an escape from the physical and psychological pain of childhood. "In her childhood she learned to leave behind pain by reading books. Sometimes they took the books away—too many words, too much pleasure. She turned to poetry. Words to learn by heart—to say over and over again in the dark" (38). Poetry becomes a powerful source of protection and even a source of healing. "Poems were the way to leave pain behind—to forget. . . . They were water to her thirst, cooling the burning sensation, soothing the red welts on her skin left by lashes from fresh young branches still green. Poetry made childhood bearable" (3). Literature is quite literally a sacred place of refuge and rebirth. "My mythic mother is Emily Dickinson. Her womb is a space of words where seeds of me enter and grow. I am born again—lost to the father, the son, and the holy ghost" (39).

Like Anzaldúa, hooks is profoundly moved by the discovery of writers who share her ethnic identity. For example, using a rhetorical style that switches back and forth between referring to herself in the first and third person, hooks says, for example, "In high school she goes to the library and finds James Weldon Johnson's *The Book of American Negro Poetry*. . . . She loves this book so much she never returns it to the library. The words of these poets are just that precious" (*Wounds* 109). She admits that she does not "know what made me keep that anthology of American Negro Poetry." But her response to this book of poems was so intense that "All I knew was that I had to have it in my possession, to concretely remind me that this wonderful poetry coming from our life existed" (*Wounds* 109–10). Perhaps like Anzaldúa, hooks realizes that her voice contains more than her private register of emotions. Rather, the shared voices found in the literature of her race provide a richer context in which her private suffering finds a voice.

In *Memories of God*, Roberta Bondi recounts a similar passion for literature. She "loved the stories of the brave Madeleine" who just said "pooh, pooh" (7). She describes herself as a "lonely child who could never seem to fit in," a child who found comfort in *Beauty and the Beast* and *The Ugly Duckling* (7). She also loved the stories of the Old Testament (7). Bondi calls these stories "her lifeblood." She remembers that these stories "helped me make sense of myself, my family, and my world" (8). Bondi finds a sense of comfort and a glimpse of liberation in her realization that her private experience can be understood from a larger perspective. However, she comes to this realization somewhat differently than Anzaldúa and hooks do. For her, it comes not by reading other writers who share her marginalized perspective. Rather, it is simply the awareness of the larger social, political, and theological context that provides her with comfort. In the introduction to *Memories of God*, she evocatively discusses the larger dimension that the personal contains:

> My own personal, private hurts were really not so private or idiosyncratic when they were seen in the context of the intersection of my theological beliefs, my family experience, and the larger world of modern and ancient cultural expectations into which my theology and my personal experience fit. (13)

Notwithstanding this strong connection with literature, Bondi's own journey toward literary creation was more prolonged. She does not describe an early childhood desire to be a writer. Perhaps this difference can be explained by Bondi's sense that elements of these beloved stories "were destructive to me as a female child" (8). She sees Dostoevsky, Hardy, and Camus in negative terms because they "reinforced the stereotypes of women I was already receiving from my larger culture of the late fifties and early sixties" (8). Perhaps, too, she had no female authorial role models in her early life. While hooks and Anzaldúa both mention the discovery of writers who share their own race as pivotal moments in their personal awakening, Bondi does not record a similar epiphany that emerges from reading a female writer. However, she does mention female writers as motivating her to overcome the confining patriarchy of her religious upbringing. For example, she refers to Rebecca Chopp (11) and mentions two other female leaders of group activities (19–20); but the most central figure for her may have been Caroline Walker Bynum, whom she cites as immensely important to *Memories of God* (19). Although Bondi has female role models in the course of her life, unlike hooks and Anzaldúa she does not have the kind of early childhood identification with a writer who communicates her own marginalized perspective. Despite this difference in early reading experiences, Bondi, too, eventually becomes a writer.

Education as a Means of Domination and Liberation

All three writers speak to the discomfort of using the personal, and to how they have been trained not to trust the personal by the academic education they received. All three speak to the false dichotomy of emotional and logical that Genevieve Lloyd helpfully explores in her now classic *Man of Reason*. All reject this dichotomy and embrace the personal voice as a means of undermining the power that this dichotomy continues to have in academia. Given their experiences, all three of these writers see education as both a means of cultural domination and a space for personal liberation. In other words, they each use the tension between public and private to create their individual voices that can speak out against oppression. Each writer focuses on a different manifestation of cultural oppression toward women. Anzaldúa talks about reclaiming her body, hooks writes of reclaiming her race, and Bondi focuses on reclaiming theology and history.

Anzaldúa explains the importance of education: "For a woman of my culture there used to be only three directions she could turn: to the Church as a nun, to the streets as a prostitute, or to the home as a mother. Today some of us have a fourth choice: entering the world by way of education and career and becoming self-autonomous persons" (16). She recognizes that education is open to "very few of us" and laments the fact that "[e]ducating our children is out of reach for most of us" (17). Lisa Bergin correctly senses the strong political motivation in Anzaldúa's understanding of mestiza consciousness. Mestiza consciousness involves "creativity and flexibility, community and coalition, growth and change" (143). Despite her awareness of the liberatory possibility of education, Anzaldúa's own early experiences with education were often constraining. She describes the mechanism of this constraint in terms of language. She "remember[s] being caught speaking Spanish at recess—that was good for three licks on the knuckles with a sharp ruler . . . and being sent to the corner of the classroom for 'talking back' to the Anglo teacher when all I was trying to do was tell her how to pronounce my name" (53). Anzaldúa also recalls her college experience at Pan American University: "I and all Chicano students were required to take two speech classes. Their purpose: to get rid of our accents" (54). Anzaldúa eventually becomes a high school English teacher. However, when she is told not to teach Chicana literature, she fights against this punishing limitation. "I swore my students to secrecy and slipped in Chicano short stories, poems, a play" (60). Like Bondi and hooks, Anzaldúa finds tremendous institutional resistance to her chosen field of study once she reaches graduate school. She has to "argue with one advisor after the other, semester after semester, before I was allowed to make Chicano literature an area of focus" (6).

As we shall see, Anzaldúa and hooks fight against the white power structure in a way that Bondi does not. Perhaps their more extreme outsider status provides them with a deeper motivation for resisting the established patriarchal system. In *Teaching to Transgress*, hooks describes her early childhood education (before the onset of desegregation) in largely affirmative terms. She describes "my all-black grade schools [which] became the location where I experienced learning as revolution . . . a counter hegemonic act, a fundamental way to resist every strategy of white racist colonization" (2). In this context, hooks experienced learning as a "sheer joy" and school as "a place of ecstasy" (3). Shehooks delineates how this experience of education "changed utterly with racial integration . . . . Knowledge was suddenly about information only. It had no relation to how one lived, behaved. It was no longer connected to antiracist struggle. Bussed to white schools, we soon learned that obedience, and not a zealous will to learn, was expected of us" (3). As a result of these two radically different experiences of education, hooks describes herself as someone who "comes to college understanding that something happened in childhood that made her separate mind and body" (*Wounds* 39). Perhaps remembering that earlier experience of education, she comes to college "imagining it to be a space where all the broken bits and pieces of her heart will come together. Learning will let her be whole" (39–40). Unfortunately, the pedagogy of oppression continues.

Though different forces undermine their pedagogical experience, both hooks and Bondi experience a similar constraint once they reach college. Explaining what happens to her, hooks says: "During college, the primary lesson was reinforced: we were to learn obedience to authority . . . The university and the classroom began to feel more like a prison, a place of punishment and confinement rather than a place of promise and possibility" (*Transgress* 4). Although hooks "had difficulty with school, with the way we were taught" (*Wounds* 73–74), she remained vitally aware of the liberating possibility of education. "Mine was my freedom, which working black folks believed came through education" (101). She does not continue her education beyond college immediately. But, eventually she comes to the realization that "I hate school but I hate dead-end jobs more" (127). Ultimately, hooks remains conflicted about the overall benefit of her educational experience. "At no time in my years as a student did I march in a graduation ceremony. I was not proud to hold degrees from institutions where I had been constantly scorned and shamed. I wanted to forget these experiences, to erase them from my consciousness. Like a prisoner set free I did not want to remember my years on the inside" (*Stand* 37). Her recollection of graduate education shares some similarity with Bondi's struggles with sexism, though unlike Bondi, hooks struggled with racism as well.

As a child, Bondi was dismissed and ridiculed for asking challenging questions about gender roles. While her brother would play, she helped her mother wash dishes. When questioning this division of labor met with no tangible result, Bondi concluded, "I was certainly smart enough to know that it was unlikely that I would be right about something and the entire adult world wrong, but what was I supposed to do with my own knowledge and experience? I thought I was crazy" (*Memories* 57).

Bondi does not write a great deal about her primary and secondary education. Instead, she mentions the indirect education she received through her relationship with her boyfriend's Unitarian family. They taught her to believe that "traditional religion was illogical, authoritarian, and impeding of progress" (59). Emboldened by this faith in "Enlightenment" rationality, Bondi thought she could "escape the murky and guilt-inducing claims of [her] childhood" (59) and "receive a well- structured and shining world of rationality" (59). Later, however, she recognizes a darker side to this "universal ethos [of rationality]" (62). Anzaldúa will describe the dark side in this way: "The Catholic and Protestant religions encourage fear and distrust of life and of the body; they encourage a split between the body and the spirit and totally ignore the soul; they encourage us to kill off parts of ourselves" (37). Bondi comes to believe that the emphasis on rationality and reason in her college education reinforces the cultural and religious stereotypes that constrained her in childhood: "The whole scheme of rationality depended upon a hierarchical division of the human race into the 'thinkers' and the 'feelers' " (64).

Unfortunately, the theological education she pursued in the seminary upheld this distinction even more firmly: "Theology was abstract, logical, propositional, and systematic, and so was its God" (9). Bondi explains the devastating effect of this theology, noting quite simply, "This hurt" (9). Even more honestly, she confesses her own complicity with the system. "I felt obligated to teach the history of early Christian thought in the same mode as I had been taught it by my own teachers" (11). She acknowledges that she was "perpetuating in my students the same problems I had had in my own education" (11). Eventually, Bondi begins to use the classroom as a space of liberation, experimenting with personal narrative in her teaching. She has to reach a place of significant success in her academic career, however, before she feels sufficiently empowered to begin this process. She would never have tried it earlier. For example, she felt so much pressure not to be a barrier to other women entering into the male realm that she missed "only one day of school when Benjamin [her son] was born" (102).

While Bondi sees this oppressive aspect of theological education mostly in terms of a dichotomy between the logical and the emotional, between the male and the female, hooks describes a similar kind of constraint operating in her educational experiences, but she tends to understand this dynamic more in terms of race and class issues and less in terms of a male oppression of female voice. In *Wounds of Passion*, hooks writes, "For no one who grows up in the apartheid south believes that the lot of black women and white women is the same, not even those who share the same class. Race makes the difference. And it is enough of a difference to preclude the possibility of common oppression" (98). Differently stated, hooks calls attention to how the interplay of race, class, and gender creates situations of oppression. She mentions that the only time she saw things purely in terms of gender dynamics was in her early family life, "living in a world of racial apartheid" (97). She expounds on this point: "I understood the meaning of male domination in patriarchal society up close and personal. I saw early on that there was a price to be paid for being taken care of" (100).

Since Bondi is not visually marked as racially different, she has the luxury of experiencing the oppressiveness of her culture simply in terms of gender. I doubt Bondi would deny any aspects of hooks's analysis of the interplay between race, class, and gender, though it is not part of her own struggle against oppression. In fact, Bondi is sensitive to the interplay of class and gender in her narrative:

> In those years of the fifties, when Freud reigned and "normal" was both a moral and a psychological judgment, only husband-centered, middle-class family life was regarded as normal. . . . Single women, divorced women, and especially women without men were supporting families of children or aged relatives where abnormal [salaries] were punishingly low. (98–99)

While Bondi attempts to articulate her real theological interests, soon she "loses badly . . . and discovers that she was actually going to have to do a dissertation in the area of theology of the early church" (70). In *Night on the Flint River*, Bondi places her fight within its cultural context:

> Back in those days of miniskirts and the Beatles, bicycles, and dining halls to which women were not permitted, an ancient understanding of the Christian life was not regarded as a properly theological topic for scholarly research, and so I reluctantly committed myself instead to studying another topic in Philoxenus, the sixth-century Monophysite Christology for which he was better known. (106)

Unlike Bondi, hooks fights back against these deeply embedded educational assumptions: "She fights with the most powerful professors. She has no idea that they are waiting for that moment when they can annihilate her. Their weapon is exclusion" (*Wounds* 132). She also encounters resistance to her desire to study and teach black female writers, at least within the English department. Nonetheless, she perseveres, changes schools, and eventually writes a dissertation on Toni Morrison, a topic of her choosing, unlike Bondi, who ends up writing on Philoxenus' monastic theology.

Bondi explains this as failure of nerve on her part: "I am not blaming my teachers for what happened. If I could have answered those words of the Word, 'be not afraid,' and brought myself to fight for what I loved, they would have let me do what I wanted, but I could not speak. Words failed me" (106). I do not mean to imply that Bondi had no real interest in this topic. Her description of her first encounters with Philoxenus is inspirational:

> Shuffling during a dreary afternoon through the enormous piles of books on the desk before me, I picked up a late-nineteenth-century volume entitled *The Thirteen Ascetical Volumes of Philoxenus of Mabbug*. Languorously, I flipped open the red-leather-spined book to its thick middle, and there, from that page written for the instruction of sixth-century monks, the Word leaped out to me, like Christ leaping down to prisoners in hell. (*Night* 105)

She continues describing the experience in painstaking detail:

> My ears were ringing and I could hardly catch my breath. In Philoxenus' text that rainy afternoon, I knew at once that I was listening to the beating heart of early monastic theology, and it was beating for me, not only to the forgotten music of the word spoken by Irenaeus, Justin, and Origen when I had met them in seminary. It was the same rhythm to which the stars were vibrating in the night sky of Iowa so many years before. I calmed myself as best I could, and committed myself at once to write on Philoxenus' ascetic theology." (106)

Psychic Unrest and Spiritual Experience

In spite of the struggles in their pedagogical experiences, Anzaldúa, hooks, and Bondi uphold the importance of education and, in varying ways and to varying degrees, articulate a vision of liberatory pedagogy. Their spiritual journeys reflect a similar tension between the awareness of the oppression inherent in their respective religious traditions and the liberatory possibility of spirituality when understood in a broader sense. Further, all three of these writers deal explicitly with the experience that Anzaldúa describes as "a prejudice and a fear of the dark, chthonic (underworld), material such as depression, illness, and death and the violations that can bring on this break" (39). Spiritual experience helps each woman heal deep emotional wounds. Though they follow different paths, each writer comes to accept the profound importance of spiritual experience in the ongoing process of human liberation.

Anzaldúa finds spiritual solace outside the Christian tradition, partly in the pre-Columbian religions of America and partly in an enthusiastic affirmation of spiritual pantheism. Anzaldúa explains her religious background: "My family, like most Chicanos, did not practice Roman Catholicism but a folk Catholicism with many pagan elements. . . . [T]he virgin of Guadalupe, the central female deity Coatlalopeuh, traces its roots back to a creator goddess, mother of the celestial deities" (26). Within this folk Catholicism, "in Texas and Mexico, this female deity, the virgin of Guadalupe, is more venerated [today] than Jesus or God the Father" (28). Anzaldúa underscores this point: "la Virgen de Guadalupe is the single most potent religious, political and cultural image of the Chicano/Mexicano. She, like my race, is a synthesis of the Old World and the new, of the religion and culture of the two races in our psyche, the conquerors and the conquered" (30). Taking this synthesis as her model, Anzaldúa finds spirituality in the indigenous roots of her culture. "Like the ancient Olmecs, I know Earth is a coiled Serpent," she explains. "Forty years it's taken me to enter into the Serpent, to acknowledge that I have a body, that I am a body and to assimilate the animal body, the animal soul" (26). Though Anzaldúa, originally the unbeliever, "scoffed at these Mexican superstitions as I was taught in Anglo school" (36), she comes to acknowledge their power within her. She explains her hesitancy in these terms:

> Like many Indians and Mexicans, I did not deem my psychic experiences real. I denied their occurrences and let my inner senses atrophy. I allowed white rationality to tell me that the existence of the "other world" was mere pagan superstition. I accepted their reality, the "official" reality of the rational, reasoning mode which is connected with external reality, the upper world, and is considered the most developed consciousness—the consciousness of duality. (36)

However, Anzaldúa eventually overcomes this cultural conditioning and narrates new visions of the divine:

> After each of my four bouts with death, I'd catch glimpses of another world Serpent. When I blinked she was gone. I realized she was in my psyche, the mental picture and symbol of the instinctual in its collective impersonal, pre-human. She, the symbol of the dark sexual drive, the chthonic (underworld), the feminine, the serpentine movement of sexuality, of creativity, the basis of all energy and life. (35)

Ann Louise Keating correctly notes that Anzaldúa "does not abandon the 'rational eye' in order to rely exclusively on the 'magical eye,' the emotional/intuitive mode of perception. Instead, she begins using her intellect differently: rather than struggle to maintain self-autonomy, she consciously struggles to let it go" ("Myth" 84). In an interview with Keating, Anzaldúa explains her spiritual views: "[Y]ou come up against an awareness that the universe is alive. It pulsates; everything's alive: nature, and trees, and the sky, and the wind. Once you connect with that, you feel like you are part of interconnecting organisms" ("Writing" 113). She explains further that the spiritual dimension is around us. "It's not that the 'spiritual' is somewhere else; it's just that right now we don't see it because of the way we're looking" (115). Anzaldúa also links the process of writing to spiritual exploration: "[W]hen you're writing, for example, you go off in alternate states" (117). Jane Hedley describes Anzaldúa's beliefs in this way: "For Anzaldúa there is just one story, to be told and retold and told again: a cosmic story of death and rebirth that functions shamanistically to induce a collective process of soul-making" (49).

Compared to Anzaldúa, bell hooks has an enviable ease with her spiritual experience. The good of religious practice is never obscure to her. It is palpable and alive.

> To be baptized in the name of the father, the son, and the holy ghost, to make one's vow to the lord and not turn back—this is the passion that calls me in childhood. Confined in my small spaces with no light I dream that I have found my true destiny—to be the bride of god, to be a contemplative. Church is one of the few public places where I feel that presence of magic. (*Wounds* 149)

From an early age, hooks finds both comfort and inspiration in the spiritual dimension of experience. She writes that "Religion inspires her. It is the place of hope—the seat of her belief that her life will be better someday, that none of her suffering will be in vain. At church she enters a world of mystery and possibility—there she learns about the mystical dimensions of Christian faith" (149–50). In *Where We Stand: Class Matters*, hooks describes this experience in evocative detail: "In my childhood fantasy life I was quite taken with notions of poverty and asceticism. At times I dreamed of joining a religious order. These fantasies were inspired by religious teachings but also by the fact that I just found it psychologically less stressful to give up attachment to material goods" (53). As an adult, hooks takes a syncretic approach to her spiritual life: "I search for the meaning of the religious life everywhere. I study Buddhism and Islamic mysticism" (*Wounds* 153). Her spiritual experience becomes a form of aesthetic expression: "I like combining liberatory narratives from Christian teachings with Buddhism. In both cases, living simply and sharing resources with others was a basic tenet of spiritual faith and action. Living simply did not mean a life without luxuries; it mean[t] a life without excess" (*Stand* 59). In *All About Love*, she affirms that "spiritual life is first and foremost about commitment to a way of thinking and behaving that honors principles of inter-being and interconnectedness" (77).

Though hooks now finds spiritual meaning in an all-encompassing universalism, the symbolism and language of Christianity resonate throughout her writing. She uses the Christian imagery of wedding altars and baptism to describe the pain she feels at the demise of a twelve-year relationship: "I confess at the heartbreak church. I tell all in the name of the father, the son, and the holy ghost" (*Wounds* 7). This Christian imagery also intermingles with her stories of childhood trauma. She mentions the lie of 1 Corinthians, that love cannot hurt (*Wounds* 8). Even the title of this memoir, *Wounds of Passion*, has deep Christian overtones, evoking the suffering of Christ: his wounds, his passion. Though hooks admits that "There is this ongoing conflict between my involvement in academic life, which seems to place so much emphasis on the ego, and my commitment to spiritual life" (158), she does not describe her spiritual journey in terms of combative struggle. Rather, she sees herself as recognizing that "there is no path I can travel on except the path of love" (156). While hooks certainly mentions the patriarchal orientation of her childhood religion, as well as the racial and class dimensions, particularly in the Western appropriation of Eastern spiritual practices, she has found her own way through these difficulties. Though she has "moved away from the conventional church," she has retained "the love of the inner life, the need to be one with the divine" (152). In contrast, Anzaldúa and Bondi struggle to find hooks's lived awareness that "the spirit has come—touched me and left my body whole" (260). Where she experiences joy and transcendence, they often experience exclusion and despair.

Roberta Bondi's story relates a lifelong and deeply painful struggle to find a space of spiritual comfort and a specifically feminine mode of expression in her chosen patriarchal Baptist religion. For Bondi, the problems with religion start early, with the belief that "my heavenly father's standards for females had to be stricter than my earthly father's" (25). She elaborates on this upbringing in her second autobiographical work, *Night on the Flint River*:

> [T]he oldest child of two young, perfectionistic parents who were both convinced that I could do very little right and that my every action at any given minute was about to reflect badly upon them, I grew up with a sense of living under a continual negative human judgment rendered or about to be rendered against me. Regular trips during summer revival to my mother's childhood country Baptist church easily convinced me that God expected far more of me than my parents and was even angrier and more disappointed than they over who I was." (61)

In *Memories of God*, she confesses that "my inadequacies filled me with guilt, and my femaleness overwhelmed me with shame" (26). She describes the overall effect of this shame: "As for God, I found that in public prayer, the very use of the name Father would regularly fill me with a sense of inadequacy, helplessness, and depression" (27). In *Night on the Flint River*, Bondi further details the experiential reasons for her despair:

> To make matters worse, once having left my childhood home, I spent the years between eighteen and thirty-five in an excruciatingly anxious marriage in which I could not please my husband. I was bitterly blamed by him for everything in the universe that made him unhappy including not only forgetting to bring home all the items on the grocery list, but also bad weather and his father's death. (61)

These experiences lead her to a series of emotional breakdowns. The first occurs during her graduate work in England. Bondi remembers, "I am not sure at what point I realized I was in a crisis. I only know that one day I woke up with a severe anxiety attack that lasted for weeks . . . I was paralyzed. I could not read, I could not write, and I could not think . . . I was afraid of my mind that had gotten me in so much trouble in the past" (*Memories* 73).

At the insistence of her adviser, Bondi goes to an Anglican Benedictine convent to rest. A process of healing begins there. Upon arrival, she is greeted by a nun. Bondi describes her as "a woman radiating intelligence, energy, and kindness, absolutely without fear, completely at home in the world and fully, unapologetically herself" (*Memories* 75). For Bondi, this woman represents the possibility of a space for the feminine within the divine. With this woman as a model, Bondi begins to reexamine the feminine role models in her life. She remembers her own mother. She begins to find comfort as she recalls that her mother constantly strove to create beauty in their world: piano and flute lessons, finding beautiful items at garage sales. Slowly, she begins to believe in her own worth and value as a creature of God. In *Night on the Flint River*, Bondi explains how these early childhood experience of beauty influenced her spiritual development: "I know that from a young age I had a very strong sense of the relationship between the transitory beauty of real individual lives, including my own, and the firm, eternal reality of what I would later learn from the early church to call God the Word which lay under, gave shape to, and supported not only those lives but everything which is" (100–101).

As part of her spiritual growth and healing, Bondi comes to value the importance of her dreams and mystical visions. She has a visually stunning epiphany looking at the Hebrew text of Genesis 1:1. "I knew that God delighted in creation" (*Memories* 66). This insight leads to graduate work in Hebrew. A similar vision solidifies her acceptance of her female nature. She writes, "behind my closed eyes, I became aware that I was looking at a living landscape. . . . In the center, under the tree . . . was a tall, dignified woman, dressed all in brown. . . . Now for the first time, I *knew* it to be true. I, as a woman—neither as a defective male nor as a generic human being, but as a woman—am made in the image of God" (*Memories* 106–7). In fact, *Memories of God* results from a mystical dream of a train station in the Egyptian desert and a snow-storm (18–19). Though Bondi finds a space for the feminine within her theological understanding, she also seeks to reconcile this belief with patriarchal conceptions of religion. Over the years, Bondi adopts "a daily discipline of prayer that committed me to facing many issues that had hurt me for a long time" (12). Though she develops a concept of God the mother, she also finds a way to pray to God the father. She believes that we must "invoke God's fatherhood as a mighty corrective against all the murderous images of the fallen fatherhood that hold our hearts and person, our churches and our world captive" (41). This commitment helps her find a way to stay in the Christian Church without submitting to the repressive patriarchy of her religious upbringing.

Anzaldúa, hooks, and Bondi each use autobiographical reflection to work through painful issues of sexism, racism, and religious oppression. In this time of cultural foment, it is particularly important for us to hear such stories and to learn from them. However, the diversity of their views illustrates the fragmentary character of the postmodern condition and signals the larger question of how to do theology or reason philo-sophically in a pluralistic world. How do we cross the boundaries? Rising to that challenge, Stanley Grenz and John Franke observe that a "theology that seeks to take seriously postmodern sensitivities views itself as conversation" (24), and suggest that ultimately "all theology is—as the 'postmodern condition' suggests—'local' or 'specific.' It is the conversation of a particular group in a particular moment of their ongoing existence in the world" (25). I believe Anzaldúa, hooks, and Bondi are saying, "Let the conversation begin." However, the dilemma remains: if all theology is "local," then how are we to resolve the more vexing prob-lems that diverse groups must face when their theological views collide as they attempt to work together, or even simply coexist. Consider, for example, the current tensions within the Episcopal Church and throughout the Anglican Communion over the recent ordination of an openly gay priest to the office of bishop. This action is so controversial theologically that several dissenting Episcopal Churches left their American dioceses, submitting instead to an African bishop more sympathetic to their understanding of scripture. One community's commitment to the authority of scripture has collided with another community's empathy for the "oppressed," made more urgent by the poignant stories of gay Christians suffering the pain of exclusion. The recent nationwide debate about gay marriage shows that this issue remains largely unresolved for the secular as well as the Christian community. How can such questions be settled? Is there an answer apart from an appeal to a grander story, which postmoderns eschew? If only local answers are acceptable, if all metanarrative is oppressive, then further fragmentation is inevitable. Still, Grenz and Franke are hopeful, arguing that various local theologies through conversation across their boundaries will gain coherence to the extent they increasingly connect their stories to the larger Christian story, which they describe as essentially trinitarian, communitarian, and eschatological (25). One thing is clear, postmodern pluralism, as demonstrated by the poignant personal narratives of thoughtful writers like Anzaldúa, hooks, and Bondi, is confronting present philosophical and theological paradigms and finding them lacking, which, in turn, is spawning a flurry of thinking and writing that is likely to have lasting impact on our times. Meanwhile, perhaps we can agree that listening to the stories of others, particularly the stories of disenfranchised and oppressed people, is an intrinsically good thing to do, an act of Christian love, or, borrowing from Miroslav Volf, a step away from "exclusion" toward "embrace."

Chapter 3

Time for Hope
The Sixth Sense, American Beauty, Memento, *and* Twelve Monkeys

D. Brent Laytham

If hope is indebted to the future, it is also funded by the past. Both temporal dimensions—past and future—continually impinge on the present. The past funds our ability to narrate our present as open to a hopeful future. The future loans us the ability to narrate our present as enabled by a hopeful past. The ability of Christians to sustain the gift of hope has always required both foci—both the past that frees and the future that beckons. Contemporary Christianity struggles to sustain hope in the midst of a culture caught in a time bind that knows neither an available future nor a usable past. Contemporary film engages that same struggle, narrating hope and hopelessness in ways that can illumine the relation of hope to time. This article will first place Christian hope in the biblical narrative of provident past and redemptive future. It will then note the closing off of both poles in contemporary culture, creating a threat to the present possibility of hope. The bulk of this essay will then examine two pairs of movies that depict the struggle for hope *in medias res*: *The Sixth Sense* (1999) and *American Beauty* (1999), which plot human life as a story of hope, and *Twelve Monkeys* (1996) and *Memento* (2000), which plot human life as a hopeless story. This examination will suggest that cinema shares with Christianity a sense of the narrative quality of both hopelessness and hope.

In popular use, hope is treated as a feeling or emotion oriented to the expectation of a positive future. The veracity of hope is judged by the likelihood of moving from this present to that hoped-for future; if my story can get from here to there, then my hope is realistic; if not, my hopes are futile. The utility of hope, on the other hand, is often judged by its effect on the present. True hope is therapeutic, a coping mechanism in the chaos of life, while false hope is pernicious, distracting or distorting real engagement with life, and lost hope produces despair. I believe that these popular notions of hope get at least three things right: first, hope is related to the future (but also to the past); second, hope does matter in the present (though it is not an outlook that one can simply choose); and third, hope is related to narrative skill (skill that can be taught or formed, suggesting that hope is no mere feeling).

In the Christian tradition, there is a more complex account of hope. It is a theological virtue that is given as gift; it does not depend on the vagaries of emotion ("he's feeling hopeful today") nor on the varieties of personality ("she was born hopeful"). Rather, it is infused by the Holy Spirit and thus received as gift. While the language of infusion sounds mystical and unpredictable, it usually occurs in and through specific practices that habituate virtue in us. These practices are often narrative in form—the Creed is narrative recital, the liturgical year a narrative (re)iteration, preaching a narrative rehearsal, and the Eucharist a narrative ritual that reenacts the story of a meal in the context of a narrative prayer stretching from the very beginning (creation) to the final end (consummation). Each practice tells, in its own way, the encompassing Christian story—a metanarrative of hope. Through these practices, hope is habituated as a narrative skill, while at the same time, communal and personal identity is situated in a narrated story. Thus hope requires a community to nurture and sustain it through particular practices; hope is nearly impossible in isolation. Put positively, hope is a gift (normally) given in community.

The Christian metanarrative presents hope in relation to a given past and a graced future—the twin foci of creation and redemption (Burrell and Malits 3–6). Thus, unlike the popular usage, the Christian metanarrative never orients hope only to the future. Rather, future expectation is grounded in past affirmation. Doctrinally, the past funding of Christian hope is expressed as creation, providence, and atonement. The Christian story begins with God creating a very good creation out of nothing. Thus, all existence is a gift, and all things are creatures of God, who is their first and final hope. Creation is a divine donation rooted in excessive love, an originary event rooted in God's original peace (passim). The Christian story begins pacifically rather than agonistically, affirming that time is predestined to be more than constant conflict (Milbank chap. 12). Thus, the very good creation is a project inaugurated; creation has a projected future which beckons, rather than some lost or mythical past perfection which fades (Gunton 19). Moreover, the Christian story continually narrates a powerful providence at work. This can never be seen prospectively. Instead, biblical narrations of providence are always retrospective, always a telling of how the hopeless story ended well in spite of circumstances and because of God (see the prototypical Joseph stories in Genesis). Prospectively, providence names the Christian conviction that no past—however hopeless—constrains a present that is beyond God's hope. Finally, the Christian story affirms that the decisive hope for all creation is an event that appears most hopeless—the crucifixion of Jesus of Nazareth. This apparent failure of hope in fact opens a hopeful future because God raises Jesus from the dead, offering, thereby, forgiveness of sins and promising to share that future with all creation. Forgiveness allows Christians to tell the truth about the past in a way that prevents "our history from becoming our fate" says Stanley Hauerwas (*Community* 10). Hauerwas argues that past evil—both what we have done and what has been done to us—is destined to become our irrevocable fate apart from a story that 1) enables us to accept responsibility for what we have done, and gives us "the skill to confess the evil that we do"; and 2) frees us from resentment for that which has been done to us, in other words to "have a stance toward [our] past without resentment" (*Reader* 219, 247 n. 37). The cross is that past event that enables a present narration of a future hope.

In summary, the Christian story rests present hope on a conviction about key features of the story's past—creation, providence, and atonement. Thus, from the perspective of Christian conviction, any hope which merely looks forward is in danger of failing 1) gratitude, by refusing to acknowledge the present as gift; 2) trust, by ignoring the provident past, and 3) truth, by denying sin and death. On the other hand, any hope that fails to look forward is shortsighted, if not illusory.

The past foundation of present hope opens to its future horizon in and through the story of Jesus Christ. Doctrinally, the future beckoning of Christian hope is expressed as resurrection, reconciliation, and

consummation. These features of the story are fundamental to any doctrine of Christian hope. Briefly, resurrection is the promise that the
self's future does not leave the body in the past, but rather finally
embraces it. Hope is, finally, for an embodied life beyond death.
Reconciliation is the promise that the self's estrangements are not permanently fixed, not even by death. Instead, justice will be done and
alienations will be mended. Consummation is the hope that all things
will be well, because all things will be gathered unto God. From the
perspective of Christian conviction, any hope that looks forward without these qualities fails to make hope adequately 1) material, 2) communal, and 3) theological.

Where does that lead us in relation to contemporary culture? I will
make three suggestions regarding contemporary culture's relationship to
past, future, and present, respectively. First, contemporary culture has
largely lost a sense of life as gift and of circumstances as providentially
ordered. This is due in part to the rise of modern science, with its apparent explanatory and predictive power, and in part to the rise of philosophical skepticism in thinkers like Hume (Gunton 20–23). While
atheism and agnosticism are clear manifestations of these trends, the
more significant issue is far more pervasive: even theists seem unable to
narrate their lives and their worlds as given, upheld, and ordered by
God. Providence has also lost ground to a culture of risk that cedes care
for present and future well-being to bureaucratic structures and technological systems of expertise, a significant source for apocalyptic tech-
nothrillers like the Terminator trilogy. This change is compounded by
exponentially escalating media coverage of bad news, lampooned in *Wag
the Dog* and *Bowling for Columbine*. Finally, Thomas Hibbs has noted a
nihilistic tendency in popular culture that is expressed in both television
and film. His book *Shows about Nothing: Nihilism in Popular Culture
from the Exorcist to Seinfeld* suggests a growing sense that either malevolent forces thwart us (e.g., *Silence of the Lambs*) or meaninglessness
mocks us (e.g., *Trainspotting*). Either way, narrating a hopeful life in this
mean time becomes increasingly difficult.

Second, the contemporary cultural outlook on the future is far from
bright. When postmodernity celebrates "incredulity toward metanarrative" (Lyotard, xxiv), it is partly a reminder of the demise of certain credulous narratives that used to focus on hope—the triumph of
communism, the spread of democracy, the elimination of poverty, disease, and war. The myth of progress dies a hard death, but current
malaise suggests the case is terminal. Because progress was our culture's
richest eschatological vision, without some replacement its demise leaves

us with nothing but death as the organizing telos of human life, and death is a future we seek to deny at almost any cost (E. Becker). Yet even where death is faced, it cannot bring meaningful coherence to a narrated life. Oliver O'Donovan rightly suggests: "Only fiction writers can integrate death pleasingly into a narrative wholeness; and that is because characters who die in fiction exist only to die, whereas characters who die in life have existed to live" (232). This claim is not an exclusively Christian conviction. Literary critic Seymour Chatman notes that "No end, in reality, is ever final in the way 'The End' of a novel or film is. Even death is not an end—biologically, historically, or in any sense one takes the word" (47). For human life, death is an inevitable end, but not a meaningful telos. In a world that has lost its eschatological horizons, hope is exceedingly difficult to sustain.

Nonetheless, my third point is that hope remains present in a variety of ways. I believe that contemporary secular culture may, in ways analogous to the Christian church, experience the cinema as a community where particular films work to offer narrative skills that habituate hope. This experience is regularly the case in films whose plot is what Seymour Chatman calls "the traditional narrative of resolution" (48). Two powerful examples are *The Shawshank Redemption* and *The Shipping News*. In movies of this sort, hope is clearly related to the past as well as the future. Past failures presently threaten the possibility of a hopeful future. The threat is broken in these movies by the gift of human relationship (sometimes relationships initiated, other times relationships reconciled). Analysis of these films would be fruitful.

Yet because they finally "hope in this life only"—that is, they lack a genuinely eschatological horizon—I will focus on four films that deal explicitly with narrative "ends": *The Sixth Sense, American Beauty, Twelve Monkeys*, and *Memento*. Each of these movies explicitly ends with death (or beyond). And each movie, in one way or another, centrally addresses the time bind that presses hope in the present—is there time for hope? My analysis will proceed by pairs. First, I will argue that *The Sixth Sense* and *American Beauty* are fundamentally hopeful movies. I will seek to demonstrate this not merely by focusing on thematic content but by displaying the way cinematic technique interacts with plot to produce a narrated past that fuels hope. Second, I will suggest that *Twelve Monkeys* and *Memento* finally refuse hope. The interaction of cinematic technique with plot in these two films suggests that there is no hope; the time bind is finally inescapable.

Both *The Sixth Sense* and *American Beauty* were highly successful films. *The Sixth Sense* was a surprisingly successful second picture for

M. Night Shyamalan; the second highest grossing picture of 1999 (over 210 million dollars), it garnered six Oscar nominations. *American Beauty* won five Oscars—best picture, actor, director, screenplay, and cinematography—and still did quite well in the box office for a serious picture (around 100 million dollars). I believe that the success of both films is related to two shared features: a hopeful narration of human life and a skillful depiction of human death.

The Sixth Sense is part thriller, inspired by childhood's fear of things that go bump in the night. Yet at a deeper level, the movie centers on the fear that death ends all hope that human relationships can be healed, that authentic communication can occur, that justice can be done. As the movie presents it, death is the horizon that seals our failures. Whether these are failures we suffer by overt evil done to us, or failures we accomplish by our own action or inaction, death seems to fix such failures beyond all hope of repair. Three of the four main characters in the movie suffer in some way because death seems to foreclose all hope of reconciliation. Child psychiatrist Malcolm Crowe (Bruce Willis) and his wife (Olivia Williams) suffer a radical estrangement in the wake of the suicide of Vincent Grey, a patient Malcolm failed to help. Lynn Sear (Toni Collett) suffers because her mother died before they reconciled. Lynn's son Cole (Haley Joel Osment) suffers because, as he finally reveals to child psychiatrist Crowe, "I see dead people." Where alienation from the dead is the problem for the adults in this story, the child would like to have more distance from the deceased than he does. Cole's visible anguish symbolizes the adults' less visible pain—their sorrow rooted in past failure. (Admittedly, some of the movie's peripheral characters represent anger rather than anguish.) For the main characters in *The Sixth Sense*, hope is caught in time's bind; it appears to be too late for a happy ending.

But it is not. The central artifice of the movie, and the reason that audiences returned again and again to see it, is that the ending changes everything. In the movie's climax, Malcolm Crowe realizes that he is dead, that he has been dead since the night he was shot by Vincent Grey (in the opening sequence of the movie). The power of the moment is due in part to the quality of acting and soundtrack. But in greater measure it is owed to two key aspects of the movie. First, there is the careful storyboarding which allows the dead Crowe to appear to interact with the living, without ever actually doing so. The primary aspect, though, is the relationship and the doubling of the lead characters. The doubling includes the fact that both have a gift that is powerful, yet not always easy to use effectively. Both are loved deeply by another, yet find that love is not sufficient to overcome alienation (which, we come to discover, is caused by death). Both need a crucial piece of information (which they finally receive as a gift from the other).

The relationship develops slowly. The opening conversation between the two makes clear that hope and trust will be intertwined. We see Crowe try to draw Cole to him, to overcome the physical and psychological distance that separates them. Through the use of subjective camera, we see Cole move slowly toward, and then slowly away, from Crowe. "You can't help me," he says. The relationship begins without trust or hope. But as Cole slowly grows to trust Crowe, and finally entrusts him with his "problem"—"I see dead people"—an impasse is reached. Hope will require that trust run in both directions: Malcolm must finally listen to what Cole tells him. When that happens, they find a way forward. Cole will assist the dead in restoring broken relationships, whether that be righting wrongs—the child poisoned by her mother—or mending fences—the estrangement between Cole's mother and grandmother. Ironically, Crowe's advice that Cole help others is finally the source of his own hope.

In the movie's penultimate scene, Cole finally trusts his mother with the truth and helps her reconcile her past estrangement with her mother. It is this success at reconciliation that lends power to Crowe's reconciliation that follows. Because Crowe is Cole's double, we expect that he will now succeed in reconciling with his wife. We are not prepared, however, to discover with Crowe what Cole has known from the start: Malcolm Crowe is dead. This revelation is accomplished by a skillful set of crosscut images and dialogue—Cole's explanation that dead people do not know that they are dead allows Crowe to "see" things in his story that he had not seen before, evidence of his own demise. This ending reframes the whole story. It forces Crowe to renarrate the story of his past and present. Because we have shared that story with him, his reframing is ours as well. Following Cole's advice, Malcolm speaks words of love and release to his wife as she sleeps. Her tension and chill are released; she is now reconciled to her past in a way that frees her for a hopeful future. It is a cathartic moment for her, for Malcolm Crowe, and for us as well. Not even death finally destroys hope.

Of course, the movie does not necessarily bring viewers to accept its spiritual vision of reality. In relation to the future, it offers a simulacrum of Christian hope for eschatological reconciliation, but no hope for a bodily future with God. In relation to the past, it invites the living to view their present as a gift given by loved ones who have gone before. I believe that the movie leaves us hoping not primarily to find some medium through which reconciliation between the living and dead can occur, but rather hoping for more honest communications in the present, for moments of truth when the other is freed because the past is forgiven. It suggests that even when our loved ones die, it might be possible for us to renegotiate the failed relationships of the past by way of cathartic renarrations of relations in the present. Short of that possibility, there is always the consolation of catharsis through watching *The Sixth Sense* again.

American Beauty is a film about the reawakening of hope in the midst of failure and futility, of death and despair. Its lead characters are all trapped, in one way or another, by mistaken notions of what constitutes hope for the good life—all except Ricky Fitts (Wes Bentley), the preternaturally calm teenager who seems to live beyond hope or despair. The hopeless condition of the other characters is revealed to us in the course of the movie. I will focus only on Lester Burnham (Kevin Spacey), since he is the primary character in the movie who wakes up to hope.

At the beginning of the movie, Lester is a pathetic loser with no real hope of escaping the smothering effects of his own life; we see it clearly in acting and image, but the voiceover narration puts a fine point on it (e.g., in noting that masturbating in the shower "will be the high point of my day"). His listless life is lustless, until he is awakened by desire for his daughter's best (only?) friend Angela. No longer apathetic, he now appears all the more pathetic (a "horny geek boy" in the eyes of his daughter Jane). This is accentuated by the cinematography, which draws a clear distinction between the real Angela—slutty in appearance, vulgar in speech, entirely self-involved—and the Angela of Lester's erotic fantasy—stunningly beautiful in lyrically filmed sequences of desire, always signaled by music and rose petals. Yet this is one of the film's subtle nuances, for in the end *American Beauty* suggests to us that Angela is neither angel nor slut—neither the essence of beauty nor the epitome of ugliness—but something in between. The movie invites us to "look closer" (a sign on Lester's desk at work, and the tagline of the movie's publicity). It is the real beauty of that something in between that finally catches Lester, and should finally catch us too.

The power of *American Beauty* is certainly multifaceted: an excellent script, powerful acting, beautiful cinematography and an unforgettable score. But the framing of the entire story as a narrated flashback may be the key to the hopefulness of the movie. Unlike *The Sixth Sense*, *American Beauty* reveals almost from the beginning the death of the protagonist. It opens with a videotape scene, in which Jane says of her father "what a lame-o. Someone really should just put him out of his misery." I would argue that though this moment introduces the themes of Lester's misery, family dysfunction, and death, it does not set the tone for the movie. The movie really begins with Lester's voice-over narration: "My name is Lester Burnham. This is my neighborhood. This is my street. This is my life. I am 42 years old. In less than a year, I'll be dead. Of course, I don't know that yet. And in a way, I'm dead already." Accompanying these words is a visual shot that glides down from heaven to earth, suggesting a transcendent perspective on all life. Lester's voice has a tranquility about it that matches the visual, a quality that is especially surprising given his frank admission that his wife is uptight, his daughter is angry, and he is a loser. The music is inviting and the mise-en-scène vibrant. The opening sequence shows at the beginning what Lester will speak at the end—a profound sense of well-being, an overwhelming awareness of beauty, and the inescapable response of gratitude. Thus as Lester's voice-over tells us that this story leads to death, the film itself is suggesting otherwise. We are thereby prepared to follow the story of the last year of Lester's life as a story of hope. (Cinematically, it seems absolutely necessary to name Lester's fate from the beginning; otherwise, it will overwhelm any possibility of a redemptive ending to the story.)

Writer Alan Ball says that he sees Lester as learning what Ricky already knows (Ball 153). I want to suggest that Lester may finally see more, and differently, than Ricky does. It is true, of course, that Lester names Ricky "my hero," that Ricky appears to give Lester the idea to quit his job, and supplies him with the freeing marijuana. It might even be mimetic desire that leads Lester to relive his own adolescence by buying a 1970 Pontiac Firebird ("the car I always wanted") and taking a job at Mr. Smiley's. Yet I would argue that Ricky's outlook is more stoical—a place beyond fear, desire, or hope—while Lester is finally converted to a richer hope.

The issue may turn on the question of beauty—both what beauty is and whether it frees us from desire, or frees us for rightly focused desire. The theme is introduced when Ricky and Jane walk home from school. As a funeral procession passes, Ricky tells Jane about seeing and filming a homeless woman who died. "It's like God is looking right at you, just for a second, and if you're careful, you can look right back." "And what do you see?" Jane asks. "Beauty," he responds. I believe that Lester's transformation comes in a surprising encounter with beauty. In the moment when Angela offers to give herself to him, she is revealed to him as both beautiful and vulnerable, an appropriate object of someone's desire, but not of his desire. Lester's gaze changes from that of a lecher to a father. In this moment, beauty effects a transformation in Lester. Both

Ricky and Lester suggest that beauty reveals itself to us, if we are willing to "look closer," and both are transformed by its revelations. The difference between them is this: Ricky sees beauty in death, while Lester is reawakened to the beauty of life—even Angela's shallow, selfish life, even his own "stupid little life."

The concluding sequence of the movie manages to convey well-being as a state Lester enters before death, a state that "stretches on forever, like an ocean of time." Just before he is murdered, he responds to Angela's query "how are you?" with "I'm great." He then sits at the table, smiling joyously at a picture of his family cradled in his hands. We see a gun slowly move toward the back of his head. We hear the shot as blood splatters the wall. Then begins a series of cross-cut edits which interpose the response of other characters to Lester's death with black and white images from Lester's past. His narration instructs the audience in appropriate response. "I guess I could be pretty pissed off at what happened to me. But it's hard to stay mad when there's so much beauty in the world." For Lester, the beauty is not in death (as it is for Ricky), but in life lived before—and remembered beyond—death. His concluding admonition is a direct address to the spectator: "You have no idea what I'm talking about I'm sure, but don't worry. You will someday." The final scene is a reversal of the opening sequence, a shot that soars up from house and tree-lined street into the transcendent heavens. As the finale of the movie, it assures us that we, too, like Lester, should feel overwhelming gratitude for the beauty of life.

Gratitude is not hope, of course, but it is the appropriate response to a gift. *American Beauty* suggests that when human beings are open to and aware of beauty, life itself is the gift. Further, it suggests that "it's never too late" for beauty, which means that there is always time for hope. Unlike the characters in *The Sixth Sense*, Lester seems contented in death even though significant relationships are not reconciled (the question of justice for his murderer, the adulterous alienation from his wife). There is a simulacrum of being gathered to God in Lester's sense of being surrounded by beauty and awash in benevolence. But this is not a bodily reality (as the soaring camera has reminded us throughout the movie), nor is it a corporate one. The movie's claim that nothing can finally put us beyond beauty's gift is powerful reason to sustain hope—come what may. For all mortals could say with Lester, "in a certain sense, I'm already dead." For many viewers who come to the movie having lost hope in a particular past, it serves as a propaedeutic for learning again the skill of narrating a hopeful present, not in spite of our past, but in light of its revealed beauty.

Both *Twelve Monkeys* and *Memento* are intensely visual movies that invite us to see the failure of hope. In both movies environment threatens and inhibits hope, while atmosphere suggests hallucination or paranoia that precludes hope. Environment and atmosphere are not the source of hope's failure, but merely the signs. They are used to suggest a failure of plot: the past is unable to produce a hopeful present. The movies use visual technique to show us just how hopeless life really is.

In *Twelve Monkeys*, director Terry Gilliam uses mise-en-scène to suggest that James Cole (Bruce Willis) is trapped by time and alienated from meaningful relationships. The movie is replete with barriers: cages, bars, fences, manacles, biohazard suits, straitjackets, plastic rain coats, locked doors. Unsurprisingly, in *Twelve Monkeys* human contact is seldom direct. Apart from the romantic relationship with Dr. Katheryn Railly (Madeline Stowe), humans hardly touch one another, except in acts of violence and coercion. Several scenes communicate the depth of human alienation. First, in Cole's repeated examinations by the team of "scientists" (or are they jailors?), he converses with persons he cannot see, while being probed and prodded like some unknown thing. The scientists use elaborate equipment—including a giant robotic eye—to keep their distance. Second, when Cole is processed at the Baltimore asylum, he is shown in a bleak and dilapidated shower, standing naked, facing the wall, being brutally scrubbed by an attendant with a long-handled brush. The alienation is clear: no face-to-face contact, touch used only to pull and push, a voice used only to threaten. These factors alone might suggest that hope is threatened only by external circumstances and heartless persons. But when this environment is coupled with the movie's twists of time, its sterile and stifling quality becomes a metaphor for time itself—for a past so constraining that it offers only a fated future.

Gilliam communicates the fatefulness of time through repeated use of a slow motion sequence in which a young boy at an airport sees security guards shoot and kill a man. The possibility that this is a bad dream fades through multiple repetitions; we realize that this is a memory whose significance remains to be seen. When that significance is finally revealed, we realize that this scene is (and was) both past and future. It is past in at least two ways. First, it is "in" the past when first shown—the dream of a man in 2035 about something that happened in 1996. Second, it is Cole's past, for he is the young boy. Yet it is also future in multiple ways. When Cole travels through time, he enters a present before the incident occurs. Thus, when he dreams it again (in 1990 and 1996), he is remembering the future. Because in the movie's denouement, Cole also turns out to be the man gunned down, this is also his future. Futhermore, because the movie's finale makes it clear that at the moment Cole dies, the destructive fate of all humanity has already been sealed by the release of deadly bioweapons, this moment is the world's future as well.

Gilliam uses the multiple repetitions of the scene to build a sense of inexorable doom. And he uses the movie's most graphic sequence—when Cole bludgeons a pimp and then pulls out all his teeth—to suggest that not even raw violence can free Cole from the grip of inevitability. There is no escape; the past has sealed fate. The multirepeated airport scene is the moment when time connects, when past and future become a unified present. Thus, when the scene finally happens—that is, when it is presented as actually occurring in the movie's story line—the audience can only interpret it as the closing of an inescapable circle. The movie's visual signature of monkeys going around in circles prepares us to see the truth: the future is fated beyond all hope, whether we try to jump off time's wheel or dutifully keep on spinning.

For *Twelve Monkeys*, there is no provident past, only a predestined one. There is no promising present, only a now governed by capricious if not malevolent powers and characterized by alienated or futile relationships. There is no hopeful future, only a final turning (or returning) to death. Meanwhile, life is essentially agonistic—a fight to the finish, not a given gift but a grasping struggle. Human tenderness may offer brief respite from these harsh realities, but it cannot withstand the destructive grind of time's wheel. Community is a possibility only for those with altered mental states; the more clearly one sees the reality of time's bind, the more impossible genuine community becomes. The vision of a hopeless world in *Twelve Monkeys* is not quite heroic, but it is unflinching.

In Christopher Nolan's *Memento*, cinematography is used to create a typically claustrophobic and confusing noir setting. In the color sequences, this setting is accomplished by using typical film noir visuals—gritty businesses in a nondescript, menacing city. In the black and white sequences, close-ups shot with a fairly unsteady steadi-cam leave us unsure what we are seeing. We need the camera to hold still long enough for us to become oriented, or to show us what lies just beyond the camera frame. The effect of the cinematography is compounded by the film editing. Reverse-chronology color sequences are interspersed with forward-chronology black and white sequences. (Most viewers notice immediately that the color sequences move backward through time; noticing that the black and white sequences move forward takes a second screening for many viewers.) Because we do not know how the two sequences are temporally related and because the color sequences work to keep us in the dark, our understanding as viewers does not progress. We have data but we cannot tell how the story should proceed. We, too, are trapped and confused, not merely by the room or the city (environment), but by time itself, which offers sequence without coherence. The film's atmosphere thus signals that the problem is not the environment but time itself, or rather our relationship to time.

The most notable feature of *Memento* is its reverse chronology in the color sequences. The movie begins where the story ends, with a brutal murder. Or is it a murder? As Seymour Chatman reminds us, the significance of action is known primarily through the contextualization of plot, something that finally requires a sense of the whole: "A killing may not be a murder but an act of mercy, or a sacrifice, . . . or one or more of a dozen other things. No battery of pre-established categories can characterize it independently of and prior to a reading of the whole" (94). That sense of the whole—what Paul Ricoeur calls the "configurational dimension" of narrative—will be tentatively construed (and reconstrued) as a story moves forward (*Time and Narrative* 66–68). The key to every such construal is the sense of an ending; a viewer's sense of where the story is going is determined by her sense of where the story will end.

The way that a story is told can make it easy or difficult to configure a sense of the whole. Film scholars sometimes differentiate between the story in a film and the discourse of the film. In this distinction, *story* means the what of a narrative and *discourse* the how of its telling (Chatman 19). In my analysis here, story means the events plotted temporally from beginning to end, while discourse means the actual order in which the story is told. If the story is told from start to finish, then discourse matches story. A discourse that follows a different order than the story allows a storyteller to do certain things to an audience.

In *Memento*, Christopher Nolan uses the difference between discourse and story to give his audience a form of amnesia. The discourse of the color sequences moves backward scene by scene. The first scene is even presented backwards, as if the filmmaker had pushed the rewind button on a video player. Thus, the discourse begins (the movie's first scene) at the story's end, and the discourse ends at the story's beginning (the movie's last scene). Nolan's reason for the inverse relation between discourse and story is simple: he wants, in a certain sense, to afflict the audience with the same problem his protagonist Leonard (Guy Pearce) has—an inability to remember. As Leonard reiterates endlessly throughout the movie, a trauma has left him unable to "make new memories"; he cannot remember the story of his own life after the trauma. Leonard cannot remember what just happened (the past) because his memory fails to record it; in viewing the movie, we cannot remember the past because it has not been shown to us yet. Thus, the reversed temporality gives us the same condition as Leonard; we are just as restricted and just as privileged as he (on strategies of privileging and restricting the viewer, see Phillips 152). Leonard becomes our surrogate, seeking the answer that will bring meaning and closure to life. Or perhaps we become his surrogate, believing that when we finally arrive at the beginning of the story, we will find the key that makes sense of the whole. We hope to find the answer, but we increasingly sense that the answer will not give Leonard—or us—hope.

Of course, noir is a genre that is notoriously short on hope. It tends to valorize the darker aspects of human existence: crime, anger, violence, lust, revenge, betrayal, and permeating deception. Certainly *Memento* is no exception. But the refusal of hope in *Memento* goes deeper than theme. Because the story is told backwards, it inverts the normal "episodic dimension" of narrative (Ricoeur, *Time and Narrative* 66–67). According to Ricoeur, the episodic dimension refers to the arrangement of events into a sequence or a series. The two main principles at work in the episodic dimension are temporal succession and causality. Normally, the episodic dimension of a plot is a mimesis of storied characters moving forward through time in ways that suggest both contingency and causality, i.e., both freedom and fate. When Nolan reverses the order of the telling, the episodic dimension loses entirely the sense of contingency. Moving forward through time appears to involve openness to the future, a range of choices, a world that is not fated. Moving backwards through the same scenes (or episodes) appears an exercise in inexorable causality, each scene inevitably caused by the previous scene.

At the end of our regress of episodes, *Memento* poses for us the question of configuring the whole story. Which end should make the difference—the end of the story (with which the movie began), or the end of the discourse (with which the movie ended)? For us it is the end of the discourse—the final scene of the movie—that makes all the difference. It finally reveals to us that misguided Leonard is his own false guide, that the deceived is himself the deceiver, that the whole story is built on a lie. And because the end of the movie is the beginning of Leonard's story, we cannot now imagine that the entire sequence is anything but an inevitable unfolding of the initiating lie. Thus Leonard is doomed not merely by his condition, nor even entirely by his deception, but finally by the inalterability of time itself. There will never be time for repentance. Even at the beginning of the story, it is already too late for hope.

There is much I have omitted from this analysis of *Memento*. The film offers a rich context for analyzing the narrative character of self-deception, for example. Clearly, the key narrative that Leonard lives is a story of revenge rooted in the myth of redemptive violence. Yet even my brief analysis demonstrates that not only the story told, but also the order of the telling combine to drive hope from *Memento*'s narrative world. As in *Twelve Monkeys*, life is seen as perpetual conflict without hope for peace. The past is our fixed fate, against which we can rail or seek revenge, but from which we can never be redeemed. Thus, the future is not an open horizon, but rather the set path of the next inevitable thing. Questions of final reconciliation are moot, since there are no real relationships of care even now. If there is a God, he stands just outside the camera frame—an antiprovidence working woe and wrath. But more likely, we wreck our own lives, with a little help from our friends (e.g., Leonard's "friend" Teddy). *Memento*'s vision could hardly be bleaker: in this mean time there is no hope.

Is life hopeful or hopeless? Answering that question requires from us a story about where life is going and from whence it has come. Contemporary film suggests what Christianity already knows—that hopelessness, like hope, is a tale that is told. Both film and faith have a stake in learning to plot hopeful lives between a benevolent, blessed past, and a beckoning, hopeful future.

Chapter 4

Beyond Futility
American Beauty *and the Book of* *Ecclesiastes*

Robert K. Johnston

*God is interested in a lot of things besides religion. God is the Lord and
Creator of all life, and there are manifestations of the holy in its celebration
or its repudiation—in every aspect of the common life.*
—*Joseph Sittler,* Gravity and Grace

In his 1996 song, "All This Useless Beauty," Elvis Costello bemoans our
repeated attempts to turn life into our "sweetheart, plaything or pet" or,
failing that, an "unveiled threat." "Nonsense prevails, modesty fails/
Grace and virtue turn into stupidity." And yet Costello plaintively asks,
"What shall we do, what shall we do with all this useless beauty?"

One of the paradoxes of postmodernity is the collapse of universal
standards of truth, beauty, and goodness—the Enlightenment dream—
with the lingering suspicion that life is, nonetheless, meaningful at its
core. Costello's question about life—how to respond to its concurrent
vanity and beauty—is a perennial one. The ancient Babylonian *Epic of*

Gilgamesh reflects on life's paradoxes as does the Egyptian *Dispute over Suicide*. But nowhere does this theme emerge with the depth and poignancy of Ecclesiastes, a biblical text that resonates powerfully with postmodern themes. Given the futility of our struggle to manipulate, order, and control our own lives and the lives of others, what shall we say about all the seemingly unwarranted and undeserved goodness life affords? "What shall we do with all this useless beauty?" Though its trenchant observations on life reveal a fragile hope, the Book of Ecclesiastes also brims with a seeming cynicism and/or despair, or as Costello will later say, "Nonsense prevails, modesty fails/ Grace and virtue turn into stupidity." One approach to reading Ecclesiastes in the context of postmodernity would be to align the speaker, Qoheleth, with those in our culture who have grown pessimistic and cynical in the wake of modernity's failed dreams. But is this the whole story? By bringing together the book of Ecclesiastes and the 1999 Academy-Award-winning film *American Beauty*, which shares similar themes, I will argue that both works, if fully understood, leave open the possibility of hope. They do so, however, in a way that is neither straightforward nor simple. Reading Ecclesiastes through the lens of *American Beauty* calls for readers to combine and hold together the contradictory trajectories of despair and joy, pessimism and hope.

Medieval commentators called Ecclesiastes one of the Bible's "two dangerous books." (The other was the Song of Songs with its overt sensuality.) Was the book's conclusion simply fatalistic like the ancient *Epic of Gilgamesh*? "Eat, drink, and be merry, for tomorrow we die." Or how were readers to understand conflicting tensions in the work between resignation (or consolation) and the seemingly pagan impulse to be merry before we die? The first thousand years of Christian interpretation found in the book support for asceticism and discipline, an encouragement to despise the things of the world and to turn in hope to the immortality of the next life. The book's commendation to enjoy food and drink was dismissed as allegorical. The advice was said to refer to the Eucharistic joy of Christ's body and blood. Luther and the Reformers challenged such an otherworldly interpretation, finding this *via negativa* rooted more in the medieval contempt for this life than in the biblical text itself. Qoheleth's purpose in writing Ecclesiastes was then thought to be the demonstration of humankind's depraved affections. According to the Reformers, Ecclesiastes showed the vanity, the futility of life "under the sun"—that is, outside of God's saving grace. Ecclesiastes might be viewed as exploring the consequences and bankruptcy of modern and/or postmodern secular thinking. Yet with the rise of postmodern literary criticism, these traditional interpretations of Ecclesiastes seemed unsatisfying to the text as text. This short book had within it both affirmation and negation, despair and hope. Moreover, God was clearly presented in and behind our lives, as Joseph Sittler insists, however problematic they might turn out to be. Thus, new interpretive strategies were tried out. Was Qoheleth a pessimist, a skeptic, a practical atheist, a relativist, a preacher of joy, a dialectical thinker, an apologist, an existentialist, a realist, someone who was simply resigned? All these interpretations have been seriously entertained. How is God to be understood as involved in human affairs? Is the book a critical corrective, a philosophical treatise, a comedy, a contextual document, a confession? Perhaps it is just confused. The questions have proliferated, as have the proposed solutions.

The interpretive quagmire of the Book of Ecclesiastes has existed right up to the present. Commentaries and monographs over the last twenty-five years offer a plethora of critical interpretations of this short book. Perhaps no other book in the Old Testament has been interpreted in such varying and contradictory ways. In fact, one is tempted to concur with the final editor of Ecclesiastes, "of making many books there is no end" (12:12), especially when it comes to trying to understand this enigmatic text. That said, readers continue to be fascinated by this short book in the Hebrew and Christian Scriptures, for it addresses our human situation with power and conviction. As Daniel Pawley has noted, Herman Melville described Ecclesiastes as "the truest of all" books, this "fine-hammered steel of woe." The novelist Thomas Wolfe believed Ecclesiastes to be "the greatest single piece of writing I have ever known." George Bernard Shaw compared it to Shakespeare. Ernest Hemingway was fascinated by the book, while John Updike has one of his characters in the *Rabbit* trilogy describing Ecclesiastes as "the Lord's last word" (Pawley 34–36).

Reversing the Hermeneutical Flow

What are we to make of our fascination with the Book of Ecclesiastes and yet our inability to interpret it convincingly? Is there another interpretive strategy at our disposal, one that might shed new light on this most enigmatic of biblical books? Is life profitless and absurd? Or are we to receive it hopefully and with joy, recognizing it as a gift from God? Could both be true? If so, how? A key to the interpretation of Ecclesiastes is to be found perhaps in the narrative structure of the first two chapters. Here Qoheleth presents life as lived, truth that is embedded and embodied, not abstracted from life's messiness. Rather than looking first to the implicit story in the biblical text and with the reflection that follows, I would like to reverse the typical hermeneutical flow. What I am proposing, in brief, is a cultural hermeneutic. I would like to begin with a narrative from outside the Scriptures—from our wider culture—and let it become the spectacles through which we view the Book of Ecclesiastes. The narrative I have chosen is the contemporary movie *American Beauty*. Like Ecclesiastes, this movie has also attracted both zeal and censure. It, too, has seemed a dangerous movie to many Christian believers. It, too, has seemed to some merely to present life's futility "under the sun."

American Beauty won best picture honors for 1999 at the Academy Awards, the Golden Globes, the British Academy Awards (BAFTA), the Producers Guild of America, and the Broadcast Film Critics Association. Shot for less than 13 million dollars, the movie grossed close to 300 million dollars worldwide. It was both a critical and a box office hit. Most Christian film critics, however, have been hard on the movie. Terry Lindvahl is perhaps representative. He writes that American Beauty casts "the corruption of the human soul in disturbing and harsh ways," diving "into its darkness and muck as if immersing oneself in whipped cream." He says, "It is flashy, flip, and hip, with a resolution that is only skin-deep." And Chuck Colson wrote in his BreakPoint Commentary on March 28, 2000, "This year's Oscar winners are, for the most part, movies that tear down values that Christians and moral conservatives hold dear. There's nothing I can recommend in *American Beauty*."

Much of contemporary religion and film criticism from a Christian perspective would believe that one looks to film for portrayals, or embodiments, of truth already understood theologically. The exercise of theology and film criticism has thus largely been a second--order analytical reflection about themes independently understood from out of the Christian tradition. The conversation, in other words, has been unidirectional, flowing from faith to film, theology to the movies. A few religion and film scholars, myself included, suggest that we might profitably reverse this hermeneutical flow, or at least make it multidirectional. Cannot the Church also learn from Hollywood? Larry Kreitzer, for example, argues in his series of four books on literature, film, and theology that our theological interpretation can profitably move from film and novel to the Bible, and not just from the Bible to film. Philip Yancey in his best selling book, *The Jesus I Never Knew*, does just that, finding in a dozen "Jesus movies" a recognition of Jesus' real humanity that has escaped many Christians in their reading of the Bible. Similarly, New Testament scholar Robert Jewett, in his book *St. Paul Returns to the*

Movies, entertains what he calls the "seemingly preposterous proposition" that "certain movies afford deeper access to the hidden heart of Paul's theology than mainstream theologians like myself have been able to penetrate" (20). Jewett's argument is with Pauline scholarship in the West that has misunderstood the discussion of grace in the Book of Romans. Such scholarship has viewed grace in terms of a guilt needing individual forgiveness, rather than understanding it in terms of a shame needing to be overcome. Our cultural blinders, Jewett believes, have kept us from hearing the text as intended by Paul.

My parallel and preposterous question is this: Could a movie such as *American Beauty* afford interpreters deeper access to the hidden heart of the theology of Ecclesiastes than most mainstream Old Testament scholars have been able to give us since the rise of modern and postmodern critical scholarship? Or to mitigate the claim slightly, can the movie *American Beauty* provide narrative glasses through which to see the paradoxes and tensions of Ecclesiastes in a new light? And might Ecclesiastes, in turn, provide an additional perspective for our viewing of *American Beauty*? That is, can this movie and this biblical text provide mutually penetrating perspectives on how viewers might concurrently hold onto the themes of despair and joy, pessimism and hope? Might they help us to discover how to celebrate all this useless beauty? To hold together affirmation and denial, meaninglessness and meaningfulness, is a vexing problem in any age. It has been particularly difficult during most of the modern period, given our commitment to a linear epistemology. Now, however, the old essentialisms are being called into question, allowing for creative reconstructions to emerge. The arts have led the way. *American Beauty* is a postmodern film that undermines linear epistemology at every turn, but especially in the lead character, Lester Burnham's inability to make sense of his seemingly futile "stupid little life."

In his book *Beholding the Glory*, Jeremy Begbie gives us an example of how music can provide interpreters with alternate, nonlinear, hermeneutical perspectives. If we consider the colors red and yellow, he explains, we believe that they cannot be seen distinctly together. If they are painted on top of each other, the two colors will merge into orange; or if the paint of one of the colors is already dry, then the paint of the new color will simply blot out the other. Such has been the typical approach to reading Ecclesiastes. Meaninglessness simply blots out meaningfulness or compromises any vibrancy and hope Ecclesiastes might possess. But, says Begbie, if we turn to music rather than painting, we note an alternate interpretive reality. When two notes are played together simultaneously, they neither merge into something else nor obliterate one or the other. Rather, the two notes both fill up the entire aural space, and yet each remains distinct. They become a chord that contains both differentiation and union (138–54). Here is an alternate hermeneutical strategy, one suited to the artistry of film, as well. For movies, like music, allow artists to portray contradictory realities in a meaningful whole.

Seeing the Movie: *American Beauty*

Turning, then, to the movie *American Beauty*, viewers are provided a narrative that helps them "see" both life's vanity and its useless beauty. (One notes as an aside that Qoheleth uses the verb *ra'ah*, which means "to see," forty-seven times in his brief essay. He too, like this movie, wants us to see life differently.) The movie tells the story of Lester, Carolyn, and Jane Burnham, a family living the American dream—the idyllic, suburban, upper-middle-class life. But beneath this rosy veneer, all is not well. Like the artificially bred "American Beauty" rose, which Carolyn (Annette Bening) tends in her front yard while wearing designer clogs to match her garden shears, their lives are a veneer, perfect to look at on the outside but lacking any scent—any soul. Lester (Kevin Spacey) is burned out in his job, trapped in a loveless marriage and unable to communicate with his teenage daughter. His falsely enclosed universe is filmed for us by Conrad Hall, who frames shot after shot to show the characters as prisoners in their own houses. "Vanity of vanities, says the Teacher [Qoheleth], vanity of vanities! All is vanity" (Eccl 1:2).

As the story continues, Lester realizes he is now one of the walking dead. He tells his boss as he quits his job, "Brad, for fourteen years I've been a whore of the advertising industry. The only way I could save myself now is if I start firebombing." Like the writer of Ecclesiastes, begin "firebombing" he does. *American Beauty* is Lester's revelation to us of his death-in-life, and paradoxically, his life in and through death. As the movie ends, Lester is heard in a voice-over: "I can't feel anything but gratitude for every single moment of my stupid little life." As with the book of Ecclesiastes, the question before the viewer/reader is how to interpret such a remark. Given life's pervasive vanity, how is one able to push through it, or perhaps find within it something more? Lester's insight comes only after a year of struggle. The movie is Lester's story, his rediscovery of life's meaning, even amidst its ongoing meaninglessness. Lester is our narrator, telling us "this is my life." He will be dead in a year, but he says, "Of course, I don't know that yet." We, the audience, are informed that we are being told Lester's story from a privileged position, one that looks back on his life in terms of a truth later learned. Lester tells us that Carolyn, his wife, was not always like this, that she used to be happy. In fact, "we used to be happy." But his family has lost that. Though the song "Bali Hi" might be playing on Musak while the family eats together, theirs is no idyllic paradise. They have "lost something," though Lester says, "I'm not exactly sure what it is." What he does know, however, is that "it's never too late to get it back."

The life that is portrayed in *American Beauty* is a life of green lawns, manicured roses, designer labels, marketing mania, and corporate greed. It looks like a world brimming with hope, but there is an overriding darkness to it. Alan Ball, the movie's screenwriter, thinks Americans have been led to believe that wealth and success and materialism ("stuff") will make people happy. But he says, "That is just an out-and-out lie" (qtd. in Longino 4). Or, as the author of Ecclesiastes informs us, "I considered all that my hands had done and the toil I had spent in doing it, and again, all was vanity, and a chasing after wind, and there was nothing to be gained under the sun" (2:11). At one level, the movie is about just that, our chasing after wind. It is a frontal attack on the absurdity of our American, materialistic values. Carolyn, more than any other character, embodies the bankruptcy of the American dream in the movie. We watch her slap herself in the face, trying to muster a "winning attitude." We see her give herself sexually to Buddy King, the successful but crass real estate agent whose financial success she craves. But success eludes her. We see her driving home from the shooting range where she has experienced the newly found adrenaline rush of firing a pistol, singing along with the radio, "Don't rain on my parade." But rain it does. When Carolyn tries to help her daughter Jane (Thora Birch) cope with life, she can only opine, "You're old enough now to learn the most important lesson in life. You cannot count on anyone except yourself. . . . It's sad but true, and the sooner you learn it the better."

Lester, on the other hand, has learned to question this American way of life. He does not know what will take the place of his present lifestyle, but he is willing to seek something, anything else. He quits his job, buys the car he has always wanted, smokes pot, starts working out with barbells to get a sexy body that his daughter's girlfriend, Angela, will like, and takes a mindless job selling "Mr. Smiley" hamburgers at a fast-food restaurant. His hero becomes Ricky Fitts (Wes Bentley), the young seventeen year old next door, who casually quits his part-time catering job when his boss wants him to stop talking to Lester in the parking lot. Lester's initial steps are regressive, to be sure, and self-indulgent. He has no clue what to do, only what not to do. When he sits down to eat with Carolyn, he observes her futile life and asks, "When did you become so joyless?" Carolyn's immediate response is, "There's plenty of joy in my life." Viewers know otherwise. Lester's question is not meant harshly. In fact, Lester reaches out to touch Carolyn, one wounded person seeking another. He is hoping to rekindle some of the passion they once had for one another. But Carolyn quenches the fire, even before it ignites, saying as Lester tries to kiss her, "Lester, you're going to spill beer on the [expensive] couch." Lester can only respond, "This isn't life. It's just stuff. And it's become more important to you than living. And honey, that's just nuts."

Despite the movie's dark humor and biting satire, despite its frontal assault on America's materialism and individualism, the film offers its viewers a sympathetic portrayal of the Burnhams. We ache for Lester and Carolyn. They have needed something, anything, to believe in—money, status, or sexuality. They have worked at making life produce for them. But life has proven futile. And so, "[Lester] hated all [his] toil in which [he] had toiled under the sun" (Eccl 2:18). Like the American Beauty rose, their lives have no scent, no soul. Lester's recognition of this emptiness is no small accomplishment. In fact, only at the movie's ninety-minute mark does Lester finally understand the saying, "Today is the first day of the rest of your life." "The Seeker" is playing in the background as Lester leaves the house to jog. Lester is still trying to figure out his life. Quitting his job is not enough, but it is a start. He has become a seeker.

Though Lester has yet to make the discovery, viewers have already been given a hint as to where meaning will be found. For parallel to the story of Lester and Carolyn, we have been shown the story of Janie, the Burnham's daughter, and her relationships with Angela and Ricky, the neighbor boy whose abusive father is a Marine sergeant. Seeking to control his son, the father has even wrongly committed Ricky to a psychiatric ward, even though Ricky is sane. Unable to live life, Ricky retreats to taking videos of it. The first time we see him, in fact, he is videotaping Jane. For her part, Jane has also retreated from life, unable to compete with her good looking, cheerleader friend, Angela, and unable to face her loveless, driven parents. These two outsiders, Ricky and Jane, discover each other, a poignant reminder that "two are better than one" (Eccl 4:9). Seeking connection with each other, Jane asks Ricky what is the most beautiful thing he has ever videotaped? Ricky shows her a clip of a chilly, fall day in which the air was "electric." As Ricky and Jane watch the tape, a plastic bag remains suspended in the air, dancing in the wind. (This is the same clip that will be played at the movie's end as

Lester talks about life's fragile beauty and meaning.) Ricky says to Jane as they watch the floating bag, "This bag was just . . . dancing with me . . . like a little kid begging me to play with it. . . . That's the day I realized there was this entire life behind things, and this incredibly benevolent force that wanted me to know there was no reason to be afraid . . . ever." Ricky confesses that, sometimes, the beauty is almost too much. It is worth noting that this "plastic bag floating in the air" was inserted into the screenplay by Alan Ball, who based it on an experience he actually had. Ball says of that moment, some might think, "It's just the wind." But for Ball, as for Ricky, it was more. Ball says, "I suddenly felt this completely unexpected sense of peace and wonder" (qtd. in Longino 4).

Viewers are, thus, prepared for a choice, even before Lester himself is let in on the options. There are two forms of beauty in life, two attempts at what the Bible calls shalom. One is the American Beauty rose; the other, the video of the dancing, plastic bag. On the surface it would not seem a real choice. The one is so ephemeral and lacks any beauty in and of itself. It seems so useless, so dependent on the *ruach* (a Hebrew word Qoheleth uses over and over, and which means "wind" or "spirit"). The one is ephemeral; the other is so tangible, and seemingly perfect, something one can work to produce, something one can take pride in. Appearances, however, are deceiving, as Jane and Ricky know too well from their own life experiences. When given the choice between these alternate beauties, Jane knows what is real—where truth, beauty, and goodness reside—and her transformation begins. Soon after viewing the plastic bag on tape, Jane stands at the window, waving across the yard to Ricky, who is again filming her from his window. On the soundtrack we hear repeated the same music that was playing while the plastic bag was floating in the air. Jane looks at Ricky and proceeds to take off her blouse and bra for him, so he can see her body. It is not a lurid act; she is not Angela. Rather, expressing both trust and vulnerability, Jane reveals to Ricky that same fragile beauty of the plastic bag, a beauty that is imperfect, yet life-transforming. Her mother Carolyn had counseled Jane not to trust anyone else, but Jane now knows better. "If two lie together, they keep warm; but how can one keep warm alone?" (Eccl 4:11).

If Carolyn represents the bankruptcy of the American Dream within the parents' generation, it is the cheerleader, Angela, who embodies the futility of such a dream among the teenagers. Carolyn's temptation is materialism; Angela's, popularity. In the process, she has become all tease and no substance. For a time Jane is taken in, and so too, is her father. But Jane learns better. Angela cannot understand what Jane sees in Ricky. "He's a freak," she tells Jane, only to have Jane yell back, "Well so am I." Jane knows that she, like Ricky, can never be part of the American Dream; nor does she want to be. She chides Angela, "You're just too perfect." But like Carolyn, Angela still does not understand how useless her beauty is, or that it is okay to be less than perfect. "Wow . . . well at least I'm not ugly," she retorts. Only for Ricky to blurt out the hurtful truth: "Yes you are and you're boring and you're ordinary and you know it." "Vanity of vanities . . . all is vanity" (Eccl 12:8). Crushed by the harsh truth, Angela retreats to the adulation of Jane's father, Lester. But when Lester discovers that Angela is all bluster and bluff— that she is in fact still a virgin—he awakens from the temptation of the American Beauty rose petals that in his dream cascaded over her body. Lester refuses her sexual offer, providing her consolation and friendship instead. Not understanding at first this fragile gift of friendship, this ephemeral expression of the windblown plastic bag, Angela cries, "I thought you said I was beautiful. I feel so stupid." But Lester's hard-won acceptance of responsibility for his actions and his genuine care for Angela provide a breakthrough for both of them. It is an alternative beauty that he now seeks to nurture.

While Angela goes to the bathroom, Lester sits alone at his kitchen table, looking at a photograph of his family. It is the same photograph that he has looked at with pain and failure as the movie opens, but now there is a smile on his face. He has offered the gift of life to another. No, he does not need to find meaning in the beauty of a blond nymph with a rose-petal covering. There is more than enough joy in the ordinary—in memories of lying on his back watching falling leaves and shooting stars, of his grandmother's papery hands and his brand new Firebird, of his young daughter Jane at Halloween, or of Carolyn laughing at a carnival. Life is, indeed, a gift. Though these insights come just seconds before Lester is cold-bloodedly shot in the head, he can still say in the voice-over as the movie ends, "It's hard to stay mad when there's so much beauty in the world." Lester says that his "heart fills up like a balloon that's about to burst . . . and then I remember to relax and stop trying to hold onto it, and then it flows through me like rain. And I can't feel anything but gratitude for every single moment of my stupid little life."

Finding Beauty: A Rereading of Ecclesiastes

Do either of these texts have anything to say about the postmodern condition? Can *American Beauty* help us to read Ecclesiastes with fresh eyes? And vice versa? Hopefully, my brief narration is enough to suggest that these two texts might be walking on the same holy ground. Stylistically, there are important similarities—both bracket their presentations with poems/monologues that move from a recognition of life's vanity to a final, joyful embrace of life's sacredness, and both qualify any call to enjoyment by quickly asserting death as our common destiny. Thematically, there are similarities, too. *American Beauty* enfleshes for its viewers a host of questions concerning life's meaning, questions central to the book of Ecclesiastes and to contemporary culture as well:

1. Given a life that refuses to yield to our attempts to produce meaning, what can we know, and what are we to do?
2. How important to the uncovering of life's significance is our "rush toward death"?
3. Though we experience the harshness and transience of this terrible world, life remains paradoxically "terribly good." Must we not, then, celebrate life, despite its futility?
4. Is not the recognition of life's beauty a holy act?

Central to both narratives is the recognition of paradox—a paradox that links life and death, joy and sadness, despair and hope. Central as well is that sacred presence that shines in and through even our bleakest human experience. Life has a sacramental quality, despite (or is it because of) its mystery. Or so Lester Burnham and his teenage avatar Ricky suggest. To "see" life well (*ra'a btov*) is to see behind and through it to Reality.

The parallel with the wisdom Ecclesiastes offers should be clear. Looking back at the end of his life with a full realization of death as the great leveler, Qoheleth must criticize the vanity, the uselessness of all the attempts to wrest meaning from life by our own efforts—whether these be wisdom, wealth, or work. But though Qoheleth can be biting in his sarcasm, though his tone is often so dark that readers mistake it for pessimism or cynicism, this Old Testament sage, like Lester, can in the same breath advise his students:

> Go ahead—eat your food and be happy; drink your wine and be cheerful. It's all right with God [or a better translation, "for God already approves what you do." In Genesis he made humankind and called them "good."] Always look happy and cheerful. Enjoy life with the woman you love, as long as you live the useless life that God has given you in this world. Enjoy every useless day of it, because that is all you will get for all your trouble. Work hard at whatever you do, because there will be no action, no thought, no knowledge, no wisdom in the world of the dead—and that is where you are going. (Eccl 9:7-10, Good News Bible)

Qoheleth recognizes that much frustrates life—death, life's amorality, life's opaqueness. Given such reality, it seems better from one perspective if we might never have been born. However, viewing this same reality from a different vantage point, life is also precious. It has so much useless beauty. As Qoheleth recognizes, "[A] living dog is better than a dead lion" (Eccl 9:4). We must speak of both life's futility and its wonder. In fact, we must speak of them in the same breath.

The transcendent vision of life in both Ecclesiastes and *American Beauty* comes without reference to the church or synagogue, without reference to traditional religion. Here is, perhaps, the reason the medieval church found it a particularly dangerous book. Although Qoheleth, writing late in Israel's history, knows the Law, he chooses not to use it in his argument. This absence, in fact, is so difficult for his readers that a later redactor inserts as an ending to Ecclesiastes: "The end of the matter; all has been heard. Fear God, and keep his commandments; for that is the whole duty of everyone" (12:13). As a Jew, Qoheleth had this answer to life's vanity in his theological quiver. He could have talked about the God of the Exodus who rescued and redeemed his people and gave them the Law. But he does not. A revelatory trump card is not played. Readers can only conjecture as to why. Perhaps Qoheleth does not want to reinforce the religious smugness of his people, something that lies behind their falsely understood gospel of prosperity. Just as money, fame, wisdom, and pleasure can be a means of shutting out God's transforming presence, so, too, can the certainty of our creeds and dogmas. Qoheleth thus does not appeal to the Law. To correct the arrogance of his readers, he instead turns to the ultimate leveler, death. Here, paradoxically, is a perspective for life. It is Qoheleth's recognition of life's ultimate uselessness that allows him to see life's grandeur and beauty. Only life's seeming hopelessness reveals life's hopefulness. Such is the paradox of life. Here, we might say, is the real American Beauty, a useless beauty upon which all our hopes can be placed. It is more ephemeral than even the rose, but also real, a beauty that will endure even beyond death, a beauty providing hope and perspective on all else.

Section Two

The Valley of Despair

There are two things that kill the soul, despair and false hope.
                    —*Augustine,* Sermon 87:10:413

Elie Wiesel, recipient of the 1986 Nobel Peace Prize, has characterized the twentieth century as a century in desperate need of hope. What began in a spirit of optimism brought on by economic prosperity, technological advances, peace, and good will ended with death camps, bombs, and, for many, a sense of despair. "When I look around the world," writes Wiesel in one of many books on the Holocaust, "I see nothing but hopelessness. And yet I must, we all must, try to find a source of hope" (qtd. in Schuster and Boschert-Kimmig 63). Since "our modern gods have failed us," writes theologian James K. A. Smith, "everything has changed, our confidence and hope have been shattered, and we late moderns find ourselves slipping under the surface, being pulled down by the eddy of despair" ("Determined Hope" 201). How does one hope again after facing the horrors of the Holocaust, or closer to home, the death of a loved one, betrayal by a friend, the collapse of a dream? The essays in this section engage stories that wrestle with life in the valley of despair, where all desire is drained away, where knees are weak and the will is sapped—where one no longer dares to hope. "Because I do not hope to turn again." T. S. Eliot writes,

> Because I do not hope
> Because I do not hope to turn
> Desiring this man's gift and that man's scope
> I no longer strive to strive towards such things
> (Why should the agèd eagle stretch its wings?)
> Why should I mourn
> The vanished power of the usual reign?" ("Ash Wednesday" 60)

When Moltmann writes of Christian hope, he means to address life in the valley, times that are beyond human fixing without God's provision in Christ, the crucified and risen One. While we may have a part to play, Moltmann makes clear that hope in the valley rests solely on the promises and faithfulness of God (*Coming of God* 194).

In chapter 5, Martha Greene Eads takes up the challenge to Christian belief posed by death in her essay "Prosaic Grace: Doris Betts's *Souls Raised from the Dead*." Betts's 1994 novel deals with the impact of the death of thirteen-year-old Mary Grace Thompson on her family, especially her father, the protagonist, Francis Thompson. Based on her reading of Glenn Tinder's *The Fabric of Hope*, Eads argues that only divine grace can enable Francis to survive this profound "theodical challenge." Although not an explicitly religious novel, *Souls Raised from the Dead* illustrates Tinder's point that the virtue of hope develops as we choose to believe in the face of doubt and despair, and more specifically, as we act on that belief. In the case of Francis Thompson, whom Betts names after the Victorian poet loved and pursued by the "Hound of Heaven" in his famous poem, this choice means performing visible acts of love, rescuing a young girl from an automobile accident, listening to his first wife grieve over the phone, and possibly remarrying and fathering other children. Such prosaic activities spark faith and rekindle hope. There is something sacramental about the message of this novel, something relating outward signs to inward grace. Never mind which comes first. As Betts explains in an interview, "[T]he soul to be raised was not that of Mary Grace from death, but the soul of her father from despair—the ultimate death." Francis Thompson's struggle to believe is not finally resolved. He does not find a satisfactory answer to his daughter's fatal illness. He does undertake disciplines of faith and love, however, and with this action he chooses to hope rather than to despair. In his classic meditation *On Hope*, Josef Pieper maintains that both the person who hopes and the person who despairs "choose these attitudes with their will and let [these attitudes] determine their conduct" (49). Eads sees in *Souls Raised from the Dead* a story that urges us to choose hope, to work out our own salvation within the context of our doubts, keeping in mind the reality and necessity of God's enabling grace.

In chapter 6, Elaine Lux's essay "Narrative Bones: Amy Tan's *Bonesetter's Daughter* and Hugh Cook's *Homecoming Man*" studies the way recurrent bone images and embedded bone-story myths release characters from familial memories of shame and guilt. Midlife protagonists Ruth Young in *Bonesetter's Daughter* and Paul Bloem in *Homecoming Man* struggle with oppressive family secrets. Learning to see hope and meaning in what has been shameful and hidden allows these characters to transform their pasts imaginatively from stories of hurt to stories of healing. Within the narrative of that transformation, according to Lux, particular emphasis is placed on the most common variant of bone myths, echoing the prophetic tradition in the Old Testament, in which dead bones are spoken or sung into flesh, breath, and life. A less common variant in which the skeleton, instead of coming back to life, tries to lure the living to their deaths is also presented. The narrative tension between hope and despair in both novels is seen in relationship to these two variants. Lux concludes her essay by reflecting on the power of mythic imagery in story and storytelling, which she identifies as the key to creating narrative worlds that live on in the reader long after the reading is over. The Tan and Cook regenerative family narratives suggest the hopefulness of biblical and folk bone tales and the skill required to convey that hope in literature. In the biblical narrative the Word becomes flesh, faces death, and overcomes it in order to redeem and restore that which was lost. The Tan and Cook narratives echo this theme in their portrayal of human suffering and the healing that comes through storytelling and story. "When our skeletons take on flesh and breath through our stories," Lux observes, "truly we live."

In chapter 7, Eric Sterling's essay "Hope from a Radio: Jurek Becker's *Jakob the Liar*" questions whether it is foolish or heroic to imagine, to pretend something is true knowing it is false, if this untruth holds back despair and enables hope. Sterling offers two reasons Jews did not resist the Nazis during the Holocaust: they lacked hope to survive, or, conversely, they possessed false hope that they would soon be rescued. In Becker's novel, set in Poland during the Holocaust, Jacob Heym offers a gift of hope that turns out to be false for despairing Jews in his Polish ghetto. Distressed to see many people losing heart and even contemplating suicide, Jacob decides to encourage them by pretending to possess a radio. Jacob provides his friends with hopeful news, concocting optimistic stories about the Russian army's steady advance against the German forces in control of their village. His hopeful stories are eagerly spread throughout the Jewish ghetto, providing the people with renewed optimism and a reason to stay alive. As hopes rise, lives are saved from despair and suicide, and people are able to bear up under the brutality of the Nazi soldiers as they await their "imminent" liberation by the Russian army. Although Jacob, a normal and unexceptional person, becomes a ghetto celebrity and hero (radios are forbidden by the Germans; the punishment for having one is death), his imaginative lie is unsustainable. Eventually, the truth is unavoidable, for reality—dependent not on his fantasies but on the actual course of the war—is beyond his control. Ultimately, Jacob must confess to his loyal but annoying friend Kowalski that he never possessed a radio. Tragically, Kowalski, upon discovering the truth, commits suicide. Sterling observes that Becker, recognizing the power of the imagination to engender hope, leaves it to the reader to determine whether Jacob is a hero for temporarily saving the lives of the ghetto inhabitants or a rogue for providing his community with a false sense of hope.

Focusing specifically on the horrors of the Holocaust, Becker's novel touches a central postmodern theme: the absurd waiting for a savior who is either ineffective or never comes. The challenge this theme poses to religious faith is taken up in Carole Lambert's concluding essay for this section, "Friendship and Hope: Elie Wiesel's *The Town Beyond the Wall*." Though not obvious on the surface, a strong similarity exists between Betts's and Wiesel's treatment of theodical themes. How does one make sense of the death of an innocent child, Betts asks, much less believe in a loving, omnipotent God who permits it? Wiesel is well known for asking similar questions about the death of millions of Jews, including his own grandparents, parents, and younger sister, during the Holocaust. In Wiesel's story, Michael, a traumatized Holocaust survivor, is deeply disillusioned with the God whom he mystically adored in his childhood. Anxious to return to his hometown, now behind the Communist Iron Curtain, he encounters Pedro, compassionate, courageous, and enigmatic, who fast becomes his closest friend. Pedro helps Michael arrive at "the town beyond the wall," but Michael is soon arrested and tortured by Communist interrogators. Having lost his earlier belief in God, Michael finds hope during his imprisonment not through prayer to God, but through remembering significant conversations with his friend. Pedro demonstrates the compassion, goodness, justice, and profound understanding that the pre-Holocaust Michael had hoped to find in God. His integrity inspires Michael to endure his own torment without betraying his friend's location to the Communists, and to assist other prisoners, particularly one even more withdrawn than he. Michael assumes Pedro's name, while bestowing his own on the mute prisoner. His friendship with Pedro not only enables Michael to imagine a sustaining narrative that allows him to survive, but also gives him hope and strength to restore another to humanity. Like Francis Thompson in Betts's novel, Michael chooses hope over despair and acts accordingly. The novel concludes with one more hopeful sign: the formerly mute prisoner receives another name change, becoming "Eliezer, which means *God has granted my prayer*." This suggests that both the Holocaust survivor Michael and possibly his creator, Eliezer Wiesel, have begun to pray to God, the friend who had once neglected or betrayed them, or so it seemed. Through Wiesel's characters, Pedro, Michael, and the mute prisoner, we see God in his "distressing disguise," as Mother Teresa calls it, seeking to restore relationships, nurturing and rekindling hope (qtd. in Muggeridge 97).

Chapter 5

Prosaic Grace
Doris Betts's Souls Raised from the Dead

Martha Greene Eads

Doris Betts's *Souls Raised from the Dead*, a novel about a highway patrol-man whose old line-of-duty injury prevents him from donating a kidney to his dying thirteen-year-old daughter, hardly sounds upbeat. Before its publication in 1994, Betts confessed to interviewer Susan Ketchin that she could barely finish writing the book, finding herself bogged down in the difficulty of depicting young Mary Grace Thompson's death:

> I wish I'd never started it. I got to the point where Mary had to die, and I just balked. I wrote descriptive passages and I prolonged the girl's illness; I did character sketches of minor people; the novel just got longer and longer without getting the least bit better. It just hid. And finally, I just had to come back and do her final scene, where she does die, and it's not even two pages long. I just had to beat around the bush a long time to write those two pages. (Ketchin 240)

Betts's turmoil is easy enough to understand; a child's death presents life's most profound—yet all too common—theodical challenge. How can humans make sense of such inexplicable pain, much less trust in a loving and omnipotent God who permits it? Betts struggled to address the topic adequately, wondering, she recounts, if she should "assign to the trooper a bookish narrator-friend who reads theodicy on the side? And if the daughter died, how could the story be anything but morbid and depressing, as even the gospel story would be if it stopped short on Good Friday or Holy Saturday?" ("Whispering Hope" 82).

Glenn Tinder's *Fabric of Hope* provides a useful framework for considering the way in which Betts's novel succeeds in showing the possibility of hope's emergence from Mary Grace's death. In his discussion of the ultimate affronts to hope, Tinder considers children's deaths resulting from both natural evil, as in Albert Camus's *Plague*, and moral evil, as in Fyodor Dostoevsky's *Brothers Karamazov* and the Holocaust. None of these tragedies is "so irredeemably meaningless as to defy the story-teller's art," Tinder argues, "for there is nothing so vile or crushing in human experience that it cannot be recounted in a way that gives it a measure of meaning." Moreover, one entirely true story "show[s] forth the meaning in every terrible detail of every tragedy in human history," and that is the story of Christ. "Every story-teller who is not simply seeking diversion is trying, however unconsciously, to replicate [that] story" (59–60). Only through the crucifixion can humans find meaning in such profound suffering: "That so dismaying an occurrence [as the crucifixion] has not only taken on meaning but has come to be seen as the key to the meaning of all human life and history suggests that nothing whatever can break out of the destiny ordained for the human race and for every human being" (134). By "destiny," Tinder means something quite different from fate, which is "meaningless, inescapable, oppressive" (60). Rather, destiny stands for God's "ultimate and unsurpassable narrative" for humanity and all of creation. Our destiny is the true and universal story which will reconcile us to all that has happened or ever will happen, and story,telling is implicitly a search for traces, hints, or rumors of that story. That said, Tinder defines Christian hope as "the faith that such a search will not prove to be in vain or ill-founded. . . . Hope is the capacity for carrying on one's life in the confidence that it will finally be seen as a story fashioned by an omnipotent and merciful God, a story therefore in which there are no unassimilated absurdities" (61).

Souls Raised from the Dead is rooted in this recognition. And yet, although the author unhesitatingly acknowledges her own Christian commitment, she publishes fiction not sermons. Citing a conversation about a draft of *Souls Raised from the Dead* with a pastor who had lost his own daughter in an automobile accident, Betts describes the danger of sermonizing:

> He told me, "Whatever you write, don't write that you get over this because there are some mornings that I get up and it just happened an hour ago." And I was really in tears listening to him. And I thought, you just can't play false to that by giving any kind of glib catechism answer. You either have to turn to hope, thin though it may be at the time, or you have to say, "To hell with this life!" and cut your throat. (Ketchin 240)

Careful to avoid catechizing, Betts nevertheless reveals that her characters' "thin hope" rests in the narrative of Christian faith. The novel's title suggests its theological foundation, and its epigraph comes from Czeslaw Milosz's poem "With Her," which alludes to the account in the Gospel of Mark of Jesus' raising a girl from the dead. *Souls Raised from the Dead* unfolds, however, not as a sunny story of Christian miracle-working but as a restrained account of the Thompsons' often torturous quest for faith in God and their persistent efforts to love other people.

In his Preface to *The Fabric of Hope*, Tinder points out that while "hope is a universal human need," the specifically Christian virtue of hope is secondary to faith and charity, or even love (xii, xi). Acknowledging the mysterious origins of faith and love in the life of a Christian, Tinder notes:

> Either they are given to us or we do not have them. When it comes to the ultimate grounds of our lives, it seems, we are not in control. Is there, then, nothing we can do? That does not quite follow, although we must recognize that no human efforts to approach God have sure results. Faith and love are given by grace, and grace has no source but God. The very word implies gratuitousness. Nonetheless, it is a vital truth pertaining to both faith and love that even though they are given by grace, human will has a role in their acquisition. (107–8)

Betts's book illustrates Tinder's claim through its characterization, showing the importance of both faith and love in the formation of hope. Even the names of the main characters, Mary Grace Thompson and Francis Thompson, serve as reminders that while humans work out their own salvation through acts of faith, love, and hope, God must initiate and enable the process.

The central figure in *Souls Raised from the Dead*, Mary Grace Thompson, challenges the adults around her to move forward toward hope through faith and love. She is not, however, a particularly pious child; indeed, she is often more smart-alecky than sweet. She addresses her father, who goes by Frank, as "General Franco," slams doors when she is cross, and "just this year" has "become very good at lying" (5, 11, 17, 19). To the interviewer who saw Mary Grace as a Christ figure come to save her mother, Christine, Betts pointed out the witty yet bitter prayer the girl utters when she finally faces up to Christine's faithlessness: "Our Mother, who art in New York, hollow be thy name" (Harmon 63). "The only relation of Mary Grace as a Christ figure to me," Betts continued, "was that she's the same age Christ was when he spoke to the elders in the temple. And it is Mary Grace who in some ways speaks to all these elders. Indeed her death does start many of them in different directions" (63). Betts does, however, admit to having chosen the girl's name for its theological and literary significance; through it, she confesses, she "managed to whisper both 'Grace' and the surname of a poet named Francis, and lift an invisible hat to a Flannery O'Connor character as well" ("Whispering Hope" 81). Critics sometimes compare Betts to O'Connor, whose short story "Revelation" features an unpleasant but insightful coed named "Mary Grace," who challenges a self-satisfied southern matron. Betts admires O'Connor's work, but explains that while O'Connor's fictional method is to "shout" for the spiritually "hard of hearing," her own approach is to whisper (79).

Betts's whispered tribute to Francis Thompson, author of "The Hound of Heaven," becomes distinctly audible, however, as *Souls* develops. At a family reunion, Frank's cousin Layla produces a genealogical chart tracing the family clan to the eighteenth-century poet who, she explains, wrote "a famous Christian poem in which Jesus, like a hunting dog, ran eternally after the scent of human souls" (134). Frank's lover, Cindy Scofield, a newspaper reporter and former English major, remembers the poem from college. "It's about how God pursued Francis Thompson's soul here on earth until He finally hunted it down," she explains to Frank's mother, Tacey, who had never heard of the poet but had named Frank "for the saint who loved animals and whose prayer was carved in the vestibule floor of her church: *Lord, make me an instrument of Thy peace*" (181, 180). Although not a member of the Thompson clan, Cindy is herself caught up in God's pursuit of human souls through her association with the family. Damaged by her own suffering, she nevertheless grows toward grace through her unwavering love for Frank.

Before the novel opens, Cindy and Frank have established a sexual relationship of convenience. "As she had saved him from ulcers," the narrator explains, "he saved her from jitters and severe female chauvinism. . . . Like an old married couple, they had to plan sex within their work schedules, build up to it, shift out of the good-buddy stage in which they had just compared their wreck reports" (85). Even such an apparently empty physical bond, however, becomes a surprising venue for grace. Frank learns that Cindy's severely autistic younger brother had injured her with a hatchet in childhood. The stress of caring for him had destroyed her parents' marriage. During one of their sexual encounters, Frank kisses Cindy's scar, "knowing how much emotion its swerve must represent. Instantly she had shivered and cried out" (85). Although she and Frank drift apart when he begins dating Mary Grace's riding instructor, Cindy finds nonintrusive ways to show kindness to him and his family: bringing him a blanket as he dozes in the hospital waiting room, taking his mother to lunch to discuss transplant options, working discreetly with his patrol partner, Elmo, to establish a medical fund for Mary Grace. Even Tacey, who disapproves of her son's sleeping with Cindy, recognizes that Cindy loves Frank and hopes that she will remain in his life (177, 178).

Betts adds to Cindy's love for Frank the possibility of her awakening religious faith. She gives Cindy no clear conversion experience, choosing instead to suggest that Cindy is opening herself to grace by considering faith. The reporter is intrigued by "The Hound of Heaven," telling Tacey she would "be proud enough to be traced back to Francis Thompson. Especially to carry his name, like Frank does" (180). After the Thompsons' neighbor Miss Lila Torrido is viciously murdered, Frank notices at the funeral that Cindy "seemed to be staring at the priest" (230). When Frank expresses skepticism about Elmo's church's prayers for Mary Grace's healing, Cindy advises, "I wouldn't knock it if I were you" (277). The book's final pages hint that Cindy's empathetic, active love and budding faith offer both her and Frank hope for a fruitful life together.

Although she appears at first to be a poor emotional risk, Cindy proves herself a far better companion than either of the other women in Frank's life: Jillian Peters, Mary Grace's riding teacher, and his ex-wife, Christine. Betts contrasts the three women through the gifts they bring Mary Grace in the hospital: Cindy offers a crossword puzzle magazine and carefully chosen poetry on tape; Jill selects a bouquet from the hospital floral cooler, and Christine presents a pink negligee—one of her own, almost certainly, and "suitable for a honeymoon" (293). Mary Grace has never hidden her dislike for Cindy, but Cindy nevertheless takes pains to select gifts a bright thirteen-year-old will enjoy. While Jill is genuinely fond of her riding pupil, she is too consumed by her own losses to attend fully to either Mary Grace or Frank. The self-absorbed Christine seems incapable of even imagining what gift a gravely ill adolescent might appreciate, much less of mothering Mary Grace as she ought.

Early in the book, Mary Grace idolizes Jill while Frank lusts after the riding instructor with her blonde good looks, teasing readers into thinking that Jill, not Cindy, will offer the love Christine denied them. Jill warns him, however, that she plans to go to veterinary school and that she "wouldn't want to get really involved in a relationship" (57). Although she and Frank become lovers soon after meeting, Jill's refusal to discuss her past with him keeps them from developing a real closeness. Like Cindy, Jill bears a scar, although hers is purely emotional: she gave up a baby for adoption and cannot stop thinking about him or the selfish man who fathered him. Comparing Jill to Cindy, Frank erroneously assumes that "Jill was probably too young to have any hurt worse than some boyfriend in a wallet photo who had ditched her at the prom" (85). Tacey compares the two women, too, concluding that Jill is too young to be a good companion to Frank (182). Although neither Frank nor Tacey ever knows Jill's story, they both recognize fairly quickly that she is unable—or at least unready—to love deeply.

Whether by coincidence or authorial intention, Jill is as closed to faith as she is to love. She mentions having been raised Roman Catholic by a mother who volunteered for parish work and a father who went to confession only once a year (31). When the Thompsons' neighbor Miss Lila correctly pegs her as Catholic, Jill responds, "I'm not a practicing Catholic. And it didn't hold me up when I needed it" (102). She resents Miss Lila's response: "Of course it did—you're still here, aren't you?— unwilling to give God credit for everything you'd done yourself the hard way" (102). Although she is a sympathetic character, Jill nevertheless shows no sign of openness to the Christian faith in the pages of the novel.

Christine Broome Thompson is a far less sympathetic character than Jill. Even before abandoning Frank and Mary Grace, she was an inattentive wife and mother. Now she goes for months on end without writing or calling her adolescent daughter. Although Betts does not address Christine's religious perspective overtly, the woman's decision to shorten her name from "Christine" to "Tina" for a radio call-in program on beauty (called "Tina's Arena") is highly suggestive (138). In a bizarre blend of naivete and arrogance, she feels as if "she had produced her particular beauty the way Henry Ford produced the Model-A car" (137). Estranged from her Creator, Christine is also cut off from those around

her. She uses a family reunion not as an opportunity to mingle with relatives but to sell them cosmetics. Considering her marriage to Frank "a
single distraction," she despises her subsequent lovers as much as she did
him, complaining to her mother that all men "get fat and they snore and
they catch diseases" (138, 294). Marveling at her relationship to Mary
Grace, she muses, "How amazing that this separate body and person had
come out of herself—though *that* experience she'd just as soon forget,
OK? Ruined her vagina" (139, 140–41). Although she obsesses over
physical appearance, she ultimately loathes physicality. Drifting off to
sleep the night before Mary Grace dies, she tries to block out the odors
of her own mother's cheap apartment: "Tomorrow at the hospital there
would be alcohol and medicine smells, thick as a mudpack, to clean out
her nostrils; and before she left Durham she would spread perfumed gel
between her breasts where her own heart would pulsate it forth, and she
could breathe the sweet fragrance of no one but herself" (298). Her
refusal to focus on "no one but herself" keeps her from meeting her own
daughter's desperate need for a transplant kidney.

Unlike Christine, Frank's father, Andrew, or "Dandy," is eager to
serve as Mary Grace's donor, secretly consulting a urologist. Outraged
to be told that high blood pressure has likely damaged his elderly kidneys, Dandy fumes at his inability to help his granddaughter. His love
for her is beyond question. Dandy's faith in God, however, is uncertain
at best. He "approves" of church, thinking it "proper that the weaker
women and children should be consoled by stories" even if he is not
(73, 317). When Tacey drags him to the hospital chapel during Mary
Grace's first renal crisis, Dandy merely mumbles instead of reciting
with her the Twenty-third Psalm. He ruminates resentfully on the tone
of the passage:

> The Twenty-third Psalm? It had always made him nervous. It gave
> in. It acquiesced. Soon as it got down to brass tacks and left the still
> waters to walk down the Valley of Death, God-as-*He* was begged to
> turn right away into God-as-*Thou*. Serious business. So wouldn't a
> need that extreme bring *Thou*, Him, It, Whoever, into the valley
> right away to fix things up?
>
> Not a bit. That psalm acquiesced to dying!
>
> For the rest of the verses no mention was made about escaping
> Death thanks to Him (thanks to Thou). The most that could be
> escaped was the fear of Death. Just the Fear. Second best. You got
> goodness and mercy the rest of your life but no insurance beyond,
> except someone to walk the last mile with you. Even convicts got
> that. (95)

Although he manages most of the time to distract himself by entering sweepstakes and telling corny jokes, Dandy carries a nearly overpowering burden: his fear of death.

Betts makes Dandy's fear and related lack of faith understandable, but she also shows how it limits his capacity to love. As he struggles to pray for Mary Grace in the chapel, his thoughts turn from his granddaughter's misery to his own. He thinks of her in her hospital bed, "all hundred pounds of her, all he would be leaving behind when he died, now lying upstairs in a state some baby intern had called preconvulsive" (97). Angrily, he addresses Jesus:

> Listen, it was bad enough when I saw she'd grow up and marry some asshole and have babies who never knew about me and they'd all forget all of it, and the ants would dig anthills on my grave that nobody visited—that was a Valley of Death, all right; but listen?
>
> Not to have anybody left able to do the forgetting? Even to send her into the ground before me?
>
> Oh, that's a torture! That's cruel and inhuman punishment, he accused.
>
> That's mean as hell! (96–97)

Again and again, Dandy reflects on his own mortality and that of those he loves, trusting only in memory as a guard against nothingness. At the family reunion on his old homeplace, he conjures up images of his long-dead mother and father and recites their names (155). "Every family needed some old maid every fifth generation or so," he speculates, "with nothing better to do than rediscover ancestors and make the others pay them homage" (157). Unable to trust in God, Dandy places his hope in memory and story.

Faced with Mary Grace's mortality, however, Dandy realizes that his hope of being remembered is unlikely to be fulfilled. He knows that unless Frank has other children, no one will remain to keep his, Dandy's, memory alive. "A name on a tombstone . . . ," Dandy frets. "Maybe no more would be left of Andrew Thompson" (157). Tinder tackles this ugly reality head-on in *The Fabric of Hope*, challenging the secular view that to be remembered is to cheat death: "Need it be said, however, that being remembered is not the same as living and is a pathetically inadequate substitute for living? And in any case, very few of us will be remembered for longer than a generation or two, or by more than a handful of people" (141). Dandy, a would-be secularist who once collected pamphlets on Darwin, Marx, Freud, and Paine, begins to recognize that mere memory will not long outlive frail flesh (156). Taking

Tacey's hand at Mary Grace's funeral, he imagines the skeleton she, too, will one day leave behind, and "by reflex he jerked when the sudden pain howled in his heart" (319). That pain points him yet again to the limitations of mortal love and human story.

A larger love and wider story worthy of his faith, nevertheless, becomes available to Dandy at the funeral. Although he sees his pastor as "a fool when he spoke as himself," Dandy observes that the Reverend Billy Ware's "personal nature dissolved when he was reading the old words most of the congregation could have read for him, even without using a Bible" (317). When the congregation begins reciting the inevitable Twenty-third Psalm, "Dandy felt his mouth moving to every one of those words he did not trust, words that after all these years were still perfectly arranged in deep storage in his throat" (319). Betts shows that when he reaches the end of his own resources, Dandy might still entrust himself to the narrative of Christian faith.

As if her suggestion that Dandy comes to rest in Christian hope were not subtle enough, Betts also tests Tacey's faith. Although the book's other characters assume that Tacey's religious conviction is unshakable, Mary Grace's illness serves as the older woman's emotional and spiritual earthquake. Like Dandy, Tacey loves Mary Grace to the limits of her ability, and her Christian commitment motivates her to try to love even her granddaughter's despicable mother, Christine. When Dandy calls Christine "that little trash. That product of trash," Tacey urges, "A little charity, Andrew" (12–13). Her charitable resources are deeper than her husband's, but she has nevertheless drained them when she hints near the novel's end that she will never forgive Christine for refusing to give Mary Grace one of her kidneys (283). She subsequently insists that she knows her Christian duty to forgive, but she also maintains that she blames not God but Christine for Mary Grace's death (287, 315). In reality, she is struggling to keep both love and faith alive as her hopes for her granddaughter die.

Tacey recognizes that her inner wranglings rival those in the oldest literary theodicy: the book of Job (315). She finds herself praying for clear weather for Mary Grace's funeral and then wonders "what kind of God might fix the weather but let a girl die so young that you would never see her wear a wedding dress?" (315). Musing on how she suggested her granddaughter's middle name—ostensibly in honor of a fictional Aunt Grace but really for "Amazing Grace"—she bitterly revises the hymn title, "Shocking Grace . . . Disappointing Grace" (326). Even so, she lectures herself about her doubts:

This isn't the first time—Tacey Thompson—you felt like giving up on God. This is like stomach flu; you've come down again with the Atheist Stomach Flu. Sick as a dog. Sick as the Devil, even. You didn't catch it from Frank, either. It's always waiting. The germ, it's always there, it's there any time your resistance drops. No wonder you know the symptoms—you've had it before, you've got it again. This time you're going to be real sick for a while . . . . But you got over it before? Last time you knew it was a lie and we all die like the lizards and bumblebees, but you got over it, didn't you? But this is the worst case ever. It's just coming on, but already you can tell it's the worst. You'll be the sickest this time that you've ever been. So you can't do anything now but hang on and be altogether sick and survive it if you can. That's all. (316)

As desperate as Tacey sounds, concluding her rebuke with "Amen" reveals her intuitive trust that grace undergirds her crumbling faith (317).

While Betts's honest exploration of Tacey's doubts helps inoculate *Souls Raised from the Dead* against a sentimentalized spirituality, it also reflects the author's experience. Betts indicates that she, too, has grappled with religious doubt. In a 1993 interview, she reveals that before returning to the church in her maturity, she "thought everybody else was very certain and very convinced and they believed every jot and tittle, and I knew I wasn't going to be able to do that" (Powell 27). Back in the church, she concludes that "what seems to be crucial is that you have decided to commit whether somebody is in charge of the universe or not, and whether that power is benevolent or not, and whether in the main the Christian story is the best revelation of that that we have" (27). In a 1995 interview, in which she discusses Blaise Pascal's understanding of faith as a wager, she sounds more confident, although still far from dogmatic, about Christianity:

I am not someone who is ever entirely free of doubt. I move in and out of doubt. I have good days and bad days. . . . But I also find in Pascal that there is a confidence behind that wager. You don't make that wager until you have already gone more than halfway. And the wager has not failed me. Although, I should say, I was out of the Church for quite a long time, and cultivated that doubt like a poisonous flower. But in the end I think the hope that Christ is just who he claimed to be is stronger than a mere bet. . . . If you decide that, having made the wager, you are now responsible for doing all the rest of it—the obedience, and the church, the prayer and the meditation—then I suspect the wager has already gone beyond you and you just didn't notice. There is a discipline, I think, that is necessary in religion as well as art. (Harmon 55)

Betts depicts such discipline in Tacey's commitment to weathering her "Atheist Stomach Flu," providing an artistic rendering of Tinder's observation that "hope is far oftener disciplinary than exalting" (81). Tacey's disciplines—habits, in some sense, of faith and love—serve as splints for her own fractured hope.

Tacey's example also aids the Hound of Heaven in catching up with the novel's modern-day Francis Thompson. "For Frank's sake, at least," Tacey decides "to pretend that with autumn the days were slowly getting better. . . . That the Prodigal Son is more than a bedtime story and that the Heavenly Father who ran out to meet him is real" (329). Unaware of Tacey's sense of having to pretend, Frank simply takes note of her loving and faithful behavior, as well as that of his partner Elmo, who, despite his own struggles, still tells his Methodist adult Sunday school class "that a good God ruled everything" (233). After declining Tacey's persistent invitations to attend church, and throwing away Elmo's countless evangelistic postcards, Frank visits his mother's church when no one is there (235, 279, 325). He begins reading the Bible she had given Mary Grace, leaving it open by his recliner (327). Again, Betts offers no explicit conversion account, but her hopeful hints about Frank are impossible to miss. Always tenderhearted, his capacity for compassion grows to the point that he takes late-night calls from Christine, whose own mother turns off her telephone rather than listen to her weeping (338). Though still mourning, he begins seeing Cindy again and returns to his work as a patrolman. He, too, undertakes disciplines of faith and love.

Frank's response to the novel's concluding crisis offers a last glimpse of life's apparently endless possibilities for both pain and hope. Answering a dispatcher's call on a rainy night, he arrives at a riverside accident scene to find a dead woman and her daughter trapped in their crushed and immersed car. With passersby and then with a rescue crew, Frank works tirelessly to free the girl and send her to the hospital. "They're Catholics," Elmo informs him, having spotted a Saint Christopher medal in the wrecked car (337). The girl's suffering reminds Frank of Mary's, but to divert himself from paralyzing grief, he thinks instead of the girl's father and then of Tacey. "Even a faith as serene as Tacey's couldn't keep parents from worrying," he realizes. "She must be as helplessly worried over [his] state of mind as he had for so long been helplessly worried over Mary's state of health" (339). Later, carrying the injured girl's identification to the hospital, he drives past his parents' dark house and considers waking Tacey to talk about Mary Grace. Confident that she is sleeping peacefully after having prayed for him, he drives on. The novel concludes: "I'll see her in the morning, he thought, before she goes to church. But now he had to go to the hospital, check on the girl, look up a suitable Catholic priest in the telephone book. Possibly call the girl's father himself" (339). His mother's faith, flawed though it may be, and Frank's own love are bearing fruit in their own lives and the lives of others.

To argue that *Souls Raised from the Dead* is a religious book in the conventional sense would be to oversimplify it. The novel's treatment of faith is vexed at best. None of the characters finds a satisfactory answer to the problem of evil, whether that evil takes the form of Mary's fatal illness, Christine's simple selfishness, or Miss Lila Torrido's murder. However, those who do grasp for some form of faith in the face of despair, over time, grow in hope. Betts discusses the slow but persistent growth of hope as it occurs in *Souls Raised from the Dead*:

> All my novel had to do was to repeat that hope or, as T. S. Eliot would have said, to "redeem the time." The soul to be raised was not that of Mary Grace from death, but the soul of her father from despair—the ultimate death. And the end of the novel does not shout about Heaven, does not draw large and startling pictures; it only whispers. In the end Mary Grace Thompson does die and her father's heart is broken, but he makes a start toward hope in divine mercy. Hope may even be whispered so softly that not every reader will notice that there are fathers and Fathers in the final paragraph. ("Whispering Hope" 84)

In this sense *Souls Raised from the Dead* is a religious novel and a distinctively Christian one.

Glenn Tinder's book offers a final insight into the way Betts has constructed a Christian narrative of hope. Tinder notes that the virtue of hope develops over time, describing the phenomenon in terms that sound much like the novel's:

> To entrust your life to time, however, is to acknowledge the impermanence and imperfection of all worlds. It is to dwell within the situation in which time has placed you, suffering and doing what you must, in the faith that by submitting to the demands of time you are submitting to the demands of God, the Lord of time. . . . Only by living faithfully within time, and by submitting to the suffering and death to which Christ submitted, is God encountered. (220)

Although they are far less conscious of their submission to suffering and death than Tacey is, Frank and Cindy join her in doing what they must: loving those around them. The grace that enables them to fulfill their obligations to love also sparks their faith and kindles their hope.

Susan Ketchin, with whom Betts discussed the difficulty of writing *Souls Raised from the Dead*, points out that Christianity is central to the novelist's artistic formation. She quotes Betts's claim from "Southern Writers and the Bible" that "'biblical narrative turns everything to purpose; events occur against a backdrop of eternity'" (231). Writing from that perspective, Ketchin explains, enables Betts "to experience the process of writing, of storytelling itself, as being 'a struggle for faith and rescue.' Stories must deal with matters of ultimate truth and must have a meaning. If endings are ambiguous, there must also be the suggestion of a mode of redemption, if the story is to be a true one" (231).

The ending of *Souls Raised from the Dead* is ambiguous; indeed, some readers might complain that Tacey's faith is fake and that Frank's dawning interest in spiritual matters is the product of her deception. In light of *The Fabric of Hope*, however, both characters' "modes of redemption" become apparent. For Tacey, the task is to wait in faith, as Tinder describes: simply to "have to bear feelings of futility—that nothing is being accomplished, not even the moral purification one can hope for in suffering. One is, so to speak, assigned by God to a station, and may have to live for years like a solitary sentinel at an outpost where little ever happens. Immobilized by darkness, one waits for light" (91). Frank's challenge is to perform more visible tasks of active love: to rescue highway accident victims, to listen to Christine cry over the phone, to talk with his mother about Mary Grace, to marry Cindy, to father more children. Tinder explains the importance of such seemingly mundane activity in the cultivation of hope:

> As with faith, grace does not preclude human will. We can wait for love, even though we cannot summon it. We do this above all by adhering to the forms of love—treating others respectfully, helping them when possible, and always paying attention to them, bearing in mind that they are not things to be used, if useful, and otherwise ignored. In other words, we can obey the requirements of love whether we feel like it or not. . . . With serious people, I would argue, this is not mere conformity with habit or observance of an unspoken social contract. It expresses a consciousness of what human relations ought to be, and in doing this it constitutes a tacit openness to grace. . . .
>
> Love is lived in families, workplaces, clubs and churches, and among relatives, fellow workers, neighbors, and friends. It is also in these places that love—and with it hope—is cultivated. (115–16)

Although he, like the pastor who bared his grief to Doris Betts, will never get over his daughter's death, Frank does have hope. Through him, his parents, and Cindy, Betts demonstrates that opening oneself to faith and love wrests meaning from even the deepest suffering. In the context of Christian grace, with its "ultimate and unsurpassable" narrative of crucifixion and resurrection, the individual, "ordinary" sufferer's story begins to make sense, too.

Chapter 6

Narrative Bones
Amy Tan's Bonesetter's Daughter *and*
Hugh Cook's Homecoming Man

Elaine Lux

"Prophesy to these bones, and say to them: O dry bones, hear the word of the
Lord! . . . I will lay sinews on you, and will cause flesh to come upon you,
and cover you with skin, and put breath in you, and you shall live. . . ."
—*Ezekiel 37:4, 6*

The Christian narrative of creation, fall, and redemption holds out the
possibility of reframing a painful past, whether it is the horrors of the
Holocaust or the personal tragedies of individuals seeking but never
quite finding forgiveness for past mistakes. Memories of shame and guilt
often remain hidden within family histories, like the proverbial skeleton
in the closet. Learning to see a hopeful meaning to a difficult family history and to envision new possibilities in it, even a new outcome, transforms that history imaginatively from a story of hurt to a story of
healing. So connected are human hope and the power of story that narrative psychologist Dan McAdams encourages people to "[construct] an

117

autobiographical *story* of the self, complete with setting, scene, character, plot, and theme" to gain a sense of forward motion and direction in their lives (151). In Amy Tan's *The Bonesetter's Daughter* (2001) and Hugh Cook's *The Homecoming Man* (1989), midlife protagonists Ruth Young and Paul Bloem each grapple with a heritage of oppressive family secrets. Echoing biblical themes of brokenness, forgiveness, and healing, both works employ recurrent bone images and embedded bone story myths to convey the powerful grip of family guilt and the redemptive movement of narrative hope to release characters from the burden of that guilt. Bones thematically interconnect various domains of experience, including physical healing, parent-child relationships, emotional healing, writing, and spiritual insight. The degree and content of the hope expressed differ according to the author's individual vision. Bones, however, are the shaping image in both works that communicate brokenness in human relationships and yet suggest the possibility of healing. In their use of bones, the authors' artistry provides what Jerome Bruner calls "metaphoric effectiveness" by linking "domains of experience that were before apart, but with the form of connectedness that has the discipline of art" (19–20). Analyzing these somewhat complementary novels together can help us appreciate the resonance of bone images and the way such powerful images allow for "contingent meanings" and "intimations of transcendence" in the world as empirically given (Leitch 22). Tan and Cook speak to our bones as they bring to life the power of their regenerative family narratives.

An inherited and essential part of genetic structure, bones naturally suggest the idea of a connection between one's essential character and one's family. Bone imagery is a particularly effective narrative device because bones are of central physical importance to our lives. Furthermore, they are embedded literally and metaphorically in the words and visual imagery of our common language. Bones serve important physical functions that are metaphorically applicable to family relationships and to our lives as writers, readers, and storytellers: bones provide shape and support, protect vital organs, and allow motion and flexibility ("The Skeletal System"). Especially pertinent here are two qualities: broken bones have the capacity to heal, and healthy bones are always in the process of resorbing old bone and creating new bone to fill the space. On an ongoing basis, and in an accelerated way when there is injury, old bone gets "munched" at and cleared away, space is made, and new bone gets formed, slowly filling the gap (Silverwood 28). "Bones grow and change. Contrary to popular belief, bone is not a lifeless structure. Bone is a living, growing tissue" (*Understanding Osteoporosis* 1).

Thus, while bones frequently evoke images of death, they also may evoke resilient images of life, vitality, and regeneration.

Consciously or unconsciously, both Tan and Cook, in their respective mother-daughter and father-son narratives, draw upon patterns of narrative hope buried in bone stories like Ezekiel's "Valley of Dry Bones" (Ezek 37:1-14) and the folk tale "Skeleton Woman" (C. Estes), in which dead, dry bones are brought to life, partly through spoken or sung words. In "Skeleton Woman," a dead woman's skeleton, inadvertently snared by a fisherman's hook, is brought up out of its watery bier. Long ago, this woman, now reduced to a mere skeleton, had been thrown off a mountain cliff to her death as punishment for some transgression. The lonely fisherman, who now ensnares her bones, is from a faraway village and, thus, has entered the waters unaware that they are taboo because of the woman's death. Terrified to discover he has hooked not a fish but a human skeleton, the fisherman paddles his kayak to land as quickly as possible, and, still carrying his fishing pole, runs toward his faraway home. In his fright and haste, he does not at first realize that she is entangled with his line. Seeing the skeleton behind him, he thinks the skeleton is chasing him. As he runs, Skeleton Woman follows over the rocks and frozen tundra. Finally, he reaches his snow house and dives in, fishing pole and all. He lies in the dark, feeling safe at last, though sobbing from the scare. When he lights his whale oil lamp, he finds the tangled skeleton there with him. Perhaps it is the way the light flickers on the skeleton, perhaps it is his loneliness and longing, but some feeling of kindness overtakes him, and he begins to gently untangle the bones, patiently setting them into proper arrangement. Out of kindness or respect, he then covers the skeleton with animal skins and falls asleep. As he sleeps, a tear appears in his eye. The skeleton woman, seeing the tear and being very thirsty, crawls over to him and drinks. Then she reaches in and takes his "mighty drum" of a heart, bangs on the heart like a drum, and sings "Flesh, Flesh, Flesh" over and over again. As she sings, her body takes on flesh. Then she returns the fisherman's heart to him and lies down beside him. When they wake, they are tangled together as lovers, and they live together ever after in a good and lasting way (129–31).

In Amy Tan's *The Bonesetter's Daughter*, we see a plot similar to that in the "Skeleton Woman" myth. *The Bonesetter's Daughter* discloses and makes a hopeful outcome for the skeleton of an unburied woman, but the novel does so figuratively, not literally. At the center of *The Bonesetter's Daughter* is the very moving story of Precious Auntie (or Bao Bomu), a young woman whose body, like the body of the skeleton woman, was thrown into an abyss that became her unmarked grave. For much of her granddaughter Ruth's life, Precious Auntie's body, her real name, and her real identity are lost. As the skeleton woman is restored to life in the myth, so is Precious Auntie brought to life, but in the novel the restoration occurs not through the recovery of her physical skeleton, but through the recovery of her name and her story. Both novel and myth end in a love story; however, in *The Bonesetter's Daughter*, the fulfilled love story is enacted symbolically through Ruth, who has taken her grandmother's story into herself and made it part of her own life story. Ruth's romantic love relationship with her long-term partner is revitalized, and they marry. In novel and myth, evil intentions that created the original disaster are thwarted, and the potentially negative outcome of the story is overcome. The novel's "metaphoric effectiveness" manifests a concept only implicitly suggested by the myth: that the ability to tell the story, to order and speak its bones into life, is a gift of hope. Ruth's writing, her metaphorical enfleshing of her grandmother's and mother's stories, resembles the work of her own great-grandfather, a bone doctor or "bonesetter," and also the bone-ordering work of the fisherman in the folk myth. It is also parallel to the interpretation of oracle bones in the novel, and to the work of the skeleton woman herself and her heart-connected, prophetic singing in the folk myth.

Although the most common variants of bone myths have the positive movement toward resurrected life and hope that is seen in "Skeleton Woman," a few negative variants exist as well. In these variations the bone person is a destructive figure, intent on luring others to destruction, usually through trickery (A. Eliot; Simms). In one Native American version, the bone man is an evil being who, years earlier, "drank the river dry" and devoured all but two of the people of the village, a boy and his grandmother (Simms 1). When the long-asleep bone man awakens, the boy is terrified. Bone man's arousal ushers in cold winds, and his steps shake the earth. The bone man devours the berries the boy has gathered in a basket, and he threatens to devour the boy. In the days following the threat, the boy practices his skills with bow and arrow, but he remains very afraid. In a dream, the boy's grandmother receives advice from their ancestors: the bone man must be shot in the heart to be killed, but his heart is in his little finger, not his chest. The grandmother warns the boy, "He will try to trick you by showing you his chest" (15). Although the bone man cunningly bares his chest, the boy is not deceived and shoots the bone man in the finger. His heart hit, it flies out of the bone man's finger; the bone man loses his power and his bones break apart. With the bone man dead, the rains come and people return to the land. Although the overall outcome of this tale is positive—the evil bone man is defeated—the bone image itself is a negative force. In yet other negative bone myths, the evil intent of the bone figure is carried out. For example, in "Talking Bone" (A. Eliot 231), a talking skull deliberately lures a passerby to his death.

The narrative pull of a negative bone tale—a tale that features an inimical bone man that would lure people to death and destruction—infiltrates the world of *The Bonesetter's Daughter* through the Chang family. Mr. Chang is a corrupt coffin-maker and a profiteer, and his son, Chang Fu Nan, is a mean-spirited opium addict. Precious Auntie's sad fate is set in motion by the evil intentions and actions of Mr. Chang. When Mr. Chang's marriage proposal to the bonesetter's daughter is rejected and she soon after agrees to marry someone else, Mr. Chang is enraged. Along with members of his family, all disguised as robbers, Mr. Chang vindictively attacks the wedding party of the bonesetter's daughter on their way to the wedding ceremony, kills her much-loved father, indirectly causes the death of her beloved bridegroom, and steals her dowry of medicinal bones. With her husband-to-be dead, the bonesetter's daughter is placed in a position of shame, for she is already pregnant with LuLing (Ruth's mother). In all their dealings, the Changs are an arrogant and mercenary family. They cheat the people for whom they make coffins by using cheap wood. They achieve fame and wealth by selling the bones that were to be the bonesetter's daughter's dowry. (In the story these bones belong to Peking Man and fetch a very good price.) Finally, and most important for our purposes, they place a curse on the bonesetter's daughter and her family.

Precious Auntie and eventually LuLing come to feel that their family is indeed cursed. Precious Auntie is mentally tormented because the ancestral bones that were stolen were not brought back for proper burial in the Monkey's Jaw, the aptly named cave where they belong. The force of the supernatural in this tormented haunting is strengthened by a dream, some time after her father's death. Precious Auntie is warned by her father's ghost that the bones, which were thought to be animal bones to be used for medicinal purposes, are actually the bones of her family. As instructed in the dream, she replaces the bones she has gathered from the cave and warns her daughter LuLing to neither disturb the bones nor tell anyone about them; however, unknown to Precious Auntie, LuLing has told Mr. Chang that she knows where more of Peking Man's bones are to be found. Naturally, to gain access to the bones, Mr. Chang tries to arrange a marriage between his son Fu Nan and LuLing. Without even knowing Mr. Chang's specific motive, Precious Auntie objects vehemently with strong gestures and the noisy banging of pots.

Unable to talk because of her severe burns and damaged vocal chords, Precious Auntie can convey to LuLing only through writing her detailed story about why LuLing must not marry into the Chang family. Thus, she writes her life story, revealing her identity as the daughter of a famous bone doctor and exposing the role of the Changs as villains and bone robbers. She then reveals to LuLing, "I am your mother." She expects these powerful words to convince and move the heart of her daughter. However, LuLing, deceived and flattered by the marriage proposal from the wealthy Chang family, spitefully does not read her mother's narrative, though she says she has read it. In response to her daughter's hardness of heart, Precious Auntie commits suicide to prevent LuLing from marrying into the coffin-maker's family. LuLing reads her mother's story too late to prevent her death. Only after her mother's suicide does LuLing realize that Mr. Chang wanted her in the family solely to gain access to the secret location of the cave from which he hoped to steal and sell the archaeologically valuable bones.

The Bonesetter's Daughter has all the potential of being a negative bone myth, with coffin-maker Mr. Chang and his family luring others to destruction. Precious Auntie's body remained unburied. Her daughter LuLing, who emigrates to the United States, marries, and has a child, is haunted by guilt even into her old age because she has not been able to return to China to search for and bury her mother's bones. Worse still, she is doubly haunted because she now cannot remember her mother's family name. She perceives the disasters of her life as emanating from the curse of her mother's unburied bones. However, in the course of the novel, the triumph of evil is thwarted. It is first thwarted through LuLing's exposure to hope through her years in an orphanage run by American missionaries to China. "To the missionaries, we were Girls of New Destiny," LuLing writes in her manuscript (231). In the orphanage, she learns that she need not be captive to curses but can have a new and different destiny. LuLing neither embraces nor rejects the Christian teachings, but she does gain hope in a Christian environment. The missionaries are sincere and kind, not hypocritical. "Miss Towler always told us that we had a choice to become Christians or not. No one would ever force us to believe in Jesus, she said. Our belief had to be genuine and sincere" (231). To the young widow LuLing, America is associated with the Christian heaven of her deceased and beloved husband, Kai Jing. Although Christianity has no perceptible influence in the lives of Ruth and her family, it is lightly sketched into the inner landscape of the novel. Among LuLing's precious mementos, stored in a hiding place below the cushion of a vinyl chair, is a Bible with a photo of Precious Auntie tucked beneath its cover.

The progress of the negative bone story is also thwarted by the gift of story. LuLing's written story is a gift to her daughter Ruth, even as her own mother's written story was a gift to LuLing. Even more significant in the novel than the role of religion to combat curses and destructive forces is Ruth's emergence as a writer. Through a confluence of forgiveness, love, and writing, Ruth recognizes that her mother's and grandmother's bones live in hers. She can shake herself free from the bondage of guilt. She shifts from being a ghostwriter for other people's books to becoming a writer who incorporates her mother's and grandmother's stories into her own story. The rival bone story, as represented by the rapacious Changs, is ultimately defeated, for Ruth is able to recover her grandmother's name, to set this bone story right, and to release herself from the shadow of the curses of the past.

Obtaining a skilled and empathetic translator is a pivotal step in preventing the negative bone story from triumphing. The information about the Changs is introduced into the novel through the written autobiographical story of Ruth's mother. Written in Chinese characters and entrusted to Ruth, LuLing's story has lain unread for six years, as Ruth herself has had neither skill nor motivation to translate it. Her mother's memory loss gives Ruth the felt urgency to obtain a translator in order to learn more about her mother. Eighty-year-old Mr. Tang is a skilled translator who has the cultural awareness of the times in which Ruth's mother and grandmother lived. A "survivor of World War Two, the civil war in China, the Cultural Revolution, and a triple coronary bypass," he had been "a famous writer in China" (299). As a character, his role is brief but essential to the hopeful resolution of the novel. His admiration for LuLing, gained in reading her life story, allows him to love her for more than her temporal self. He unlocks the stories of her mother and grandmother for Ruth, and he discovers the oracle bone in the museum. The oracle bone opens a way for Mr. Tang and later Ruth to recapture Precious Auntie's name, thus forging a connection between the family's identity and a new future that emerges from affirming one's relation to the past. His perspective is vital to fulfilling Tan's expressed intent for *The Bonesetter's Daughter*: "I wanted to do a book about memory. . . . I also wanted to write a book about hope" (Tan, Ruiz Interview).

In *The Bonesetter's Daughter*, as E. D. Huntley has observed about Tan's other novels, "painful experiences are recast in the language of folk tale; . . . real life takes on the contours of myth." Through her use of "details, allusions, aural and visual motifs, image clusters, fragments of myth, linguistic wordplay, [Tan] alerts her readers to the multiple layers of meaning that reside in her prose" (34). In particular, bone motifs give Tan's novel the vitality of an archetypal drama in which good and evil vie for the ancestral bones of the bonesetter and his family. Tan's artistic awareness of the importance of the bones is clear. Asked by an interviewer why she took the already finished novel back from her publisher and "virtually rewrote it," Tan says her changes added "structure [and] a depth to it—that I didn't have in the first go-round. The whole beginning of not knowing the name of the woman, Precious Auntie, was not there; I added that later. The voice business and the imagery of bones were all added in the new draft" (Tan, Edwards Interview). Perhaps Tan's inspiration for bone imagery came from real life, as it was only in her mother's last days that she discovered her mother's and her grandmother's birth names, which she never knew before. Her grandmother's name was Gu Jinmei (Tan, Ruiz Interview); the word *gu*, as the novel explains, means "bone."

Interestingly, the seeds of the positive and negative bone tales, as well as the revivifying hope that emerges in most variants of bone myths, can be seen in Richard Rosen's discussion of the Latin word *sacer*:

> The Latin word *sacer* means both "holy" and "cursed." It is the ancestor of familiar English words like "sacred" and "sacrifice," as well as the name of a small triangular bone that forms both the back of the pelvis and the base of the spine. Known to anatomists as the *os sacrum*, literally the "holy bone," it was given this appellation, according to one legend, because it was believed to be eternal and so the "seat" of the body's resurrection. (qtd. in Woodman 198)

In Chinese, too, the word for bone is metaphorically rich, and the discussion of its meanings becomes important to reenvisioning Ruth's family story. The fulfillment of LuLing's quest and then Ruth's quest to discover the birth name of Precious Auntie is connected to bone imagery and to the subtleties of the word *gu:* "Gu Liu Xin . . . The family name had been there all along, like a bone stuck in the crevices of a gorge" (Tan, *Bonesetter's* 350). As do most Chinese words, this name has multiple meanings through its composite ideographic characters. The key meaning of *Liu Xin* is "remain true" (350), and its connotation of essential truth and character is related to the concept of bones in English and in Chinese. Regarding the family name *Gu*, Ruth's aunt GaoLing explains to her:

Gu as in "gorge." It's a different *gu*. It sounds the same as the bone *gu*, but it's written a different way. The third-tone *gu* can mean many things: "old," "gorge," "bone," also "thigh," "blind," "grain," "merchant," lots of things. And the way "bone" is written can also stand for "character." That's why we use that expression "It's in your bones." It means, "That's your character." (349)

As the daughter of two cultures—Chinese by heritage and maternal upbringing, and American by place of birth and cultural environment—Ruth struggles to define her own character. She is haunted by memories of her past with her mother, mutual wounds, but especially by two incidents in which she rejected and betrayed her mother through her words spoken and written. Both of these are bone-connected incidents and emanate from the power of words to harm and to heal. In the first, when Ruth was a young child in the playground at school recess, her mother stood outside the fence and shouted warnings to her daughter not to go down the slide. Ruth not only ignored her mother's warning, but she denied her relationship to her mother, telling her friends: "She's not my mother! . . . I don't know who she is" (69). Ruth "threw herself down the slide. . . . And . . . crashed face first, with such force that she bit her lip, bumped her nose, bent her glasses, and broke her arm" (69). In the second incident, when she was a teenager, in response to her mother's snooping in her diary, Ruth wrote these words that she knew her mother would read, "You talk about killing yourself. . . . I wish you would. . . . " (141). The next day, Ruth returned home to learn that her mother did try to kill herself. Her aunt greeted her by saying, "Your mother is hurt. . . . She fell out the window. . . . Her body is broken, and something is wrong with her head" (142).

Like her mother before her (although she does not realize this at the time), Ruth at first puts off reading the story of her mother's life that LuLing gives her; thus, in a significant way, compounding the family misunderstandings and rejecting her mother again. After suddenly recognizing how much her mother means to her and how little time they have left, she reads the translated manuscript of her mother's life story. She learns her grandmother's story, as well. LuLing's story becomes Ruth's link to her grandmother and to the setting right of the relational bones in her life: with her mother, with the man in her life, and with herself. The novel tells Ruth's story, by telling her mother's story and her mother's mother's story—both through autobiographical narratives that form an integral part of the ongoing story of the next generation. Always in the process of resorption and formation, bones are wonderful physiological images to convey the complex process of integrating Ruth's cultural roots into her bicultural life in America. As she learns how to take into herself and rescript the stories of the women in her past, Ruth's own story gains power, and this rescripting leads to the hopeful resolution of the bone story.

Significant to the cycle of redemption embodied in the novel, Precious Auntie's father, the bone doctor, was skilled at healing many others, but he could not save his own family from a rampant illness. Early in the novel, someone calls Ruth a "book doctor," rather than "ghostwriter" or "book collaborator." Ruth prefers the term, even before understanding her family's link to her bone doctor great-grandfather. Important to theme and image, this parallel between writing and bone setting is made clear through this phrasing. In her life, Ruth becomes someone who can help others and her own family and herself. Through her visit home, she learns about her mother's similar fear of receiving love and gains the ability to move past her relational impasse. In contrast to other images of scattered bones in the novel, her mother and her grandmother are perceived as part of Ruth's own living skeleton. They are "the women who shaped her life, who are in her bones. . . . [Their] warnings were passed down, not simply to scare her, but to force her to avoid their footsteps, to hope for something better. They wanted her to get rid of the curses" (352). In the end, Ruth sees that her broken arm and her subsequent use of the sand tray to write messages, presumably for her grandmother Precious Auntie to her mother LuLing, are linked to her ultimate freedom as she moves from ghostwriter of other people's books to writer of her own book. After Ruth's mother tells her daughter, "I hope you can forgive me, because if I hurt you, I'm sorry," Ruth cries with happiness because "It was not too late for them to forgive each other and themselves" (352). In forgiving and receiving forgiveness, injured story-bones of the past can be resorbed and a new story formed, free from curses. Thinking about her mother and grandmother, Ruth reflects that their sufferings have been transmuted for good.

With its story layers embedded within and encircling one another, the narrative returns to its beginning, as it fulfills LuLing's quest for her mother's name. The answer to that quest is conveyed in the epilogue through bone imagery:

> [Ruth's] laptop becomes a sand tray. Ruth is six years old again. . . . her broken arm healed, her other hand holding a chopstick, ready to divine the words. Bao Bomu comes, as always, and sits next to her. . . . "Think about your intentions," Bao Bomu says. . . . And

side by side, Ruth and her grandmother . . . have become the same person. . . . They write of a past that can be changed. . . . They can choose not to hide it, to take what's broken, to feel the pain and know that it will heal. (352–53)

While bone imagery is used to help convey both haunting and healing in the novel, the prevalent emphasis is on the capacity for bones to be set right. The protagonist and the reader discover the esemplastic reworking of the past into a new pattern, in large part through bringing the intention of the heart into the art of telling a family story and making it new. Although the residual sorrow of LuLing's progressive dementia forms a cloud in the background, the linkage of writing, bone setting, and relational healing, as well as the promise of marriage for Ruth and her partner, Art, and the late-life love between Mr. Tang and LuLing, leave the reader with a sense of cautious optimism and hope.

By contrast, in Hugh Cook's *The Homecoming Man*, the cycle of relational healing is only partially completed. In this work, the sense of hope is more muted. With *The Homecoming Man*, readers must work harder, as narrative theorist Thomas Leitch might put it, to "impute" (38) the hopefulness of the narrative "through [supplying] the unspecified connections, extrapolations, and resonances they require in order to make sense" (39). Before considering the "unspecified connections," we will explore the way bone imagery is interwoven into the text in ways that elucidate themes of brokenness and healing. Throughout the novel missing and broken bones communicate the fallen and damaged condition in which humankind lives, in both personal and societal contexts. Accidental and intentional evils are part of the fallen world, in Gerrit Bloem's words, a world of "things forever breaking"(Cook 23). Physical brokenness is a reality of and metaphor for the human condition. Gerrit limps as a result of a mowing accident long ago in which "he'd sliced off most of his first two toes, so that now he walked with a slight wobble" (108). Paul, the younger of Gerrit's two sons, remembers the sight of the "decapitated head, still helmeted" of one of the men in his church, killed in a motorcycle accident (174). A fawn is accidentally caught in the blades of the mower while Paul is driving the tractor, and "the bottom part of one of its hind legs [is severed]" and the other leg "badly mangled" (179).

Moral and emotional brokenness is conveyed through bone imagery as well. In reflecting on the accident that caused his limp, Gerrit considers himself lucky to have emerged with such minimal loss: "Lucky, at least compared to the things that had happened to him during the War . . ." (108). He moves from nearly skeletal images of himself and other emaciated prisoners at the end of World War II to a more recent war-connected memory concerning the televised news coverage when the body of Jozef Mengele, one of his captors, was found:

> They had opened the grave in the cemetery and . . . taken out . . .
> the white casket containing nothing more than a little pile of bones
> and tattered brown rags, then several days later a man holding a
> skull in his hands and saying without doubt it was the skull of Jozef
> Mengele. . . . The Angel of Death himself. (151)

This link is significant because Gerrit's experience during the war is part of his private torment throughout the novel. Although Gerrit's son does not know about his father's experience in a Nazi camp, Paul finds his mind filling with the ghastly bone images he is translating into English from the writings of Dutch-Jewish poet and Auschwitz survivor Abel Rozenberg:

> and suddenly I can make him out
> in the dark, the grizzled old
> Russian, embracing—
> the skull of a cow,
> gnawing, gnawing on it.
> In the moonlight the teeth
> in the jaws of the cow
> skull *glitter*. (254)

The bone imagery suggests the images contained in his father's memories of Holocaust inmates, "walking skeletons sapped of all strength and resistance" (255).

Gerrit is haunted by a guilt that he never expresses to his son Paul. Under torture by the Nazis forty-five years earlier, he confessed the names of two of the members of the Dutch underground resistance. Subsequently, they were killed. His effort to block out the memory of this betrayal, rather than to deal with it, is symbolized by the padlock he has placed on a room he recently created in the basement of the house, as if to wall off memories from his consciousness.

Like his father, Paul is haunted by a spirit of self-recrimination, for he was the driver in a car accident that killed his young son Quentin. "Sitting in the tractor seat with the bush hog's blades whirling behind him like some voracious animal perpetually at his heels, he [knows] he had never forgiven himself for his son's death" (Cook 178). Suddenly he recognizes that, like his father, he "had made a habit of retreating to his work and the solitude [of it] . . . at the expense of the rest of the family" (178). While he is busy in these thoughts, the sudden maiming of the fawn occurs. Thinking about the driving accident that caused his son's death, Paul symbolically reenacts the tragedy in the maiming of the animal. In addition to the guilt over his son's death, Paul feels guilty about his relationships with his other children and his estranged wife. His awareness of this guilt surfaces in connection with the wounded fawn as he nurses it back to health after its surgery, "its body all hard angles of bone under tawny fur" (198).

Although images of hurt are certainly conveyed in connection with bone imagery, so, too, are images of healing. The healing use of bone imagery in *The Homecoming Man* centers around the fawn. At the level of plot and emotional resolution, the fawn recovers; that is, it experiences as full a healing as is possible in the situation. In addition the fawn's healing brings about a metaphorical resorption of old destructive relational patterns and a movement toward creating new and healthy ones. Despite Gerrit's first impulse "to put the thing out of its misery" when he sees the "mangled" hind leg and "the other sliced off completely above the fetlock . . . [with] the white bone stick[ing] out" (182), he joins in Paul's attempt to save the fawn. In caring for the fawn, Paul learns about his own locked doors, so that he gains personal insight for growth and begins to share his inner emotions. He invites his new acquaintance, Lena, to his home to see his translations of Rozenberg's poetry and the fawn. He shares with her his concern about his father's odd behavior, including the padlocked room that is empty but for three freezers loaded with food. Lena recognizes in the description a pattern known to her because of her Jewish background: survivor's guilt. Though Paul knows none of the details of his father's personal haunting, he now has an imaginative clue into his father's story, and is more empathetic. Lena understands suffering, for she is a daughter of Holocaust survivors and is the niece of poet Abel Rozenberg.Lena stares at the fawn, "as if [it] might be a holy thing and she were in the presence of a fearful mystery" (258). In terms of the novel, the fawn does embody the mystery of the power to heal despite damage. When the fawn takes its "first steps," Lena's face is "transfixed with wonder." Paul "[does] not know what to say; he [feels] only as if for the first time in a long while a burden [has] been removed from somewhere deep inside him" (259). This time he has the opportunity to help repair the damage he has caused.

In terms of Paul's relationship with his father, the fawn provides more than an opportunity for the two men to join together to bring about healing. Its injury serves as a catalyst that evokes the biblical parable of the prodigal son. As is appropriate to the novel's worldview, this earthly version is an imperfect enactment of its heavenly prototype. However, without a mutual exchange of stories, this enactment is the closest Paul and Gerrit come to a shared expression of vulnerability and tenderness. When Paul first gathers the fawn in his arms after the mowing accident, he feels lost and confused. "He did not know where to go," but as he "waded . . . through the tall grass . . . he saw his father standing far off at the doorway of the tool shed, [and] then a constriction formed in his throat as he saw his father come running gimpily towards him" (180). Seeing his father, Paul "began to cry . . . and the words *I'm sorry, forgive me* stuck like a stone in his throat" (180). The importance of this scene is highlighted by its being told twice, first from Paul's perspective and then from Gerrit's. The severed bone image is even more conspicuous in the rendering through Gerrit's consciousness in the following chapter: "He ran towards Paul as fast as his legs permitted him, the missing toes of his left foot turning his strides into a limping run" (182). Father and son rush the fawn to the veterinarian for surgery, and they provide its aftercare. Together they build a pen for it. Significantly, Gerrit feels "the sudden need for forgiveness . . . and remembering how [Paul] had cried coming down the grassy slope with the fawn in his arms, Gerrit [feels] an urge to rush forward and embrace his son" (194). Although Gerrit does not act on this urge, the incident of the fawn has already begun its healing work. Gerrit experiences his dual role in the parable, as the father offering and as the son needing forgiveness.

In the fallen world of the novel, the healing of a damaged creature is not a full restoration, but it does bring possibility for a good life. While Paul cannot literally heal his dead son, by helping the fawn, he ritualistically brings life out of his son's death. Although Gerrit dies without sharing his story with Paul and without having taken communion at the last church service he attends, the ending has a distinctly hopeful tone. The words *forehead* and *frame* continue the bone imagery. Paul tells his dying father, "'I love you, Dad,'" and "place[s] his hand on his father's forehead, as if he [were] . . . a priest giving absolution, then he [feels] a wave of forgiveness wash over him, of being forgiven and of forgiving in return, and he ben[ds] forward, embrace[s] his father's thin frame, and [weeps]" (312). This scene marks a completion of Paul's role in the parable; for now he stands in the role of forgiver as well as forgiven, father as well as son. In the epilogue, he lovingly creates a monument of stone in memory of his father. He writes his love wordlessly, expressing it through the land—in his father's language. Then he moves from his isolation and, sharing the occasion with Lena, takes the fawn to live in a children's zoo. Not only is Lena beside him sharing the moment of the fawn's release from the pen, but Lena's words express the thematic note of healing in this fallen world: "When a creature's been hurt, sometimes a limited freedom is as much as it can handle" (324). The maimed fawn, so central to this multilevel narrative of hope, is the novel's final image: "The fawn stood still a moment, then took several quick running steps through the grass" (324).

In contrast to the exuberant restorative movement of the bone story "Skeleton Woman," characters here live in the stages of limited restoration. A potential love story is implied between Paul and Lena, but their relationship exists only as a future possibility. Although he cannot bring his son Quentin back to life, Paul's heartache and sense of guilt are partially eased through his symbolic atonement in helping the wounded fawn's broken bone to heal and granting the maimed animal a limited freedom. Although writing (symbolically related to the Skeleton Woman's singing of "Flesh, Flesh, Flesh") provides a form of connection with others, being able to write does not, as it does in Tan's novel, lead to relational newness or restoration. Indeed, Abel Rozenberg, the Auschwitz survivor, cannot overcome the trauma of surviving the Holocaust and, despite his writing, commits suicide. In Cook, the evil bone man / "Talking Head," with its malevolent pull of the bones to a final grave, is epitomized by the Nazi destruction and cruelty; yet even without the Nazis, motifs of illness, death, and relational fragmentation provide negative bone story images. Hope in this novel, however, emerges most fully in the stories implied behind the expressed narrative. Just as the scene that evokes the parable of the prodigal son implies that there is another (heavenly) homecoming that will be fully joyful, so the incomplete bone story in Cook's novel, showing only partial restoration and healing, evokes yet another bone story that is told in the Bible: the resurrection.

Without compromising its sober portrayal of a fallen world, *The Homecoming Man* invites readers to construct hope as the implied hermeneutic of the novel. Cook's readers must construct what it all means by also drawing upon the absent but implied bone story. In this way, the unexpressed bone story is, to draw upon Leitch, a "tactful or provocative omission" through which "an audience [can] enjoy the latitude it requires to appreciate whatever the story is displaying" (38). Positive bone imagery in Tan's novel suggests hope for human healing, including physical and spiritual healing, deliverance from curses, and healing across generations. The bone imagery in Cook's novel is more ambivalent, suggesting limited physical and emotional healing, but at the same time pointing to the limitless healing of perfected faith. In

Cook's world, total healing and restoration will come through the implied bone tale/love story that begins with Eve being fashioned out of Adam's ribs. It begins again in a world beyond time with the bones of the bride of Christ (believers) being resurrected into eternal life.

Largely because of Tan's and Cook's artistry, and partly because of the resonance of bone imagery itself, these narratives move and encourage us. The concrete and unique characteristics of bones make them a powerful literary image to portray renewal, particularly family renewal, for "bone is constantly changing. . . . Old bone is removed and new bone is laid down" (*Understanding Osteoporosis* 2). Through an examination of the power of bone imagery in these two novels, we can appreciate Pat Allen's observation: "Our images reveal that we are holographic creatures, living multiple stories. . . . Images are a means of coming to know the richness and variety of our stories, their shadows and nuances" (10). We know in our bones the cycle of death-in-life and life-in-death. By embedding bone imagery and myth in the narrative bones of their protagonists' metaphorical recasting and resorption of the past and remodeling of their futures, Tan and Cook enhance the vitality of their fictional worlds. In his work on narrative theory, Leitch speculates that "Despite the end nearly every story predicates, the end which gives it unitary impact and often makes it tellable, a fundamental wish of every storyteller is to create a world without end" (82). This hope is the hope of narrative: to create a world that lives on, a world that readers may enter into for a time and that may live on in them afterwards. Indeed, in the power of the image may lie buried the secret of fiction: endings that open, rather than close, and that generate and regenerate in readers their own stories of hope, perhaps even redemptive stories that endure. For when our skeletons take on flesh and breath through our stories, truly we live.

Chapter 7

Hope from a Radio
Jurek Becker's Jakob the Liar

Eric Sterling

Hope is a human emotion that can aid someone psychologically during times of crisis, serving as a defense mechanism. During the Holocaust, hope helped Jews to survive and, to some extent, served as a means of resistance against their Nazi oppressors. Hope also gave some Jews a false sense of security, thus hindering their opportunities to survive. This point is particularly relevant during the Holocaust because hope often involved passivity, not action—some individuals hoped for help to arrive rather than working actively themselves to survive. Michael R. Steele notes that the stubborn refusal of some Jews to accept their fate derived "from the simple hope that 'things would get better' to various forms of denial and psychic numbing" (44). Arthur Koestler adds that false hope is tantamount to a "smug and smiling voice in us, which whispers in our ear the gentle lie that we shall never die, and that tomorrow will be like yesterday. It is time that we learnt to distrust that voice" (247). The argument has been made often that Jews failed to resist their captors during the Holocaust. Two primary reasons are offered for this failure to resist the Nazis: Jews either lacked hope to survive or, conversely, possessed the false hope that they would be rescued and thus decided to be patient and accommodating.

Jurek Becker's poignant award-winning novel *Jakob the Liar* (and the 1974 East German film *Jacob der Lügner* that uses Becker's Academy-Award-nominated screenplay and stars Vlastimil Brodsky, as well as the 1999 Robin Williams remake written by Peter Kassovitz and Didier Decoin) tells the story of a despairing and melancholic community of Jews living in a Polish ghetto during the Holocaust. These Jews believe that they have nothing to live for—until they receive a glimmer of hope, the gift of story, from Jacob Heym and his radio. Jacob (spelled "Jacob" in the text but "Jakob" in the title) is an ordinary person who becomes the only source of hope in the ghetto as well as becoming a celebrity. He claims to have a radio and to have heard the optimistic news that the Russian army has advanced against the Nazis and are twelve miles past Bezanika. Jacob has actually heard this radio report in the German administration office where he had been taken into custody for breaking curfew. Jacob does not actually possess a radio; ownership of a radio violates Nazi regulations and is regarded as a crime punishable by death. The Jews in the ghetto consider a Russian victory over the Germans, with a concomitant liberation of Poland, to be their only hope. This hope derives from historical truth: the Jews in the Lodz ghetto in Poland (Becker himself was a Holocaust survivor from this ghetto) also placed all their hopes on a liberation by the Russian army— a liberation that never happened. The Jews in Jacob's ghetto greet the news with great enthusiasm, which, in turn, incites him to claim falsely to have a radio and to invent optimistic news reports. In both film versions, the characters become excited when they hear Jacob's radio reports. Jews who previously have been resigned to their grim, deadly fate begin to smile and are invigorated after they hear Heym narrate hopeful news. They start to think optimistically about their future, about what they will do after the war. As the narrator of Becker's novel reveals, "Old debts raise their heads again, diffidently the debtors are reminded, daughters turn into brides, weddings are planned for the week before New Year's, people have gone stark staring mad, suicide rates have dropped to zero" (67).

As the novel concludes, Jacob confides to the narrator, while they ride in the railcar that transports them to a concentration camp, that he had witnessed the hope and excitement in the eyes of his fellow Jews and thus had decided to pretend that he had a radio. Periodically, he

invented news, which he claimed to have heard on the radio, and dis-
seminated the bulletins to his coworkers.

Although the people initially welcome the news that originates from
Jacob's supposed radio, Becker's text poses the dilemma of whether this
false sense of hope actually helps or injures the inhabitants of this Polish
ghetto, whether hope benefited Jews during the Holocaust or aided the
Nazis by rendering their Jewish victims passive and unwilling to resist.
Becker's screenplay (the basis for the Brodsky film) posits the same
quandary. In fact, Becker's screenplay portrays an even more passive
Jewish community than in his novel because the film conspicuously
omits a key scene from the novel—Professor Kirschbaum's act of resistance, his suicide. The Robin Williams version, however, restores the
professor's suicide yet deviates markedly from the novel by inventing
another act of Jewish resistance. In this second film, Heym's concocted
radio reports incite the Jews to create their own resistance movement in
order to protect themselves before and during the alleged Russian
advance, even though they possess only one gun while the Nazis are
heavily armed. In the second version, the Jews elect a reluctant Jacob as
leader of their uprising, based on his knowledge of the radio reports and
the hope he has given them. Although Jurek Becker's novel and film
indicate that false hope is dangerous because it can render people passive, the Williams film contradicts this point by suggesting that Heym's
gift of hope actually makes the Jews more eager to resist their oppressors.
The Williams film actually undercuts its own argument, however, by
creating a farcical tone in the resistance scene, which suggests the hopeless nature both of the resistance movement and of the future of the
ghetto inhabitants. Becker's novel differs significantly from the Williams
remake in that the author of the book indicates that the false hope para-
lyzes the Jews emotionally, hindering them from acting or resisting, and
encouraging them to wait passively for the arrival of the Russian army.

The novel begins with the narrator presenting to the reader a ghetto
permeated with hopelessness. Like both film versions, the novel portrays
the setting as dark, austere, run down, and sterile—symbolic of the
despair of the people. The narrator laments that Sturmbannführer
Hardtloff, the Nazi leader of the ghetto, prohibits trees, food-bearing
plants, pets, jewelry, watches, and clocks—the things that the narrator
believes make life pleasurable and possible. The narrator does not exist
in the two films, probably because employing a narrator is more difficult
and more intrusive in a movie than in a novel. Trees and plants bear fruit
and vegetables that contain nourishment and thus, if allowed, could
have sustained the starving ghetto Jews. Trees possess beauty and house

animals such as birds. Trees are also special to the narrator because of memories—he used to climb trees; he first made love to a woman under a tree; and his wife, Hannah, was shot to death by Nazis under a tree. (In the Williams film, Hannah was Jacob's wife; in Becker's novel Hannah was the narrator's wife.) Pets would provide the ghetto inhabitants with love and companionship, which becomes more significant as family members die or are deported to the camps. Jewelry often contains material value as well as sentimental value, which means that it can be bartered for food or used to bribe a Nazi in the case of a life-threatening emergency.

The prohibition of watches and clocks is essential to the Nazi plot to destroy the hope of the Jewish ghetto inhabitants. Without watches and clocks, time loses meaning, and the people cannot provide their lives with temporal structure. Furthermore, the narrator mentions that Jews can be severely punished for arriving to work late and are killed by Nazi sentries if they are seen out of their homes after the eight o'clock curfew, and yet Jews are not permitted to own clocks and watches. With this theme of timelessness, the narrator links his own sense of hopelessness to the story of Jacob, the radio, and false hope. On the night in which Jacob hears the news on the radio, he is confronted by a Nazi sentry and a duty officer, both of whom initiate the conversation by asking him a question regarding the time. The sentry asks, "Am I mistaken, or is it forbidden to be on the street after eight o'clock?" (4). Jacob, of course, cannot know what time it is. Becker demonstrates that the inability to know the time renders the Jews vulnerable and helpless when he shows that Jacob Heym is to receive a severe punishment, probably death, in the German administration building for being out after eight o'clock, even though it is actually only seven thirty. Although the sentry merely plays a joke on Jacob, allowing him to be released, the Jew understands that the trick almost cost him his life (during the Nazi occupation, no Jew has left the edifice alive). Thus, all of the prohibitions mentioned by the narrator, along with starvation, persecution, deportations, and hard physical labor, have left the Jews without hope—until Jacob transforms the mood of the ghetto by creating news reports.

After his release from the German administration building, Jacob works with his friend Mischa in the freight yard. He discerns that Mischa is so desperate for food that he is about to risk his life to steal a few potatoes from a railcar. In the novel and in the Brodsky film, Jacob trips Mischa to save his life, preventing his friend from being killed by the Nazis. Knowing that he lacks the strength to keep the muscular Mischa from running to the railcar, Jacob blurts out that he possesses a radio. If Mischa has hope that the Russians will rescue the Jews in the ghetto, he will not be foolish enough to risk his life for a few potatoes; instead, he will endure adversity. In Becker's novel, when Professor Kirschbaum, the celebrated heart specialist, lecturer, and head of a Kraków hospital, urges Jacob to stop disseminating radio reports, Jacob replies indignantly:

> Have you ever once seen their eyes when they beg me for news? No? And do you know how badly they need some good news? . . . Isn't it enough for you that we have almost nothing to eat, that in winter one in five of us freezes to death, that every day half a street gets taken away in transports? . . . And when I try to make use of the very last possibility that keeps them from just lying down and dying—with words, do you understand? I try to do that with words! Because that's all that I have!—then you come in and tell me it's prohibited! . . . Since the news has been passed around in the ghetto, I haven't heard of a single suicide. . . . And before that there were many. (164–66)

Mischa's reckless decision to steal a few potatoes while under the watchful eye of Nazi sentries can be interpreted as an attempted suicide, an unequivocal sign of despair and hopelessness. This desperation is transformed immediately into optimism and hope after Jacob tells his friend that he has a radio and that the Russians are advancing.

The news that Jacob creates on his "radio" helps cure the Jews of their despair and incites them once again to think about life and the future. The narrator informs the reader that Mischa, upon hearing Jacob's news report (the first and only truthful one), experiences joy and hope for the future. Only minutes after hearing Jacob's news, Mischa, the narrator believes, would like to shout words of encouragement to his fellow suffering Jews: "Stop taking your own lives, you'll soon be needing them again! Stop living without hope, our days of misery are numbered! Make an effort to survive, you've had plenty of practice, you're familiar with all the thousands of tricks that can cheat death—after all, you've managed so far" (24). Then Mischa goes to the apartment of his girlfriend, Rosa Frankfurter, to tell her and her parents about Jacob's news concerning the Russian army's advancement to Bezanika, just as she and her parents are lamenting what Mr. Frankfurter considers a tragedy—the birth of a child into the ghetto. During the conversation between Mischa and the Frankfurters, hope and despair intermingle. Initially believing that the Frankfurters are discussing Jacob's news, Mischa asks them if they are glad. Mr. Frankfurter, who is actually speaking about the news concerning the birth, rebukes Mischa: "In my opinion, it's all a big calamity, my lad, almost a disaster for those people [the parents of the baby], and you're asking why I'm not glad?" (38). Frankfurter signifies that it is hopeless and tragic to attempt to raise a baby in a ghetto where people are starving and dying, and where deportations to concentration camps are beginning. The baby will not only die, Frankfurter assumes, but will also indirectly cause the deaths of his unfortunate parents. But Mischa, with Jacob's news, brings hope. Speaking from the perspective of Mischa's optimism, the narrator informs the reader:

> Apparently two crazy people have brought a child into this world, without having heard the news—in normal ghetto times, certainly a subject for discussion. But as of yesterday [when Jacob first tells Mischa the news that he heard on the radio in the German administration building] the times are no longer normal, a different wind is blowing, we [Mischa and the narrator] tell you about things that will make you forget child and husband and wife and eating and drinking: as of yesterday, tomorrow will be another day. (38)

Hearing from Jacob that the Russian army is advancing, Mischa, unlike Rosa and her parents, believes that there is hope for the lives of the newborn baby and its parents, as well as for everyone else in the ghetto. Only recently, Mischa has experienced despair like everyone else and would literally have died for a few potatoes, but Jacob's news has markedly altered his view of the future, particularly because now he believes that he has one. Manifesting the hope that he now exudes, Mischa, in a moment of ecstatic optimism, asks the Frankfurters for permission to marry their daughter, a proposal that earlier in the day would never have crossed his mind. His impromptu decision to marry Rosa derives from his hope for the future and his exuberant hope of liberation by the Russians. Upon hearing the news about the advancement into Bezanika, Mr. Frankfurter, an actor who thought that his career was over because of the Nazi occupation, contemplates a return to the stage upon liberation. (In the Williams remake, Mr. Frankfurter [Alan Arkin] fears the radio because he believes that it will cause the liquidation of the ghetto; thus he embarks on a farcical crusade to destroy it. The scene is not in Becker's novel and is the invention of the screenwriters.) Similarly, Kowalski, Jacob's loyal but annoying friend, becomes upbeat and asks Jacob about whether to reopen his barber shop and what financial investments to make upon liberation from the Nazi occupation.

Thus Jacob Heym's news restores vitality and the hope for a future to the Jewish people's lives

Jacob's surname "Heym" is a form of the word *Chaim*, the Hebrew word for "life." The two letters of the Hebrew alphabet of which the word consists are *het* and *yud*, which together signify long life. Het is the eighth letter of the Jewish alphabet, and yud is the tenth; together the numbers add up to eighteen. According to the Jewish mystical and rabbinical belief known as *gematria*, long life is symbolized in numbers that are multiples of eighteen. Ellen Frankel and Betsy Platkin Teutsch correctly point out that such combinations are "not seen merely as coincidental; they represent purposeful conjunctions of the higher and lower worlds. . . . [Eighteen and multiples of eighteen] ha[ve] long been important in Jewish liturgy" (47). Jacob overhears that Russian troops are twelve miles away from Bezanika, which he estimates is 300 miles away (7). If the troops are twelve miles past Bezanika, they are only 288 miles away from liberating Jacob's ghetto, and 288 is a multiple of 18. Although the novel never mentions gematria, the Judaic mystical numerological belief would be well known to Jacob and the other characters. They would realize that, according to *gematria*, the Russian army, upon liberating the Jews from its position 288 miles away, would enable them to live long lives by destroying the German army.

Because Jacob wants his fellow Jews to enjoy long lives, he attempts to give them the gift of hope for the future so that they will have the desire to survive. Consequently, Jacob, who previously prevents Mischa from risking his life for a few potatoes, jeopardizes his own life to steal a newspaper. Desperate for real news to disseminate to his fellow Jews, Jacob sneaks into a Nazi outhouse upon seeing that an officer has left his newspaper there. While Jacob is in the process of purloining the newspaper, another Nazi officer, one impatient because he suffers from diarrhea, attempts to use the outhouse, trapping Jacob inside. The officer paces impatiently outside the lavatory, knowing that someone is inside but not realizing that the occupant is a Jew. Kowalski, realizing that Jacob will be killed when he is discovered in a Nazi outhouse, purposefully knocks down a tower of crates, distracting the officer and allowing Jacob to escape from the outhouse. Kowalski acts heroically, and consequently, endures a brutal and bloody beating, primarily because Jacob is his friend and possesses, Kowalski believes, a secret radio that brings them good and hopeful news. Jacob is embarrassed that he has caused Kowalski's beating and grateful that his friend has saved his life, so he rewards him with uplifting, albeit untrue, news: "By the way, did I tell you that the Germans are suffering huge losses?" (92). This "news" provides Kowalski with false hope, serving as Jacob's way of thanking his friend and suggesting that God is punishing the Nazis for the kind of brutal treatment that Kowalski has endured. In Becker's novel—as in the Holocaust itself—hope is allied, to some extent, with divine retribution. The narrator illuminates this point when he describes Kowalski's reaction upon being beaten up by a Nazi officer and then hearing news from Jacob. In the novel, as in both film versions, Jacob's hopeful news brings a smile to the battered face of Kowalski. The narrator of the novel states that upon hearing Jacob's news, "Kowalski turns around to him, and in the midst of his bruises, a hint of a grateful smile—grateful in spite of everything—blooms fleetingly" (92). The narrator is ambiguous concerning to whom Kowalski is grateful—Jacob or God. The report regarding Nazi casualties that Kowalski receives gives him hope and compensation for the brutal beating that he suffers at the hands of a Nazi.

In the novel, Becker effectively juxtaposes hope and faith. Jacob Heym provides hope to the Polish ghetto inhabitants by telling them that the Russian army is steadily advancing and will liberate them soon from German oppression, that the end of their suffering is within reach. Jacob's coworker Herschel Schtamm, however, considers the radio dangerous because he believes that it diverts the attention of the people away from God and their belief in divine intervention. He believes that in order for Jews to survive, they must, as in the past, maintain their faith in God, not in false idols. Schtamm hopes that like Job, the Jews in the ghetto will endure their suffering. Schtamm worries about the ramifications if the Jews give up hope in God because they do not witness a sign that he cares about them. As Jacques Ellul says, "it is God who questions us and who awaits a response from us, not the other way around" (vii). God declares, "[I]f you obey the LORD your God, . . . the LORD your God will set you high above all the nations of the earth; all these blessings shall come upon you and overtake you, if you obey the voice of the LORD your God. . . . But if you do not obey the the LORD your God by diligently observing all his commandments and decrees . . . all these curses shall come upon you and overtake you" (Deut 28:1-2, 15). Schtamm also knows the scriptural passage that states:

> Blessed are those who trust in the LORD,
>   whose trust is the LORD.
> They shall be like a tree planted by water,
>   sending out its roots by the stream,
> It shall not fear when heat comes. (Jer 17:7-8)

Schtamm worries that the radio has superseded God in the hearts of the ghetto inhabitants and that there will be repercussions if the Jews place their faith in the Russian army and in the radio rather than in God's authority. In fact, Sander L. Gilman claims that Jacob's radio "literally is the *deus ex machina* [god out of a machine]" (18).

Furthermore, Schtamm expresses concern that many Jews will be murdered by the Nazis if the enemy discovers that a ghetto inhabitant possesses and listens to a radio. (Schtamm, like the others, does not realize that Jacob's radio does not exist.) Consequently, Schtamm prays for the destruction of the radio so that the Jews in the ghetto will restore their faith in God. While Schtamm prays to the Lord for the destruction of the radio, a power failure occurs, preventing the radio from working and the people from receiving news from Jacob. In his prayer, Schtamm tells God the serious consequences if gossips inadvertently reveal the radio's existence to German ears: "[B]efore you know it, it's happened. . . . Or someone wants to save his own skin and betrays on his own initiative the existence of the radio. There are scoundrels everywhere, You know that too; without Your consent they would not be in this world. Don't permit the great disaster to overwhelm us, so close to the end, seeing that all these years You have held Your sheltering hand over us and saved us from the worst. . . . [I]f I may make a suggestion, destroy that cursed radio" (70). As the light bulb in the ceiling flickers, Schtamm assumes God has heard his prayer. "[A]t the appropriate moment He sends His sign, the acknowledgment of receipt, truly a sign that could not be more practical; this proves He is God!" (70). Jacob's building across the street is also dark. Schtamm sees this as added confirmation, which is implied by his further reflection: "We have silenced you, my friend, heavenly silence will reign, take your terrible box and give it to the devil; it's of no further use to you. And don't imagine that the power, the loss of which you innocently assume to be a breakdown, will be restored tomorrow: short circuits instigated by the Supreme Being take their time" (71). Schtamm sincerely believes that God has answered his prayers, manifesting His omnipotence by disabling the threat that the radio, and thus hope deriving from a worldly or earthly source, poses. Schtamm actually does not disapprove of hope. He simply believes that it should come from faith in God and providence, not from a radio.

Although Schtamm clearly disapproves of the radio's presence, he nonetheless comprehends its significance to others. In a poignant scene, Schtamm realizes that one of the railcars in the work area where the Jews load crates contains live human beings. Despite strict orders from a sentry to avoid walking near this particular railcar, Schtamm sneaks over and converses with the Jews within—Jews who are in the process, no doubt, of being deported to a concentration camp and subsequently to their deaths. Recognizing that the Jews are scared and feeling hopeless, Schtamm reassures them, "You must hang on; only for a short time, you must hang on. The Russians have already advanced past Bezanika! . . . You can believe me. We have a secret radio" (115). Feeling pity for the deported Jews, Schtamm offers them a glimmer of hope, thinking that it will provide them with the courage to survive. He does not realize that in so doing, he acts in the same manner as Jacob Heym, the man whom he condemns. Even though he sincerely believes that he has incited God to temporarily disable the radio, he instinctively recognizes the value of the hopeful news to Jews who despair. Consequently, he proudly informs the Jews trapped in the railcar that "*We* have a secret radio"—as if he is partly responsible for the hope that the radio offers. Because Schtamm disobeys the sentry's order to stay away from the railcar, he is killed.

In Becker's novel, Jacob assumes that Schtamm's twin brother blames him for the death, but in the Brodsky film version and in the Williams remake, there is no doubt that the brother and others blame Jacob for Schtamm's death. The characters accuse Jacob because Schtamm died while providing hope to deported Jews—hope that originated with Jacob's radio and news reports. In the Brodsky version, Schtamm's twin brother turns and stares angrily at Jacob. The Williams remake is much more explicit in the condemnation of Jacob. Schtamm comforts the Jews in the railcar by telling them to remain patient because he knows for a fact that the Russians are coming to rescue them: "We have a radio." As he utters the word *radio*, he is shot dead by a Nazi guard. The simultaneous timing of the word and the shot indicates a connection between the hope Jacob offers and Schtamm's death. Schtamm's twin brother faces Jacob accusingly and shrieks, "You did this! Did you have to shout from the rooftops that the war is over. Look where it got us." The Williams film, therefore, suggests that the false hope offered by Jacob proves disastrous for the people and that he is to blame. Although Professor Kirschbaum consoles Jacob by claiming that he is not to blame and that Schtamm has acted on his own accord, the film suggests that Schtamm would still be alive had Jacob not lied about having a radio. In the remake, as in the novel and the Brodsky film, Schtamm is a devoutly religious Jew who wishes to place his faith in God, not a radio, but he, like Jacob, succumbs to the need to offer optimism and hope to his fellow Jews in a time of dire and hopeless circumstances.

Witnessing atrocities on a daily basis causes people to yearn for good news—something for which they can be hopeful. Joshua Sobol, arguably Israel's greatest playwright and an authority on the Vilna Jewish ghetto in Lithuania, mentions that the ghetto librarian Herman Kruk wrote in his diary of "the disease of hope." Kruk suggested that hope can become a disease if it renders people passive, inhibiting them from taking action. Kruk lived in the Vilna ghetto at the same time that *Jakob the Liar* is set; in both Poland and Lithuania, some Jews did not try to escape from the ghettos because they naively hoped—and believed rumors—that the Russian army would soon rescue them. As Rhys W. Williams remarks, "Any reader familiar with *Jakob der Lügner* will be aware of how story-telling in the sense of invention (and untruth) is an existential necessity" (93). Even though the information is not verifiable or even credible, the desperate and hopeful will accept it as truth. Consequently, their judgment and interpretation of events can be skewed, and they can be fooled into feeling false hope. Becker's screenplay includes a scene, not present in his novel, that supports this point. After Jacob informs Kowalski that the Russians have advanced two miles closer to their town, the friend, in turn, reports to other Jews that the Russians have advanced five miles. It seems that Kowalski even believes this exaggeration that he himself concocts and disseminates. Unsatisfied with a gain of a mere two miles, Kowalski becomes an accomplice by enhancing the advancement. (At this time Kowalski does not realize that he is exaggerating a lie.) George M. Kren and Leon Rappoport claim that "like all emotional defense mechanisms, the tendency to normalize extraordinary events reduces anxiety only by falsifying reality" (14). Because of the widespread despair, hope supersedes truth. As Patrick Shade says, "Hoping may be a natural and attractive human activity, especially when we are at a loss to readily secure desired ends on our own. Yet those who pursue hopes play a dangerous game, for hope is unpredictable and typically prodigal in nature" (3–4). Similarly, Sara R. Horowitz notes that "the victims grasp at the flimsiest of explanations rather than acknowledge the horror in store" (162). Ghetto inhabitants believe Jacob Heym's false news reports even though he is unable to provide them with any details or answer questions concerning the reports that he disseminates. Becker thus maintains that people in precarious situations are so desperate to survive that they are credulous enough to accept optimistic rumors as fact. It never occurs to the people that the Russians might bypass their town and leave them at the mercy of their Nazi oppressors.

Becker explores the false hope of the inhabitants by including the character of Leonard Schmidt, an intelligent but naive Jew. Schmidt is an assimilated and wealthy Jew who earned an Iron Cross medal during

World War I. His parents do not attend synagogue and do not call attention to themselves as Jews. Schmidt believes, therefore, that he and his
family are immune from Nazi persecution and that the German government will act respectfully toward them. His temporarily successful
assimilation causes him to have the false hope that while virtually all
other Jews will be persecuted, he and his family will be spared. Paul
O'Doherty claims that even the Germanic surname "Schmidt" suggests
assimilation (47). The narrator observes that the fact that Schmidt has
been arrested and placed in a ghetto "transcended anything he could
ever have imagined. . . . In Schmidt's mind the whole thing persists like
some idiotic joke. . . . He had been well on the way to becoming a
German nationalist. But they didn't let him" (106–7). Like other Jews
who would endure terrible fates during the Holocaust, Schmidt hopes
that although others will suffer, he will somehow be treated differently. J.
Christiaan Beker observes that when we "divorce hope from suffering,
then we become victims of illusion and create images of false hope" (30).
Schmidt hopes that his wealth and assimilation will allow others to perceive him as a German, not as a Jew, particularly when he works toward
German nationalism. Such a cause suggests, perhaps, that he, to some
extent, supports the Nazi government until his arrest. He is so hopeful
that he allows himself to believe that the suffering will not affect him.
While working at the freight yard, he foolishly decides one day to wear
his Iron Cross, hoping to receive respect and better treatment from Nazi
soldiers; the narrator and other workers are amazed when a sentry seizes
it gently yet decides to spare his life for this offense. The narrator
observes that Schmidt exudes a haughty attitude toward his fellow Jews,
who refer to him mockingly as "Leonard Assimilinski" (110). As with
the other characters in the novel, false hope is eventually crushed; assimilation signifies nothing to a government that judges its people strictly
by their ethnicity and religious affiliation.

Jacob finally gives up on his invented radio reports and his dissemination of false hope—which seem to have inspired not only the other
ghetto Jews but also himself—when Professor Kirschbaum dies in Nazi
custody and the professor's sister is arrested by German soldiers. After
these incidents, Jacob recognizes unequivocally the insurmountable
Nazi power over the Jews and the depth of the adversary's cruelty. Miss
Kirschbaum is arrested and will, no doubt, be killed because her
brother chooses to die rather than care for the dying Hardtloff, the
German commandant. The professor, being a heart surgeon, realizes
that he lacks the medical equipment necessary to save the life of the
Sturmbannführer and that the ghetto chief's death will cause him to be

tortured and murdered. He therefore relinquishes any hope for survival and commits suicide. The professor's sister is then arrested in revenge for the professor's failure to treat Hardtloff. The loss of the professor and his sister greatly affects Jacob. As J. Christiaan Beker notes, "If we divorce suffering from hope, then we become victims of cynicism or despair and surrender hope altogether" (30). Discerning no end to the deportations and killings, Jacob Heym simply gives up hope—and gives up providing it to others.

Jacob finally confides to Kowalski that he never owned a radio or heard news reports, save the initial one. Seemingly wallowing in false hope to the end, Kowalski smiles. The narrator remarks that even though Kowalski's "eyes smile less than his mouth, they still do not proclaim the end of all hope" (217). Kowalski seemingly believes that Jacob does possess a radio but, knowing that people caught with one are murdered, wants people to think that he never owned one. Kowalski says conspiratorially, "If I'd had a radio here, I don't suppose a single soul would ever have heard a word. . . . To keep an entire ghetto supplied with news! I would never have gone that far—you never know who else is listening. If I have ever in my life understood anybody, I can understand you now" (217). Jacob is amazed that Kowalski seems to cling irrationally to hope, refusing to accept Jacob's confession. But Jacob is even more shocked when he realizes that he has misjudged Kowalski, that his friend has actually understood him. The next morning, Jacob discovers that just after he confessed his lie to Kowalski, his friend hanged himself. Having lost the hope which Jacob has supplied him, Kowalski can no longer survive. Before experiencing the hope that derived from Jacob's radio reports and his now questionable gift of stories, Kowalski merely trudged through life in the ghetto. Now that he has lost the hope that inspired him, he simply gives up. What destroys Kowalski is not the lack of hope (he had none before Jacob started to spread news), but rather the loss of hope and the realization that Jacob's narration of hope has been a lie.

Early in the Robin Williams remake of *Jakob the Liar* (1999), Jacob walks into Kowalski's old barber shop and sees that his friend is about to commit suicide. Jacob prevents Kowalski's death by sharing with him the optimistic radio report that he heard in the German administration building; thus Jacob, according to the Williams film, devises the idea of spreading false hope. This interpretation is problematic because it indicates that Kowalski is already suicidal and thus has no hope from the beginning. According to the novel and Jurek Becker's film version, Kowalski never entertains the idea of suicide until he realizes that his hopes have rested solely on lies. In Becker's novel and screenplay, Jacob blames himself because Kowalski never considered suicide until Jacob started to disseminate false news reports. In Becker's novel but particularly in his screenplay, Jacob realizes that he is largely responsible for the death of his friend. In the Becker film, Jacob feels culpable and projects his guilt onto his dead friend: "How could you [Kowalski] do this to me? Aren't there enough murderers in the world? Why did you have to choose me of all people on the earth?" Jacob implies that by committing suicide upon hearing his confession, Kowalski has made Jacob responsible for his death. This interpretation suggests, again, that Kowalski is destroyed not by the absence of hope, but by the realization that his hope has been unfounded and based on Jacob's lies.

After reading the novel, it is difficult to determine Jurek Becker's view of Jacob's behavior. Does the author consider his protagonist heroic or misguided? One must bear in mind that Becker devised the title *Jakob der Lügner [Jacob the Liar]*, not *Jakob the Hero* or *Jakob the Bringer of Hope*. During the conclusion of Becker's screenplay, the Jews stare angrily and accusatively at Jacob when they learn that they are being deported, suggesting that they, to some extent, blame him for their unhappy fate. The Williams remake condemns Jacob more than the novel and the Brodsky film because Professor Kirschbaum dies in an effort to protect Jacob. Furthermore, unlike in the other two versions in which the Nazis deport the ghetto's Jews to the death camps, in the Williams film, the Nazis deport the Jews *because of* Jacob Heym's radio—a radio that never existed. The Williams movie indicates, therefore, that Heym is, to some extent, responsible for the death of thousands of people. Writing about the culpability of Jacob in the Brodsky movie, Annette Insdorf believes that "though well-meaning, he offered illusions that kept the Jews from banding together and fighting. His lies prevented not only suicides . . . but also the will to organize and resist. . . . On an individual level, the escape into imagination might be a means to survive. For the survival of a group, however, Jacob's lies are pernicious" (143–44).

Insdorf's criticism of Jacob is somewhat unwarranted, for she implies incorrectly that his lies prevented the Jews from militarily resisting their Nazi oppressors. Even before Jacob invents his false news reports, the ghetto inhabitants lacked weapons and never considered the possibility of armed resistance. With or without Jacob Heym, no armed resistance would occur. Jacob's lies possess the potential to help Jews because his false hope temporarily prevents suicides and provides Jews with a will to live. If the Russian army had, in fact, liberated the town,

Jacob's false hope could have made him a hero. But as Sarah Horowitz notes, "[F]abricated broadcasts prove no match for history. The confabulated narrative of hope that Jacob produced for the ghetto masked but could not ultimately displace the narrative of destruction" (68). Historically, the Russians, who did not make the liberation of Jews one of their priorities, advanced into Jewish ghettos months after their liquidation; Jacob, of course, could not have known that. Jacob realizes that his dissemination of hope is temporary because if the Russians stand 288 miles away and advance several miles per week, they must arrive soon. Although Horowitz correctly states that Jacob's "fabricated news is configured not so much to represent reality as to match the contours of the ghetto dwellers' hopes" (67), it can be argued that Jacob wants history to represent his news reports—that if the Jews find the hope that provides them with the will to live, his lies will become reality.

Hope for the future does in fact exist at the conclusion of the novel because the narrator survives and is able to relate the story of Jacob and the other ghetto inhabitants to the reader. The Jews in the Polish town live on through memory and through the novel itself. The fact that Becker, a Holocaust survivor, wrote this novel, and the narrator, who is an important character, still lives at the end indicates triumphantly that the Nazi "Final Solution"—the plan to destroy all the Jews in Europe—fails. The narrator survives not merely to tell Jacob's story of why he lied about having a radio, but also to signify that there is still hope for the Jewish people. Jurek Becker thus replaces Jacob Heym as the narrator of hope who provides the gift of story.

Chapter 8

Friendship and Hope
Elie Wiesel's The Town Beyond the Wall

Carole J. Lambert

I have written several novels—among them The Town Beyond the
Wall—*solely to celebrate friendship. I love the character of Pedro
because he evolves in a world illuminated by friendship*
                                        —Elie Wiesel, Memoirs

According to sociologist Zygmunt Bauman, the twentieth century was
the "Age of the Camps," since "the shadows cast by Auschwitz and the
Gulag seem by far the longest and [most] likely to dominate any picture
[future historians] may paint" (*Life in Fragments* 193). Microcosms of
totalitarian society, Bauman argues, the camps were the offspring of "the
modern dream of total order, domination and mastery run wild,
cleansed of the last vestiges of that wayward and unpredictable human
freedom, spontaneity and unpredictability that held it back" (201). If
the Holocaust casts a dark shadow on the Enlighten-ment narrative of
progress for its Jewish victims, it shattered faith in the biblical narrative

as well. Where was the God of Abraham during the extermination of over six million of his chosen people? One does not think immediately of finding God, friendship, or hope in the ashes of Auschwitz. Yet these are recurring themes in the novels of Holocaust survivor Elie Wiesel. Given his horrific experiences with injustice during what he calls the "Event" (Wiesel, *And the Sea* 18)—which resulted in the deaths of his beloved grandparents, parents, and younger sister—understandably Wiesel appreciates deep friendships in his own life and describes them in detail in his writings. Michael's and Pedro's relationship in *The Town Beyond the Wall* (*La Ville de la chance*) is just one example of a profound and life-changing friendship that provides hope for a Holocaust survivor whose trust in God has been severely damaged.

Friendship can certainly be a consolation to the two individuals sharing it, but it can also become a means of fighting both injustice and indifference to the suffering of others beyond the two bonded together in this relationship. We shall see how even the recollection of Pedro's wise words leads the imprisoned Michael to emerge from his own emotional entrapment in misery to save another prisoner's life. Having been choked by an insane bully, the introverted, unnamed victim is led by Michael from an unresponsive, incoherent state of being into a new life of relationship with others. Thus the experience of a deep, fulfilling friendship, for example, that between Pedro and Michael, can instill values in one of the friends (Michael) upon which he acts at great cost to himself to save another even during the absence of the cherished other friend (Pedro). True friendship hence leads to personal hope shared with despairing others and may even renew one's hope and trust in God.

Elie Wiesel wants to be a link between all people:

> I want to bring people together from all sides: Buddhists and Arabs and Europeans and Americans. Because, again, a witness is what? A witness is a link. A link between the event and the other person who has not participated in it. A witness is a link between past and present, between man and man, and man and God. Being a witness I would like to be that link between the Arabs and the Jews, and the Jews and the Christians, and the Jews among themselves. (Cargas, "What Is" 157)

In *The Town Beyond the Wall*, awarded the Prix Rivarol in 1964, Michael is a Jew, a Holocaust survivor, who, having lost most of his family in the camps, longs to return to Szerencseváros, his village in the Carpathian mountains, now behind the Iron Curtain. Pedro is a Spanish Christian, a professional smuggler, who orchestrates the plan to make

Michael's dream come true, even accompanying him back to "the town beyond the wall."

Hasidism, which has attracted Wiesel all of his life, teaches that God may be in the stranger, and hence every stranger becomes worthy of respect and potential friendship. Ted L. Estess remarks:

> The Hasids believe that God hides in the least likely stranger, ready to surprise the unsuspecting. Wiesel's attribution of religious intensity to friendship reflects this notion. Michael—the name means "Who is like God"—discovers the divine presence in those persons close to him. (53)

Both Jews and Christians recall Abraham's entertaining the three holy figures in Genesis 18 as a paradigm for finding God in the guest.

Wiesel's Michael at first wants to avoid meeting Pedro in Tangier, having received his phone number from Meir, Pedro's shady employer who is also Michael's formerly honorable friend from childhood. On the telephone Pedro insists that Michael appear that very night in Soco Chico at The Black Cat, a humble bar where men enjoy drinking and telling stories about their life experiences (*Town* 101).

It cannot be argued that Pedro is God, although Simon P. Sibelman notes that "[i]n Judaism, another of God's names is *Tzur* . . . or *rock*, which is Pedro's name" (72). Pedro is unlike the strangers that Abraham honors in the biblical theophany, and yet, the qualities of a good, compassionate, and wise God are in Pedro. The men drinking with Pedro "take him for God. . . . That's why he's so alone; why he sees so far" (*Town* 109). When Michael asks "'Who are you?'" "Pedro would have answered, 'I am. Isn't that enough?'" (113). The "I am" of course echoes the biblical response of God to Moses (Exod 3:14). Although Pedro drinks heavily and involves himself in covert international smuggling operations, he commands the respect of his fellow drinkers and immediately of Michael who has, up until their meeting at The Black Cat, maintained no profound friendships. Pedro infuses hope into Michael instantaneously: "The power of that man, . . . is the power to awaken me to freedom," thinks Michael prophetically (*Town* 109), and Pedro does indeed do this for Michael, despite his ending up imprisoned in Szerencseváros, Michael's hometown. Pedro's compassion and hope, transmitted through their deep friendship, liberate Michael from himself and help him to liberate another. Wiesel himself has called Pedro "an existentialist Hasid" (*Conversations* 74). He continues. "Pedro is the ideal friend or the friend idealized. You write only about people you don't have, people you want to have" (74). At one point in the novel,

"Michael felt an impulse to ask [Pedro], 'Tell me the truth, Pedro: are *you* God?'" (115).

I shall analyze Pedro's qualities as a hopeful friend, and I shall illuminate the enigma of how friendship is a spiritual and even godly experience, especially for a Holocaust survivor who may have already given up on God. In one interview Wiesel affirmed: "I cannot speak of God without speaking of man, or of man without speaking of God. God has always been my central problem in everything I have written." He further explains, "In [*The Town Beyond the Wall*] I tried to deal with man's relation to God, because God is always there. When man talks to man, somehow, God is there" (Cargas, *Responses* 151).

In a personal interview with this author, Wiesel stated that "God cannot be put into words, . . . God is a mystery . . . [and] God's love is shown in men's love for others." The relationship between Pedro and Michael has something godly about it. It does not describe a particular biographical relationship that Wiesel had with a friend in his own life (Wiesel, *Memoirs* 197, 357–58), but rather it announces the possibility of God's presence still being in the post-Holocaust world; it portrays the values, conduct, and integrity of two exemplary friends in their relationship to each other and with others, and it shows their response to the unjust. A close study of *The Town Beyond the Wall* may provide insights into the most hoped-for qualities of God as reflected in a compassionate, responsible friendship founded on a strong ethical base. The Holocaust has left Michael with no hope in God. Once again undergoing torture, this time administered by the Communists, he thinks of his friend Pedro, not God.

Michael endures a peculiar torture ironically called "Prayers," as he refuses to state why he returned to his homeland and who, namely Pedro, arranged and accompanied him on this visit (*Town* 8). The Communist tormentors require three days of Prayers during which the victim stands, facing a wall, forbidden to lean on it or to sit down, while submitting to the relentless questions of his torturers. "Able to confront moral torment with his head high, [Michael] was afraid of physical torture. . . . He thought of Pedro and kept silent. He remembered his friend's face and his lips remained shut" (*Town* 8).

An understanding of Pedro and Michael's relationship is necessary in order to grasp Michael's intense loyalty. Their friendship has been built on intimate hours spent together, often walking: "[H]e became Pedro's friend for the simple reason that Pedro knew how to walk; few people did" (*Town* 67). During their all-night walks they often discuss profound topics, such as God and men:

"Talk to me about God."
"God, little brother, is the weakness of strong men and the strength of weak men."
"What about men? Do you like to talk about men too?"
"You know I do."
"Then talk to me about men."
"Man is God's strength. Also His weakness." (9)

Throughout the novel Wiesel italicizes the fragments of Pedro's conversations with Michael which he recollects as he undergoes this torture. The italics signal that the narration shifts from third person omniscient to the first person speaker (Michael). The reader discovers oxymorons at every turn: God *"is the weakness of strong men and the strength of weak men,"* and *"[m]an is God's strength. Also His weakness."*

An oxymoron, the combining of contradictory words, rhetorically tends to push the reader beyond the rational comprehension of language to the realm of irrational mysticism. Here Wiesel suggests that both God and man cannot be defined or described simplistically in words, nor can life itself, for why is prayer, normally understood as man's sacred communication with God, here transmuted into "Prayers," a cruel Communist torture? Michael never prays to God during his three days of Prayers, but he does silently converse with his friend Pedro *in absentia*. A post-Holocaust world is one that defies both old and new definitions of prayer and of God and man, but fortunately it is illuminated by the loving warmth of friendship.

"Michael sees his friend's eyes. Deep-set eyes, where joy and despair wage a silent, implacable, eternal battle" (*Town* 9). Pedro's soul, accessed through his "[d]eep-set eyes," is also a dynamic, perpetual oxymoron. The two friends share a respect for each other's wide range of emotions: "I was always sad when I recalled Szerencseváros, which means the city of luck. But Pedro was my friend. He felt no need, no duty, to join me in my sadness. If he felt like laughing, he laughed" (12). And yet, Pedro's laughter may actually signify sadness: "I was sad, but he was laughing. Maybe that was how he showed sadness" (18).

The repetitious circulation of oxymorons in this text unbalances the reader as the emphasis on the irrational intensifies. It then becomes logical, in this illogical universe, that madmen take precedence over the sane. After Michael has told Pedro about Moishe the Madman, his village's honored crazy man, Pedro admits the deceased Moishe into their intimate company: "Pedro spoke of Moishe as if he had known him, as if the madman were still alive, there, with us; Pedro spoke the same way of all my dead friends: he gave them immortality" (*Town* 19). Here

Wiesel introduces another positive quality found within Michael and Pedro's exemplary friendship: one's friends, even though dead, become the other's friends eternally. No sense of jealousy, desire for exclusion, or limitation by mortality is demonstrated by this friendship.

Curiously, yet perhaps fittingly, madmen are beloved by God: "They're the only ones he allows near him," Michael explains to Pedro (*Town* 19). "Since the beginning of history madmen have represented the divine presence; the light in the eyes comes bathed in the source" (94). As Wiesel's oxymorons suggest an increasingly irrational world, it becomes understandable why madmen may be God's chosen. Following a tradition dating back through the Middle Ages to the "God-demented" (137) biblical prophets, Wiesel esteems the madman for his enigmatic language, which may contain profound but hidden truths, and for his proximity to God, who also may communicate truth through mysterious language. Yet the conclusion to which the reader may arrive is terrifying: could God be insane, too, as appear to be his prophets and his creation? "'God is not madness,' . . . Who knows? And if, after all, He were? That would explain so much" (137). The theme of God's possible madness here is explored more fully in *Twilight*, Wiesel's later novel of 1988.

After this discussion of madmen, Michael recalls fragments of his conversation with Pedro about sexuality. Michael has related the story of Varady, the eccentric neighbor of Michael's family, who was said to have lived over a hundred years and who was nursed by the beautiful, young Milika, to whom the adolescent Michael is attracted. Pedro boldly inquires, "*Could you have made love to her?*" (*Town* 35). Even more noteworthy than their discussion of a potential sexual relationship is Michael's freedom to tell Pedro to shut up:

> "*I think so. But then the joke* [Varady's scheme to unite Milika and Michael] *would have been perfect.*"
>
> "Are you sure? Sure it was a joke? Sure you didn't run purely and simply because you were afraid? Afraid of committing a mortal sin? Afraid of being happy and sharing that happiness with a woman, at the very moment when you were sinning against God? Afraid of finding Good in Evil?"
>
> I knew I was turning pale. "Shut up, Pedro," I begged him. (35)

Michael's anguished "*Shut up*," which Pedro honors, is less an angry command than a passionate plea not to trespass on an emotionally vulnerable area of his friend's soul. Pedro, again thinking and speaking in oxymorons, elides happiness and immorality, good and evil, and challenges Michael to explore, at a deeper level, his real reason for fleeing from Milika—was it fear more than righteousness, or perhaps both?

Michael's recollection of this conversation is important because it exemplifies that true friends can both push each other to deep levels of awareness and yet respect each other's emotional boundaries. In his second volume of *Memoirs*, Wiesel states, "Every human being is a sanctuary, for God resides there. And nobody has the right to violate it" (*And the Sea* 94). Michael's closing the door to his close friend Pedro on the subject of sexuality and sin is hopeful not only because it demonstrates that friends can maintain boundaries with each other but also because it reveals Michael's ongoing sensitivity to immorality despite his acute alienation from God, the source of his ethics.

After Pedro forces Michael to a deeper self-realization, he respects his "Shut up" and drops this subject, only shortly thereafter to introduce yet another difficult question, which Michael hesitates to answer, the very question with which his Marxist torturers assault him: "Why this desire to go back in time [to your hometown]?" (*Town* 38). Toward the close of the novel, Michael finally reveals to the reader, by way of yet one more remembered conversation with Pedro, that he has returned to his hometown to encounter again the indifferent spectator who had watched from his upper window the Jews in the synagogue courtyard, including Michael and his family. This man had been "gazing out, reflecting no pity, no pleasure, no shock, not even anger or interest. Impassive, cold, impersonal" (150).

Michael, understanding the persecutors and victims, had been intensely curious about and angry with this indifferent spectator. Unmoved by the two glasses of wine that Michael has thrown in his face, this observer remarks, "'I had a shocked feeling that I was a spectator at some sort of game—a game I didn't understand: a game you had all begun playing, you on one side, the Germans and the police on the other. I had nothing to do with it'" (*Town* 157).

After his unexpected harsh encounter with Michael, the spectator at least does move into action—he denounces Michael to the Communist police, and thus he is the reason behind Michael's imprisonment and torture with Prayers. Spectators do not have the compassion to become authentic friends. They cannot move out of themselves to join emotionally and spiritually with others. Michael, on the other hand, sought to unite himself to God and friends, seeking God intensely in his childhood.

The adolescent Michael who had abandoned Milika was, at that time in his life, absorbed in religious studies and mysticism. Kalman, his spiritual guide, "renounces reason at the start in order to find it later, embellished and vigorous, at the heart of madness" (*Town* 41). Thirteen-year-old Michael longs to be fully united with God, and "[t]he year that he spent beside the master was for Michael the most wondrous of his life. The most profound, the fullest" (41). The omniscient narrator, who reliably relates all of Michael's thoughts and actions except for the first person excurses in italics, indeed affirms here Michael's adult conversations with Pedro, stressing the boy's hunger for God and willingness to deprive his physical body if this would enhance his spiritual quest.

Now the reader begins to understand the depth of disillusionment that Michael has suffered as a result of the horrors of the camps. Rather than finding "reason . . . embellished and vigorous, at the heart of madness," as Kalman had predicted, he finds only madness. What remains for Michael are his father's wise words: "Who does not live for man—for the man of today, for him who walks beside you and whom you can see, touch, love and hate—creates for himself a false image of God" (*Town* 43). The words of Michael's father are similar to Pedro's striking revelation: "He who thinks about God, forgetting man, runs the risk of mistaking his goal: God may be your next-door neighbor" (115). The post-Holocaust Michael is angry with and deeply disappointed in God. What remains for him is friendship. Feeling hopeless before God's lack of compassion, he finds truth, understanding, loyal love, and, of course, hope in his new friend Pedro.

The adult Michael, deeply wounded in his adolescent quest for union with God, now lives—and is ready even to die—for man, in particular one man, his friend Pedro. This positive experience alone guides his life as he endures the torture of a new set of tormentors, this time not Nazis but Communists. At the close of his first day of "Prayers," and also the first section of Wiesel's novel, Michael commends Pedro's personal prayer:

> "'Oh God, give me the strength to sin against you, to oppose your will! Give me the strength to deny you, reject you, imprison you, ridicule you!' That's my prayer."
> "I like it," I said. "It's a madman's prayer." (*Town* 48)

The shadow of the ideal friendship exemplified by the relationship between Michael and Pedro is the connection with Michael sought by Yankel in the "Second Prayer," Wiesel's second chapter. A survivor of the camps, Yankel announces in Paris, where he sees Michael again after several years, "I was your friend" (*Town* 51). Yet, in the perverted atmosphere of the camps, Yankel, the favorite of the overseers, had imposed his childish will on whomever met with his disapproval. Michael still fears him and despises him: "I'm afraid of you; of the bit of me that's part of you," he explains to Yankel (51). The honesty of the statement provides a seed for genuine friendship; Michael admits that the thoughtless cruelty he witnessed in Yankel may also reside in himself. No wonder he hates to open his door to this creature from his dark past who embodies his own weakness.

Michael has also made casual friendships with the clochards, the omnipresent street people: he "accepted their bread, their wine, their incoherent confessions" while "[t]hey accepted his silences" (*Town* 69). Friendship, however, needs more than poverty, incoherence, and silence.

As much as Yankel annoys Michael, the potential for friendship between them remains because they share the same horrific past, something in which even Pedro has not participated. Yet Michael hates Yankel for having observed him in his most vulnerable moment: "Michael was jumpy, all his nerves exposed. This is the only person in the world who knows, he thought. He was right there, that close. He saw me. He saw me as I am, as I am when the skin is stripped away" (*Town* 71). Yankel saw Michael "right there, that close" when Michael's father died: "I looked on and didn't cry. And you saw it. And I can't forgive you that" (75). Michael has not yet forgiven himself for not having, to his mind, adequately helped and comforted his father at this poignant transitional moment. He hates Yankel for being a witness to the event about which he feels the most shame. Yet Yankel claims to have interpreted this tragic situation differently from Michael's self-condemnation: "I'm telling you the truth. I thought that you were probably crying inside. Like you did when Karl whipped you. When we're very badly hurt we prefer to keep our tears to ourselves" (78).

Yankel's divergent reading of that tragic situation has the potential to help Michael find healing from his own self-condemnation: "Let me transform the image he carried congealed in his memory," Michael reflects. "I could justify myself very simply" (*Town* 76). Michael's thinking is aberrant, however, because Yankel already believes what Michael intends to justify for him, namely "that sometimes the fount of tears dries up" (76). Michael himself needs to be persuaded that he was, indeed, even without shedding tears, deeply moved by his father's death. In fact, a real-life survivor, Miso Vogel, admits to mourning profoundly for his father, Heinrich Vogel, and the rest of his family, but he also refused to cry: "In Auschwitz," he recalls, "[if] you cried, you died" (qtd. in Sydnor 15). In 1977, Wiesel again spoke about the absence of tears: "There comes a moment when you do not cry, because you *are* your own crying. And you know very well that should you start to cry you will never finish, so you do not start. Jeremiah did not know how to cry, and the children of my generation did not know how to cry either" (Abrahamson 336).

Yankel exits quietly before Michael can turn to him to speak his self-justifying remarks. The moment for self-healing and hope through the compassion of a friend who has witnessed an extraordinarily painful moment passes. Yankel resurfaces in a hospital bed in Paris, having suffered a near fatality after being hit by a car. Rushing to his bedside, Michael announces to the doctor that he is not a relative but "[a] friend" (*Town* 88). Hate has turned into love. Vainly he tries to communicate to the comatose patient:

> Little prince, you're slipping away, and taking the memory of me with you, the memory of someone who didn't cry when his father met death. I hated you, I loved you; I hated you because I hated myself, and I love you for the same reason. (89)

Once again Wiesel uses oxymorons to communicate the mystery of friendship, which includes both hate and love. Perhaps hate and love synthesize to produce the self-sacrificing love Michael is living out for Pedro, but this was already expressed to Yankel: for seven days Michael remains at Yankel's bedside, begging God to take his life rather than his friend's: " 'Leave the boy alone! Take me! Don't be so sly; you want a battle; I'm ready; but leave the boy alone!' " (*Town* 91). When Yankel finally dies, Michael laughs despairingly, strangely, "a powerful, manly laugh, a blood-chilling laugh" (90). He still has trouble crying when someone he loves deeply dies.

Yankel's death almost drives Michael insane; he later tells Pedro: "*I was on the verge of madness. . . . I could see myself in it. I saw myself as I was and as I wanted to be. I was at once myself and another. I'd finally been freed from myself*" (*Town* 93). Choosing madness and death is, in an oblique way, opting for freedom: "*The man who chooses death is following an impulse of liberation from the self; so is the man who chooses madness. A last resort, it awaits us open-armed. . . . To keep our balance then is the most difficult and absurd struggle in human existence*" (93). Michael has hated the self that did not cry when his father died. After offering to die in Yankel's place and, following the child's death as he fights against madness, he offers a third option for freedom: the struggle to "keep our balance."

Coming from a very different past, Pedro compares Michael to Christ: "*You go beyond the Nazarene. . . . You want to do better, surpass him, exceed. You have the soul of a priest. . . . Christ said no only to men; you say no to God. You're jealous of God*" (*Town* 94). Rather than be offended by his friend's remarks, Michael acknowledges that Pedro's analysis may be true. Their conversation ends, predictably, with another oxymoron. Pedro exclaims, "*I like you, my friend! You're trying to drive God mad,*" to which Michael replies, "*And God too is trying to drive me mad*" (94).

Since the italicized reminiscences of Michael's conversations with Pedro are all being silently recreated in the former's mind, one wonders if Pedro may be a fictive idealized friend created as both a comfort and a challenge to the suffering prisoner. Wiesel has stated that he has never had a real friend like Pedro: "Tangier, for me, was Pedro, my friend, the man who to me embodies the ideal of friendship, as much madman as sage, as brave as he was philosophical, as sad as he was triumphant over all sadness. I created Pedro because I missed him. I still do" (*Memoirs* 177). Pedro shows many qualities of Wiesel himself: an honest questioner unafraid to probe ever more deeply with his questions, even if it may be painful for his respondent or considered blasphemous of his God. For example, Pedro, recalling Michael's intense animosity toward Yankel, dares to ask, "Did you want the little prince to die? Answer me!" Again Michael asks him to shut up, and Pedro again honors his plea (*Town* 97).

Pedro also acknowledges that the "*dialogue—or the duel, if you like—between man and his God doesn't end in nothingness*" (*Town* 98). A real friend, or, in his absence, the voice of a friend in one's mind, relishes the "*duel*" with God and creatively uses it. As fearful as profound encounters with man or God may be, the "artists, ascetics . . . attacking fear . . . mold their works of art, their visions of God," Pedro explains (108). In contrast to choosing suicide or madness, " 'What you must say is "I suffer, therefore you are." Camus wrote somewhere that to protest against a universe of unhappiness you had to create happiness. That's an arrow pointing the way: it leads to another human being' " (*Town* 118). Pedro demonstrates this philosophy in his care for Michael, both in words and actions, and Michael is fundamentally changed as a result. Almost as if commissioning him, "Pedro set his heavy hands on his friend's shoulders, as if to anoint him, and said, 'Try to help others. Many others'" (123).

Is Pedro, "the perfect friend" (127), a real human friend to Michael, or the voice of an imaginary, idealized friend inside Michael's head, or the voice of God residing in the very center of Michael's being?

After his three days of torture, Michael meets in his cell Menachem from Marmaroszighet, he whose "handsome Christlike face radiated compassion" (*Town* 165). Menachem inquires if during Michael's torment he had heard "the voice of God" (135). "I heard his Voice," Menachem assures Michael, who has replied negatively. Menachem affirms, "It asked me questions and gave me the answers. Thanks to that, I held out; I wasn't alone" (135). Both Menachem, whose name in Hebrew means "to console" (Berenbaum 41), and Michael have survived their torture because of the friends in their souls: God and Pedro, respectively. They were never totally alone.

Perhaps for one who desires to learn about friendship and hope from Wiesel's text it is not important to answer the question of exactly who belongs to Pedro's voice—a real man, an idealized imaginary friend, or even God. "When two solitudes unite, there is the world on the one hand, and they on the other—and they are stronger than the world. More solid. More real," Michael reflects (*Town* 125). The "two solitudes" may be one's best friend and one's self, or one's inner child and adult self, or God's Spirit and oneself. This union of solitudes is powerful and discerning. It knows who to help, and it recognizes who is a fraudulent friend.

At the close of his three days of torture, Michael is invited to sit down—a major privilege—and chat with a Marxist officer who also claims to be a writer:

> "One day," the officer said dreamily, "I'll be sitting across from someone like you and we'll be talking about literature and art. There'll be no distrust between us. The gaps will be bridged. We'll be able to look each other in the eye without afterthoughts. Everything will be frank and open." (*Town* 129)

Is this another example of two solitudes merging? Cleverly, Wiesel places in the torturer's mouth a description of the relationship Michael has shared with Pedro, but the choices this officer has already made—to be a Communist and an interrogator—eliminate the foundation on which the two seekers of love, goodness, and justice, namely Pedro and Michael, have built their relationship. The true friend must never be betrayed to the false friend:

> Keep talking, Michael thought. Go on. I'm naïve, but not to that point. You do it well, anyway. Your buddies—the tough ones—laid the groundwork for you: "They're disgusting, but I'm goodhearted and understanding; I'm your friend." Well, no. It won't wash. I know those tricks. (129)

The Marxist officer with the literary bent cannot be trusted; he plays the fradulent role of a friend in the last act of the drama called *Prayers*. Alone in his cell, having finally cried (not laughed as at Yankel's death) over the removal of the gentle, compassionate Menachem, who was fast becoming a new friend, Michael senses profound solitude. He is left with an autistic introvert and a violent bully; Pedro's remembered words are becoming foggy (*Town* 168–69). Michael is fast becoming totally alone and friendless.

One night "the Impatient One" beats up "the Silent One" (*Town* 171), as he had previously tried to suffocate Menachem until Michael had rescued him (167). Choking the crazed bully in his effort to save the introvert, Michael almost kills him. Later, "Pedro came to visit" (171), this time no longer speaking as a memory but rather giving his advice about the current crisis: "*You saved a human life, little brother. I'm proud of you. . . . Save his soul. You can do it . . . re-create the universe. Restore that boy's sanity. Cure him. He'll save you*" (171–72).

Despite Michael's being exhausted and nearly insane himself, he takes Pedro's advice, working daily with the introvert to draw him out of himself and back to reality and society. Symbolically, Michael "changed corners immediately; now he was living where Menachem had lived" (*Town* 172) before being removed to another cell, Menachem, who had kindly and sincerely drawn Michael out of his solitude. Curiously, the mute's response is for a long time like the spectator's, he who had watched the Jews gathered in the courtyard of the synagogue: "Imperturbable, the other stared, as if all this were no concern of his" (175), the very reaction that Michael hates. Nevertheless, Michael persists in talking daily to his self-enclosed cellmate about love, God, friends, questions. "A man is a man only when he is among men. It's harder to remain human than to try to leap beyond humanity. . . . Don't stay at the window" (176–77).

Michael even renames both himself and this seemingly unyielding introvert: Michael becomes "Pedro," and the introvert becomes "Michael," later to be called "Eliezer, which means God has granted my prayer" (*Town* 178). These concluding words of the novel suggest that true friendship has instilled new, life-giving qualities into Michael and his mute cell mate. They do indeed take on the qualities of compassion and hope, first transmitted from Pedro to Michael and then from Michael to the newly named Eliezer. Friendship has left such an indelible mark that the befriended even assumes the name of his original friend, the name characterizing the essence of that person's very being. In conversation with Harry James Cargas, Wiesel acknowledged that giving another person one's name means "[h]e gives him his destiny. He gives him the most precious thing that he has and that he has received" (Cargas, *Harry* 50). In Wiesel's universe, the gift of the name signifies renewed hope in the future of both the giver and the recipient.

Pedro, in his final apparition, had told Michael to "*[r]estore that boy's sanity. Cure him. He'll save you*" (*Town* 172). The daily challenge of drawing his new friend out of himself prevents Michael from sinking into a narcissistic abyss. Ending the novel with the new Michael's name being transformed yet again into Eliezer, Wiesel's own name, which announces "*God has granted my prayer*" and which means "help of God" (Leizman 63), affirms that God has somehow mystically been in these friendships all along; he may manifest himself, paradoxically, most powerfully in authentic friendships filled with love and hope, not hatred, despair, or madness. Such friendships create links of genuine relationships, excluding only the false (like the Communist connoisseur of literature) and the indifferent (like the cold spectator in the window). By resurrecting his mute cellmate, Michael has angrily uttered, finally, a prayer: "God of Adam and of Abraham, this time, I beg you, don't be against us!" (*Town* 172). Perhaps this is the meaning of "*God has granted my prayer*" and "help of God," the mute's new name. God, whoever he is, at least has not opposed the re-creation of his universe through human friendship.

Robert McAfee Brown proposes another meaning for the mute's new name: "By introducing his own name, Wiesel indicates to the reader that he too has moved from solitary to solidary, and that in a world full of corpses, it is now more than corpses that he sees" (88–89). Michael's initial impression that Pedro had "the power to awaken me to freedom" (*Town* 109) is justified, and this "power" is so infused into Michael that he can awaken another, the withdrawn cellmate, also to the freedom of health and social interaction. Michael is not at all disappointed in Pedro as he was tragically disillusioned with God after the Holocaust. If we define "hope" as "the power to awaken [others] to freedom," then we see the chain reaction set in motion from Pedro to Michael to the healed prisoner and perhaps to the reader.

Thus authentic friendship engenders the hope that illuminates a dark world, even the universe of torturers, madmen, and imprisoned cellmates, and it preserves in the friends the best qualities of the God who seems to have been absent and silent during the Holocaust. This absent, silent God can arouse fear in those like Michael who had sought him with all their "heart, and with all [their] soul, and with all [their] might" (Deut 6:5) in the pre-Holocaust days. The warm, genuine compassion of Pedro for Michael can no longer be found in a child's union with God. Pedro always gives Michael hope, a hope which draws him away from the temptation to yield to insanity or suicide. However, one other danger exists for Michael: will he remain a disillusioned, indifferent, hence incommunicative spectator before God?

Wiesel's novel ends without showing Michael daring to communicate, one on one, to God, as Menachem had during his interrogation. The author, nevertheless, speaks openly of his own faith in God and of his belief in the necessity of friendship. Of faith, he affirms:

> I have never renounced my faith in God. I have risen against His justice, protested His silence and sometimes His absence, but my anger rises up within faith and not outside it. . . . I have always aspired to follow in the footsteps of my father and those who went before him. . . . [I]t is permissible for man to accuse God, provided it be done in the name of faith in God. (*Memoirs* 84)

More simply, he states: "It is because I still believe in God that I argue with Him" (*And the Sea* 70).

On friendship, Wiesel attests: "For me friendship has always been a necessity, an obsession. . . . Friendship or death, the Talmud says. Without friends, existence is empty, sterile, pointless" (*Memoirs* 45). The original version of the first volume of his *Memoirs, Tous les Fleuves Vont à la Mer*, includes an affirmation of friendship not found in the English translation: "Le pire des malédictions? . . . Pour tout être humain, l'absence d'amis. Sans amis, la liberté n'a ni sens ni portée. Qui n'a pas d'amis n'est qu'un prisonnier hors de prison" ("The worst of curses? . . . For every human being, the absence of friends. Without friends, liberty has neither sense nor significance. Whoever has no friends is only a prisoner outside of prison") (63; my translation). Wiesel even remarks in his second volume of memoirs, *And the Sea Is Never Full: Memoirs, 1969–*, that he soon intends to write a new book entitled *My Masters and My Friends* (6). Obviously, friendship is a key theme in his life and literature, but it may also be a hidden means of finding God, or at least his best qualities—love, hope, goodness, justice, and profound understanding—in a post-Holocaust world rife with hate, despair, violence, injustice, madness, falsity, and indifference. Authentic friendship, as portrayed by Pedro and Michael in *The Town Beyond the Wall*, illuminates the moral darkness, for it encompasses friends deceased but alive in one's memories, friends present and absent, friends imagined, and friends still hoped for—including God.

Section Three

Resisting the Night

Because hope is much more than a mood, it involves a commitment to action. Its moral character implies that what we hope for should be what we are prepared to work for and so bring about, as far as that power lies in us.

—*John Polkinghorne*

The proposition that story and storytelling are essential to hope forms a common thread throughout the essays in this book. Richard Bauckham and Trevor Hart make a slightly different claim, arguing that hope is "a vital function of imagination," indeed, that all purposeful human action requires hope, which is "the capacity to imagine otherwise, to transcend the boundaries of the present in a quest for something more, something better, than the present affords" (72). As Richard Middleton and Brian Walsh make clear, the Christian story abounds in hope: "This is the story of the unswerving narrative intent of the Author of creation to

165

liberate his creatures from their bondage, untangling the dead-end plots of their stories by incorporating them into his grand design, through what Jesus has done" (107). A biblical understanding of hope presupposes a "moral universe in which there is normative direction for human life; it tells us that parting from such direction results in nothing less than death" (162). Thus there are limits to what we in our human-ness can realistically achieve. Moreover, Christianity boldly asserts that there is a right and just order to life that can be good news in a disinte-grating, fragmented postmodern world. In the scriptures such righteous-ness, justice, and order are called shalom (162). The horizon of Christian hope, then, as indicated in the introduction, is the coming of shalom, the unfolding of God's peaceable kingdom. However, as long as sin in its various forms, personal and political, continues to hinder God's just and righteous purposes, those who are willing to resist the night are called upon. In *Nehemiah: The Courage to Face Opposition*, Don Fields tells of an occasion when American evangelist Dwight L. Moody was on a voyage and a fire broke out on his ship. When asked by a frightened companion to pray, Moody said, "You can go and pray, brother, but I am going to man the water buckets. There is a time to pray and a time to put the fire out!" (12). Essays in this section deal with the power of story to inspire courageous hope that energizes action, anticipating and enabling shalom.

Hal Bush leads off this section in chapter 9 with his essay "A Passion for the Impossible: Richard Rorty, John Okada, and James Baldwin." Relating recent trends in literary theory to the history of American cul-ture, he specifically engages the works of Andrew Delbanco and Richard Rorty, and the eschatologically oriented theologians Jürgen Moltmann, Paul Fiddes, and Glenn Tinder. With Delbanco, Bush contends that postmodernism's wholesale rejection of metanarrative has led to a "diminution of hope" in American culture, having followed a trajectory from communal hope, invested in the Christian God; to social and political hope, invested in utopian America; to self-absorbed hope, invested in the autonomous individual. Up to a point, Bush shares the postmodern suspicion of grand narratives, the majority of which, he says, are "wolfish metanarratives dressed up in sheep's clothing" but, in agreement with Delbanco, he laments the diminished capacity for story and storytelling and the attendant decline of communal vision and com-munal hope. Insofar as the object of American hope looked upward and not simply forward, it had much in common with the goal or teleologi-cal endpoint of Christian eschatology. Drawing on Moltmann's insight that Christian theology is for "combatants not onlookers," Bush challenges Rorty's position that American visionaries, like John Dewey and Walt Whitman, were right in urging that "utopian America replace God as the unconditional object of desire." According to Bush, to suggest, as Rorty does, that we must choose either immanent and secularized "utopian America" or a transcendent, supernatural God is a false dilemma. Though America has not always lived up to or even agreed upon what constitutes the American dream, is it not possible, Bush asks, to conceive of a utopian vision of America that is in line with God's utopian vision for all of humanity? Such a view has been commonplace among American writers until very recently, from Abraham Lincoln in the nineteenth century to John Okada and James Baldwin in the twentieth. These writers, Bush explains, all shared a passionate belief in the possibilities of America, including its sublime and ultimately supernatural features, and it is this passionate desire for "the possibility of the impossible" that his essay aims to rekindle.

The theme of hope for America continues in chapter 10 with Kelvin Beliele's essay "The Prophetic Burden: James Baldwin as a Latter-Day Jeremiah." Beliele profiles the prophetic voice of James Baldwin—both his condemnation of racism and its effects on America, and his recipe for change. Baldwin believes that if America, even though riddled with racism, is willing to tell the truth about itself, to walk the walk and pay the price, then it will be able to realize its "sublime possibilities," as Bush urged in chapter 9. Beliele notes the truly prophetic character of Baldwin's writings, both his fiction, which can be read as parables, and his essays, which are like sermons. Much like Jeremiah of old, Baldwin proclaims the hope of redemption, in this case from America's manifest sins. Identifying three prophetic roles—the Witness, the Doomsayer, and the Agitator—Beliele shows how Baldwin conveys his own political and religious messages through the characters in his novels, which reveal his love for his people and his hope that they will become more fearless and kind. As Witness, Baldwin weaves a narrative tapestry that tells of his people's trouble, pain, anger, and despair at the hands of a largely ignorant, myopic, and uncaring white culture. As Doomsayer, he warns his people against continuing on their blind path, which leads to despair, and urges them to hold out for hope in a future based on honesty, love, and fearless commitment consistent with Christian principles. As Agitator, he exhorts his people to tell their stories, to mobilize their justifiable anger and hatred, and to engage society's oppressive forces and compel change, or as Moltmann has said, to be social and political "resistance fighters, struggling against the godless powers on this earth" (*Coming of God* 153). Though Baldwin is at best ambivalent about the church, his application of Christian principles to personal and social issues clearly illustrates Moltmann's profound insight that "faith, wherever it develops into hope, causes not rest but unrest, not patience but impatience. . . . Those who hope in Christ can no longer put up with reality as it is, but begin to suffer under it, to contradict it. . . . [F]or the goad of the promised future stabs inexorably into the flesh of every unfulfilled present" (*Theology of Hope* 21).

Susan VanZanten Gallagher's essay "Reconciliation and Hope: Confessional Narratives in South Africa" concludes this section. Here we turn our attention from Baldwin's hope for America, to South Africa's attempt, through the Truth and Reconciliation Commission (TRC), to put its shameful apartheid past behind it and to construct a more hopeful vision of the future. Gallagher visited postapartheid South Africa in 1996, six years after the release of Nelson Mandela and the official recognition of the African National Congress (ANC) and two years after South Africa's first democratic election. What she witnessed and later described in her book *Truth and Reconciliation in South Africa* (2002) was the work of the TRC, established during the presidency of Mandela and headed by Anglican Archbishop Desmond Tutu. In this essay she revisits some of this material, focusing especially on the role of story and storytelling in helping to reconcile the victims and victimizers of apartheid to the truth of the atrocities that occurred, and to release the nation from the burden of suffering and guilt so it can move forward into a more just and humane future. Taking issue with philosopher Michel Foucault, who sees confession as a form of oppressive discourse, Gallagher demonstrates how this form of story and storytelling opens opportunities for reconciliation, healing, and hope. Most important to the theme of this volume is Gallagher's understanding of the way even stories of lamentation and grief may be a gift to people struggling to let go of a painful past and to believe in some kind of future. This idea was behind the TRC, which organized thousands of hearings where victims told their stories and put their truth on record, and where members of the National Party, who originally wanted "blanket amnesty," could be pardoned only by confessing to their own crimes or complicity in the crimes of others. As Gallagher notes, those proceedings, which are not over by any means, amount to reimagining and rewriting the "metanarrative" of an entire nation. The power of story to sustain hope during an exceedingly dark time is evident in Gallagher's compelling account of the confessional narratives she heard and witnessed in 1996 at the TRC hearings. "If hope is for God," writes Glenn Tinder, "then it is manifest in listening for the Word in which the depths of divine reality are expressed. It is manifest also in attempting to respond" (36).

Chapter 9

A Passion for the Impossible
Richard Rorty, John Okada, and James Baldwin

Harold K. Bush, Jr.

Today, many cultural critics lament the disappearance of hope in the general American culture—one widely read account of this being Andrew Delbanco's *The Real American Dream*. There, Delbanco chastises the influence of postmodern critics, many of whom hang their hats on the widely quoted formulation of Lyotard—we are now officially a culture marked by a deep-seated "incredulity toward metanarratives" (xxiv). Delbanco's book, ostensibly the crucial beginning point for this entire book project as well as the conference that preceded it, is a concise and suggestive treatment of the movement of American cultural and intellectual decline, specifically with regard to hope. As Delbanco argues, the problem with a wholesale rejection of metanarrative is that metanarratives are undoubtedly our best source for hope—at least, communal hope. According to Delbanco's account of the demise of a hopeful vision in American cultural history, the movement is from a vision of the Christian church to a vision of the Christian republic to the isolated hopes of autonomous individuals, cut off from the communal visions of earlier days. Hope has moved conspicuously from the realms of God to nation and finally to self. In other words, most Americans today simply do not view any collaborative effort with anything approaching real hope. Instead, any hope that Americans have is aimed purely at the progress of the self.

Such an account is consistent with aspects of Harold Bloom's far-reaching argument in his controversial book *The American Religion*. Bloom describes American belief as fully post-Christian insofar as it is obsessed only with personal salvation and immortality, and thus engrossed only in matters of selfhood. Personal salvation, or individual hope, does not take into account, however, the true nature of hope, which is always communal. Indeed, one might say, an obsession with personal salvation might be considered antithetical to any communal objectives or goals. The sad result, in Delbanco's mind, is a growth of melancholy that is unprecedented in American cultural history. These developments constitute, unfortunately, a breakdown of the true American dream, according to Delbanco.

As such, we might sadly note how Americans have come to use the notions of hope and vision—and surely this is one of Delbanco's points. In a word, after Abraham Lincoln's emphatic and, at times, almost sublime enlistments of hope, American culture in general has moved further and further away from the eschatological nature of its true greatness. Of course, our current suspicion of metanarrative and all the violence that has been done in its many names must be asserted and respected. As the twentieth century has made abundantly clear, Americans really should have a healthy skepticism toward the claims of any metanarrative—we must be skeptical of any assertion of an objectively true system of belief, in almost every case. Perhaps Delbanco's major burden is to have us consider the danger of extreme measures. Simply because we have discovered the vanity and implausibility of the vast majority of wolfish metanarratives does not give us the right to think that all metanarratives are by definition false and oppressive and violent. We should also not conclude, as so many theorists apparently have, that we must give up the possibility of metanarrative. *The Real American Dream* participates in an eschatological critique of American cultural history in two major ways: 1) it asserts both the centrality of metanarrative and its concomitant hopefulness in American history and culture; and 2) it asks important questions about the sources of hope for today and for future generations of Americans in light of the current stress on cultural suspicion toward metanarratives.

It must surely be one of the greatest ironies of the contemporary academy that English departments have intensely critiqued, if not entirely rejected, the power and wonder of storytelling. This is a sweeping statement to say the least, and yet it may after all merely constitute the pragmatic realization of the postmodern pronouncements by the likes of Jean-François Lyotard. In a sense, postmodern fundamentalism, in its utter and final rejection of metanarrative, has deluded us temporarily into believing that we have lost our way and that stories can no longer contain wisdom or truth. Despite the fact that literary critics have violently forsaken the power of storytelling, we should be cheered by the fact that in certain pockets of the humanities, a number of thinkers are attempting to reinvigorate the concept of hope in a mostly hopeless culture such as ours. In the ensuing years, it is highly likely that the results of their labor will influence the English classroom, popular culture, and the pragmatics of youth ministry and urban renewal. Certainly in the field of biblical and systematic theology, an emphasis on eschatology has become one of the most distinctive features. Numerous writers as diverse as Jürgen Moltmann, Ernst Bloch, Ernst Kasemann, Paul Ricoeur, John Polkinghorne, Paul Fiddes, George Eldon Ladd, Hans Frei, George Steiner, Mary Grey, and Wolfhart Pannenberg have developed theories of culture foregrounded in eschatology. In this century, Bloch, in his massive three-volume study of the principle of hope in human cultures (*The Principle of Hope*), leads directly to Moltmann's concept of a "Theology of Hope." Derived from the title of his book in 1964, Moltmann's phrase has become almost a mantra for a movement that has emerged as one of the most influential and wide-ranging approaches to Christianity and culture in the past half-century.

The full details of these grand movements to understand hope and to envision human culture as an outgrowth of eschatological concerns, largely ignored by literary scholars in the 1980s and 1990s but now gaining momentum in a new century, are well beyond the scope of this essay. In large part the results remain to be seen. Ricoeur has become one of the most profound expositors of Moltmann's basic ideas in the context of a study of literature and culture. Frank Kermode, in his seminal work of literary criticism *The Sense of an Ending*, and Northrop Frye, with his study of biblical archetypes and his ruminations on cultural theory in such volumes as *The Critical Path,* have both emphasized the significance of imagining the future and the apocalypse for writers of many genres and nationalities. But for many of today's younger critics, sadly, Kermode and Frye have been mostly left behind. Recently, we should be heartened to see some further exploration of these issues by critics like

Paul Fiddes, who discusses a variety of authors in his book *The Promised End*, as well as Delbanco and Richard Rorty, mentioned in more detail in this essay. However, we should compare the excitement being aroused among theologians by offshoots of Moltmann's "theology of hope" with the current cul-de-sac of postmodern literary theory and criticism that I have briefly mentioned above. In its archest forms, it long ago became hopeless, almost nihilistic. Some observers have remarked that postmodern theory, especially its epistemological aspects, has peaked in the academic world, has played out its influence, and indeed has shown itself to be powerless to explain fully our predicament as humans, let alone our meaning or purpose. More simply stated, postmodern epistemology has nowhere else to go, but almost nobody seems to be trying to do anything about it. Perhaps the problem, in literary studies at least, is that we have not had, or considered with urgency, the tools and/or vocabulary necessary to create and sustain an eschatological theory of literature and culture.

Those who are trying to sketch a response, like Fiddes and Delbanco, point us directly to that musty old concept of hope. Indeed, it is truly a remarkable event in very recent American literary theory to witness among the antifoundationalist faithful what appears to be the resurrection of the category of hope and the intense need for a narrative account of America. An exemplary moment in this reemergence is certainly Rorty's profoundly hopeful volume *Achieving Our Country: Leftist Thought in Twentieth-Century America* (1998). This slim set of essays pulsates with a hopefulness for our nation and a narrative quality shaping that hope. Literature professors will be interested to see the great amount of attention given by Rorty to America's literary tradition. The book begins with Rorty's extended rebuke of a number of recent novelists, including Thomas Pynchon, Neal Stephenson, and Leslie Marmon Silko, whom he considers to be typical of the failure of the AmericanLeft since the sixties. Their work can be summarized, according to Rorty, by its "rueful acquiescence in the end of American hope" (6). Rorty associates writers of this ilk with the dastardly works of philosophers such as Michel Foucault whose "proto-Heideggerian cultural pessimism" leads their followers to view America merely as a "violent, inhuman, corrupt country" (9, 7). Rorty appears to be in agreement with one of the book's heroes, William James, in calling such a position "decadent and cowardly" (9), and this analysis leads up to Rorty's provocative opposition between the "agents" and "spectators" of the American left. Rorty would like to champion the agency of the pre-1960s Left at the expense of the spectatorial role played out by today's dissipated and theory-burdened cultural Left. In many ways, Rorty's argument is another in the long line of American jeremiads that hearken back to the good old days of rolling up our sleeves and getting things done, as opposed to just sitting around and theorizing about the sad state of affairs. For Rorty, "The academic Left has no projects to propose to America, no vision of a country to be achieved by building a consensus on the need for specific reforms. . . . Insofar as a Left becomes spectatorial and retrospective, it ceases to be a Left" (15, 14).

Of interest in all of this is the manner in which Rorty's plea to the Left mirrors, in important ways, the pleas of many in the Christian church for reform among the faithful. If we substitute the word *Church* for the word *Left* in the passages above, this similarity becomes rather clear (significantly, Rorty continually capitalizes the term *Left* throughout the book). Rorty's distinction between the agents and the spectators of the Left sounds almost identical to Moltmann's critique of a similar phenomenon among Christians: Christian theology, says Moltmann, is "a theology of combatants, and not of onlookers" (*Coming of God* 146). Moreover, Rorty often cites with apparent endorsement formulations of early commentators who unapologetically associate their politics with religion. For instance, he quotes in this manner both William James ("Democracy is a kind of religion") and Herbert Croly ("The faith of Americans in their own country is religious") (*Achieving* 9–10). He describes Whitman's belief that "the Golgotha of the Spirit was in the past" and "the American Declaration of Independence is an Easter dawn" (qtd. in Rorty, *Achieving* 22). The great hero of Rorty's book, John Dewey, is quoted appreciatively as saying, "Democracy is neither a form of government nor a social expediency, but a metaphysic of the relation of man and his experience in nature" (qtd. in *Achieving* 18). The title of Dewey's most famous volume, *A Common Faith*, promises a teleological fulfillment of that metaphysical quest, secular though it surely is. Indeed, Rorty agrees with Steven Rockefeller's conclusion that Dewey's "goal was to integrate fully the religious life with the American democratic life" (qtd. in Rorty, *Achieving* 18). Surprisingly, Rorty even mentions that his own maternal grandfather is the great social gospeller Walter Rauschenbusch, whom he applauds in his stance against capitalistic greed and antimilitarism (59–60). All of these heroic figures share, for Rorty, the crucial missing ingredient among today's cultural Left and academic elite: the desperate need to envision America as an unfolding, quasireligious story whose end is hope. Such a story, says Rorty, is the greatest need of our generation.

As much as I believe we should admire Rorty's plea for hope and the authentic and ennobling baring of his soul at this late stage of his career, there is a great deal to criticize in this argument. By now, we must all be fairly weary of the emptiness of generic terms like *left* and *right*, *radical*, and *conservative*—and Rorty is guilty of using "Left" in such a way, for example, as to eliminate any possibility of it being religious in any meaningful sense. More specifically, he also seems unaware of how the two kinds of leftists (observers versus participants) might actually complement each other. Rorty also occasionally handles carelessly facts of American literary history. It might surprise some literary historians, for instance, to hear that there is "little difference in doctrine between Dewey and Whitman" (*Achieving* 25). Such a remark can only come from crass naiveté, inept historicism, or worst of all, willful irresponsibility. This sort of brazen misappropriation of a major figure like Whitman is similar to the common disingenuousness with which numerous recent theorists have deployed Ralph Waldo Emerson as some sort of agnostic, naturalistic pragmatist. Rorty's enlistment of Whitman into the neopragmatist camp may be compelling in certain ways, but the differences with Dewey are quite staggering. The greatest difference is surely at the heart of my argument here—Whitman's profound ties to Transcenden-talism and its inherently theistic foundations, and Dewey's status as chief secularist and naturalist of the past century.

According to philosopher Glenn Tinder, secularism's reluctance to consider this crucial difference, or somehow to pass over it almost silently, is exactly the problem with versions of modern hope. Putting that aside for now, I would suggest that this casual statement is symptomatic of another weakness of Rorty's volume: his entire lack of any version, beyond mere platitude, of what the object of hope for Americans might actually look like. As Tinder points out in *The Fabric of Hope*, hope always requires some noun as object, an object for which we yearn and work and aspire. Tinder provides a long and painstaking critique of "modern hope," which he considers to be a sort of secularized, naturalistic, and finally vague sense of expectation that is neither universally nor communally anchored. In this sense, Tinder's version of a declension of the concept of hope from a transcendental to a naturalistic phenomenon echoes what nearly all of these books have to tell us about the critical illness of modern hope. The book's profound opening discussion of the failures of modernity, and in particular the heady considerations of the "subversion of wisdom" by modern concepts of hope, sets the stage for his presentation of what he calls "authentic hope" (25–29). In particular, the vast majority of Tinder's volume provides a deep and multilayered description of what the object of hope might actually look like.

What is the object of Rorty's hope for America? In the few passages where he attempts to sketch a vision of the object of hope, Rorty puts it this way: "America is destined to become the first cooperative commonwealth, the first classless society. This America would be one in which income and wealth are equitably distributed, and in which government ensures equality of opportunity as well as individual liberty" (*Achieving* 8). For Rorty, the beauty of the combined visionary achievement of the likes of Dewey and Whitman (and presumably of Baldwin's *The Fire Next Time*, which provides Rorty with his title) was that these writers "wanted to put hope for a casteless and classless America in the place traditionally occupied by knowledge of the will of God. They wanted that utopian America to replace God as the unconditional object of desire" (18). Thus, says Rorty, we must desire earnestly "to take time and finitude as seriously as any Hobbesian materialist . . . to look forward rather than upward" (19).

But surely this is exactly the false dilemma that theologians like Moltmann are crying out against in the church itself. Must we necessarily choose between a focus on a utopian America as opposed to a focus on God or the transcendent? Must we decide to look merely forward to the exclusion of upward? In my view, this logical slipup has become a commonplace in the marketplace of ideas, so much so that it appears to be having devastating effects among not just the postmodernists and the general American citizenry, but among Christian believers as well. Is it impossible to conceive of the pursuit of a utopian vision of America that is somehow also subordinate to God's utopian promises for all of mankind? To put it in Ricoeur's terms,

> There is a great risk of reducing the rich content of eschatology to a kind of instantaneousness of the present decision at the expense of the temporal, historical, communitarian, and cosmic aspects contained in the hope of the Resurrection. . . . [I]t will be necessary to speak, with Kierkegaard again, of the passion for the possible. . . . [A] new ethics marks the linkage of freedom to hope—what Moltmann calls the ethics of the mission . . . [I]n the mission, the obligation which engages the present proceeds from the promise, opens the future. . . . "Christian freedom"—to take a phrase from Luther—is to belong existentially to the order of the Resurrection. (*Conflict* 408, 409)

Rorty's secularized position fundamentally lacks the "passion for the possible" insofar as it utterly denies the potentially astonishing effects of a sovereign God's agency in the world we inhabit. Somehow, mystically, we must also have a passion for the impossible because if we are only passionate about what is possible, we limit ourselves. The postmodern theorist Slavoj Zizek has formulated this paradox memorably, drawing upon Ernesto LaClau's and Chantal Mouffe's concept of radical democracy: "[W]e can save democracy only by taking into account its own radical impossibility" (6). Zizek is onto something important about the very nature of what makes humans, after all, human, and what makes ideology, after all the politically correct gestures, sublime. Democracy, like Christianity, is brimming with impossibility, and it is this feature that attracts us and that we as humans seek and need. At its core, ideology is sublime and mystical. Thus we can never be truly and fully satisfied—at least on this side of the great divide.

The grave omission of Rorty's eschatology constitutes a full rejection of this paradox. Rorty (like other secular and/or atheistic theorists) does not believe in the possibility of the impossible. More generally, postmodernist theory, in a sense, is similarly mistaken in its premises—eschatologically speaking. At the risk of simplifying in the extreme, it is certainly noteworthy how frequently Lyotard's well-known quote is invoked as the great starting place for understanding postmodern theory. We have become, said Lyotard, simply incredulous regarding metanarratives. But metanarratives are by definition narratives leading to some set of social and political ends. Metanarratives are teleological—they are leading somewhere that is presumably better and more humane. Of course, metanarratives can also be dangerous, imposing their grand visions in an oppressive and often violent manner. That competing "local" narratives are less oppressive and that all metanarratives are intrinsically violent, as some postmodernists claim, is not at all clear. More to the point, metanarratives advocate an object of hope—they are, in effect, our access to and our source for hope. The mistake of postmodernists is to suggest that somehow we humans can get beyond our desperate need for hope. But in certain ways, hope is our most human need. We simply cannot live without hope; we are designed as hope-bearing and hope-hunting creatures. Indeed, Paul says in Romans that "the creation was subjected to futility . . . in hope that the creation itself will be set free from its bondage" (8:20-21). These verses attempt to express the crucial center of the entire biblical tradition—a center upon which Jürgen Moltmann has constructed arguably the most influential theological system of our lifetime.

These insights are not limited to Christian thinkers. A number of psychologists have identified the need for hope and meaning, sometimes despite their own naturalistic and secular presuppositions. Viktor Frankl's famous theory of "logotherapy" focuses on the need of all humans to discover the meaning and purpose of their lives. His most widely read exposition of this psychological approach is in *Man's Search for Meaning*, much of which consists of first-person depictions of his experience in the Auschwitz death camp during World War II. There, as a young doctor, Frankl tried to determine why some of the prisoners seemed to find the mental strength to survive, while others simply were unable to cope. Frankl's conclusion was that the strongest survivors were marked by a continual "will to meaning." According to Frankl,

> this striving to find meaning in one's life is the primary motiva-
> tional force in man. . . . This meaning is unique and specific in that
> it must and can be fulfilled by him alone. . . . I would not be will-
> ing to live merely for the sake of my "defense mechanisms," nor
> would I be ready to die merely for the sake of my "reaction forma-
> tions." Man, however, is able to live and even to die for the sake of
> his ideals and values! (104–5).

Frankl's analysis is helpful in explaining how meaning is not just a crucial category of human existence, but perhaps the most crucial, especially in light of the most dire and horrific circumstances. "There is nothing in the world, I venture to say, that would so effectively help one to survive even the worst conditions as the knowledge that there is a meaning in one's life. . . . In the Nazi concentration camps, one could have witnessed that those who knew that there was a task waiting for them to fulfill were most apt to survive" (109). Recent psychologists have extended Frankl's basic insights to suggest the centrality of hope and optimism to human existence. Among the more prominent examples are Martin Seligman's exposition of what he calls "learned optimism" and the "science of hope" (*Learned Optimism*), as well as C. R. Snyder's extended treatment of what he calls "hope theory." These approaches echo Frankl's interest in the maintenance of mental health resulting from an emphasis on hope and meaning for the individual. If Frankl's conclusions are correct, then the postmodern denial of such meaning or purpose, as in the utter denial of metanarrative, may be regarded as a sustained denunciation of that which makes us most human.

However, a key word in the previous paragraph is the word *individual*. One might argue that Frankl's concerns are intact to the extent that constructing individual meaning and purpose is still possible. The post-modern complaint, such critics might stress, is against the positing of a meaning or purpose for an entire group or community, let alone a nation-state the size of the United States. But the Christian faith is firmly rooted in a sense of communal hope, meaning, and purpose; indeed, it is rooted in group destiny. Thus, we might ask, is it possible to extrapolate from Frankl's theory of the individual's mental health to a consideration of the "will to meaning" of a given community, whether it be small or as large as America? We might begin by changing just a few words from the Frankl quote above; we might state that

> this striving to find meaning in *a community's* life is the primary motivational force in *a community*. . . . This meaning is unique and specific in that it must and can be fulfilled by *a community* alone. . . . *a community* would not be willing to live merely for the sake of *its* "defense mechanisms," nor would *a community* be ready to die merely for the sake of *its* "reaction formations." *A community*, however, is able to live and even to die for the sake of its ideals and values! . . . There is nothing in the world, I venture to say, that would so effectively help *a community* to survive even the worst conditions as the knowledge that there is a meaning in *a community's* life.

Certainly, this revision has much in common with commentary by the likes of Delbanco that yearns for the revival of American communal meaning and purpose. Another critic Zachary Karabell has echoed Delbanco's concerns recently by insisting that at heart, America is a visionary community seeking a utopian "connectedness," and that this visionary quality is on the verge of a reawakening.

Karabell is correct in noting that the critical eulogies in honor of the death of American vision, as in Russell Jacoby's *The End of Utopia*, are premature. All of this suggests that any postmodernism that dismisses or diminishes authentic hope may ultimately be doomed to marginalization in the big picture of intellectual history, not to mention cultural and literary theory. What will take its place and attempt to fill the vacuum it creates? Authentic hope, and its eschatological implications, may be due for a revival of interest. Furthermore, Christians can be forthright to suggest that the hope of the cross is the truest kind of hope. Literary critics should begin in earnest to take up what Ricoeur has called "the task of a hermeneutics of the Resurrection," which is "to reinstitute the potential of hope, to tell the future of the Resurrection" (*Conflict* 406). Tinder's vision of hope is clearly one that emerges from his own explicitly Christian philosophical position: "Christ is the ultimate ground of all human hope" (xii). However, Tinder is quick to add the spirit of humility and curiosity that informs his approach:

> [There is] a great danger that arises whenever Christians address the vast human multitudes who are not Christian: that of failing to accord full respect to those they address. . . . [T]hey are condescending when they assume that there is no deep truth outside of explicitly Christian truth. In doing this they falsify their relations with the human race as a whole. And they falsify hope, which for Christians is hope for all humanity. (xii)

Thus, Christians cannot assume that they know this hope more fully than they actually do know it.

So far I have outlined a theoretical approach for identifying and analyzing expressions of hope in American culture. By way of illustration, I will use the remainder of this essay to discuss a handful of authors who have given utterance to some of these impulses. Surprisingly, very little attention has been given to the concept of hope by literary critics. A major category used by nineteenth-century Americans to understand their own literature and culture, hope has been ignored or neglected by recent, post-1960s Americanists, even though many of our finest literary achievements are obviously laden with hope. Some expressions of hope in American literature of the past fifty years are astonishing, almost beyond belief, given the nature of the opposition and trial faced by the authors and characters. For instance, the powerful post-World War II novel *No-No Boy* (1957) by John Okada records some of the most stinging criticisms of racialized America of the twentieth century. Ichiro, the novel's Japanese American narrator, has witnessed the imprisonment of his Seattle family by the United States government. Furthermore, Ichiro, a native-born U.S. citizen—in what must surely be considered one of the great ironies in American history—is drafted by the U.S. government to fight against Japan. Although it is an historical fact that the majority of young male Japanese Americans agreed to fight, a substantial number refused to serve in the U.S. military: the so-called "no-no boys," who because of their refusal were sent from the Japanese internment camps to prison. Ichiro is one of these young Japanese men who refuses to fight, and as a result, serves time in prison. Upon his release after the war, he returns to his family home in Seattle, only to be chastised and sometimes physically assaulted as a traitor by those around him, including his old Japanese American friends who are veterans of the war. During the course of the novel, Ichiro faces constant physical and emotional abuse, along with other traumatic events such as the death of his best friend, Ken, from war injuries; the psychological illness and ultimately suicide of his mother; the constant inability to find work because of his criminal record; and the heated anti-Japanese prejudice of the postwar era. *No-No Boy* is a greatly underrated novel of emotional passion written with style and skill, and it reveals a level of racial hatred and marginalization that has caused numerous critics to compare it favorably with other similar twentieth-century masterworks, such as Ralph Ellison's *Invisible Man*.

I begin with a quick summary of this novel in order to note the remarkable manner in which Okada brings his story to a close. The narrative ends as Ichiro tries to stop a fistfight between his friend Freddie and their joint enemy, a Chinese character named "Bull," who has been taunting and threatening them throughout the novel. Freddie jumps into his car, accelerates into Seattle traffic, and dashes his car against a wall, killing himself—a grisly scene witnessed by many of the celebrants at the Club Oriental. Oddly, Bull, who is nothing more than a grotesque bully throughout the story, experiences a moment of grief and horror in witnessing this tragedy. Moments later, Okada presents the following benediction that brings the novel to a close:

> Ichiro put a hand on Bull's shoulder, sharing the empty sorrow in the hulking body, feeling the terrible loneliness of the distressed wails, and saying nothing. He gave the shoulder a tender squeeze, patted the head once tenderly, and began to walk slowly down the alley away from the brightness of the club and the morbidity of the crowd. He wanted to think about Ken and Freddie and Mr. Carrick and the man who had bought the drinks for him and Emi, about the Negro who stood up for Gary, and about Bull, who was an infant crying in the darkness. A glimmer of hope—was that it? It was there, someplace. He couldn't see it to put it into words, but the feeling was pretty strong.
>
> He walked along, thinking, searching, thinking and probing, and, in the darkness of the alley of the community that was a tiny bit of America, he chased that faint and elusive insinuation of promise as it continued to take shape in mind and in heart. (250–51)

Considering Ichiro's hardships, what is the reader to make of such an ending? Our only conclusion must surely be that, even in the face of constant disappointment, outright social injustice, and even sustained emotional terror, Americans can still take comfort in an illumined hope by which they can be guided onward and upward as Americans. *No-No Boy* illustrates that the mean streets of urban decay, racial nightmare, and world war cannot erase the eschatological urge of the American project.

There remains, even for the likes of Ichiro, "that faint and elusive insinuation of promise," and it continues "to take shape."

We might compare Okada's ending with the far more well-known conclusion to James Baldwin's classic essay *The Fire Next Time* (1963). Baldwin's autobiographical volume shares much with Okada in terms of racial tensions, marginalization, class issues, and historical abuse. While it would be wrong to formulate a simplistic comparison of the plights of African Americans and Japanese Americans, the structural relations between these two books are striking. Baldwin and Okada spend the vast majority of their time outlining and analyzing the terrible treatment that they have had to endure as members of an oppressed and racialized class in mainstream American society. And yet, as in Okada's novel, Baldwin ends his essay by rising again to the level of benediction in finally endorsing with passion the hope upon which America was ostensibly founded, in one of the great passages of twentieth-century American prose:

> I know that what I am asking is impossible. But in our time, as in every time, the impossible is the least that one can demand—and one is, after all, emboldened by the spectacle of human history in general, and American Negro history in particular, for it testifies to nothing less than the perpetual achievement of the impossible. . . .
>
> Everything now, we must assume, is in our hands; we have no right to assume otherwise. If we—and now I mean the relatively conscious whites and the relatively conscious blacks, who must, like lovers, insist on, or create, the consciousness of the others—do not falter in our duty now, we may be able, handful that we are, to end the racial nightmare, and achieve our country, and change the history of the world. If we do not now dare everything, the fulfillment of that prophecy, recreated from the Bible in song by a slave, is upon us: "God gave Noah the rainbow sign, No more water, the fire next time!" (104, 105–6)

Again, as with Okada, Baldwin's language is memorable and moving, after such a long litany of horror and hatred, in its insistence on bringing the reader face to face with such a brazen statement of American hopefulness. Baldwin agrees here with Okada, insofar as both, despite having faced far more unimaginable prejudice and rejection than most people, assert the abiding mission of America and the comfort that such hope avails. Both believe that it is still possible, indeed even compulsory, to continue to hope. Baldwin's words are even more daring than Okada's, however, in their remarkable use of biblical and prophetic motifs, which bring to bear a particularly religious sensibility on the topic of American hope.

For instance, several times Baldwin remarks on the "impossible" aspect of hope. Here I should like to mention once more Zizek's concept of radical democracy: "[W]e can save democracy only by taking into account its own radical impossibility" (6). The overarching image of the Baldwin passage presents whites and blacks as "lovers [who] insist on, or create, the consciousness of the others." This sublime vision of citizenship in loving embrace constitutes for Baldwin the supreme challenge of the American idea of hope for the future. Baldwin's concept has affinities with Mirâslôv Volf's intriguing depiction of Christian "embrace" and "self-donation," as outlined in his study *Exclusion and Embrace* (22–28). Volf's concept shares with Baldwin's powerful expression an acute awareness of the "impossibility" of such a directive—at least, within the confines of modern hope. Only within the context of a supernatural, resurrected version of cosmic hope can we make any sense of Baldwin's or Volf's proclamations that we must demand the impossible. Indeed, it is certainly typical of the times we live in that virtually no critic has remarked on how Baldwin's work has transcendental implications. Michael Lynch has noted, "his [Baldwin's] implicit, deep faith in (some) God and in Christian ideals has gone all but unrecognized and certainly unexplored" ("Just Above My Head" 284). It is important to recall that Baldwin began his young adulthood as a Pentecostal preacher, and that much of his greatest writing takes the form of the jeremiad, railing against society's grave injustices. In this context, the first line quoted above—"I know that what I am asking is impossible"—resonates powerfully with Jesus' insistence that the kingdom of God is impossible with men, but with God, all things are possible.

Furthermore, Baldwin insists that the achievement of the impossible must be regarded as "perpetual"—a term bringing to mind some of Abraham Lincoln's arguments in his First Inaugural Address (1861) and elsewhere, insofar as the finite historical America becomes transposed to the realm of the eternal. The perpetuity of the American vision, says both Baldwin and Lincoln, must eventually "change the history of the world." Finally, Baldwin implies, we must long for the achievement of our nation, or else we must face the certainty of a judgment of God not unlike the cataclysms of the book of Genesis—this time, as the book's title reminds us, not by water but by fire. Thus, the final words of *The Fire Next Time*, and its title, place the book's argument firmly in the biblical tradition of the jeremiad, meaning that we must look again to the very foundations of the vision or else be relegated to the growing decline that comes from the removal of God's good graces and the substitution of God's wrath. Put more simply, Baldwin agrees with Okada in his powerful desire to continue regarding America as a story still unfolding, whose end is the promised land of hope.

What precisely is this "perpetual achievement of the impossible"? How does Baldwin define it? And how will this vision of human community, whatever form it takes, contribute to "change the history of the world"? Baldwin never says, except by implication. And yet such an evasion is not uncommon among some of the greatest visionaries of the American spirit. For example, here is the master of evasion himself, Abraham Lincoln, describing the sublime object of desire that made the Declaration of Independence such a special document:

> I have often inquired of myself, what great principle or idea it was that kept this confederacy so long together. It was . . . *something* in that Declaration giving liberty, not alone to the people of this country, but hope to the world for all future times. (213; emphasis added)

The American hope for Lincoln is somehow subordinate to a greater hope, a cosmic hope in which the American version is perhaps the great exemplar in human society. Furthermore, this cosmic hope transcends the ability of language to contain or confine it. Even for Lincoln, the object of American hope is, to some extent, impossible: impossible to name, impossible to define, and impossible to embody completely.

Finally, the object of American hope can be understood as merely one of the world's great expressions of the sublime object of cosmic, human hope. We would be gravely mistaken to think that American hope is somehow the sum of cosmic hope. We must utterly reject attempts to maintain an exclusively American franchise on what this cosmic hope might actually look like. It has been all too easy throughout our history to confuse U.S. nationalism with cosmic hope. John Okada and James Baldwin never made this mistake (although the debate is still open regarding Lincoln and certainly Whitman). For Christians, American hope is authentic only insofar as it participates in and reflects the "future of the Resurrection." But we must also refuse to accept anything less than the possibility of embodying an impossibly cosmic hope in real, actual human communities. Authentic hope is never merely otherworldly: it constitutes a yearning to be embodied. Alasdair MacIntyre has reminded us that any living tradition is best defined as "an historically extended, socially embodied argument" (222). In this sense, the church has partly misunderstood 1 Peter 3:15, which challenges believers "always to be ready to make your defense to anyone who demands from you an accounting for the hope that is in you." The mistake is in seeing this as a call merely to intellectual arguments, or apologetics, rather than also the call to embody, to the best of our abilities, the object of our hope. In other words, we defend our hope in the lives we lead. Richard Middleton and Brian Walsh make a similar point in their defense of the Christian metanarrative, noting that "the charge of total-ization addressed to Christianity [by postmodernists] can only be answered by the concrete, non-totalizing life of actual Christians, the body of Christ who as living epistles (as Paul calls the church in 2 Cor 3:1-3) take up and continue the ministry of Jesus to a suffering and bro-ken world" (107). The failure of the Church to do this is precisely what Baldwin laments in American religion—just as Rorty laments the failure of the cultural Left to embody, and thus defend, their own versions of hope. But this charge to embody fully any truly cosmic hope is impossi-ble, one might say. Authentic hope, however, must always maintain its edge through its audacious mystery and wonder. Hope, finally, is tran-scendental. To combine the thought of Ricoeur and Zizek, hope consists of the possibility of the impossible, and we must be passionate about it. This yearning for the possibility of the impossible—meaning, in Christian terms, a yearning for incarnation and embodiment—consti-tutes the sublime object of all human hope, American and otherwise.

Chapter 10

The Prophetic Burden
James Baldwin as a Latter-Day Jeremiah

Kelvin Beliele

Hope is the belief that the heart's deepest yearnings may one day be fulfilled, the belief that tomorrow will be better than today. Hope strengthens weak knees and emboldens believers to overcome obstacles in order to effect and embrace change. Rightly understood, Christian hope embodies shalom, as Harold Bush says in the previous essay, "the possibility of the impossible," a future that is assured by the crucified and resurrected Christ. Jürgen Moltmann explains that Christian hope is not idealistic but pragmatic: "Hope alone is to be called 'realistic,' because it alone takes seriously the possibilities with which all reality is fraught. It does not take things as they happen to stand or to lie, but as progressing, moving things with possibilities of change" (*Theology of Hope* 25). Both Christianity and modernity are deep in America's DNA, giving rise to the great American dream of prosperity, health, and opportunity, coupled with self-restraint and communal accountability. In *The Real American Dream*, Andrew Delbanco observes that religion and government, when responsible and perceptive, are intent upon the same goals: "[W]hat Christianity and democracy share is the idea that to live in a purely instrumental relation with other human beings, to exploit and discard them, is to give in entirely to the predatory instinct and to leave unmet the need for fellowship and reciprocity" (91). That said, nationalism and Christian hope are not the same, and, when conflated, they can result in the kinds of oppression postmodern critics rightly fear.

This marriage of patriotism and religion that James Baldwin strongly protests, insisting that uncritical adherence to such doctrine perpetuates the weaknesses in what Baldwin regards as the evil extremes of Christian fundamentalism and American nationalism. In his essay "A Glimpse of the Hidden God," Michael F. Lynch makes clear that Baldwin, at least in his early work attacks widely held perversions of Christian doctrine, not the Christian church itself. In *Go Tell It on the Mountain*, Baldwin "censures not Christian theology per se but its misapplication among many of the professed in Christendom. Nor does he target the white church specifically, as he does with considerable stridency in many later works, but the black fundamentalist church, the site of his initiation and early service in the faith" (M. Lynch, "Glimpse" 37). Baldwin believes that the Christian church has the potential to protect and save what is best about American life by reviving the ideals of compassion and faith. Likewise, he believes that the United States government and the American people are capable of returning to the American values of democracy and hope for the future. To this end, he speaks out prophetically as a latter-day Jeremiah, proclaiming the hope of redemption from America's manifest sins as he perceives them.

In Baldwin's *Tell Me How Long the Train's Been Gone*, Mr. Proudhammer tells his sons Leo and Caleb, "But our people ain't never going to learn. I don't know what's wrong with our people. We need a prophet to straighten out our minds and lead us out of this hell" (28). Baldwin describes himself as just such a prophet in *The Price of the Ticket: Collected Nonfiction 1948–1985*: "I find myself, not for the first time, in the position of a kind of Jeremiah" (403). Later, he tells Margaret Mead in *A Rap on Race*, "Maybe I am an Old New England, Old Testament prophet" (James and Mead 174). In addition, almost within the same breath, he adds, "No, I don't think I was as merciless as the Old Testament prophets. But I do agree with Malcolm X, that sin demands atonement" (175). Baldwin's characters, too, often speak as prophets, voicing his hopeful concern for America. His deep faith in the American spirit, especially the African American spirit, sustains him.

Even at his darkest and most pessimistic, James Baldwin never loses hope that America can learn from the past and build a better future.

As a modern prophet, Baldwin rails against the sins of America and insists on the need to make amends, to correct the past, and to forge a more honest and loving future. His stories are like parables, his essays like sermons, dense with prophetic rhetoric and hyperbole, sometimes a series of polemics. As a social and political critic, he shows his people their faults, shortcomings, and sins, and he teaches them to solve their own problems. As such, Baldwin assumes three important prophetic roles: the Witness, the Doomsayer, and the Agitator. These three roles emanate from his love for his people and his hope that they can mend their unloving ways and become the best people that they can be, both fearless and kind. Even Jeremiah, who had many hard words to deliver, had hope for his people and their ability to change: "The LORD appeared to him from far away. I have loved you with an everlasting love; therefore I have continued my faithfulness to you." (Jer 31:3). Jeremiah's angry God acts out of love: "For thus says the LORD: Just as I have brought all this great disaster upon this people, so I will bring upon them all the good fortune that I now promised them" (Jer 32:42).

The voice of the Witness entails the act of testifying, first in a legal and a political sense ("I am the man, I was there, I suffered"), but also in a religious sense, as a witness to God's word and character. Speaking rhetorically as a Witness, Baldwin, in "The American Dream and the American Negro," says, "I am speaking very seriously, and this is not an overstatement: I picked the cotton, I carried it to market, I built the railroads under someone else's whip for nothing" (*Price* 404). In "Conversation: Ida Lewis and James Baldwin," he stresses the difference between an observer and a witness: "An observer has no passion. It doesn't mean I saw it. It means I was there. I don't have to observe the life and death of Martin Luther King. I am a witness to it" (I. Lewis 92). Further, in "James Baldwin—Reflections of a Maverick," Baldwin makes clear that he is "witness to whence I came, where I am. Witness to what I've seen and the possibilities that I think I see" (qtd. in Lester 225). "I have never seen myself as a spokesman. I am a witness. In the church in which I was raised you were supposed to bear witness to the truth. Now, later on, you wonder what in the world the truth is, but you do know what a lie is. A spokesman assumes that he is speaking for others. I never assumed that—I never assumed that I could" (226).

Furthermore, a spokesman acts on behalf of a cause and those who align themselves with that cause. Baldwin categorically renounces causes: "Causes, as we know, are notoriously bloodthirsty" (*Price* 29). The prophet, as Witness, records and denounces the thoughtless, blood-thirsty behavior created by causes and their adherents. Indeed, for Baldwin, the disciples of causes are the divisive forces determined to destroy America and the ideals that Baldwin represents. Joshua L. Miller stresses that Baldwin's position as Witness is a direct result of his being American: "Baldwin thus clarifies his status as a vocal American, simul-taneously claiming and challenging his ambiguous heritage through an active witnessing of U.S. culture and society" (333). Bearing witness to the experience of an oppressed people, however, is costly and deeply troubling. In *Another Country*, Baldwin presents the anguish of the young, black, American male in Rufus Scott, a desperate yet resigned character. Rufus is at best spiritually flat, at worst spiritually dead. For Baldwin "death" signifies more than death of the physical body; it is a spiritual and metaphysical reality, hardly uncommon in Baldwin's America. "When I was seventeen, working for the Army, I could not have been a threat to any white man alive. So it wasn't me, it was some-thing he didn't want to see. And you know what that was? It was ulti-mately, yes, his own death. Or call it trouble. Trouble is an excellent metaphor for death" (Auchincloss and Lynch 73). Many of Baldwin's troubled, dead-in-life characters seem beyond redemption, having lost their religion and lost their direction. In the case of Rufus, Baldwin mourns these losses and the high toll taken on the American spirit. But, like the prophets of old, he is confident that spiritual death is avoidable, that his audience is capable of change; and, if they listen and heed him, they can escape this death and bring new hope to a dying world. Because of his deep love and compassion, the prophet bears the pain he witnesses in order to warn and to point a way out.

As a Doomsayer, the prophet raises his voice to alert his people to the nature of their plight, warning them of the price of continuing on their blind, neglectful path. In "The Fire Next Time," Baldwin soberly warns, "If we do not now dare everything, the fulfillment of that prophecy, recreated from the Bible in song by a slave, is upon us: 'God gave Noah the rainbow sign, No more water, the fire next time!'" (*Price* 379). In clarifying this disaster, Baldwin, drawing on his background as a minister, continually relies upon biblical imagery. In his preface to *Blues for Mister Charlie*, he explains, "[T]he play then, for me, takes place in Plaguetown U.S.A., now. The plague is race, the plague is our concept of Christianity: and this raging plague has the power to destroy every human relationship" (xv). Again, in *The Evidence of Things Not Seen*, Baldwin revisits, with chilling poignancy, his plague imagery, referring to "the plague years of the child murders" (3), and noting that "a plague may be no respecter of persons, but that means, only, that there are two sides to every coin" (52). Though relentless, a plague does not pick and choose: everyone is susceptible and equally responsible and faultless. Finally, for Baldwin, the plague "is, really, the American Dream. The doctrine of White Supremacy—which, in America, translated itself into the doctrine of Manifest Destiny, having returned to Europe, and like a plague carried by the wind, infests all the cities of Europe—is all that now unites the so-called Old World with the so-called New" (93–94).

Clearly, doom, the cynical sense of despair and loss—the dark place of sin with no hope of redemption—is the opposite of a state of grace. Delbanco reasons that only belief in a transcendent reality beyond our own lives can dispel the suspicion that we are alone in an absurd world: "The name for that suspicion—for the absence or diminution of hope—is melancholy. Melancholy is the dark twin of hope" (2). Christian theologian Jürgen Moltmann extends this idea beyond the psychological or emotional sphere, taking the position that despair and melancholy are not just signs of hopelessness, but they are, in fact, sin, and obstacles to hope and to redemption:

> If faith thus depends on hope for its life, then the sin of unbelief is manifestly grounded in hopelessness. To be sure, it is usually said that sin in its original form is man's wanting to be as God. But that is only the one side of sin. The other side of such pride is hopelessness, resignation, inertia and melancholy. From this arise the *tristesse* and frustration which fill all living things with the seeds of a sweet decay. (*Theology of Hope* 22)

Thus, doom and melancholy dwell in the absence of transcending faith and spiritually beneficial hope. Like Moltmann, however, Baldwin is fired by an eschatological vision that relentlessly pursues transformation, especially in the face of the despair and melancholy he has witnessed in America. He remains persistently optimistic and hopeful, even as he warns that transforming the future will be costly. No cheap grace in Baldwin's economy! In his view, the plague is pervasive, touching every aspect of our human existence. In *Giovanni's Room*, Jacques, by some standards an unlikable character, takes on the voice of the prophet, a doomsayer, dwelling on the past in a kind of bitter longing and remorse. "'Nobody can stay in the garden of Eden,' Jacques said. And then: 'I wonder why'" (35). Yet, his bitterness is a warning to David, the narrator: "'You play it safe enough,' [Jacques] said, in a different tone, 'and you'll end up trapped in your own dirty body, forever and forever and forever—like me'" (77). In "Stranger in the Village," Baldwin asserts that "[p]eople who shut their eyes to reality simply invite their own destruction, and anyone who insists on remaining in a state of innocence long after that innocence is dead turns himself into a monster" (*Price* 89).

Like Baldwin's symbolic plague, his monster imagery is dependent upon the traditional discourse of biblical prophecy. In a conversation with Margaret Mead, he says, "[I]f I had tried to become a Christian by imitating what the Christians did, I would be dead, or a monster" (Baldwin and Mead, *Rap* 88). This fear of becoming a monster is echoed by Cass Silenski in *Another Country*. She tells Eric, "I felt betrayed, I felt that I'd betrayed myself, and you, and everything—of value, everything, anyway, that one aspires to become, one doesn't want to be simply another grey, shapeless monster" (404). Cynicism and despair are at the very heart of being a monster. The prophet must claim his own inherently human capacity for despair and his own potential to be a monster in order to empathize with his people's fear and shame at their own monstrous tendencies. Dishonesty, to self and others, results in betrayal, which eventually creates a monster.

Thus, David, the narrator of *Giovanni's Room*, can be seen as a monster. He is fleeing from reality and behaving, at least on the surface, as he thinks others expect. He says, "people who believe that they are strong-willed and the masters of their own destiny can only continue to believe this by becoming specialists in self-deception" (30). He is a pessimistic Doomsayer, one who has never known joy like that which Jacques seems to have experienced in some distant past. David has not traveled from another emotional or spiritual state to this despair. He is resigned, a passive character with no sense of direction or commitment. Near the beginning of his reminiscences, he states, "But people can't, unhappily, invent their mooring posts, their lovers and their friends, anymore than they can invent their parents. Life gives these and also takes them away and the great difficulty is to say Yes to life" (10). David's wisdom—if it is wisdom—is a wisdom of hindsight, gained through the suffering of those who love him. He has betrayed and forsaken both Giovanni and Helga. He continues: "It takes strength to remember, it takes another kind of strength to forget, it takes a hero to do both" and "[h]eroes are rare" (36). David, however, is no hero. Regrettably, he seems to remember what he should forget—the faults and mistakes of others—and to forget what he should remember (if he ever knew in the first place): love and honor and what makes a decent man. Thus, he becomes doomed in his dishonesty and self-distrust. Even so, David is not past redemption. In the final passage of *Giovanni's Room*, he remarks, "[t]he morning weighs on my shoulders with the dreadful weight of hope" (224). Hope, in Baldwin's world, is akin to forgiveness and enlightenment.

Rufus Scott of *Another Country* does not share David's weight of hope. He, like David, is doomed, and in some ways a monster. He is abusive to those who love him, motivated by self-loathing and anger. A prisoner of hatred and lies, he is unable to journey from despair to hope. Regrettably, Rufus is beyond redemption; he can find no hope. Baldwin has explained that there are no antecedents for Rufus: "He was in the novel because I didn't think anyone had ever watched the disintegration of a black boy from that particular point of view. Rufus was partly responsible for his doom, and in presenting him as partly responsible, I was attempting to break out of the whole sentimental image of the afflicted nigger driven that way (to suicide) by white people" (Hall 104). Rufus, like Bigger Thomas in Richard Wright's *Native Son*, has willingly bought into the prevalent stereotypes of race and religion: "Bigger's tragedy is not that he is cold or black or hungry, not even that he is American, black; but that he has accepted a theology that denies him life, that he admits the possibility of being sub-human and feels constrained, therefore, to battle for his humanity according to those brutal criteria bequeathed him at his birth" (*Price* 33).

In addition, as part of this unyielding theology, Rufus is doomed because he cannot accept his sexuality and its possible consequences:

> He [Rufus] remembered only that Eric had loved him; as he now remembered that Leona had loved him. He had despised Eric's manhood by treating him as a woman, by telling him how inferior he was to a woman, by treating him as nothing more than a hideous sexual deformity. But Leona had not been a deformity. And he had used against her the very same epithets he had used against Eric. (*Another* 46)

Rufus has treated his sexual partners not as equals but as inferiors, despising them for his sexual attraction to them. In Baldwin's view, he is destroyed by the hostility of certain prevailing American myths of race and sexuality. He must see himself as the superior aggressor, not what he considers an emasculated imitation of malehood. When he cannot be the superior sexual being, he is weakened and demoralized.

Rufus and Richard of *Go Tell It on the Mountain*, two of Baldwin's suicides, are defeated by their color and their gender. Rufus's confusion and despair about his sexual and social roles lead, in part, to his suicide.

Richard's suicide, however, stems from his humiliation during his confinement and trial when falsely accused of assaulting a white man. He realizes, like Rufus, that he is condemned by his skin color: "Then Richard shouted: 'But *I* wasn't there! Look at me, goddammit—I wasn't *there!*' 'You black bastards,' the man said, looking at him, 'you're all the same'" (171). Richard's realization that he is condemned by the white man for all crimes committed by all blacks drives him to his final act of self-destruction: "He fell asleep at last clinging to [Elizabeth] as though he were going down into the water for the last time. And it was the last time. That night he cut his wrists with his razor and he was found in the morning by his landlady, staring upward with no light, dead among the scarlet sheets" (174).

Baldwin maintains that suicide is a symptom of the doomed culture, of the young black man overwhelmed by, and unable to escape from, the blatant racism of America. These suicidal characters, however, are not to be considered heroes or even admirable:

> If one can reach back, reach down—into oneself, into one's life—and find there some witness, however unexpected or ambivalent, to one's reality, one will be enabled, though perhaps not very spiritedly, to face another day. . . . What one must be enabled to realize, at four o'clock in the morning, is that one has no right, at least not for reasons of personal anguish, to take one's life. (*Price* 389)

These defeated black men, therefore, fail to accept their inherent dignity; they are incapable, or unwilling, to reach down for that personal witness to save themselves. Baldwin further expands on his feelings toward suicide and ways to avoid suicide: "My best friend committed suicide when I was twenty-two, and I could see that I was with him on that road. I knew exactly what happened to him—everything that happened to me. The great battle was not to interiorize the world's condemnation, not to see yourself as the world saw you" (D. Estes 275–76). Ironically, the tragic act of suicide can allow the survivors to discover new life and compassion. Rufus's suicide eventually brings the other characters together into communication and understanding. Elizabeth's isolation after Richard's death draws her to Florence, also isolated and unpopular, even despised, like many strong, self-sufficient blacks. Thus, Elizabeth and Florence become lasting, lifelong friends: "Elizabeth thought that she [Florence] must have once been very rich and lost her money; and she felt for her, as one fallen woman for another, a certain kinship" (*Go Tell It* 177).

Sonny, of "Sonny's Blues," is another desperate young black man, but he has learned to cope, on some levels, with the pain and the anguish. He has a deeper self-knowledge than Rufus or Richard because he has not internalized the world's view of him. Granted, he is a junkie and an ex-convict, but he also has his music, and it gives him hope and energy. More importantly, he has something inside himself, a sense of survival, a spiritual strength, or perhaps just plain stubbornness. Sonny has maintained his human dignity; he has struggled to define himself and not rely on exterior definitions. He explains to his brother: "[T]here's no way not to suffer. But you try all kinds of ways to keep from drowning in it, to keep on top of it, and to make it seem—well, like you. Like you did something, all right, and now you're suffering for it. . . . [W]hy do people suffer? Maybe it's better to do something to give it a reason, *any* reason" (*Going* 115). A moment later, he continues: "You walk these streets, black and funky and cold, and there's not really a living ass to talk to, and there's nothing shaking, and there's no way of getting it out—that storm inside. You can't talk it out and you can't make love with it, and when you finally try to get with it and play it, you realize nobody's listening. So you've got to listen. You got to find a way to listen" (115). Through Sonny, Baldwin's own prophetic voice is heard—a cautionary Witness.

Baldwin's women characters, in sharp contrast to these seemingly doomed men, are "uppity females" willing to face the world and take their chances. As Ida Scott, Rufus's sister in *Another Country*, tells her lover, Vivaldo, "Oh. All you white boys make me sick. You want to find out what's happening, baby, all you got to do is pay your dues!" (277). She does not believe, however, that this reproach applies only to Vivaldo and other white boys: "I know you're not responsible for—for the world. And, listen: I don't blame you for not being willing. I'm not willing, nobody's willing. Nobody's willing to pay their dues" (325). In a conversation with Cass, Ida again warns of the ultimate dangers of socially accepted naiveté: "'What you [white] people don't know,' she said, 'is that life is a bitch, baby. It's the biggest hype going. You don't have any experience in paying your dues and it's going to be rough on you, baby, when the deal goes down. There're lots of back dues to be collected, and I know damn well you haven't got a penny (350). Baldwin uses Ida to call the other characters into account. Her forceful voice, as an extension of his own, has the credibility and authority required to convey the message. She, as a black woman, has seen the world differently than the other characters have:

"*You* don't know, and there's no way in the world for you to find out, what it's like to be a black girl in this world, and the way white men, and black men, too, baby, treat you. You've never decided that the whole world was just one big whorehouse and so the only way for you to make it was to decide to be the biggest, coolest, hardest whore around, and make the world pay you back that way." (347)

The black woman is among the most disenfranchised of Americans, and her sexuality is only one of the treacherous lies that Baldwin confronts. Ida, and her historical sisters and mothers, have paid their dues by virtue, or curse, of their race and gender. Florence, of *Go Tell It on the Mountain*, one of Baldwin's angrier women, discovers at a young age that "all women had been cursed from the cradle; all, in one fashion or another, being given the same cruel destiny, born to suffer the weight of men" (83). And, Juanita, of *Blues for Mister Charlie*, underscores the defiance of a black woman in a white world: "Mama is afraid I'm pregnant. Mama is afraid of so much. I'm not afraid. I hope I'm pregnant. I hope I am! One more illegitimate black baby—that's right, you jive mothers! And I am going to raise my baby to be a man. A *man*, you dig? Oh, let me be pregnant" (94). Baldwin consistently comes to the defense of the black woman in America:

> The black woman has been accused of something I don't think she is guilty of, a certain kind of domination, a certain kind of dominance. She did have to hold the family together, she had to deal with her father, her mother her son, somehow. . . . Her terrible dilemma was to treat a man as a man and protect him from being lynched, which is quite an assignment. And I resent in a way the whole myth against black women, the myth being made about them. They are much more various than that. (qtd. in Binder 196)

He maintains that African American females are given a burden of living well beyond the stereotypical roles of the mammy and the prostitute. Not only must they endure the historical burden, but they must also create new avenues of endeavor. They, like their men folk, must listen to their hearts and their deep, inner selves; they must listen to the world and its demands. Only then can they show the courageous love necessary for change.

The message is clear: The way to survive, to learn about life and one's self, and to start living, begins by listening. Americans must listen to themselves individually and to one another, to brothers and sisters of all colors. The narrator in "Sonny's Blues," Sonny's brother, says of

Sonny's band, "He and his boys up there were keeping it new, at the risk of ruin, destruction, madness, and death, in order to find new ways to make us listen. For, while the tale of how we suffer, and how we are delighted, and how we may triumph is never new, it always must be heard. There isn't any other tale to tell, it's the only light we've got in all this darkness" (*Going* 121).

Baldwin also bears witness to the place of anger, even hatred, in the life experience of his people: "[T]here is not a Negro alive who does not have this rage in his blood—one has the choice, merely, of living with it consciously or surrendering to it (*Price* 133). From Baldwin's perspective, this rage is not the bigot's blind, generalized hatred, but a righteous, cleansing, and empowering hatred for all injustice and evil. Often Baldwin's characters, especially the women, hold on to this anger. They remember it, finding something beyond the pain and horror of existence. After Richard is jailed, Elizabeth, sitting in a coffee shop looking out the window at the street, feels the fear, loneliness, and anger which allow her to continue:

> [F]or the first time in her life she hated it all—the white city, the white world. She could not, that day, think of one decent white person in the whole world. She sat there, and she hoped that one day God, with tortures inconceivable, would grind them utterly into humility, and make them know that black boys and black girls, whom they treated with such condescension, such disdain, and such good humor, had hearts like human beings, too, more human hearts than theirs. (*Go Tell It* 173)

Of course, such hatred is not only the province of female experience, as Leo Proudhammer makes clear: "Because I could love, I realized that I could hate. And I realized that I would feed my hatred, feed it every day and every hour. I would keep it healthy, I would keep it strong, and I would find a use for it one day" (*Tell Me How Long* 241).

In addressing hatred, its causes and what to do with it, Baldwin makes some important distinctions. The hatred that causes lynching is a hatred of humans, of skin color, and of a perception of the "other" that is threatening and must be controlled; this hatred is sinful. Elizabeth and Leo are praying for a new strength and justice, which they have never known. The lynch mob's hatred is blind and violent, void of any human, or humane, consideration: "Hatred, which could destroy so much, never failed to destroy the man who hated and this was an immutable law" (*Price* 145). In contrast, the hatred of African Americans (at least in the world of Baldwin's fiction) serves as a catalyst for change, for their need to perceive of themselves and the world differently. Righteous hatred must always be directed toward the unjust and hostile society. Another striking difference between black hate and white hate is that black hate has a sense of weary resignation about it. White hate, for James Baldwin, pulses with exuberant joy. In the short story "Going to Meet the Man," Baldwin uses the character of Jesse, a young white boy in the deep South, to relate the joyful hatred he despises:

> [Jesse] turned his head a little and saw the field of faces. He watched his mother's face. Her eyes were very bright, her mouth was open: she was more beautiful than he had ever seen her, and more strange. He began to feel a joy he had never felt before. He watched the hanging, gleaming body, the most beautiful and terrible object he had ever seen till then. One of his father's friends reached up and in his hands he held a knife: and Jesse wished that he had been that man. It was a long, bright knife and the sun seemed to catch it, to play with it, to caress it—it was brighter than the fire. And a wave of laughter swept the crowd. (*Going* 216)

In essence, a vital difference exists between these two forms of hatred, and Baldwin labors to clarify this difference. Only with the eradication of bigotry and racial hatred can Americans find any peace or communication among the races and between individuals. Black hate is founded on a hope for the future, a belief that love will eventually prevail; white hate is a product of despair, a longing for an idealized version of the past. Without this difference in perception, Baldwin's black characters would perish. Without anger—strong, energizing, hopeful anger—Baldwin's characters, and American culture, are doomed to violence, hatred, and wholesale spiritual destruction. This pervasive sense of doom—the plague of modern America—goes beyond any individual loss or destruction. It is a universal, communal condition. Baldwin virtually echoes the words of Jeremiah: "Hear, O earth; I am going to bring disaster on this people, the fruit of their schemes, because they have not given heed to my words; and as for my teaching, they have rejected it" (Jer 6:19).

In *Another Country*, Cass says, "This isn't a country at all, it's a collection of football players and Eagle Scouts. Cowards. We think we're happy. We're not. We're doomed" (406). Baldwin, however, does not lay blame, but rather he wants his readers to move beyond any blame or guilt. "I'm not interested in anybody's guilt," he states in "Words of a Native Son" (*Price* 400). "Guilt is a luxury that we can no longer afford. I know you didn't do it, and I didn't do it either, but I am responsible for it because I am a man and a citizen of this country and you are responsible for it, too, for the very same reason" (400). His message is clear: to escape our doom, Americans must think and act with responsibility and maturity. They must heal their deep, potentially fatal wounds by acts of pragmatism, not idealism. Jacques, the jaded, unenthusiastic prophet of *Giovanni's Room*, warns David, the immature narrator, against seeking any soft way out: "Confusion is a luxury which only the very, very young can possibly afford and you are not that young anymore" (57). Baldwin, in a speech at Cambridge University, warns against confusion and denial: "Until the moment comes when we, the Americans, are able to accept the fact that [our] ancestors are both black and white, . . . until this moment comes there is scarcely any hope for the American dream. If the people are denied participation in it, by their very presence they will wreck it. And if that happens it is a very grave moment for the West" (*Price* 407).

Although Baldwin's voice as Doomsayer often permeates his work, the coin of doom has another side. The opposite of debilitating despair is invigorating hope. Love, forgiveness, and commitment can assure hope for changing and improving our nation. "It is the miracle of love, long strong enough to guide or drive one into the great estate of maturity, or, to put it another way, into apprehension and acceptance of one's own identity" (*Price* 389). In much of his writing, Baldwin demonstrates his hope that love can liberate and rejuvenate his characters, race relations in America, and eventually the spirit of this nation. "If the Negro doesn't save this country, then nobody else can. And if I can find another word than Negro it might be closer to what I mean. I don't mean the Negro as a person: I mean the Negro as an experience—a level of experience Americans always deny" (Auchincloss and Lynch 73). In addition, Baldwin believes that black Americans have a higher need and responsibility, a burning obligation: "Black people did not invent the legend of color, but only Black people can destroy it. Blacks being the only people who do not need it" (*Evidence* 99).

Baldwin's genuine concern and fear for the future of America led him to write, often forcefully and articulately, as a Doomsayer. This prompted Horace A. Porter to conclude that Baldwin "moves from the Promethean figure, the man who stole the fire of 'Notes of a Native Son,' the powerful writer of 'The Fire Next Time,' to the embittered and self-indulgent naysayer of *No Name in the Street* and *Evidence of Things Not Seen*" (160). Yet, by so readily dismissing Baldwin's later work, one risks becoming another embittered naysayer. Baldwin's prophetic message is difficult to receive and accept, like a religious message deliv-

ered to a reluctant congregation. Americans are the reluctant congregation to Baldwin's discomforting message. "I have too much faith in people to be hopeless but we are in for some very difficult times. The whole
great power syndrome may be obsolete but nobody knows it yet. The
world is heading for a certain kind of decentralization which I think is
its only hope" (Walker 140).

Indeed, the Prophet has unpleasant messages to convey to his people; that is the difficult position of a prophet. A true prophet, however,
must replace the doom and despair with something else, something
greater, something that will inspire and sustain hope for his people. To
this end, Baldwin articulates a better future based on honesty, love, and
the commitment to move beyond this country's historic bigotry.
Energized by this hope, he courageously expresses his concern and compassion for his people, challenging his listeners to act to prevent destruction, and so fulfills his prophetic role as Agitator. As he puts it, "For,
intellectual activity, according to me, is, and must be, disinterested—the
truth is a two-edged sword—and if one is not willing to be pierced by
that sword, even to the extreme of dying on it, then all of one's intellectual activity is a masturbatory delusion and a wicked and dangerous
fraud" (*Price* 465). This is clearly akin to what Moltmann has in mind
when he calls Christians to work proactively for the coming of God's
kingdom—to be "combatants" not just "onlookers." When viewed
squarely, the injustices of this world provide a "goad to resistance," energizing believers to enter the universal struggle for shalom. Like
Moltmann, Baldwin's vision is eschatological, viewing the eschaton not
so much as apocalyptic but as teleological, not concerned as much with
the catastrophic end of the world, though he surveys that possibility, but
with the "moral and political ideal which human beings can approach by
working unremittingly on themselves and the world" (*Coming of God*
186). Thus, as a prophetic Agitator, Baldwin must stir up his people and
engage them in the struggle for justice, truth, and love. He and his characters are unflinchingly direct: "To act," he says, "is to be committed, to
be committed is to be in danger" (*Price* 336). Baldwin considers this
danger inevitable in order for Americans to attain the redemption that
we so urgently need. Our survival is dependent upon learning to endure
the pain and to persevere. Only by acknowledging our shameful past
and accepting the dangerous present, can we survive and find Salvation
(absolutely with a capital "S"), our salvation from sin and damnation.

As the Agitator, Baldwin often uses his characters to express his own
deep-seated anger and frustration with the injustices and consequences
of racial oppression. For instance, Leo Proudhammer, the narrator of

Tell Me How Long the Train's Been Gone, lashes out against the theological perversions that keep his people down: "And one always felt: maybe they're right. Maybe you are nothing but a nigger, and the life you lead, or the life they make you lead, is the only life you deserve. They say that God said so—and if God said so, then you mean about as much to God as you do to this red-faced, black-haired, fat white man. Fuck God. Fuck you, too, mister" (226). On another occasion, Leo vents his anger over the conduct of the police: "I've often thought if Hitler had had the California police force work for him, he would surely be in business still—not that I am persuaded that he ever retired" (324).

Baldwin's characters, however, also recognize the difficult choices and changes that Americans must face to accept their history and create a decidedly different, more truthful and loving, future. Although Daniel Vivaldo Moore of *Another Country* is often dismissed as a near caricature of the intellectual white liberal, he occasionally articulates hope. After having sex with Eric, Vivaldo tells him about revenge and integrity: "'[Y]ou can begin to *become* admirable, if, when you're hurt, you don't try to pay back.' He looked at Eric and put one hand on the back of Eric's neck. 'Do you know what I mean? Perhaps if you can accept the pain that almost kills you, you can use it, you can become better'" (391). Likewise, Leo Proudhammer states:

> Some moments in a life, and they needn't be very long or seem very important, can make up for so much in that life: can redeem, justify, that pain, that bewilderment, with which one lives, and invest one with the courage not only to endure it, but profit from it; some moments teach one the price of the human connection; if one can live with one's own pain, then one respects the pain of others, and so, briefly, but transcendentally, we can release each other from pain. (*Tell Me How Long* 312)

This pain, in the tradition of the self-denying prophets and saints, can lead to greater understanding of the pain and humanity of others. Appreciating the pain of others can embolden us to move beyond our individual pain to a place of understanding and forgiveness. This place, merely by its nature, requires humility.

The changes that Baldwin sees as essential for personal and national survival require courage and honesty, self-knowledge and self-acceptance. As Eric Jones puts it in *Another Country*, "Maybe I'm crying because I wanted to believe that, somewhere, for some people, life and love are easier—than they were for me, than they are. Maybe it was easier to call myself a faggot and blame my sorrow on that" (337).

Certainly, none of Baldwin's characters has an easy life, but those who accept their feelings and their destinies are the survivors, even if they are scarred and torn. Through her pain and anger, Cass, like Eric, has arrived at a place of sorrow and wisdom, and world-weary humility. She, too, speaks with Baldwin's prophetic voice, warning of the responsibility and vigilance that love demands: It is "[t]errifying that the loss of intimacy with one person results in the freezing over of the world, and the loss of oneself! And terrifying that the terms of love are so rigorous, its checks and liberties so tightly bound together" (*Another* 363).

As Baldwin sees it, once people take responsibility for themselves and their history, they can work to achieve change. Addressing the denial that incapacitates us—and creates monsters—he says, "[I]f the word *integration* means anything, this is what it means; that we, with love, shall force our [white] brothers to see themselves as they are, to cease fleeing from reality and begin to change it" (*Price* 336). By "love," he explains, "I don't mean anything passive. I mean something active, something more like a fire, like the wind, something which can change you. I mean energy. I mean a passionate belief, a passionate knowledge of what a human being can do, and become, what a human being can do to change the world in which he finds himself" (qtd. in Mossman 48). Elaborating further in "The Fire Next Time," Baldwin remarks, "I use the word 'love' here not merely in the personal sense but as a state of being, or a state of grace—not in the infantile American sense of being made happy but in the tough and universal sense of quest and daring and growth" (*Price* 375). Love, therefore, is not merely an emotion, but a somber endeavor, a difficult mission ordained by God. Love that perseveres is the way of salvation, the path to both personal and social redemption.

Baldwin sometimes challenges conventional sexual mores in ways that are sure to put off many conservative Christians, but in doing so, he seems often to be making a larger point. For instance, in *Another Country*, Baldwin contends that his characters must tread a fine line between passivity, which is viewed as femininity or lack of maleness in our culture, and aggression, a more macho American view of masculinity. So, before engaging in sex, Eric tells Vivaldo something about sex between two men: "'[I]f you went to bed with a guy just because he wanted you to, you wouldn't take any responsibility for it; you wouldn't be doing any of the work. He'd do all the work. And the idea of being passive is very attractive to many men, maybe to most men'" (337). This creates a dilemma for the American male and the male characters in *Another Country*, which Baldwin, as Witness, depicts as struggling for a self-definition that is neither demeaning nor violent. All of Baldwin's men, regardless of sexual orientation, must engage in this search. After Eric and Vivaldo have sex, we are told that "Vivaldo seemed to have fallen through a great hole in time, back to his innocence, he felt clear, washed, and empty, waiting to be filled. He stroked the rough hair at the base of Eric's skull, delighted and amazed by the love he felt" (*Another* 386). Vivaldo, the prototypical heterosexual male, symbolically becomes the dark and passive woman to Eric's white, essentially homosexual, male figure. The "innocence" which Vivaldo has briefly experienced with Eric is not to be sustained, for this is not Vivaldo's principal relationship. The love that Vivaldo and Ida share, regardless of its uncertain and volatile nature, proves to be the foundation for the healing and redemption Vivaldo needs.

For Vivaldo Moore and for James Baldwin, innocence is not a desired state. Baldwin regards ignorance and innocence as synonymous. The real love that Baldwin advocates is built upon quest, daring, and growth, and thus requires a loss of innocence. When Ida and Vivaldo are last seen, they have moved into a new and deeper plane of relationship: "[Vivaldo] thought to himself that he had at last got what he wanted, the truth out of Ida, or the true Ida: and he did not know how he was going to live with it" (*Another* 430). A short while later, Ida and Vivaldo hold each other "like two weary children. And it was she who was comforting him. Her long fingers stroked his back, and he began, slowly, with a horrible strangling sound, to weep, for she was stroking his innocence out of him" (431). In Vivaldo's search for truth is a painful loss of naiveté and self-centeredness that is indicative of the complex personal journey he has undertaken in the course of a few days, "and something in him was breaking; he was, briefly and horribly, in a region where there were no definitions of any kind, neither color, nor of male and female. There was only the leap and the rending and the terror and the surrender" (302). After this encounter with Ida, Vivaldo's writer's block is vanquished, and he is able to write deep into the night. He has begun to bridge the gap between his perception of Ida and her true presence. He has begun to see Ida as an individual with a past, not merely as a black (sexual) woman. He has lost his innocence and engaged the truth.

Baldwin would have all Americans acknowledge the shameful and discouraging truth of race relations in the United States. He would have them courageously accept the fault of white America and admit the unspeakable wrongs committed against black America, often in the name of patriotism and religion; and, he would have each American accept the reality of his or her own irrefutable racism. To commit ourselves to a love of daring and growth—a love that dispels our illusions and lies—is the great challenge set before us by this modern prophet of hope. In the words of Sister Margaret Alexander in her final speech, a sort of farewell sermon, in *The Amen Corner*,

> "I'm just finding out what it means to love the Lord. It ain't all in the singing and the shouting. It ain't all in the reading of the Bible. *(She unclenches her fist a little.)* It ain't even—it ain't even—in running all over everybody trying to get to heaven. To love the Lord is to love all his children—all of them, everyone!—and to suffer with them and rejoice with them and never count the cost!" (88)

Baldwin would have us also understand that there are serious obstacles to this vision, deep-seated prejudices, amply supported by "bad theology." The members of Margaret's own congregation—particularly Sister Moore—believe that this statement is clear and definite proof of Margaret's failure as a minister and of her continuing and inevitable decline into sin and damnation. Baldwin persistently censures Sister Moore's type of superficial, judgmental Christianity. In "The Fire Next Time," Baldwin argues,

> It is not too much to say that whoever wishes to become a truly moral human being (and let us not ask whether or not this is possible; I think we must believe that it is possible) must first divorce himself from all the prohibitions, crimes, and hypocrisies of the Christian church. If the concept of God has any validity or any use, it can only be to make us larger, freer, and more loving. If God cannot do this, then it is time we got rid of Him. (*Price* 352)

He can say this because he truly believes that the love Christ modeled was far more expansive and inclusive than the narrow expressions of many who profess to follow him. About Margaret's speech, Baldwin comments, "[A]lthough she has lost everything, she also gains the keys to the kingdom. The kingdom is love, and love is selfless, although only the self can lead one there. She gains herself" (*Amen* xvi). Michael F. Lynch, in "Staying Out of the Temple," states: "As she acknowledges her failings and sins, Margaret emphasizes the universality of Christian love, the absence of which in Baldwin's church prompted his departure" (66). Margaret's son David has learned the transcendent power of Christian love: "In leaving the church, David rejects the shameful practice of his mother and most of the congregation, but not the essence of Christian principles, which inform his implicit theology" (59).

The distinction between religion and religiosity, Christianity and "churchianity," proves to be a driving force in much of Baldwin's work.

He is determined to distinguish hypocritical Christians who claim to be "born again" but live shallow, bigoted lives, from those who look to the love and teachings of Christ to guide their lives and shape their conduct. Like many "backslid" individuals, Baldwin employs Christian symbology and language while he remains ambivalent toward the Christian church as he has experienced it:

> I am also speaking as an ex-minister of the Gospel, and therefore, as one of the born again. I was instructed to feed the hungry, clothe the naked, and visit those in prison. I am far indeed from my youth, and from my father's house, but I have not forgotten these instructions, and I pray upon my soul that I never will. The people who call themselves "born again" today have simply become members of the richest, most exclusive private club in the world, a club that the man from Galilee could not possibly hope—or wish—to enter. (*Price* 654)

Likewise, Baldwin's characters, in their personal spiritual journeys, often remain conflicted toward the church. These postmodern agnostics are weighing Christian virtues and values against the harsh judgments that characterize too many fundamentalist Christians they encounter. Again, Michael Lynch addresses this conflict within Baldwin and within his characters:

> The experiences of John Grimes, David, Margaret, and even Luke Alexander, as well as Baldwin himself, suggest that only the person with the courage to defy the church and become an outsider can hope for a life of spiritual growth and for knowledge of the loving God. In spite of the gloomy prognosis for the church, Baldwin's first two texts convey an optimistic theology centered on following one's calling wherever it leads and serving others and God even in obscure ways that may seem antithetical to salvation. ("Staying" 66–67)

Baldwin is nothing if not courageous, and he calls on all his readers, all his people, indeed, on all America to enlist in the Lord's army by serving one another in love and in truth. His vision is grand: "This is the only nation in the world that can hope to liberate—to begin to liberate—mankind from the strangling idea of the national identity and the tyranny of the territorial dispute" (*Evidence* 125). Speaking first as an African American, but also as an American to Americans, he challenges our national stereotypes and myths, demonstrating their deadly and corrosive effects on American life and culture, reminding us of our own disturbing culpability, but ultimately holding out for the salvation of

America through love and perseverance. He has said that "hope—the hope that we, human beings, can be better than we are—dies hard; perhaps one can no longer live if one allows that hope to die" (*Price* 467). James Baldwin is not about to let that hope die. Though his words are hard, his message deserves deeper consideration. Like Jeremiah of old, James Baldwin is for our times a prophet of hope.

Chapter 11

Reconciliation and Hope
Confessional Narratives in South Africa

Susan VanZanten Gallagher

Our capacity to imagine a future is, in large part, dependent on an ability to confess, for in confession we construct a narrative of responsible community that is capable of instilling hope. Perhaps this is why as a society we are so obsessed with confession, from the sleazy confessions of movie stars and politicians, to the dramatic revelations of political parties and government agencies, to the carefully timed admissions of athletes who wish to enter the Baseball Hall of Fame despite a history of gambling. The West, wrote Michel Foucault in 1978, is "a singularly confessing society. The confession has spread its effects far and wide. It plays a part in justice, medicine, education, family relationships, and love relations, in the most ordinary affairs of everyday life, and in the most solemn rites: one confesses one's crimes, one's sins, one's thoughts and desires, one's illnesses and troubles . . . " (1:59). Today we even have "DailyConfession.com," which describes itself as "the world's Largest OnLine Confessional . . . the only place in the world that you can go to truly confess your sin (or sins), your transgressions, your humanity, in complete anonymity." Such thirst for confession is yet another manifestation of our common "unslaked craving for transcendence" (Delbanco 114), our human longing for hope. Similar longings pervade James Baldwin's prophetic "Witness" in the previous chapter, as well as the personal autobiographical narratives of Gloria Anzaldúa, bell hooks, and Roberta Bondi in chapter 3. Such desires also lie behind the remarkable confessional discourse that has occurred in South Africa during the past ten years.

In the Hebraic-Christian tradition, the word *confession* refers to two complementary acts: "testimony"—as in a confession of faith—and "admission"—as in a confession of sin. Early liturgical practices of confession evolved into what I call "the confessional mode in literature," in a manner similar to the way Greek religious rituals that were first embodied in the formal genres of Greek drama (such as the classical tragedy) developed into more general literary modes (such as the tragic). In the confessional mode, a speaker both testifies to and admits guilt about life events in such a way as to construct, or reconstruct, a "self." A confession is ontological: "It is personal history that seeks to communicate or express the essential nature, the truth, of the self" (F. Hart 227). As a personal history, confession takes the form of a narrative rather than a set of propositional truths. Typically, the confessional mode marks a move from silence to speech, even as the silence of the confessional stall is broken by the words, "Father, forgive me, for I have sinned." In confessional writing, that silence has been imposed by some power that is rejected or reversed by the confessional articulation. The self that had been denied speech reconstitutes itself through speech and thus constructs a story by which to navigate life.

As testimony, the confessional mode includes factual information. But it goes beyond a mere documentary presentation of these facts. With both religious and legal connotations, testimony rhetorically calls for action in a way that simple information does not. Shoshana Felman, speaking of Holocaust memoirs, says, "To bear witness is to take responsibility for truth: to speak, implicitly, from within the legal pledge and the juridical imperative of the witness's oath. . . . To testify is thus not merely to narrate but to commit to oneself, and to commit the narrative to others" (Felman and Laub 204). The term implies moral obligation, ethical responsibility, and larger legal, social, or religious consequences.

Furthermore, confession is directed toward a specific audience, or community, which the speaker needs for existence and affirmation. As Terrence Doody states, "A confession is the deliberate, self-conscious attempt of an individual to explain his nature to the audience who represents the kind of community he needs to exist in and to confirm him. Confession is always an act of community" (4–5). Often this communal dimension involves a degree of mediation, as a facilitator—the confessor—prompts or assists in the confession. The confessional mode consciously directs itself toward an identifiable audience and has a particular motivation for doing so; it is not the introspective self-examination found in a private journal or the ego gratification of an anonymous posting at DailyConfession.com. The audience hears the testimony, attends to the guilt, and incorporates the confessant back into itself, re-affirming the posited identity. True confessions are thus both communicative speech-acts as well as performative speech-acts.

For a variety of reasons, discussed more extensively in my *Truth and Reconciliation: The Confessional Mode in South African Literature* (2002), the literature produced in South Africa during the past sixty years often has been in the confessional mode. In this essay, however, I want to consider briefly the way in which South African narratives emerging since the collapse of the apartheid system have employed the symbolic structure and rhetoric of the confessional narrative to articulate hope. Since 1994, the adoption of a new Constitution and Bill of Human Rights has redefined what it means to be a South African. Former "non-Europeans" are now citizens. Those of European ancestry are no longer in the political majority. In legal terms, South Africans are now defined as unique individuals belonging to groups rather than as anonymous and similar members of groups. Although political documents establish the contours of this new identity, the idea of being a South African still needs to be inhabited and enacted; it needs a story, or narrative.

Political violence, such as that previously exercised by the apartheid system for almost fifty years, attempts "to destroy the narratives that sustain people's identities and substitute narratives of its own," according to theologian Robert J. Schreiter (34). "The narrative of the lie" must be overcome. The first step is testimony. "We begin," Schreiter explains, "by acknowledging the violence that is being done to us, and we cry out in protest and lament against it. Silence is the friend of oppression and crying out names the perpetrator of the violence. . . . Crying out gives voice to our pain and calls others to our side, to help us be restored to the larger social network" (36–37). After testimony and lamentation, new narratives need to be told. Schreiter warns that

> the reconstruction of memory, however, is not simply a retrieval of memory. That old memory becomes so associated with violence

> that it becomes too painful to evoke. What must be done to over-
> come this suffering is to disengage the older memory from those
> acts of violence. That is done by repeating the narrative of the vio-
> lence over and over again to ease the burden of trauma that it car-
> ries. Such an activity begins to put a boundary around the violence,
> as it were, to separate it from the memory. (38)

Repeated public recitations of the former violence facilitate reconstruc-
tion by creating the necessary boundaries.

The confessional discourse of the South African Truth and
Reconciliation Commission (TRC) is one way in which a new South
African identity—a new national narrative—has been constructed.
Created by the National Unity and Reconciliation Act, the TRC was
established to facilitate national reconciliation by establishing a public
record of human rights violations. During the first stage of its work,
from the spring of 1996 through 1997, victims recounted their stories at
hearings held in packed courtrooms, city halls, and community centers
across South Africa. Later, the Amnesty Committee began evaluating
amnesty applications, which it had the legal authority to grant if the perpetrator submitted a full confession and demonstrated that the violations were committed in pursuit of political objectives. The TRC
process was designed to write a communal narrative by weaving together
numerous individual stories: those of victims, perpetrators, politicians,
the media, the medical establishment, the business community, the
political parties, and the church. In essence, it would construct a new
story of what it meant to be a South African.

Faced with the massive human rights abuses committed during
apartheid and the compromises necessary for a negotiated settlement,
South Africa established the TRC process rather than pursue legal pros-
ecutions along the lines of the Nuremberg trials. Harvard Law professor
Martha Minow notes that such a choice elevates a therapeutic goal over
a legal goal, working toward healing rather than justice:

> [T]he working hypothesis is that testimony of victims and perpe-
> trators, offered publicly to a truth commission, affords opportuni-
> ties for individuals and the nation as a whole to heal. With the aim
> of producing a fair and thorough account of the atrocities, a truth
> commission proceeds on the assumption that it helps individuals
> to tell their stories and to have them acknowledged officially. Also
> assumed here is the premise that a final report can create a frame-
> work for the nation to deal with its past. Echoing the assumptions
> of psychotherapy, religious confession, and journalistic muckrak-

ing, truth commissions presume that telling and hearing truth is
healing. (61)

The parliamentary act that established the TRC demonstrates these principles in its declaration: "there is a need for understanding but not for
vengeance, a need for reparation but not for retaliation . . ." (Truth and
Reconciliation Web site). Choosing truth and reconciliation instead of
justice, the TRC instituted a massive, communal, confessional narrative.

One significant way in which the TRC differed from previous truth
commissions was in the fact that its hearings were public events, open to
anyone who wished to attend, endlessly discussed in public forums and
updated on an official Website. Each Sunday evening during the hearings, a popular weekly wrap-up appeared on television, and the South
African Broadcasting Company aired reports in eleven languages over
national radio. The unprecedented procedure gripped the imagination
of South Africa as well as the international media. A few South Africans
grew tired of the country's obsession with the TRC (one writer notoriously complained about having to mix "breakfast and blood" in the
mornings), but others were appalled by the extent of the corruption that
was revealed. Many black South Africans found the lamentations given
voice by the TRC an important part of claiming a new identity. South
African Constitutional Court Judge Richard J. Goldstone reported, "I
have not heard a black South African complain that the Truth and
Reconciliation Commission has gone on too long or suggest that it
should come to a premature end" (xii). From silence to storytelling—the
confessional discourse of the TRC, through both the testimony of victims and the admissions of perpetrators, tried to create a new community of shared humanity.

Over a two-year period, approximately 20,000 South Africans
spoke before the TRC about their experiences of apartheid, abuse, torture, and murder. As confessional discourse, the victims' stories centered
on testimony and lament, although occasional admissions of guilt also
emerged. Their narratives were rambling, repetitive, and sometimes
almost incomprehensible, not tightly constructed legal arguments.
Peripheral stories caused distracting diversions from the primary narrative, as with one woman who insisted on describing in great detail—to
the delight of her audience—the strange way her dog shook as her husband died. Important factual details, necessary for further judicial proceedings, were often omitted until elicited by a commissioner's question.
As their testimony became public, some victims experienced a degree of
healing. Lucas Baba Sikwepere, who was blinded by an apartheid-era

police officer, told the Truth Commission: "I feel what has been making me sick all the time is the fact that I couldn't tell my story. But now I— it feels like I got my sight back by coming here and telling you the story" (Krog 43).

The confessions of perpetrators, on the other hand, involved both testimony and admission. Warrant Officer Paul van Vuuren, a member of the Vlakplaas 5, a notorious government hit squad that committed over forty murders, also experienced a change in identity as a result of his testimony: "It is not easy to sit in this chair. You expose your soul to the nation of South Africa, white and black. And they look at me and they think I am a monster . . . for sure I can feel it" (Krog 117). Some perpetrators, such as one of the murderers of American Fulbright exchange student Amy Biehl, repeatedly admitted their sorrow and asked for forgiveness. Others are struck with the futility of such acts of contrition; van Vuuren told a journalist, "You know, you say you're sorry, but on the other hand, it is also empty words. . . . Do you understand what I am trying to say? I mean here I walk up to a person I don't even know . . . and I say, 'Listen here, I'm sorry,' I mean isn't it just empty words?" (Krog 117). Nowhere are the moral struggles of perpetrators as bleakly portrayed as in *A Human Being Died That Night*, in which psychologist Pumla Gobodo-Madikizela recounts her conversations with the imprisoned Eugene de Kock, the notorious commanding officer of a government-sponsored death squad. Gobodo-Madikizela notes, "Much as some perpetrators might try to ask forgiveness, receiving it is unsettling for them. If they have hearts to feel remorse, how can their hearts allow them to forget?" (45).

Ultimately, however, the national narrative impact of the TRC is more important than the resolution of these individual stories. Even though admissions of wrongdoing may be made without asking for forgiveness, such testimony is a vital contribution to the construction of a national narrative that includes new standards of morality. Minow explains, "A truth commission is charged to produce a public report that recounts the facts gathered, and [to] render moral assessment. It casts its findings and conclusions not in terms of individual blame but instead in terms of what was wrong and never justifiable" (78). The cumulative effect of the hearings, then, was to produce a new national narrative in which oppression is outlawed, human rights will flourish, and democratic civil values will emerge. As Gobodo-Madikizela notes, "The question is no longer *whether* victims can forgive 'evildoers' but whether we—our symbols, language, and politics, our legal, media, and academic institutions—are creating the conditions that encourage alternatives to revenge" (118). South Africa's hope for the future lies in the development of such alternatives.

The crafting of the new South African story has not been without its critics. When the commission began its work, an extended legal battle was waged over its power to grant amnesties. Relatives and friends of several of the victims, including the family of murdered black activist Steve Biko, refused to participate and attempted to stop the process. International human rights advocates, including the Human Rights Watch, also opposed the granting of amnesties as a travesty of justice. Both the National Party and the Inkatha Freedom Party were slow to endorse the TRC, arguing that the process would lead to a witch hunt in which African National Congress (ANC) abuses would be overlooked. Others suggested that publicly rehearsing the grim details of the past would lead to more violence and hatred, work against reconciliation, and revictimize the victims. Former ANC President P. W. Botha refused to appear before the commission and was charged with contempt of court.

Other controversies arose because of the unmistakable religious roots and elements of the TRC process. Nowhere was this more apparent than in the choice of the charismatic former Anglican Archbishop Desmond Tutu as the commission chair, propelling him into the role of chief national confessor. Some questioned imposing the particularly Christian paradigm of confession, reconciliation, and forgiveness upon a process that should be secular. For example, one South African professor complained about the way that "religious style and symbolism supplanted political and human rights concerns" (qtd. in Minow 55). Several South African academics with whom I have spoken have criticized the "religious cooption" of the process. A day at the Truth Commission does contain much religious symbolism and rhetoric, but for the most part that arises spontaneously from the victims.

In the summer of 1996, I attended a Human Rights Abuse hearing held in the historic town of Pietermaritzburg, Natal, a site of ongoing violence between the ANC and the Inkatha Freedom Party. The hearing was held in an ornate red-brick, Victorian city hall. Bright television camera lights flooded a raised platform with three long tables covered in white linen. To the left were two crude wooden booths for the translators, who provided simultaneous translations into both Zulu and English. The proceedings opened with a prayer, recited in Zulu by a commissioner, who was a Methodist church leader, followed by the solemn lighting of a white candle symbolizing the presence of truth (much like the candle lit in many Christian church services representing the presence of Christ). Next, we were asked to rise out of respect for the victims, as they filed into the front rows of the hall. As victims testified, they were often flanked by family members and were always accompanied by a psychotherapist. Most of the testimony and questioning occurred in Zulu, simultaneously translated into English. After a witness was sworn in, a commissioner would begin by asking about his or her family. Besides putting the victim at ease, this ritual grounded or located the victim as a person in the fullest African sense—with a family, a community, a place. Then the story was told.

The narratives were overwhelming: intimidation, assault, abduction, disappearances, rape, torture, murder. The commissioners briefly asked questions at the conclusion of each story, attempting to elicit the names of corroborating witnesses, as well as asking what kind of reparation the victim was requesting. Finally, a commissioner responded formally, summing up the story that had been told, thanking the witness, and declaring that an evil had occurred. "We have a system that needs overhauling, a system that needs to reearn your trust," one commissioner said in thanks to a witness. "Testimony such as yours will assist in the process of creating a just system." "May the Lord help you through these hardships," concluded another. The serious listening, the tone of caregiving, and the sense of safety instilled by these rituals all served to "reestablish . . . a moral framework in which wrongs are correctly named and condemned" (Minow 71).

With only a few exceptions, most victims I heard testify during two days in Pietermaritzburg understood their lives as part of the Christian story and described suffering and endurance in Christian terms. Biblical citations, references to impassioned prayer, narrow escapes attributed to God's miraculous intervention were common. "When I think of the things that have happened," one matronly woman said with great dignity, "I just open the Bible and pray Psalm 71." Another woman, accompanied by her son, who sat during her entire testimony with closed eyes seeping tears, told about her husband who was gunned down when he opened the door to their home. As he lay in the hallway, bleeding to death, he asked for his rosary. Such stories are not surprising when we remember that over 80 percent of the black population is Christian. The formal, almost liturgical, tone of the proceedings provided the necessary ritual to mark a time of transition, and the Christian resonances added an even deeper significance for these victims.

While the TRC process relies on the psychological, social, and rhetorical efficacy of religious confession, it differs from religious confession in one significant aspect: it does not require either personal contrition or personal forgiveness. Although Bishop Tutu's infectious advocacy of Christian forgiveness and moral commitments of the victims themselves inspired them to embrace perpetrators in almost transcendental acts of forgiveness, others have found themselves unable to forgive, and the process did not require it. One woman, whose son was killed and set on fire, refused to forgive the perpetrator, commenting, "It is easy for Mandela and Tutu to forgive . . . they lead vindicated lives. In my life, nothing, not a single thing, has changed since my son was burnt by barbarians . . . nothing. Therefore I cannot forgive" (Krog 142). Similarly, perpetrators are not required to demonstrate contrition or ask for forgiveness in order to be given amnesty. South Africa's judicial confessional discourse often does become religious, when contrition and grace are freely offered and accepted, but it is not necessarily so.

Minow suggests that the confessional discourse produced by the TRC process steers a middle course between vengeance and forgiveness, declining to punish but also refusing to forget. Any discourse that takes such a middle way is a discourse without closure, she continues, "it is imperative for people to render as truthful an account as documents and testimonials will allow, *without giving in to the temptations of closure,* because that would avoid what remains inevitably indeterminate, elusive, and inexplicable about collective horrors" (24). Language heals but also fails. Listen to the struggle in the words of one witness: "This inside me . . . fights my tongue. It is . . . unshareable. It destroys . . . words. Before he was blown up, they cut off his hands so he could not be fingerprinted . . . So how do I say this?—this terrible . . . I want his hands back" (Krog 39). A victim that I heard in Pietermaritzburg simply announced, "Some parts cannot be said." Even partial accounts, however, are valuable. Notice the way in which the appalling details of an almost unbearable story nonetheless provide some comfort to one mother: "Sonnyboy was already dead. He [the perpetrator] was holding him by his legs like a dog. I saw him digging a hole, scraping Sonnyboy's brains into that hole, and closing it with his boot. The sun was bright   . . . but it went dark when I saw him lying there. It's an everlasting pain. It will stop never in my heart. It always comes back. It eats me apart. Sonnyboy, rest well, my child. I've translated you from the dead" (Krog 40). This mother will always mourn, but she believes that the public account of her son's brutal death has in some way brought rest to her child. In Pietermaritzburg, one commissioner told an anguished witness, "When you are telling people your pain, you leave part of it with them. We will take part of your pain with us." Confessional testimony allows lament and facilitates healing, but still remains incomplete. The truth that has been uncovered is complex, ambiguous, and, at times, contradictory. A narrative truth rather than a propositional one, it resists closure.

This public drama of confession has inspired many literary works employing the confessional mode. The activities of the TRC have proved fertile ground for fiction, drama, visual art, and memoirs. One of South Africa's most famous satirists, Pieter-Dirk Uys, has a one-man show in which he plays a brassy, overdressed woman named Evita Bezuidenhout, somewhat in the style of Flip Wilson's "Geraldine." In 1995–1996, he sent Evita to the Truth Commission in a hilarious, popular production called *Truth Omissions*. In stark contrast is *The Story I Am about to Tell*, a play in which three victims played themselves, reciting the words of their testimony on stage, repeating their stories of imprisonment, rape, and murder. Another dramatic response was the play *Ubu and Truth Commission*, which also used testimony, but has the victims portrayed by puppets, with speaking manipulators next to them, visibly delivering lines based on the testimonial record. Author Jane Taylor explains, "Puppets . . . declare that they are being 'spoken through.' They thus very poignantly and compellingly capture complex relations of testimony, translation and documentation apparent in the processes of the Commission itself" (vii). As every gesture of the puppet becomes a metaphor, so the individual story of each victim becomes representative of many other victims and segments of society, contributing to the new national narrative.

One of the most powerful literary responses is Antjie Krog's highly confessional book, *Country of My Skull* (1998). Krog, a respected Afrikaans poet, covered the TRC proceedings for SABC radio, and she has produced a remarkable text concerning this experience. *Country of My Skull* does not provide a straightforward historical account of the TRC process. Rather, it is constructed as a sprawling verbal collage of genres and voices. Reading *Country of My Skull* is more emotional than cognitive, recreating some of the feelings experienced by an Afrikaner glimpsing some of the horror of the apartheid past. Extensive passages of testimony directly quoted from both victims and perpetrators are interspersed with descriptions of unfolding events, personal reflections, political analysis, and social commentary. Krog also includes fragments of poems, letters, and newspaper stories. Her text includes the nitty-gritty details of covering the TRC hearings: translation problems, security issues, quarrels about seating arrangements, and scrambling to file a story on a deadline. It also reveals the incongruities: by day Krog listens to stories of the most unbelievable vileness, and at night she helps her children with their homework.

Many of the grim depositions of victims poured out before the Truth Commission are once again brought into the public sphere in Krog's text. These stories appear now as literary testimony, reinforcing their earlier status as legal testimony. Some of these very same accounts also are used in Jane Taylor's *Ubu and the Truth Commission* (for which Krog received research credit). These stories, along with those I heard in Pietermaritzburg, are being repeated again in this essay. Such performed repetitions may be seen as attempts to inscribe boundaries around violence and turn it into a "new narrative," in Schreiter's terms. Repetition both ritually inscribes the testimony and simultaneously mediates it. There are multiple layers of mediation. The mechanical transcription into typographical signs printed on the page in ink distances the testimony from the faltering, strained, impassioned voices that originally spoke. Yet even in the original moment, mediation occurred through the voices of the translators. While these multiple levels of translation mean that such confessional testimony will never be pure, unmediated, or authentic, neither is identity, which always is found in community, in relationship. In South Africa, to alter a well-worn saying, "it takes a village to tell a story."

Perhaps the most striking aspect of *Country of My Skull*, however, is how Krog moves beyond the disturbing docudrama of the hearings to her own internal drama. The book is not only about Krog's country, but also about her skull, her innermost being. When Krog begins covering the activities of the TRC, she is skeptical about the process—its inability to achieve justice, to elicit confessions from high officials, to achieve significant reparations, to escape political entanglements. She—like many of us—longs to assign clear culpability, to name "the guilty party." Horrified by the stream of atrocities retold by the victims in the first months of the hearings, Krog anticipates listening to the accounts of the perpetrators, hoping that they will reveal how one human being could do such things to another. "When the amnesty hearing begins,' she writes, "I go sit in a bench close to them. To look for signs—their hands, their fingernails, in their eyes, on their lips—signs that these are the faces of killers, of the Other. For future reference: the Face of Evil" (114). She interviews each member of the Vlakplaas 5. "I want to know," she writes, "whether they are deranged freaks, murderers who committed crimes in the name of the government, or whether they are forcing the Afrikaner to confront himself. More to the point—what do I have in common with the men I hate the most?" (116). These men are "the Other" in Krog's universe, yet they also are—perhaps even literally—her family.

When their testimony and interviews establish that they are not monsters but men, Krog ponders,

> What do I do with this? They are as familiar as my brothers, cousins, and school friends. Between us all distance is erased. Was there perhaps never a distance except the one I have built up with great effort within myself over the years? . . . In some way or another, all Afrikaners are related. . . . From the accents, I can guess where they buy their clothes, where they go on holiday, what car they drive, what music they listen to. What I have in common with them is a culture—and part of that culture over decades hatched the abominations for which they are responsible.
>
> In a sense, it is not these men but a culture that is asking for amnesty. (121)

As a prominent figure in that culture, due both to her family connections and to her celebrated poetry, Krog finds herself at fault despite her previous political opposition to apartheid. Her confession of the complicity of cultural identity is made simply in her dedication of her book—"For every victim / who had an Afrikaner surname on her lips." That admission gains more emotional urgency in subsequent entreaties: "[H]undreds of Afrikaners are walking this road—on their own with their own fears and shame and guilt. And some say it; most just live it. We are so utterly sorry. We are deeply ashamed and gripped with remorse. But hear us, we are from here. We will live it right—here—with you, for you" (125). *Country of My Skull* concludes with a poetic litany in which Krog confeses her own complicity in apartheid and openly seeks forgiveness from those she has wronged.

Speaking to all who make up the new South Africa, but especially to those who suffered under the words and hands of Afrikaners, Krog defines the new Afrikaner as someone who will live with people from various cultural backgrounds in the geographical space called "South Africa." Her voice is both strikingly personal but also representative, employing both the "I" and the "we."

The personal, however, dominates another part of her confession. One of the most controversial aspects of *Country of My Skull* is Krog's account of confessing an extramarital affair to her husband. The controversy arises because the entire episode is fictional, an imaginary conversation with symbolic resonances. When Krog offers philosophical explanations of forgiveness and truth, her husband responds, "Stop talking crap" (261). He employs emotional rather than theoretical language: "I need to know everything. I need detail. I need to churn it over and over in my mind until it stops hurting and humiliating me. I need to have language for it in order to pack it neatly away. I want the truth. Who, where, when, and how" (261). When she questions whether any narrative can be true, given every speaker's intentions to frame a story in a certain way, he retorts, "Rubbish. There is always a basic truth: you cheated on me. Why? Where? How? From when to when—all of that is negotiable with the things I already know. So the more I know, the more you will confess. What truth I don't know, you will never tell me. More pertinent: when I know the full truth, will I be able to share a space with you?" (262). Fabricated in order to explore confessional discourse in another, extremely personal, venue, this episode succinctly summarizes many of the contending opinions and feelings about the confessional aspect of the Truth and Reconciliation process, down to the final question of whether a particular physical space can be shared.

Debating the possibility of accessing truth in a fictional dialogue inserted into a text presented as a journalistic account is ironic, to say the least. Krog admittedly employs such fictions at several points, admitting near the end, "I have told many lies in this book about the truth" (368). Such rhetorical strategies, refusing to differentiate between true and false, fact and fiction, have dismayed some readers, who see Krog's postmodern perspectivalism concerning the nature of truth at odds with the Truth and Reconciliation Commission's philosophy, which privileges truth. In fact, some claim, Krog's postmodern disbelief echoes the overtly political cynicism of the National Party (Braude). For if we all see truth differently, who is to condemn apartheid?

To some degree, Krog does appear to be a good postmodern in her approach to the question of truth. She admits, "The word 'truth' makes me uncomfortable," and finds it difficult to say on her radio broadcasts: "Your voice tightens up when you approach the word 'truth,'" her technical assistant tells her. "Repeat it twenty times so that you become familiar with it. . . . (Truth is your job, after all!) I hesitate at the word; I am not used to using it. Even when I type it, it ends up as either *turth* or *trth*." She adds a telling admission: "I have never bedded that word in a poem" (50).

At two points, Krog includes long excerpts from TRC testimony followed by a lengthy formal analysis of each narrative. Her analysis demonstrates how telling a story is never a neutral activity: one chooses a particular order; one selects certain details to highlight, emphasize, or repeat; one draws on personal experiences and contexts. Yet in comparing two differing accounts about a particular murder, two perpetrators' "versions of truth," Krog admits. "Either Hechter or Mamasela killed Irene Mutase. The truth does not lie in between. There cannot be a compromise between the two versions. Is the truth known only to the dead?" (112). We might think that Hechter and Mamasela know the truth, but even those who have committed horrendous acts, a psychiatrist tells Krog, can reconstruct their memory—either deliberately or involuntarily as a result of trauma or stress. Nonetheless, although perspective can influence how a narrative is told, the language in which it is couched, even the moral judgments that one makes, someone killed Irene Mutase. The physical fact of her death remains.

As is typical of confession, then, Krog's account does not attempt to reach closure. Rather, she affirms the value of the experience of telling; the experience of confessing leads to new personal and corporate identities. Krog believes that the Truth Commission will produce another "version of the truth," but it is a version that has not been told before and that—in its very telling—will reshape South Africa (112). While white South Africans can still deny their own responsibility, they can no longer deny that atrocities occurred. These are modest ambitions for confession, as Krog admits, "The absolution one has given up on, the hope for a catharsis, the ideal of reconciliation, the dream of a powerful reparation policy. . . . Maybe this is all that is important—that I and my child know Vlakplaas and Mamasela. That we know what happened there" (172). The TRC process has succeeded by creating what one philosopher calls an "archive of atrocity" (Herwitz 31).

The limits of such truth not withstanding, Krog sees hope in what she calls "the birth of a new language" for South Africa. This new language draws on the resources of the Christian tradition and rhetoric of confession. From the beginning of the process, Krog notes, Bishop Tutu "unambiguously mantled the commission in Christian language," despite the opposition of some of the commissioners (202). And his language and vision worked. Krog continues:

> The process is unthinkable without Tutu. Impossible. Whatever role others might play, it is Tutu who is the compass. He guides us in several ways, the most important of which is language. It is he who finds language for what is happening. And it is not the language of statements, news reports, and submissions. It is language that shoots up like fire—wrought from a vision of where we must go and from a grip on where we are now. And it is this language that drags people along with the process. (201)

Language shooting up like fire—it occurs in the stories of both the victims and the perpetrators, in Krog's own personal reflections and those of others, in the new plays, memoirs, and novels of the post-apartheid period. In the fictional, autobiographical, and judicial confessional discourse of South Africa, we find hope for a new identity.

Section Four

Adversity and Grace

All sorrows can be borne if you put them into a story or tell a story about them.

—*Isak Dinesen*

In his book *The Fabric of Hope*, Glenn Tinder contends that because true hope is eschatological, we can expect to see foreshadowings of the "last things" breaking into history, however fragmentary or ephemeral they may be. Yet by just such glimpses, "God carries those who are attentive through the crucifixions inherent in temporal life" (78). While the secularizing forces of modernity have made it difficult to discern such "signposts" or "pointers," as Peter Berger in *A Far Glory* (138–40) calls them, the testimony of Christians through the ages has been that God does indeed signal his presence here and now in this world. "On the other side of a Christian act of belief the world discloses itself as a sacramental world; that is, a world in which the visible reality contains many signs of the invisible presence of God. Christian faith not only affirms that God will not abandon us, but that he has left scattered evidence of that promise in all sorts of places" (Berger, *A Far Glory* 142). Berger refers to "prototypical human gestures" and "certain reiterated acts and experiences," including, we would argue, the act of reading, writing, and telling stories, that "reach out in hope toward transcendence" (*Rumor* 100). To see such gestures as possible "pointers" toward God requires an act of faith, to be sure, and nowhere is such faith tested as severely than in times of great trial, illness, suffering, and death. "Human hope has always asserted itself most intensely in the face of experiences that seemed to spell utter defeat," Berger continues, "most intensely of all in the face of the final defeat of death" (69). The psalmist speaks of a divine presence even then: "Even though I walk through the darkest valley, I fear no evil, for you art with me" (Ps 23:4). When trouble comes, however, faith is always challenged. The essays in this section deal with the challenge of adversity and the evidence of grace.

In the first essay, "Hope in Hard Times: Moments of Epiphany in Illness Narratives," Marilyn Chandler McEntyre examines two nonfictional accounts of illness that are representative of a large and growing literature written by patients, caregivers, and witnesses to life-changing experiences of ill health. Drawing from Anne Hunsaker Hawkins's 1993 study of pathographies, or illness narratives, McEntyre looks at several metaphors in *A Whole New Life* by novelist and poet Reynolds Price, including illness as battle, illness as journey, and illness as symbol of death and rebirth. The "epiphanies of hope" experienced by Price during his diagnosis, treatment, and excruciating recovery from spinal cancer come to him as miraculous gifts, one of the most remarkable being a waking vision of Jesus. Serious illness is always baffling and mysterious, sometimes enraging, and illness narratives are about coming to terms with that bafflement. But with surprising frequency we also find wonderment and hope. While Price records his own story of pain in *A Whole New Life*, neurologist Oliver Sacks uses his considerable literary skills in *The Man Who Mistook His Wife for a Hat* to tell the stories of patients with mental disabilities who are under his care. Both narratives complicate our understanding of hope by revealing how hope comes, how it is sustained, and how it may coexist with a full reckoning of the worst. Having been tried in the fire, writes McEntyre, hope "may emerge not only renewed but utterly reconfigured, . . . caus[ing] us to reframe our expectations radically." Among the insights she offers on hope in hard times, the following speak most eloquently to the theme of this volume: that "hope may be found in story—both plumbing our own stories of suffering, reprieve and recovery, and in understanding our own stories as part of the larger, ongoing story to which we all belong," and that hope is "always an open door, inviting us to walk in trust over a new threshold."

The next essay in this section, "Geographies of Hope: Kathleen Norris and David Lynch," by Kevin Cole, focuses on what may at first seem an unlikely pair of literary works: Kathleen Norris's novel *Dakota: A Spiritual Geography* (1993) and David Lynch's film *The Straight Story* (1998). Cole argues, however, that they are strikingly similar in that each juxtaposes the possibility of hope against the challenging physical and spiritual geographies of the upper Midwest. *Dakota* is a meditation on the relationship between hope and sight—literal sight and metaphorical sight. For Coles, Norris is a seer, a "quiet prophet of the plains," who teaches her readers how to see, read, and interpret the terrain, illustrating that hope comes with understanding (i.e., seeing) the relationship between spiritual and physical landscapes. Even amid the despair of the severest physical and spiritual obstacles, Norris finds reason to hope.

Like *Dakota*, the film *The Straight Story* also focuses on the relationship between literal and metaphorical sight. Lynch's film centers on the true story of Alvin Straight (played by the late Richard Farnsworth) who, in 1994, drove a riding mower with a makeshift trailer 300 miles from Iowa to Wisconsin to reconcile with his estranged brother. Straight drove the mower because, as a result of poor eyesight, he was not allowed a driver's license. The elegant paradox, though, is that Straight's odyssey—"the straight story"—demonstrates that he, more than others around him, was able to see what others could not, which enabled him to share his insight with those he encountered throughout his journey. One of the most poignant in American cinema, the final scene hinges on the pathos of Straight's intensely human gaze into blinding sunlight, which alludes to his extraordinary insight in the face of life's tangled web of love, regret, failure, and hope.

In chapter 14, Michael Herzog's essay "Attunement and Healing in *The Fisher King*" examines Terry Gilliam's adaptation of the ancient myth of the grail to a contemporary setting in his 1991 film *The Fisher King*, demonstrating how attunement with others brings hope and healing both to wounded individuals and suffering society. In the traditional versions of this story the hero saves a wounded king and a dying land by demonstrating compassion. In this rendition, Gilliam elucidates the wounds of both hero and king and shows how they heal each other by sharing one another's experience and learning to love unconditionally. The unlikely friendship between Jack, a cynical shock-talk radio host, and Parry, an idealistic homeless person, projected against modern New York, constitutes an effective reminder that the diseases to which humanity is prey can be healed. The evils that humans themselves produce can be turned to good if they are willing to accept and love one another at a deeply human level. The film relies on a combination of realism and fantasy, evocative music, visual symbolism, and, of course, the power of the grail story, to remind viewers that forgiveness, romance, and sacrifice will always win out over cynicism, greed, and anger, and that hope resides in the faith such stories evoke and require. *The Fisher King* does not end with societal healing on the level of the grail myth, where the wasteland of the wounded king becomes fruitful, but Herzog argues for an "intensely hopeful" ending, nevertheless, in the mutual transformation of the wounded (Jack) and the healer (Parry). Consistent with the theme of this collection, *The Fisher King* refuses to write off compassion and hope as outmoded, sentimental, or romantic notions, but courageously depicts such ideals as not only realistic but necessary to life in our contemporary secular culture. Viewers are left to ponder how such ideals can be practiced without the enabling power of God's love. In the grail myth, Gilliam points toward an answer, the idea that love came into the world in Christ, who first drank from the grail, taking on the suffering of humanity, that we might know love and show love to others.

In chapter 15, which concludes this section, Maire Mullins' essay "The Gift of Grace: Isak Dinesen's *Babette's Feast*" focuses on the relation between hope, grace, and reconciliation. Not unlike the wounded characters discussed in the preceding two essays, Dinesen's "maid-of-all-work," Babette, bears sorrow for the tragic loss of her husband and son, killed during an unsuccessful revolutionary coup in France. Once a famous Parisian chef, Babette now lives in exile in the Norwegian village of Berlevaag, where she works as a maid for two sisters, Martine and Philippa, who, along with other members of the congregation for whom their late father served as pastor, are burdened by the memory of past choices. Mullins traces the path of reconciliation for the sisters, for Babette, and eventually for the entire community. The presence of hope and grace is evident throughout the original story (first published in 1950) and in the film (directed by Gabriel Axel in 1987), which culminates in the transformation that occurs during the sumptuous feast prepared by Babette at the end. Drawing on theological insights from David Tracy's *The Analogical Imagination*, Mullins identifies moments in the story where characters and/or the reader experience the "presence of the uncanny as the presence of a power not one's own" (Tracy 374). This presence is especially strong during Babette's feast, where "theologies of the concrete, the ordinary, the everyday," and the theology of the "proclaimed word" blend into each other (Tracy 381). According to Mullins, the feast embodies and reenacts a moment of grace, gift, and favor that manifests God's presence. Distinctions between Berlevaag and Paris, the sisters and Babette, the past and the present, are erased. The feast brings the community together, allowing characters to reconcile with their past, cementing the bond between the sisters and Babette. Mullins notes that the transforming power of grace can be seen in the effect the feast has on the community, the joy Babette experiences in preparing the meal, and the exquisite unity that takes place between the collective body and soul of those who partake in the feast. Whether fully intended or not, the story taps into mythic images from the recorded life of Christ—the wedding at Cana, the loaves and fishes, the feeding of the five thousand, the institution of the Eucharist—and foreshadows the great banquet, the wedding feast in the *eschaton*, to which all are invited. In this and the other stories considered in this section, we can discern gestures and evidence of God's promised presence, enabling and sustaining hope. For, in the words of Moltmann, "No one can assure us that the worst will not happen. According to all the laws of experience: it will. We can only trust that even the end of the world hides a new beginning if we trust the God who calls into being the things that are not, and out of death creates new life" (*Coming of God* 234).

Chapter 12

Hope in Hard Times
Moments of Epiphany in Illness Narratives

Marilyn Chandler McEntyre

Shortly after undergoing surgery for a malignant spinal tumor in 1984, novelist and poet Reynolds Price found himself one morning lying on the shore of the Sea of Galilee among Jesus' disciples where Jesus himself approached and addressed him. Jesus told him, "Your sins are forgiven," and began to walk away. "I came on behind him," Price writes,

> thinking in standard greedy fashion. It's not my sins I'm worried about. So to Jesus' receding back, I had the gall to say, "Am I also cured?" He turned to face me, no sign of a smile, and finally said two words—"That too." Then he climbed from the water, not looking around. (43)

This account of a waking visionary experience—palpable, vivid, and shockingly real to the writer—is recorded in Price's illness narrative, *A Whole New Life*. The vision, which he describes as having "a concrete visual and tactile reality unlike any sleeping or waking dream I've known or heard of" (44), occurred on the eve of his first searing course of postsurgical radiation therapy, a precarious and dreadful moment in an illness which has left him neurologically impaired, but alive against strong odds.

Most of *A Whole New Life* is a record of felt responses to the long succession of symptoms, diagnoses, prognoses, treatments, reassessments, and more treatments familiar to anyone who has lived close to cancer. Most of it—exquisitely written though it is—is unsensational. But Price does record a few remarkable, life-changing moments, the encounter with Jesus being the most dramatic. One other is an unexpected phone call from a remote acquaintance one morning who, with no introductory word of explanation, announced, "I've called to tell you you are not going to die of this cancer." Then she quoted the words from Psalm 91, "He shall give his angels charge over thee; to keep thee in all thy ways" (64–65). Though he had heard similar words of comfort from other sources, he was suddenly filled with conviction that the woman spoke the truth.

How many of us, watching a friend or loved one struggle with disease, have wished for such dramatic reassurances? How many of us, reading the gospels, have had the thought that just one direct encounter with Jesus might be enough to shore up waning hope in the bleak midwinter of illness or pain? How many of us have wondered why such blessings seem to be distributed so inequitably? Illness is always baffling, mysterious, sometimes enraging. Consequently, illness narratives are usually stories about coming to terms with that bafflement. Sometimes, in the midst of suffering, bafflement turns to wonder.

Not too many illness narratives include encounters with Jesus himself, but surprisingly consistent in them are epiphanies of hope. Even in some that record a steady sinking toward death and experiences of depression or despair, the hope enacted in the writing of the story often surfaces in unexpected ways. I think of Samuel Beckett's darkly comic story, "Malone Dies," where the ray of hope lies in the writing itself: the dying patient's determination to keep writing is his way of choosing life. To say hope is a common feature of illness narratives may stretch the point in some instances; yet having spent the last fifteen years reading them, I continue to be amazed and edified by the manifold ways in which hope, often paradoxically, survives suffering and impending death. Hope, like love, it seems, has a thousand faces. And stories of illness often unveil new dimensions of hope. In the midst of serious illness, those who do not despair seem to learn something about hope.

In order to consider what illness narratives have to teach us about hope in hard times, I have chosen two nonfictional accounts of illness ("pathographies" is the term of choice among medical humanists to describe this genre) that I believe to be fairly representative of a large and growing literature written by patients, caregivers, and witnesses to life-changing experiences of illness. What is consistent in the stories I've chosen—*A Whole New Life* by Reynolds Price and *The Man Who Mistook His Wife for a Hat* by Oliver Sacks—and in many other such narratives, is the way they complicate our understanding of hope: how hope comes, how it is sustained, how it may coexist with a full reckoning of direst possibility. Hope, tried in the fire of life-threatening illness, may emerge not only renewed but utterly reconfigured. Hope is marked, like all biblical precepts, with paradox and puzzlement, and it may cause us to reframe our expectations radically. Eliot's words in *Four Quartets*, "I said to my soul . . . wait without hope / For hope would be hope for the wrong thing" ("East Coker" 23–24), might serve as an epigraph to many of these stories in which renewal of hope has sometimes meant a complete relinquishment of the wishes, desires, and expectations with which the journey of illness began.

We do tend to approach the experience of illness with expectations, many of them culturally conditioned, not all of them medically tenable, and some of them even theologically questionable. We learn from our culture how to be sick, and since the culture itself is not completely healthy, some of what we learn may not serve us well in a crisis.

The idea that illness is socially constructed may sound obnoxiously postmodern, but in fact our norms of health, acceptable treatment, and longevity fluctuate not only with the tides of scientific studies but also according to much more dubious sources of popular wisdom such as magazines and slick ads sponsored by pharmaceutical companies. For readers interested in a fine exploration of the ways in which illness reflects cultural ideas, I recommend Claudine Herzlich and Janine Pierret's *Illness and Self in Society* and Lynn Payer's *Medicine and Culture: Varieties of Treatment in the United States, England, West Germany, and France*, both of which examine the expectations we learn to bring to medical practices and the ways these practices respond to and reinforce conditioned expectations.

Illness narratives—the good ones—often provide correctives to conventional ideas of what to expect and what to hope for. They are similar in this respect to war stories that take the protagonist from idealistic expectations of conquest and glory through profoundly disillusioning and disorienting experiences of combat, to a radically modified understanding of the ways we talk and think about war. Illness narratives have a great deal to teach us about how we talk and think about suffering. Our theology of suffering is often too simplistic, our hopes too sentimental, our decisions too driven by dubious medical conventions. We need the stories of those who have weathered serious illness and those who have imagined it deeply in order to open our hearts to compassion and to challenge us to a strenuous understanding of suffering. First among these may be the book of Job; the biblical narrative as the source of our deepest hope serves also to complicate our understanding of what hope looks like and how it reasserts itself against death and despair. Human stories of suffering continue to find their precedents and roots in biblical stories, which continue to challenge us to understand our own stories more complexly. As Daniel Taylor puts it in *The Healing Power of Stories*, "When our own ability to narrate our story falters, we can lean on the shared story to sustain us" (114). To lean on the foundation stories we share means to take from them knowledge and meaning that apply directly or indirectly to our own lives and suffering.

The conventionalized hopes and expectations we bring with us into illness arise partly from the metaphors we commonly use to describe illness and suffering. In her 1993 study of pathographies, or illness narratives, Anne Hunsaker Hawkins identifies and discusses the most common of these metaphors: illness as a battle, illness as a journey, or illness as a symbolic experience of death and rebirth ("Introduction"). These metaphors can either enable or disable; each provides a way of understanding what is inherently disorienting and disruptive, and each has its limitations. The idea of illness as a battle is certainly the dominant metaphor in American medicine and one which, though it may be invigorating and challenging, can also be inappropriate to kinds of suffering that must be borne, managed, and endured.

The language of the battle occurs throughout Price's *A Whole New Life*, but not uncritically. Just after diagnosis, he recalls "the laughing atmosphere of the X-ray tank gave me a brief whiff of hope that now I'd entered some big joint effort to rescue my spinal cord and legs—the kind of World War II alliance I'd known as a boy, to stop the marauder and reclaim lost ground" (20). He recalls this, however, with a gentle irony that must inevitably accompany words about "victory" over an illness whose course is highly unpredictable and whose outcome is most often a painful and disabling diminishment of powers on the likely way to death. He goes on to testify to deeper experiences of hope that came not always on the crest of a new treatment strategy, but more often in the times when control seemed least possible and medical means least promising—times when, in fact, he was not in fighting mode.

The book chronicles a journey through discouragement pain, false hope, and spurious offers of comfort interspersed with moments of insight that came as gifts—hope appearing in unexpected ways and at odd moments. I would like briefly to consider the accounts he gives of two of those moments when hope emerged, subsequent to the visionary experience already recounted which was to serve him as a reliable, never-doubted point of reference for the long course of his illness and treatment. These epiphanic events are detailed against a background of escalating losses, daily pain management, rituals self-consciously constructed to shore up a shattered life, and the drug-induced mood swings that confused him at the time, but that served as foils to the more authentic experiences of hope that came as astonishing gifts.

There were, of course, sources of more "garden variety" hope—the presence of faithful friends who shored him up in days of very black depression and moments of despair, some who dared to bring laughter into the sick room. Of these friends, Price writes, "I thought I could sense their hope like a firm wind at my back. It felt like the pressure of transmitted courage . . . and that was the thing I needed most now—that and the effort to string a usable line of communication with what I call God" (22).

This simple, lovely description of the "pressure" of the hope of others reminds us that hope, like faith and love, may, mysteriously, be borrowed. Like the abbot who told a young monk who thought he was losing his faith, "Then come worship with mine," Price testifies to what it means to "lean" on the faith and hope of others when one's own have faltered. He speaks humorously of letters he received, even from people he didn't know, that provided sustenance along the way, one from a "strange woman who said that she had 'a whole convent of nuns' praying for me and that 'they get results!'" "Such homely assurance in the midst of a trial," he comments, "can sound like a far-off but usable message, helpful for anywhere from seconds to weeks" (61).

But his hope was sustained more unusually by two other experiences, both encounters with the God in whom he had always trusted, albeit with what he acknowledged to be an unorthodox and "unchurchly" faith. The first of these was a practice he initiated in bed when few activities were available to him, when even periods of reading were too demanding. He began to draw. Drawing, he writes, "had been the main work of my childhood." "I honestly think," he goes on, "that, like all drawing children, I unconsciously shared the aim of the cave art of Cro-Magnon man. If I could truly make a world as nearly like the visible world as human hands and paints could manage, then the world beyond me would do my will or would at least let me pass as I went my way on private missions of hunger and daring" (74).

Price takes this primitive faith in the power of art quite seriously, as, I believe, we should, who believe that such gifts come from the source of all life. Though no image, literary or visual, can control the world it represents, images are a powerful means of putting us in touch with the world Hopkins saw as "charged with the grandeur of God." Think, for instance, of Van Gogh's luminous trees, bursting almost into fire, like matter straining to become pure energy.

After a few days of drawing, Price sketches a likeness of the Jesus he saw in his vision. "As the lines moved down in ink on the paper," he writes, "I knew I was suddenly concentrating for more than ten seconds on something better than the pain that roared all down my spine" (75). The moment of self-abandonment becomes the seed of a deeply significant period in his recovery:

> The fact of regaining just that much on paper triggered the subject of all the dozens of drawings I'd make in the next two years. They were all, every one, meditations on the face of Jesus; and looking back through them now, I can wonder how I narrowed so much of my limited strength and hope for survival down to the space of a sheet of paper with a few brushed lines in search of the face that had driven Western art for more than a thousand years. . . .
> . . . what I was doing in so much time and with such intense effort, I'm still by no means sure I can fathom.
> I do know, however, . . . that the drawings became my main new means of prayer when my earlier means were near exhaustion. By now I'd asked a thousand times for healing, for ease and a longer life. But calamity proceeded, and even the repetition of "Your will be done" had come to sound empty. So the drawings were a sudden better way, an outcry and an offering. If they asked for anything, I suppose it was what I still ask for daily—for life as long as I have work to do, and work as long as I have life. (75–76)

What comes clear in this moving passage is that hope lies in action as well as in attitude—more precisely, that hope can come as a byproduct of action—perhaps any action that involves the wholehearted giving of oneself to the call of the moment. The practice of drawing begun more or less as a conventional diversion from the bleak boredom of the sickroom becomes a spiritual practice of significant healing value, in this case, for two reasons. First, the patient finds within himself and reclaims a defining desire of childhood—to attend to the world as it is given and, see it truly. This desire, which I believe underlies all authentic artistic impulses, orients one toward the created order in a disposition of profound receptivity.

Second, the patient reclaims a childlike curiosity. Like desire, curiosity is a reaching for truth, for clarity, for disclosure, indeed, for revelation. And what is affirmed in Price's experience here is the way the biblical story evokes the curiosity that brings us back and back to it, seeking the face of Christ. Literal as that seeking is here—where the face of Christ is the very material of his seeking—Price's account works powerfully as a parable: it recalls the admonition to become like little children; it reminds us that the Spirit can transform our work to prayer; and it suggests how healing may come in the very midst of pain—not to dispel it, but to suspend it and provide unforeseen relief along the hard way.

A third experience recounted in Price's story completes the triad of spiritual epiphanies that mark his narrative of recovery—full as it otherwise is with more predictable musings on illness and its discontents—as a miracle tale. The simplicity with which he recounts his moments of divine encounter and the skill with which he avoids sensationalizing them, underscore their credibility as entirely possible gifts of grace in the midst of great pain.

The third breakthrough experience comes in the first days after realizing he is losing the use of both legs, "almost surely for good." Up until this time, he has sustained some hope that all his limbs will remain usable, even if diminished in strength and mobility. Realistically, a new prognosis seems to include "paralysis, dependence on others, untouchable pain and the absence of work." He reflects darkly:

> Maybe I'd really been tricked in my "vision." Maybe death or worse was near; quadriplegia now seemed worse than death. Death would solve at least the other quandaries. In that black trough, I remember looking up to the ceiling and addressing what I must have thought was God, the last unchangeable bafflement—"How much more do I take?"
>
> A long silent pause, then a voice at normal speaking strength said the one word "More." Neither male, female nor repellently neuter, but thoroughly real and near at hand. (80)

This word uttered in the night, however one may assess the claim to literal audibility, impels the afflicted man to ask, the next morning, that communion be brought to him. When it is brought, he recalls,

> [I]n the slow eating that one morning, I experienced again the almost overwhelming force which has always felt to me like God's presence. Whether the force would confirm my healing or go on devastating, for the moment I barely cared. No prior taste in my old life had meant as much as this new chance at a washed and clarified view of my fate. . . . In many calmer hours to come, I'd know that my answer to the one word *More* was three words anyhow—*Bring it on.* (81–82)

This is, we must admit, a curiously paradoxical kind of reassurance. Taken at face value, all it consists of is a promise of more suffering. Yet it is exactly the kind of reassurance Jesus gives the disciples when he promises them persecution, suffering, pain, perhaps violent death. They have suffered; there will be more. And he will be there with them.

Price's response once again provides a clear teaching about what it may mean to hope: in his "barely caring" about the outcome, he is given a surprising gift of trust he could not possibly have summoned at will. The "taste" of truth he receives as a "washed and clarified view of my fate" is enough. Even very hard truth can, because it is truth, be empowering.

These remarkable events in the four years of strenuous recovery recounted in *A Whole New Life* all preceded months of escalating pain, a second surgery, and torturous rehabilitation. Price makes it very clear that the pain and darkness of those months were by no means less physically painful or emotionally variegated than anyone else's might be in a similar condition. Yet he lived them with a clear sense of purpose, a memory of guidance that held even in the hardest times. Little in the narrative other than these three stories can be called "religious" in either tone or content. Price's reflections at the end, having survived to return to a full life of teaching and writing, wheelchair bound but fully alive and energized by his work, are modest in their offering of what companionship and encouragement his story might provide to others in hours of suffering. His self-representation is decidedly unheroic. "Even my handwriting," he writes in the conclusion, musing on what in him has changed, "looks very little like the script of the man I was in June of '84. Cranky as it is, it's taller, more legible, with more air and stride. It comes down the arm of a grateful man" (193).

I offer Price's story for the particular clarity with which it illustrates several truths about hope: that hope, and the courage it makes possible, are gifts, not achievements; that hope is separable from common sense—indeed that it relies upon quite uncommon sense; that hope arises within community and can be shared and passed along a current of love as surely as the electricity that lights this room; and that hope is profoundly personal—rooted in the particularities of personal history and disposition, and borne, certainly in this instance, of encounter with a personal God.

In these respects, his story is unusual, but not unique. Exquisitely written, it meets every criterion of good literature, and indeed, in my opinion, exceeds the literary achievement of some of his other work. Finding words for pain, fear, loss, and personal transformation challenges the best wordsmith, and some of the best wordsmiths, Reynolds Price among them, have risen to the challenge.

Another of the growing number of very fine writers who have focused considerable literary gifts on the problem of pain is a man now well known for the "clinical tales" he has produced—one as a patient, most as a doctor. Neurologist Oliver Sacks is probably best known for *The Man Who Mistook His Wife for a Hat,* a collection of superbly told stories of encounters with neurologically impaired patients who had no hope of full recovery. Sacks's basic task as a physician to these patients has been first to imagine their illnesses and secondly to help them determine what might enable them to live with a sense of wholeness and psychosomatic integrity.

Working with patients who by definition will not be "cured" as most of us understand that term, Sacks holds out none of the hope other physicians might who can offer the means of complete recovery. Yet within the harsh terms of incurable disease or dysfunction, he has found remarkable ways of imparting hope of a different kind. His capacity to empower patients seems to come largely from the breadth of his own compassionate curiosity, his ability to empathize, and his inventiveness in reframing what presents itself as a hopeless condition.

Not incidental to these traits are his exceptional literary skills. Sacks's clinical tales are fine stories by any measure—witty, allusive, suspenseful, rich with surprising metaphor and astute characterization. Thus, what he imparts to patients he also, by extension, imparts to readers by inviting them radically to reconsider both the practical challenges of disease and the ways both patient and doctor may find meaning in it.

Sacks's approach to his patients is based on implicit questions he pursues which are not part of the standard medical repertoire: Who are you? What is your story? What does it feel like to be you? What are you compensating for, and how? How is your experience of your condition different from my observations about it? What are your most familiar frames of reference or contexts of action? How have you organized your environment? How can I help you if I can't cure you? What would real "help" look like? This, I believe, is what it means to practice hope: to seek to see each patient in terms of his or her life strategies, desires, and purposes. To practice hope means to believe that each life has meaning and to assume that what one sees as caregiver is always only partial and not necessarily definitive.

Such questions recognize story as the context of meaning and illness as part of a larger story. In telling his patients' stories, Sacks wields his considerable arsenal of literary tools as precisely as he might a scalpel. He often provides a series of verbs or descriptors in a single sentence as a way of probing for the word that will name what he is looking at adequately and precisely. He writes, for instance, about an autistic patient at work on a drawing, "Now, for the first time, he was bold, without hesitation, composed, not distracted. He drew swiftly but minutely, with a clear line, without erasures" (215). He does the same with images, trying different images out in turn to see what each yields in understanding. In both his medical and literary capacities, Sacks's patience and precision are liberating and generative for both patient and reader. He draws us, as well as his patients, into a kind of partnership as fellow seekers of understanding.

The stories collected in *The Man Who Mistook his Wife for a Hat* focus on four different kinds of neurological impairment: "Losses," which details cases of patients who have lost particular brain functions, resulting in distorted perceptions and behavior; "Excesses," which focuses on conditions of excessive affective or neurological response, resulting in compulsive behavior, tics, and outbreaks; "Transports," which has to do with patients who live in what we might describe as dream states or isolated mental worlds; and "The World of the Simple," which focuses on phenomena like autism or the strange genius of the "idiot savant" who is exceptionally gifted in one area and essentially retarded or incapacitated in most all others. Sacks's obvious fascination with his patients is accompanied by respect and even affection for them. His scientific curiosity is informed and shaped by caring that expresses itself in a kind of poesis that departs boldly from professional discourse or even the reportage of popular medicine in its imaginative, speculative, playful reflection on what it must be like to live with a dysfunctional body or mind. He spends a great deal of his time in diagnosis, which is to say, upon the business of naming what he sees, not only assigning a clinical term, but describing and discerning the process. In his book *Stories of Sickness*, physician Howard Brody asserts that "great comfort results when the physician is able to give a name to the complaint—if it has a name, it must have an existence apart from me; so then I can struggle against it" (8). That naming and the struggle that may ensue—or even the accommodation—become, in a sense, shared rituals of hope.

I would like to consider a few of these clinical tales in terms of how Sacks, both as doctor and as writer, discovers avenues of hope in seeking to *heal* what cannot be *cured*. Indeed, distinguishing between these terms may open the first door to hope for those who have thought of incurable as a medical and spiritual dead end.

"Witty Ticcy Ray," as Sacks calls him, was one of the first cases of Tourette's syndrome in his clinical practice. It is a condition, now more generally recognized, thanks to Sacks, which is

> characterized by an excess of nervous energy, and a great production and extravagance of strange motions and notions: tics, jerks, mannerisms, grimaces, noises, curses, involuntary imitations and compulsions of all sorts, with an odd elfin humour and a tendency to antic and outlandish kinds of play. In its "highest" forms, Tourette's syndrome involves every aspect of the affective, the instinctual and the imaginative life; in its "lower" and perhaps commoner, forms, there may be little more than abnormal movements and impulsivity, though even here there is an element of strangeness. (92)

Notice how the passage moves from a simple inventory of symptomatic manifestations to the more poetic description of "elfin" humor and antic play. Throughout his diagnostic and descriptive passages, Sacks borrows language from the discourses of literature, folklore, myth, art, philosophy, and religion. In the act of description itself, he seems always to be reaching for a way of framing what he observes that will reveal new meaning. Indeed, he regards description as an essential part of diagnostic practice: he quotes A. R. Luria, a predecessor and mentor: "The power to describe, which was so common to the great nineteenth-century neurologists and psychiatrists, is almost gone now. . . . It must be revived" (viii). Why is this? Perhaps because careful description involves long looking, and looking again, involving one in a search for the precise word that presses beyond crude categories to fine distinctions that reveal successive layers of subtlety invisible to the less patient eye. Practiced in this way, description itself can become an act of love—even a way of putting on the mind of Christ, who saw beyond the crude behaviors of the damaged human rabble he came to save, to cast out their demons, and to read their hearts.

Consider Sacks's description of Ray recalled from their first encounter:

> When I first saw Ray he was 24 years old, and almost incapacitated by multiple tics of extreme violence coming in volleys every few

seconds. He had been subject to these since the age of four and severely stigmatized by the attention they aroused, though his high intelligence, his wit, his strength of character and sense of reality enabled him to pass successfully through school and college, and to be valued and loved by a few friends and his wife. Since leaving college, however, he had been fired from a dozen jobs—always because of tics, never for incompetence—was continually in crises of one sort and another, usually caused by his impatience, his pugnacity, and his coarse, brilliant "chutzpah" and had found his marriage threatened by involuntary cries of "Fuck!" "Shit!", and so on, which would burst from him at times of sexual excitement. He was (like many Touretters) remarkably musical, and could scarcely have survived—emotionally or economically—had he not been a weekend jazz drummer of real virtuosity, famous for his sudden and wild extemporizations, which would arise from a tic or a compulsive hitting of a drum and would instantly be made the nucleus of a wild and wonderful improvisation, so that the "sudden intruder" would be turned to brilliant advantage. His Tourette's was also of advantage in various games, especially ping-pong, at which he excelled, partly in consequence of his abnormal quickness of reflex and reaction, but especially, again, because of "improvisations," "very sudden, nervous *frivolous* shots" (in his own words), which were so unexpected and startling as to be virtually unanswerable. The only time he was free from tics was in post-coital quiescence or in sleep; or when he swam or sang or worked, evenly and rhythmically, and found "a kinetic melody," a play, which was tension-free, tic-free and free.

Under an ebullient, eruptive, clownish surface, he was a deeply serious man—and a man in despair. (97)

Several features of this description are worth noting for what they reveal about Sacks's own searching gaze. First, consider how much information he includes that might ordinarily be viewed as medically irrelevant. Even discounting the fact that these accounts are reconstructions of the clinical encounter, the wide reach of observations about his patients, the evident interest in personal history, family, emotional life, and even the patient's own language (Sacks frequently quotes what he hears as telling phrases or terms) all suggest a basic assumption that life is whole and that disease should not be viewed apart from a whole life context. Much of his treatment consists of helping patients adapt more effectively to the social and cultural environments they inhabit, so that they might live and move in them more comfortably and freely. In this way he seeks not so much to set them free of the disease itself (since, in this case and many others he treated, not much could be done to effect an actual cure), but of ineffectual and self-defeating strategies of self-protection and of despair.

Second, notice again how Sacks's own language betrays a basic attitude of fascination, even delight in the unusual—a capacity to see debility as the dark side of a possible gift. He comments on Ray's wit, strength of character, and sense of reality as survival skills. He recognizes what has enabled him to be "valued and loved." He sees even in the abrasive, shocking verbal outbreaks a "coarse, brilliant 'chutzpah.'" And in his "wild extemporizations" as a drummer a wonderful capacity for improvisation upon which he had capitalized. One of the words that recurs frequently in this narrative and others is "play." And another is "free." The kind of healing he effects almost invariably has to do with enabling patients to play—to devise strategies of accommodation that often have exactly the wild, brilliant character he here attributes to Ray's improvisations. Not all of his patients, of course, are capable of play. But since Sacks himself is eminently playful, he permits those who can to experiment. Sacks, for instance, devised an attachment for the frame of the glasses worn by a patient whose sense of balance was so far off that he leaned far to one side when he walked. Sacks affixed a carpenter's level to the glasses with a piece of wire as a simple feedback device. Both were pleased with the result. In another case, he put a pen in the hand of a young man locked in a mental institution and dismissed as incompetent, encouraged him to draw, and discovered not only that he was a fine artist but that his drawings communicated vital information about how he saw the world—to a doctor willing to read and interpret it.

This willingness to spend time in the discovery process, allowing patients to experiment and witnessing their efforts, repeatedly reinforces the biblical truth that healing occurs in relationship and indeed involves a kind of intimacy. Both healer and patient become vulnerable in negotiating the terms of change. In the case of Witty Ticcy Ray, Sacks prescribed Haldol, the most effective drug available at the time, but found that it deprived the patient of his habitual means of accommodation:

> Even this minute dose, he said, had thrown him off balance, interfered with his speed, his timing, his preternaturally quick reflexes. Like many Touretters, he was attracted to spinning things, and to revolving doors in particular, which he would dodge in and out of like lightning: he had lost this knack on the Haldol, had mistimed his movements, and had been bashed on the nose. Further, many of his tics, far from disappearing, had simply become slow, and enormously extended: he might get "transfixed in mid-tic" as he put it, and find himself in almost catatonic postures. (98)

Here again, Sacks is unusual in recognizing two things: that a closer approximation to behavior we consider normal may not, in all cases, be the most desirable outcome. Furthermore, how the patient feels about the change is as important to the effectiveness of a treatment as how the doctor understands it. Ray is loath to relinquish some of the benefits of his affliction, and Sacks is willing to acknowledge them as benefits and work toward preserving what Ray has claimed and adjusted to. In this instance, as in many of the other stories, Jesus' important question, "Do you want to be healed?" is implicit and central to the decisions Sacks makes.

Another way of putting the question might be, "What do you hope for?"—a question that might often yield surprising answers if one did not leap too quickly to conventional assumptions about what one should hope for. After trying a medication that helped him normalize his behavior, Ray said "he could not imagine life without Tourette's, nor was he sure he would care for it." "Suppose you could take away the tics," he said. "What would be left? I consist of tics—there is nothing else" (98). Sacks, who sees in his patient a great deal more than his tics, eventually worked out an arrangement with him over three months of "deep and patient exploration" during which "(often against much resistance and spite and lack of faith in self and life) all sorts of healthy and human potentials came to light: potentials which had somehow survived twenty years of severe Tourette's and 'Touretty' life, hidden in the deepest and strongest core of the personality. This deep exploration was exciting and encouraging in itself and gave us, at least, a limited hope" (99). When they try the medication after this period of exploration, it works much more effectively.

Finally, Sacks worked out an agreement with Ray whereby he took medication during the week to help him keep a job and work more effectively with his family, and on weekends went off it to allow himself periods of higher, wilder creative play as a jazz drummer. Sacks describes the subsequent nine years in Ray's life as "happy ones for Ray—a liberation beyond any possible expectation. . . . he enjoys a spaciousness and freedom he would never have thought possible. . . . His marriage is tender and stable . . . he has many good friends, who love and value him as a person—and not simply as an accomplished Tourettic clown" (101). Sacks concludes that Ray has achieved "what Nietzsche liked to call 'The Great Health'—rare humour, valour, and resilience of spirit: despite being, or because he is, afflicted with Tourette's" (101). The shift from "despite" to "because" in the final sentence tells us a lot about the importance of paradox in Sacks's work, both as physician and as writer. In the diseases he sees, wheat and tares grow up together, and conventional diagnostic categories are often inadequate to describe the curious ways human beings build lives around their wounds in processes that articulate strange forms of spiritual beauty. Sacks is unabashed in making beauty, elegance, delight, wit, inventiveness, and uniqueness criteria for medical success. He is never far, in discussing biomedical problems, from some comment upon the life of the spirit.

Sacks's recognition of the power of spiritual orientation becomes most explicit in his story of "The Lost Mariner"—a man who had severe amnesia, and could only live from moment to moment in a state of perpetual disorientation or forgetfulness. With no identity, Sacks wonders in some anguish himself over the question, whether the man has a soul. When he puts the question to the nuns who run the care facility in which his patient is living, they are "outraged," and tell him to watch Jimmie in chapel and judge for himself. He does, and this is his report:

> I was moved, profoundly moved and impressed, because I saw here an intensity and steadiness of attention and concentration that I had never seen before in him or conceived him capable of. I watched him kneel and take the Sacrament on his tongue, and could not doubt the fullness and totality of Communion, the perfect alignment of his spirit with the spirit of the Mass. Fully, intensely, quietly, in the quietude of absolute concentration and attention, he entered and partook of the Holy Communion. He was wholly held, absorbed, by a feeling. There was no forgetting, no Korsakov's [the name of the amnesiac syndrome from which he suffered] then, nor did it seem possible or imaginable that there should be; for he was no longer at the mercy of a faulty and fallible mechanism—that of meaningless sequences and memory traces—but was absorbed in an act, an act of the whole being, which carried feeling and meaning in an organic continuity and unity, a continuity and unity so seamless it could not permit any break. (38)

Sacks's language of wholeness, his acknowledgement of the reality of spiritual encounter, and the humility with which he recognizes his own limitation in what he had conceived possible come to the threshold of a kind of statement of faith. He is a deeply hopeful man whose hope is expressed in the inventiveness that chooses life on altered terms where the usual terms do not apply. His hope has enabled many patients to accept and reconceive their lives with disabilities. It has also given an ever-widening number of readers not only the hope exemplified in the outcomes of his clinical tales, but also the hope modeled in the way he waits for revelation and seizes upon the epiphanies, practices expectation without judgment, and remains aware of the limitations of professional and personal assumptions in the face of what will always be a mystery.

Illness narratives like these by patients, doctors, and caregivers, are nothing new. The history of fiction and memoir is rife with stories of physical suffering, care, and healing. The practice of medicine in our time has profoundly changed the nature of healing and complicated our expectations by offering a dazzling array of technological options. Perhaps by the same token, it has deepened our distrust and disappointments and confused our notions of what is normal or natural. I chose these two works for the ways they represented that complexity and for the insights they offer on hope in hard times. That if hope is a virtue it is because it is first, like grace, a gift. That true hope corrects false hopes and exposes the fallacy of optimism. That hope comes from careful discernment and takes a full reckoning of evil, or as Thomas Hardy put it, "If way to the Better there be, it exacts a full look at the Worst" ("In Tenebris" line 14). That hope is related to humor. That hope is generated and sustained in community. That hope is often counterintuitive, sudden, epiphanic. It sometimes actually comes when original expectations are defected. That hope results from reframing. That hope can survive even severe disappointment. Finally, that hope may be found in story—both plumbing our own stories of suffering, reprieve, and recovery, and in understanding our own stories as part of the larger, ongoing story to which we all belong. Hope has very little to do with risk assessment, "odds," or statistics. Hope is always an open door, inviting us to walk in trust over a new threshold.

I want to close with the reminder that many illness narratives are now available; the genre has blossomed over the past couple of decades. Two things, it seems to me, should motivate all of us to be interested in reflective writing about disease and healing. One is simply that the sick we have always with us, and what they have to tell us about sickness may enable us to be more effective healers, and when it is our turn to suffer, to approach our own suffering with informed intelligence and imagination as well as with prayers for patience and courage. The other reason is that pain can push language to its limits. Stories about pain involve us with language in unique ways as writers; searching for adequate metaphors and treading the fine line between self-pity and sterile stoicism help develop a discourse for a dimension of being human we all inherit. The best pathographies offer profound lessons in spiritual resourcefulness, and each can provide its own avenue of grace. What Mark Van Doren wrote about love might also be said about each experience of human suffering: "There is no single way it can be told" (*Sonnet*

25). The best of the pathographies that chronicle our generation's struggle with rampant cancer, diabetes, environmental toxicities, and stress-related diseases can, indeed, provide a sobering and insightful but also a hopeful word for all of us who will, very likely, be among those who suffer and those who, by prayer, presence, medicine, and imagination, act as agents for the One who has promised finally to heal all our diseases.

Chapter 13

Geographies of Hope
Kathleen Norris and David Lynch

Kevin L. Cole

If *hope* has an antonym, it is *despair*. Their etymologies suggest as much. *Desperare* means "to give up hope." The etymology of hope can be found in three Old English words. *Hopa*, or *tôhopa*, means an expectation of something desired, a feeling of expectation and desire combined, and *hopian* means to entertain an expectation of something desired. Most dictionaries continue to define despair as a complete loss or absence of hope, a feeling of hopelessness. Nevertheless, it would not be at all unusual for one to say, "I hope to climb out of this despair." In other words, despite its denotation, despair is not an absolute; despair does not preclude, eliminate, or cancel hope.

One sees this connotative facet of despair in Western literature. In the third canto of *The Inferno*, for instance, despair is inscribed above the gates of hell: "ABANDON EVERY HOPE, WHO ENTER HERE" (line 9). Put another way: "Get ready to encounter some serious despair." Despite the despair of hell, Dante and Virgil repeatedly encounter souls who hope to escape. In Milton's hell, the fallen angels have reason to hope only because they are in such utter despair, a condition their motivated leader makes them aware of in his speeches. Jane Eyre and Huckleberry Finn—optimists that they are—preserve their hope and idealism despite the crushing societal despair around them. Amid the despair and nihilism of the crew of expatriates in Spain, Hemingway's Jake wants to have hope, even if it is only "pretty" to think he can (251). In these works and many others in Western literature, characters negotiate their way through a spiritual geography created by the tension between despair and hope.

This is the geography traversed by Kathleen Norris's memoir *Dakota: A Spiritual Geography* (1993) and David Lynch's film *The Straight Story* (1998). Exploring the relationship between despair and hope, both works chart journeys across physical and spiritual geographies in the upper Midwest. For obvious reasons, Norris and Lynch at first seem an unlikely pair. However, each explores the anatomy of hope with the same elegant, powerful metaphor: literal and figurative sight. The metaphor is, of course, ancient. One thinks of Tiresias, the blind but omniscient prophet; of Oedipus who can truly see—truly know—only after blinding himself; of Saul who sees only after he is blinded; of Rochester who sees Jane as a complete, complex human only after being partially blinded. In recent literature, one thinks of Cormac McCarthy's blind prophets who impart their terrible wisdom through the art of seeing. Using this rich metaphor, Norris and Lynch illuminate the tragic, comic, and redemptive relationship between despair and hope. Although these works concern a specific region—the upper Midwest—the vision and significance of each extend far beyond geographic boundaries.

Dakota: A Spiritual Geography

Ask people not from the upper Midwest how they imagine the region, and they respond predictably: the heartland of America, Rockwell's America, a bucolic and harmonious America, a land of plenty. Yes, Rockwellian towns do still exist, but the sense of despair among rural upper Midwesterners is palpable, in large part because small towns and family farms are on the brink of extinction, especially in the Dakotas. The southeastern corner of South Dakota—Minnehaha and Lincoln Counties and the city of Sioux Falls—has experienced sustained economic and population growth over the last fifteen years. It is a prosperous, thriving sector. Most other parts of South Dakota (with the exception of Rapid City in the Black Hills), however, have experienced sustained population loss. The same is true for North Dakota. The bleak situation is abundantly documented, for example, by statistics from the Census Data Center's *South Dakota Population, Housing, and Farm Census Facts*, as well as from numerous articles including pieces by Bryan Hodgson, James Saterlee, Gary A. Goreham, Katherine Hutt Scott, and Terry Woster. Other studies corroborate the disappearance and shrinkage of small towns and farms in the Midwest as a whole, including, the work of Timothy Egan, Osha Gray Davidson, Marvin Duncan, Dennis Fisher, Mark Drabenspott, Harlow Hyde, Jake Goldberg, and Lonnie Harp. So, yes, this is still the heartland, a land of plenty, but farmers often cannot sell the grain in their overflowing silos because of flooded markets; for many, in fact, survival means relying on government programs that pay them not to plant. Yes, Native Americans and whites get along better now than they did just ten years ago, but turmoil, strife, and poverty still characterize life on the reservation. None of this is hyperbole. No one is crying wolf.

Kathleen Norris, a New York poet who moved to northwestern South Dakota to live on the homestead of her ancestors, writes a memoir about finding hope amid despair. *Dakota* is a meditation on discovering hope through geography, no matter the landscape: physical or spiritual, natural or human. It maps out a course of hope, and Norris's cartographic strategy, if you will, is to instruct her readers in the art of looking intently, the art of seeing.

In terms of physical geography, Norris must necessarily emphasize the art of looking intently because she is not writing about the bucolic harmony of, say, Vermont, the dreamy mists of the Smoky Mountains, or the romantic wildness of the Rockies—all conventional images of beauty. Rather, Norris is writing about the seeming barrenness of the Northern Great Plains, the high desert plains that to the untutored eye appear desolate and ominously vast. But the seeming barrenness is her point: if one educates oneself in the art of seeing, the Plains are anything but barren, and being able truly to see them expands one's spiritual vistas. As Diane D. Quantic explains, Norris is not unusual in this regard among Plains writers: "In most Great Plains works, the landscape is the constant against which authors measure their characters' abilities to adapt to radically new conditions" (59). For Norris, "radically new conditions" refers to both physical and spiritual landscapes.

First, the physical landscapes. According to Norris, finding hope on the Northern Plains requires that one see and understand the spiritual offerings of the landscape—the physical geography. This is not easy, even for its residents. She writes, "The High Plains, the beginning of the desert West, often act as a crucible. . . . Like Jacob's angel, the region requires that you wrestle with it before it bestows a blessing" (1). Whether one is truly seeing the High Plains for the first or for the hundredth time, experiencing its numinous power is epiphanic: "Suddenly you know what you're seeing: the earth has turned to face the center of the galaxy, and many more stars are visible than the ones we usually see on our wing of the spiral. . . . Nature, in Dakota, can indeed be an experience of the holy" (1).

Dakota is replete with the words *see* and *seeing*, as well as imagery and metaphors related to sight, especially in the opening chapter. In "The Beautiful Places," Norris prepares the audience for the message of her humbling homily: most people fail dismally at seeing, but this memoir will teach us how to see keenly and intently. In the second paragraph, for instance, she recalls a passage from Thoreau's *Walden*: we "need to witness our limits transgressed." For Norris, the geography of Dakota represents "limits transgressed," but she will show readers how to be witnesses to it—and to any geography for that matter. Using words associated with sight, Norris illustrates the degree to which we fail to see. She writes that most Americans tend "*to see* Plains land as empty." "*Looking* at the expanse of the land in between, they may wonder why a person would choose to live in such a barren place, let alone love it. But mostly they are bored: they turn up the car stereo, count the miles to civilization, and *look away*" (emphasis mine) (2). The implication is clear. We the readers have been deprived of seeing, have been made blind by the business of "our fast-paced, anything-for-a-buck society" (9). Norris's sometime belligerent tone has been overlooked or ignored by reviewers and critics, but it is undoubtedly present, strengthening the force of her admonition.

Toward the end of chapter 1, though, Norris makes it clear that her ultimate objective is not to admonish or lament but rather to instruct. Relying again on the language of sight, she first quotes the Dakotan monk Terrence Kardong, whose sentences rest on the word *see*: "We who are permanently camped here see things you don't see at 55 m.p.h. . . . We see white-faced calves basking in the spring grass like the lilies of the field. We see a chinook wind in January make rivulets run. We see dust-devils and lots of little things" (10). Norris follows with her own words, beginning a series of participial phrases with the verb *see*: "One might see a herd of white-tailed deer jumping a fence; fox cubs wrestling at the door of their lair; cock pheasants stepping out of a medieval tapestry into windrowed hay; cattle bunched in the southeast corner of a pasture, anticipating a storm in the approaching thunderheads. And above all, one notices the quiet, the near-absence of human noise" (10). Thus, in the opening chapter, Norris first calls attention to our failure to see and then initiates her method of instruction in the art of seeing. As the memoir progresses, she constructs more elaborate tropes and metaphors, further illustrating how to see the spiritual world in the physical.

Not surprisingly, we see the culmination of this rhetorical strategy in the chapter entitled "Seeing." All along, Norris has been training her audience how to use their eyes. In the following paragraph, she uses metonymy—the human and the eye are now one and the same—to reiterate her thesis, that the art of seeing entails a process of learning to appreciate:

> The landscape of western Dakota is not as abstract as the flats of Kansas, but it presents a similar challenge to the eye that appreciates the vertical definition of mountains or skyscrapers; that defines beauty in terms of the spectacular or the busy: hills, trees, buildings, highways, people. We seem empty by comparison.
>
> Here, the eye learns to appreciate slight variations, the possibilities inherent in emptiness. It sees that the emptiness is full of small things, like grasshoppers in their samurai armor, clicking and jumping as you pass. This empty land is full of grasses: sedges, switch grass, needlegrass, wheatgrass. Brome can grow waist-high by early summer. Fields of wheat, rye, oats, barley, flax, alfalfa. Acres of sunflowers brighten the land in summer, their heads alert, expectant. By fall they droop like sad children, waiting patiently for the first frost and harvest. (155–56)

The passage itself is a harvest of images that illustrate how to look intently and see keenly into what Gerard Manley Hopkins calls the "dearest freshness deep down things" ("God's Grandeur" line 10). This harvest of things physical presages the central aim of her instruction: an articulation of the relationship between physical and spiritual geography. Near the end of the chapter, Norris moves seamlessly from the physical to the spiritual geography. Comparing the spiritual richness of Dakota's geography to an icon, she suggests that to find hope in the geography, one must seek out and yearn for the spiritual:

> Along with the largeness of the visible—too much horizon, too much sky—this land's essential indifference to the human can be unnerving. . . .
>
> A person is forced inward by the spareness of what is outward and visible in all this land and sky. The beauty of the Plains is like that of an icon; it does not give an inch to sentiment or romance. The flow of the land, with its odd twists and buttes, is like the flow

of Gregorian chant that rises and falls beyond melody, beyond reason or human expectation, but perfectly.

Maybe seeing the Plains is like seeing an icon: what seems stern and almost empty is merely open, a door into some simple and holy state. (156–57)

This passage recalls the last sentence of the second paragraph in chapter 1: "Nature, in Dakota, can indeed be an experience of the holy" (2). Seeing requires that one be open to the spiritual because the land itself—as much as the person observing it—is spiritual. The geography of Dakota, then, is one of only seeming desolation and despair; hope lies in seeing, understanding, and accepting its spiritual offerings. Norris describes nothing less than a sacramental relationship: the land offers up its gifts to the communicant seeking hope.

Another concern of *Dakota* is, of course, the spiritual geography of humans, and it, too, is a place where hope must reside. Dakota is as much about the human, spiritual geography—especially the geography of despair—as it is about physical geography. Quantic correctly states that Norris is "aware of the tolls exacted in the spiritual health of people who lose contact with or grow indifferent to Nature" (61) and that she does not have an idyllic, utopian view of the prairie (62). In Norris's own words, "The Plains are not forgiving. Anything that is shallow—the easy optimism of a homesteader; the false hope that denies geography, climate, history; the tree whose roots don't reach ground water—will dry up and blow away" (38). In short, Norris is not a naive romantic; she is a realist. In the same way that she instructs her readers to embrace unflinchingly the geography, she also instructs her readers to face despair unflinchingly—all in the pursuit of hope. One might think of this as Norris's *Dakota* ethic.

Despair is nothing new under the sun in the Dakotas, particularly since the wave of immigration that began in the 1880s. Brutal winters, drought, pestilence and blight, wind, and insanity have made failure central to the region's history. But *Dakota* educates readers on what the residents of the Northern Plains have learned in order to survive: persist, hope, and do not fall victim to despair. More important, *Dakota* reminds readers that although the region has been one of despair, it has also been a fertile region of hope, an iconic region of hope, as Norris might put it.

In chapters such as "Evidence of Failure"—a rather disconcerting chapter—Norris instructs her readers on how to look despair courageously in the face. Writing from her ranch, she contemplates the vestigial objects of her ancestors, relics of the despair that accompanied life on the Plains in the early twentieth century: her grandmother's rotting rain barrel; an old piano; auction notices from the 1840s and 1850s; photographs of two gravestones of boys who died in the influenza epidemics of the 1920s; a photograph of a baby in a coffin, inserted in the Psalms of the family Bible whose bindings and covers are crumbling (102–3). These objects are what they are: signs of despair, evidence of failure. Throughout the memoir, Norris points to the continuity of despair, reminding readers that little has changed in rural Dakota. Daily, family farms go under, small towns grow smaller, Dakota's youth leave in droves, whites and Native Americans live separately in what Norris calls a "deafening silence between the two worlds, a silence exacerbated by ignorance and intolerance on both sides" (108). "Signs of hope are few," she bluntly states, and at times, she herself is "tempted to despair" (109–10).

If signs of hope are few, where and why does Norris find reason to hope? What gives her reason to chart a map of hope? What one must not do is rely on naive platitudes about hope; instead, one must be a realist. Consider the following passage:

> Where I am is a place where the human fabric is worn thin, farms and ranches and little towns scattered over miles of seemingly endless, empty grassland. . . . Some have come to prefer the treelessness and isolation, becoming monks of the land, knowing that loneliness is an honest reflection of the essential human loneliness. The willingly embraced desert fosters realism, not despair. (110)

The last sentence is critical. It embodies the hard realism of Norris's *Dakota* ethic, but it is also optimistic and looks toward hope. Again, Norris is instructing readers how to face despair, how to search for and find hope where others would find only reason to lament. Norris, then, looks for signs of hope not only in the landscape—seeing it, contemplating it, writing about it, and understanding the spiritual metaphors it offers—but also in the determined people of the Dakotas.

No matter the degree of despair, Norris believes there is always reason to have hope and to search for hope. To yield to despair is to die. This sensibility permeates *Dakota*, and the clearest expression of it occurs in "Getting to Hope," a chapter about a dying community, centered around a church that tenaciously holds onto hope, despite the bleakness of its future. Hope, South Dakota, is a tiny town, a stamp of a sparsely populated territory, at the center of which is an old Presbyterian church: Hope Church. Like many upper Midwestern towns, both the community of Hope and Hope Church embody a poignant paradox:

although dying, they are "beautifully alive" (170). They are "beautifully alive" because the community of Hope and the members of Hope Church—in some ways, one and the same—unflinchingly stare down insidious despair and insist on Hope's future.

Because of the precipitous fall in population in the last half of the twentieth century, the steady flight of its young people, and its sheer geographic isolation, one might assume hope is dead to the world, that the people of Hope see the world as irrelevant to them and see themselves as irrelevant to the world. But according to Norris they do not, and she sees this attitude as Hope's greatest expression. On the one hand, the people of Hope remain curious about the world because they know that their economic well-being is tied to it: their farming and ranching livelihoods depend on the health of world markets. Thus, they keep abreast of world events and are conversant with the complex conditions of the world's agricultural and livestock markets. On the other hand, their religious and ethical sensibilities also make them curious about and concerned for the world. For example, this seemingly insignificant community actively pursues ways to reduce world hunger. Moreover, despite difficult economic times in the last decade, Hope Church ranks "near the top in per capita giving among Presbyterian churches in the state of South Dakota" (164). In every way, they are alive to the world; their vitality is an essential element of hope.

Quantic writes that Great Plains writers—Ole Rølvaag, Willa Cather, Wright Morris, Larry Woiwode, Sharon Butala, and Kathleen Norris—explore and articulate the absolute necessity of the residents of the Plains to establish and maintain a connectedness to place and to understand the relationship between one's existence and place (59). This realization describes the tenor of "Getting to Hope." America needs places like Hope, Norris argues, because, juxtaposed against the barrenness of the banal American urban landscapes, dying towns such as Hope embody hope itself. Its residents understand and appreciate the land from which they have sprung and on which they still make their living:

> The power of Hope Church and country churches like it is subtle and not easily quantifiable. It's a power derived from smallness and lack of power, a concept the apostle Paul would appreciate, even if modern church bureaucrats lose sight of it. (165)

Norris associates this particular kind of power with an understanding of place:

> Hope's people are traditional people, country people, and they know that the spirits of a place cannot be transported or replaced.

> . . . Hope's people have become one with their place: this is not
> romanticism, but truth. You can hear it in the way people speak,
> referring to their land in the first person: "I'm so dry I'm starting to
> blow," or "I'm so wet now I'll be a month to seeding." (169)

To my knowledge, Norris and *Dakota* have yet to be described as
hard as nails. Such a statement is perhaps heretical among those taken
with *Dakota*'s lyricism and powerful, elegant evocation of place. Like the
Northern Plains itself, though, there is a stark but elegant duality to her
message: it is lyrical and poetic but hard as nails. One cannot face
despair and arrive at hope—on the Plains or elsewhere—unless one is
tough and steely. Take, for instance, the following passage, which foreshadows the chapter on Hope, South Dakota: "Maybe the desert wisdom of the Dakotas can teach us to love anyway, to love what is dying,
in the face of death, and not pretend that things are other than they are"
(121). "Getting to Hope" profiles a place that is dying, but it also profiles a people who are strong, a people who are not afraid "to look into
the heart of their pain" and have hope in the face of despair (173).

Norris is a seer and an instructor, a quiet prophet of the Plains who
teaches her readers how to see, read, and interpret geography and how to
have hope in the face of spiritual despair. This instruction culminates in
"Getting to Hope":

> When these people ask, "Who will replace us?" the answer is, "who
> knows, maybe no one," and it's not easy to live with that truth. The
> temptation is to deny it or to look for scapegoats. The challenge is
> to go on living graciously and thankfully, cultivating love. Not sen-
> timental love but true charity, which, as Flannery O'Connor said,
> "is hard but endures." (174)

What O'Connor saw in charity, Norris sees in hope: hope is hard but
endures.

David Lynch: *The Straight Story*

David Lynch's film *The Straight Story* is intriguingly similar to *Dakota* in
that it, too, explores the relationship between hope and despair in the
upper Midwest. Lynch, however, unlike Norris, is ambivalent about
hope: the degree to which it exists and the degree to which it can overcome or respond to despair. Kathleen Norris has different sensibilities.
Based on actual events, *The Straight Story* opens with a perspective from
the air, a perspective of Elysium: cornfields bathed in the light of the setting sun, manicured plots of brightly colored crops, combines harvesting

the earth's plenty, and mainstreet U.S.A.: Laurens, Iowa. In Tim Kreider and Rob Content's words, the opening is "cinematographer Freddie Francis filling in for Norman Rockwell and composer Angelo Badalamenti for Aaron Copeland" (26). Indeed, from the air, Iowa appears to be a paradise of plenty, a land bereft of despair. But of course it is not. Of these opening shots, Charles Taylor writes that "there's a fragility to it all" ("Every Moment's"). That fragility is a result of devastating and paralyzing despair, a despair that the protagonist, Alvin Straight, negotiates in a heroic expression of hope.

Alvin (played by the late Richard Farnsworth) lives in a very modest house in Laurens with his daughter Rose (Sissy Spacek). Alvin has experienced a bad fall, and the doctor, to whom Alvin is averse, orders him to get a walker, to stop smoking, and to change his diet, which consists primarily of braunschweiger. Alvin will have none of it, but he does acquire a second cane. More than a tacit concession of his disability, Alvin's act establishes a theme related to the larger theme of insight: the symbolic relationship between physical and spiritual disability. Alvin's literal fall, which serves as the exposition of the plot, symbolizes his fallenness, presaging his quest for redemption, a quest driven by hope.

One evening, in the middle of a thunderstorm, Rose and Alvin receive word that Lyle (Harry Dean Stanton), Alvin's brother who lives in Mt. Zion, Wisconsin, has suffered a severe stroke. Alvin looks out into the rainstorm with a countenance of despair, a look of despair that—in my estimation—few actors other than Farnsworth could capture. As Howard Hampton puts it, "Farnsworth's eyes articulate what Straight himself can't put into words, conveying what it means to bear witness to decades of silent tragedy, shame, fear, and loss" (21). Alvin's countenance suggests that this new element of despair, while unexpected, was inevitable, given the despair in his life before the news of the stroke. Not surprisingly, Lynch does not lay out Alvin's history of despair like condiments on a picnic table. Viewers must be alert to clues in the dialogue in order to piece together Alvin's past. Kreider and Content's review is exceptional in this regard because throughout they explain what we can infer about Alvin's past. Among other problems, his former alcoholism is to blame not only for his estrangement from Lyle, but also for Rose's children being badly burned and, subsequently, being taken from her. His alcoholism is probably the root of other elements of despair. Alvin indicates, for example, that he and his wife had fourteen children, seven of whom are dead, but clues in the film suggest that only one of the surviving children, Rose, still speaks to him. Of his spouse, little is mentioned, and we assume she is dead. Thus, the most recent bout of despair—Lyle's stroke—is only the latest in a life of despair.

Refusing at first to tell the doting, protective Rose about his plans, Alvin begins working on his riding mower. They work side by side in their small backyard—Rose building and painting birdhouses, Alvin tinkering with his mower—until it becomes clear to Rose that Alvin, who has also built a sleeping trailer to attach to the riding mower, intends to drive it 300 miles to Wisconsin to reconcile with his brother.

At this point, we see the metaphor of literal and figurative sight emerge, along with signs of hope. Alvin cannot drive himself to Wisconsin, and he refuses to allow Rose to drive him. He cannot drive himself because he does not own a driver's license: his eyes are too weak. Therein lies the elegant paradox of *The Straight Story*: Alvin's eyesight is literally weak, but his human, spiritual insight is keen. He sees that he must make one last journey; he sees that he must make amends with his brother before he dies; and he sees that he must take this journey alone. This keen insight, this ability to truly see, makes finding hope amidst despair a prominent theme of *The Straight Story*. Alvin's last journey will be an odyssey fueled by gasoline and hope.

Alvin does not get off to an auspicious start: just a few miles out of town, his mower breaks down. In a Lynchian, comic scene, Alvin disposes of the old riding mower with dispatch. In the quietness of his own backyard, he shoots the gas tank of the decrepit machine, igniting an inferno of metal. Undeterred, he purchases a "new" riding mower: a 1965 John Deere, the best that he can afford. And so Alvin sets out again, equipped with a new vessel, two canes, a sleeping trailer, and a hearty supply of Swisher Sweets and braunschweiger.

I have suggested—as many reviewers have—that Alvin's journey is an odyssey. Perhaps picaresque odyssey is more accurate or, as Howard Hampton refers to it, a "plangent spiritual odyssey" (21). Whatever the genre, Alvin's journey is an odyssey. That an elderly man on a riding mower could experience an odyssey might seem unlikely at first. But Lynch, through the episodic nature of the plot and the characters and situations Alvin encounters, clearly wants us to think of Alvin's travels in odyssean terms. And, after all, if Stephen Dedalus and Leopold Bloom can experience an odyssey in a single day, then surely over the course of several weeks and 300 miles, Alvin can experience an odyssey on a riding mower.

This discussion of odyssey should not imply that hope wins out in the end. Far from it. Tragedy in *The Straight Story* persistently threatens to snuff out hope. So tragic is Alvin's own life that the tension between despair and hope is at times almost unbearable. Moreover, his despair intersects with the despair of others. For example, Alvin and Lyle know they will soon die, yet they have been estranged for ten years—and only because of an alcohol-induced argument. Rose's life is the epitome of tragedy, and Rose herself the epitome of heroism in her quiet suffering and noble endurance. Alvin encounters many people on his journey who also have experienced tragedy, and they relate their stories to him as if they had all been destined to meet Alvin for this purpose. At first glance, in fact, Lynch seems to have characterized Alvin as a benevolent, itinerant sage, doling out wisdom and existential observations that address the problem of despair. But Kreider and Content write that "the situations Alvin encounters are reiterations of his own crimes and failures, confrontations with his own denial" (29). In either interpretation, tragedy and despair are still at the center of the characters' lives. Furthermore, if we recall that the film is based on actual events, the tragedy is even more poignant.

In light of my thesis—that hope is a major theme in *The Straight Story*—I would be remiss if I did not discuss Kreider and Content's review of *The Straight Story*. For a host of reasons, it is the most informed, insightful, and compelling review of the film I have read. They discuss crucial aspects of the film that others miss or ignore, and they illustrate the significance of what at first seems to be irrelevant and/or Lynchian minutiae. Additionally, their review is iconoclastic because they argue that, in truth, viewers have little reason to find hope or happiness in the film. Whereas most if not all reviewers have thought *The Straight Story* a bucolic, "meandering picaresque," Kreider and Content argue otherwise: "There is darkness here beneath the bright autumn colors, and evil concealed in Alvin's heart. There is the history of a family destroyed by alcoholism and abuse. There is fire and death" (26).

Good reader-response critics, Kreider and Content read Alvin as an unreliable first-person narrator who does not tell the story straight. The title of the film is more a warning than a pun: "[I]t warns us not to be deceived by appearances—in this case, by an ingenuous claim of forthrightness, a frank demeanor, or an honest face" (27). If viewers want the straight story, they have to interpret Alvin's coded language.

Kreider and Content point first to Alvin's duplicity. The stories he tells to the people he meets are full of "conspicuous gaps and contradictions." For example, Alvin admits that before WWII—in which he fought—he had a problem with alcohol but that after the war a minister helped him forsake it. This claim contradicts his explanation that his and Lyle's excessive drinking before and after the War resulted in their estrangement. Moreover, he divulges enough information (intentionally or not?) for the audience to infer that Alvin, because of his heavy drinking, is responsible for Rose's children being taken away from her. He gives just enough information to allow the audience to infer that, while inebriated, he left them unattended and that they consequently were seriously burned. Finally, Alvin may come across as a kind, patriarchal raconteur, but viewers must remember that he did father fourteen children (quite a burden on one spouse) and that apparently only one of the surviving children, Rose, still talks to him. Viewers should be asking, then, "Where has all his family gone?" Kreider and Content also encourage viewers not to assume what most reviewers have assumed: that Rose and Alvin's life together is "tender and innocent." Rather, "we might see instead a stunted and bereaved Cordelia alongside a middle-American Lear." Viewers do not know what motivates Rose to care for a father who has apparently caused her so much pain, and, moreover, Lynch's portrayal of their life together does not intimate happiness. Instead, contend Kreider and Content, there is a palpable sadness and despair beneath the image of the kind daughter caring for the aging father (28–32).

The most insightful, convincing element of Kreider and Content's case against Alvin is their deconstruction of the deer episode (29–30). First, a reckless driver roars past Alvin, who is putting along in a no-passing zone on a two-lane highway. A few moments later, Alvin encounters the same car, now parked on the shoulder of the highway. All is remarkably still and quiet, except for the visibly distraught driver, who motions between the damaged hood and the dead deer on the side of the road. She wails out in despair, lamenting to Alvin that she has now killed thirteen deer in only seven weeks. Her despair is convincing. As Kreider and Content explain, although the audience might be tempted to sympathize with her (as most reviewers have), she does not deserve sympathy because she is a reckless driver. She has killed all thirteen deer during the day, a time when deer are rarely out. Experience alone should tell her that, for whatever reason, deer populate this stretch of highway during the daytime and that she should slow down if she truly wants to avoid killing them. Moreover she drives much too fast on the two-lane highway, evident in the speed at which she has passed Alvin in a no-passing zone, just before she hits the deer. Her story is not straight and her despair incongruent with her complicity in the slaughter of the deer.

Alvin's dishonesty parallels hers because he himself has not been straight, and Lynch suggests as much. Still bewailing her fate as a deer-slayer, the woman roars off in her car. The next scene opens with Alvin cooking venison over an open fire. At first, the scene is darkly comic, but then it becomes simply dark. Alvin is visited by the ghosts of four deer, appearing as statues. At first, viewers naturally associate the ghosts with the deer killed by the reckless driver or perhaps with the deer that Alvin is eating. Kreider and Content, however, write that these four statues should remind viewers of Rose's four children, now only a ghostly presence in the Straight household. The scene suggests that Alvin is responsible for their unhappy fate.

Because they see little possibility for hope in *The Straight Story*, Kreider and Content's argument seems to contradict and perhaps preclude my own. Such is not the case, however. On the one hand, they see Alvin's quest as a quest for atonement. One seeks atonement because one hopes to receive forgiveness and achieve redemption. Simply put, one cannot seek atonement without having hope. On the other, Kreider and Content do not explore fully the thematic significance of the film's comic elements, which sustain hope throughout the film. The picaresque—the comic—in *The Straight Story* stubbornly reminds the audience of Alvin's hope and raises expectations that this hope will be fulfilled. Stressing the horrifically thin line that divides the tragic and comic in human existence, throughout *The Straight Story*, Lynch elegantly juxtaposes the elements of tragedy with elements of comedy.

On the very first day of Alvin's journey, for instance, a bevy of cyclists—all dressed as if they were in the Tour de France—overtakes Alvin on a lonely highway as he putts along on his John Deere. "On your left! On your left!" they yell out as they pass a dismayed, bewildered Alvin. The message is clear: youth, modernity, and agility have raced by Alvin. (One senses that Lynch is also satirizing the amateur cyclists and their gear.) Notwithstanding Kreider and Content's analysis of the deer scene, it, too, has comic elements. Standing in the middle of the highway, the irrational, distraught woman yells out to Alvin that her emotions can no longer endure this daily slaughter. As they both look at the carcass and the crumpled hood of the car, Alvin patiently listens to her lament until she throws herself back into her car and roars away. She leaves Alvin standing in the middle of the road, not suspecting that he has been much less concerned about her emotional state and much more concerned about preserving the deer for his next meal, which he does. In the next scene Alvin is roasting a shank over a campfire. The following day, he attaches the antlers to the front of his trailer, adding a darkly comical ornament. We find humor, too, in the bumbling, bickering twins, riding-lawnmower repairmen who foolishly attempt to swindle the wily Alvin after the brakes on his mower malfunction. In the end Alvin gets his price and delivers a soft, admonitory sermon about why the two brothers should not argue with one another.

I am not being ungenerous when I say that at times the image of Alvin himself is a comic image—a comic image of hope. On this aspect of Farnsworth's performance, Taylor writes: "It's a measure of the grace of Farnsworth's performance—and the love Lynch has for the character—that Alvin is never a figure of fun" ("Every Moment's"). Instead of a strapping Ulysses, the hero of *The Straight Story* is an old man sitting upright in a riding mower with a homemade sleeping trailer—bedecked with a set of antlers—in tow. Wisps of white hair spring out from under his cowboy hat as he holds tightly to the steering wheel, a Swisher Sweet planted firmly between his lips. He is a small-town Iowan on his last odyssey, bound for Wisconsin. Farnsworth's acting, countenance, and demeanor are remarkable because they contain the nuances of comedy and tragedy and at the same time convey hope.

Some might be surprised to hear that *The Straight Story* was produced by Disney and is rated "G"; thus, they might also be surprised to hear that the conclusion of *The Straight Story* is not maudlin. (Then again, it is hard to imagine any conclusion featuring Harry Dean Stanton and Richard Farnsworth being maudlin.) Stanton-as-Lyle makes his first appearance at the end of the film when he emerges from his shack to greet the penitent Alvin. Stanton's actual time on the screen is minimal, but his presence is enormous and his performance exceptional. The audience immediately understands what Lynch saw in the pairing, the power of which Hampton best articulates: "Together, these two aged character actors embody a range of American experience that encompasses the iconic and the breathtakingly quotidian" (22). When I refer to the "conclusion," I do not mean the "resolution" of the conflict—because there arguably is no resolution—but to the very last scene and the very last images of the film. When Lyle does appear, we see the specter of a human whose mobility has been severely impaired and who now awkwardly relies on a walker. The two say little. In unreserved amazement, Lyle asks Alvin if he has traveled this far on a lawn mower just to see him, to which Alvin quietly replies, "Yes." The last image of the film is of Alvin looking up into the sky and the sun, wincing from the blinding light. His countenance is inscrutable. It reminds one of Oedipus, Saul, or Ivan Ilych being blinded by insight; it reminds one of the speaker in Dylan Thomas's "Do Not Go Gentle into that Good Night," passionately exclaiming to his father: "Grave men, near death, who see with blinding sight / Blind eyes could blaze like meteors and be gay / Rage, rage against the dying of the light" (lines 13–15). It is one of the most poignant concluding scenes in American cinema.

Presumably, most viewers want to read hope in Farnsworth's expression, just as I did the first time I saw *The Straight Story*. But the inscrutability of his gaze and of his expression defies labels. It is not at all clear what Alvin is feeling, and it is not at all clear that Lynch wants to conclude with an unambiguous image of hope. It would be safer to say that the rhetorical strategy of *The Straight Story* is to seek out the possibility of hope along the journey, not to see it as a final destination. Perhaps because *Dakota* is informed by a religious ethic, its rhetorical strategy is to arrive at hope. Hope is more than a possibility in *Dakota*; it is a destination, no matter the degree and history of despair. Nevertheless, these differences emphasize the degree to which hope is central to the vision of each work. Both Norris and Lynch, in their love of region and in their quiet, poetic expressions of hope, remind us that hope emerges in the places where we least expect to find it: in geography, in dying churches, and on the back of a riding lawn mower.

Chapter 14

Attunement and Healing
The Fisher King

Michael B. Herzog

While stories are told for as many different reasons as there are story-tellers, the very act of telling and retelling stories implies the presence of hope, as stories arise from our past experiences to inform our present and provide guidance for the future we must anticipate. While, again, there are innumerable ways of creating or nourishing hope in narratives, one of the most basic emerges from stories about healing or being healed from incapacitating wounds or illnesses. Social scientists have long recognized the crucial role of fairy tales and myths in human maturation and in the creation and operation of healthy social units, even specifically acknowledging the role of imaginative literature in developmental theory. Some physicians now acknowledge the role of storytelling in the healing of serious illness, and the therapeutic results of modern psychotherapy are possible largely because of patient narratives. Of course, imaginative literature is replete with inspirational stories, and some of the best-known and longest-lived narratives clearly create hope with characters and situations that involve healing. Jesus employs parables in his healing ministry in the New Testament, and it is the power to heal (physically and spiritually) that Jesus promises to the apostles in Matthew 10:7-8 and Luke 9:2 when they are sent out to spread the "good news," the term itself proclaiming hope as a substantive element of narrative.

The story of the grail, already ancient by the time it appears in its earliest written forms, tells of physical and spiritual healing; its hero must save a wounded king and a dying land by demonstrating compassion: the quality most necessary if human beings are to live in community. This is a tale with a multitude of reincarnations and variants, told and retold by Celts (*Mabinogion*), medieval bards (Chrétien de Troyes, Wolfram von Eschenbach, Thomas Malory), Victorian poets (Tennyson), and our own contemporaries (T. H. White and, yes, Walt Disney)—and in every version its essence is the creation of hope through healing.

The grail story makes an unexpected reappearance in *The Fisher King*, a 1991 film in which director Terry Gilliam evokes a medieval city from the stone- and glass-encased canyons of late twentieth-century New York. The director relies on the intersection of shock-talk radio host and homeless idealist to revive the legend of wounded individual and suffering society healed through the compassionate intervention of an unlikely hero. Consistent with the basic traditions of the grail story, the film's screenplay, by Richard LaGravenese, depicts the mutual transformation of the wounded and of the healer, but in a postmodern world. Here medieval ideals of courtly love and sacrifice for others might seem impractical and hopelessly unfashionable. Yet this film manages to show the triumph of these values in a gritty, realistic presentation that makes use of the romantic, or fantastic, only as counterpoint. In other words, the film refuses to let us write off compassion and hope as outmoded, sentimental, or romantic notions that have no place in contemporary culture.

The protagonist of *The Fisher King* is Jack Lucas (played by Jeff Bridges), a narcissistic, in-your-face New York radio talk show host on his way to media stardom. His shtick is to antagonize, deride, and goad his listeners, signing off at the end of his show with a self-assured: "Thank God I'm me." One day, after he releases a diatribe against Yuppies ("they're not human—they don't feel love—they only negotiate love moments—they're evil—they must be stopped before it's too late,"), one of his listeners acts on this suggestion. Lonely and pathetic Edwin Malnick seeks out an upscale restaurant filled with those very Yuppies he thinks Jack has told him to eradicate, shreds seven people with a shotgun, and then blows his own brains out all over the bistro's glass walls. Faced with these horrendous consequences of his comments, Jack is devastated and takes the advice of his radio show's closing signature song to "Hit the Road, Jack" (an ironic allusion to the quest motif at the heart of the grail story). As unlikely as it may seem, Jack's situation is actually analogous to that of the typical grail hero, who begins to seek the grail when his previously successful life implodes and he finds that he must change everything that may have worked for him in the past.

Three years later, Jack is living with Anne (Mercedes Ruehl) above the seamy little video store Anne owns. She treats Jack much better than he deserves, but Jack still lives under a cloud of hate and disgust—at humanity and himself. In a drunken storm of self-pity, he decides to kill himself. Along the way, an unfamiliar little boy gives him a puppet of Pinocchio, which he ties to his foot next to the cement block that is meant to weigh him down once he lands in the East River. His attempted suicide is thwarted, however, by two young male Yuppies who pour gasoline over him to teach him a civics lesson but are stopped from immolating their sacrificial bum by Parry (Robin Williams), a street person who appears as a modern Arthurian hero in rags—backed up by a veritable army of the lame and the halt. Brandishing a garbage can lid as a shield, Parry accosts Jack's assailants with: "Hold, Varlet, or feel the sting of my shaft—in the name of Blanche de Fleur unhand that errant knight." Then he proceeds to tame the would-be vandals, all the while belting out "New York in June," accompanied by his merry band of street people.

Suspicious of his demented knight-in-rusty-armor, Jack helplessly participates in a wild parody of a medieval banquet, held in a cavernous courtyard, replete with food scavenged from garbage containers and drink several grades below Mad Dog 20-20. Jack's concerns are not assuaged when he awakens in Parry's "apartment," a subbasement storage space lit by candles and decorated with an eclectic collection of tourist junk masquerading as grail-memorabilia. Parry seeks the Holy Grail; furthermore, he has located it, and proudly displays its photo, which he had found in the pages of *Progressive Architecture*. In the photo the grail appears on the library shelf of an upper East Side millionaire. Parry would like nothing better than to claim it himself, but he is prevented from doing so by his nightmarish nemesis, the Red Knight. But now all will be well, Parry informs Jack, as the little people, whom only Parry can see, agree that Jack is the one—the hero who will not be stopped by the terrifying Red Knight who makes it impossible for Parry to achieve this quest for the good of all humanity.

Unlike the usual grail hero, Jack has no interest in securing the grail, real or imaginary. He easily dismisses Parry's ravings, but then discovers that Parry is really Henry Sagan, a college teacher who survived the restaurant massacre in which his wife and six others were gunned down by the killer whom Jack inspired with his anti-Yuppie radio rant. Convinced that he is truly cursed, Jack believes this may be his chance to redeem himself. Jack tries unsuccessfully to salve his conscience by giving Parry money. (Just as the grail hero's efforts to make up for past mistakes by seeking the grail are futile, so is Jack's attempt to pay his way out of his guilt.) Mystified by Jack's act, Parry is nevertheless deeply touched by this gesture and begins to admit Jack into his life, introducing him to his secret love, Lydia (Amanda Plummer), a walking disaster of a young woman with no social graces and few qualities anyone besides Parry could find attractive. Parry's love for Lydia is so secret that they have never met; but, like the ideal medieval courtly lover, Parry is happy to worship from afar, admiring her sloppy eating habits and the destruction she unwittingly leaves in her wake as she clumsily navigates through her world.

Fed up by Parry's insistence that he must procure the grail, Jack reminds Parry of his real identity. Unwittingly he conjures up the Red Knight, an imaginary monster that haunts Parry whenever he feels threatened, either by the horrible past that he denies successfully most of the time, or by anyone who gets too close to him personally. But Parry is convinced that the Red Knight fears Jack and, thus emboldened, chases his imaginary nemesis through Central Park (followed by a very confused Jack). In the process Parry rescues yet another homeless person, a gay male cabaret singer who aspires to be Katherine Hepburn. Jack finds this character to be absolutely revolting, but Parry's exhortations are beginning to change Jack into the kind of person he must become if he is, indeed, to be the grail hero. To help Jack understand the importance of the grail, Parry tells him the story of the Fisher King (given here verbatim, as the specifics of Parry's version matter):

> It begins with the king as a boy having to spend the night alone in the forest to prove his courage so he can become king. And while he's spending the night alone, he's visited by a sacred vision: out of the fire appears the Holy Grail, the symbol of God's divine grace, and a voice said to the boy: "You shall be keeper of the grail so that it may heal the hearts of men." But the boy was blinded by greater visions of a life filled with power and glory and beauty, and in this state of radical amazement, he felt, for a brief moment, not like a boy, but invincible, like God. So he reached in the fire to take the

grail and the grail vanished, leaving him with his hand in the fire, to be terribly wounded. Now, as this boy grew older, his wound grew deeper, until one day, life for him lost its reason. He had no faith in any man, not even himself; he couldn't love or feel loved; he was sick with experience—he began to die. One day a fool wandered into the castle and found the king alone. Now, being a fool, he was simple-minded. He didn't see a king—he only saw a man alone and in pain. And he asked the king, "what ails you, friend?" The king replied, "I'm thirsty. I need some water to cool my throat." So the fool took a cup from beside his bed, filled it with water and handed it to the king. As the king began to drink he realized that his wound was healed. He looked in his hands and there was the Holy Grail—that which he had sought all of his life. He turned to the fool and said with amazement, "How could you find that which my brightest and bravest could not?" The fool replied, "I don't know. I only knew that you were thirsty."

Perhaps in response to this story, but certainly out of guilt, Jack devises a plan to get Parry and Lydia together, explaining to Anne: "I feel indebted to the guy. I thought if I could help him in some way, get him this girl that he loves—that maybe, you know, things would change for me." Jack and Anne arrange a successful (and hilarious) double date with Parry and Lydia. At evening's end, however, when Parry allows himself to become vulnerable to Lydia, the Red Knight appears and chases him to the spot where he first saved Jack. This time Parry is beaten into a coma by the same two Yuppie vigilantes who earlier tried to immolate Jack.

At this point, all of Parry's efforts to turn Jack into the grail hero apparently have failed, as Jack, who believes that he has squared his debt by bringing Parry and Lydia together, has dropped Anne. He has returned to his former life, where he is being considered for the lead in "Home Free," a television sitcom about the homeless. When he learns that Parry is in the hospital in a catatonic state—condemned to perpetually replaying the mental tapes of his wife's death—Jack reluctantly decides to help. In the middle of the night, he breaks into the millionaire's castle in the heart of New York and liberates the grail—in actuality an unimposing silver cup from a 1932 grade school Christmas pageant. Before he escapes with the cup, Jack finds Langdon Carmichael (the owner of the cup) unconscious in an easy chair, with an empty bottle of pills lying next to him on the floor. Unable to awaken the drugged old man, Jack bolts from the mansion, intentionally setting off the electronic burglar alarms. At the hospital he places the cup in Parry's unresponsive hands and falls asleep next to his bed. In the morning, Parry awakens from his catatonic state, refreshed and now able to grieve the loss of his wife without having to escape into a fantasy world. The newspaper headline tells us that millionaire Langdon Carmichael's life was inadvertently saved by a midnight prowler, and we see a restored Parry teaching the other members of the hospital ward how to sing: "New York in June." Jack returns to Anne, able for the first time in his life to tell another human being that he loves her, and the film ends with Jack and Parry lying naked, at night, on the grass in Central Park, singing "New York in June."

By the end of the film, the reluctant and ill-equipped protagonist has not only been turned into a hero but also a Christ figure who has accepted the power of unconditional love to heal. Moreover, Gilliam and LaGravenes have added yet another layer of significance to this ancient story by shaping the virtue of compassion that is traditionally assigned only to the hero into mutual attunement that brings about reciprocal healing for both main characters.

As a member of that zany group that brought us "Monty Python and the Holy Grail," Gilliam knows how to find and exploit the humor in the grail story, but he also understands how to adapt many elements of the traditional story to make his point—beginning with the names of the main characters. The grail seeker, usually named "Perceval" or "Parzival" in the medieval stories, here is named "Parry," and the achiever of the grail is "Jack," a variant of the most common male name in many cultures—making him an "everyman" figure who represents us all in our lack of attunement. More thought-provoking names for other characters in the film include the killer (Malnick), a word that contains the root *mal* for "evil"; the owner of the grail in this story has a name which associates him with God ("Carmichael"—"Michael" echoing the question with which one archangel challenges the other: "who is like God?"); even "Lydia" and "Anne" have interesting biblical associations: Lydia is a woman converted by St. Paul, and Anne is the name of the Virgin Mary's mother. But it goes beyond names: the Red Knight is transformed from victim into terror; the grail seeker's beautiful courtly beloved becomes a klutz who is rather pleased by the suggestion that she may just be enough of a bitch to have an attitude; the knights of old have become street people who treat Jack's panicky dance (actually his effort to put out his burning sleeve at their impromptu banquet) as if it were entertainment by a court jester. Interestingly, the film's title comes from a part of the medieval story that Parry does not relate to Jack: the wounded grail king who finds relief from excruciating and constant pain only in fishing—an activity engaged in by many (who are not grail kings) in contemporary society for its restorative and healing powers.

In Chrétien de Troyes's seminal grail story, *Le Conte de Gral*, Perceval is a prince whose family is dedicated to maintaining the grail, but Perceval himself is intentionally kept unaware of his heritage by his mother (382ff.). She raises him to be a fool, so that he cannot lose his life (as did his father) or be wounded (as was his uncle) in knightly service. De Troyes' story sets the pattern for grail heroes who are fools, or at least characters who have much to learn. Gilliam's version gives us two heroes, one of them diminished by intermittent insanity and the other by crippling selfishness. Parry assumes multiple roles: he is at once the grail seeker, the wounded Fisher King, and the grail inspirer: the storyteller who invites Jack into the circle of grail seekers, realizing immediately that Jack is the one. Jack (the main character) is the unprepared and unwilling common man who—just as many medieval grail heroes do initially— attempts to win the grail (in Jack's case by doing a good deed or two with the specific goal of assuaging his guilt feelings and removing the curse from which he believes he suffers). Instead, like all grail heroes before him, he must develop humility, compassion, and selflessness; he must become a person, a human being, a "Mensch" who is ready to assume his proper role—at which point he will achieve the grail.

In grail stories, the wounded king is healed by the hero, and the hero is often rewarded with the crown. He becomes the next grail king, restoring fruitfulness to the wasted land and hope to its inhabitants. The focus is upon the recovery of the grail king, while any healing that the erstwhile fool has undergone in his transformation into the ruler of a powerful semispiritual kingdom is merely implicit. By providing us with dual protagonists, this film makes explicit the mutual healing inherent in the narrative. The similarities in the two characters prepare us for Gilliam's conclusion. Thus, Parry and Jack are both terribly wounded (ironically, Jack is the person responsible for Parry's wound, and the villains who put Parry in a coma are the same people from whom Parry has saved Jack), and each heals the other: Jack heals Parry by entering Parry's distorted world and seeking, at great personal risk, the cup that Parry believes to be the grail. In doing so, Jack heals Parry's emotional illness by virtue of his sacrifice on behalf of another. Parry heals Jack by leading him (partly by example and partly through his suffering) to personal responsibility, compassion, and attunement with other human beings.

When Jack finally accedes to Parry's insistence that he must obtain the grail, it is an act Jack carries out in blind faith. Certainly, the entire series of events clearly makes no sense: stealing a grade school loving cup from the library shelf of a rich recluse in the middle of New York and presenting it to a comatose man—these actions do not inherently seem to carry much healing power. They do demonstrate, however, Jack's willingness to risk his own well-being to help a seriously damaged fellow human. Jack's words (expletives deleted) to the nonresponsive, comatose Parry, before he sets off on his quest, make clear his change of heart.

> You think you're going to make me do this—well, forget it—I don't feel responsible for you or anybody—I'm not God—people survive. Don't [lie] there in your comfortable coma and think I'm going to risk all that because I feel responsible for you. I'm not responsible. . . . So I won't do it—don't give me that stuff about me being the one—there's nothing special about me. I control my own destiny—not some floating overweight fairies. I decide what I'm going to do—and I'm not going to risk my life getting some . . . cup for some . . . vegetable.

He turns to ask, rhetorically, the inmates silently surrounding them in the mental ward of the hospital: "What am I supposed to do?" and then unwittingly speaks to the heart of the issue, as he addresses Parry again:

> All right, for the sake of argument, let's say I do do this. . . . OK? If I do this I want you to know it wouldn't be because I felt I had to or because I felt cursed or guilty or responsible. If I do this . . . if I do this and I mean IF, it's because I want to do this for you. That's all, for YOU!

While Jack's change of heart does not occur solely in this two-minute speech, his words strikingly demonstrate that he is moving from someone who sought to buy peace of mind and earn forgiveness to someone who needs no reward. He wants to go on record that he is not doing this out of obligation but by his own choice. And he is doing it for Parry—not for Jack. Lest this be interpreted as too fast a turnaround, Gilliam shows that Jack has integrated the lesson, for he saves not only Parry but the overdosed millionaire, as well—the latter by intentionally setting off the alarm, thereby risking capture but also bringing immediate medical assistance to a desperate individual attempting suicide. Even this event, which may seem gratuitous, focuses us on the central issue of hope; suicide is a sin of despair—the final giving in to hopelessness—and Jack's action frustrates that hopeless outcome.

The winning of the loving cup completes Parry's healing of Jack, as it demonstrates the achievement of the direct and active learning process through which Parry has taken Jack, teaching him attunement. The process is initiated when Parry persuades Jack to help someone Jack finds absolutely repulsive: the would-be cabaret singer in Central Park, who is literally buried in horse manure. In a replay of the Good Samaritan story, Jack wants to leave him by the wayside, saying "someone will take care of him," to which Parry replies: "Who? Mother Theresa? She's retired." This incident signals the beginning of change in Jack, visually suggested by his holding of this person he despises in a pieta-like tableau. Parry's narration of the Fisher King's story follows immediately, prompted by Parry's direct identification of his new friend's wound: "Jack, I may be going out on a limb here but you don't seem like a happy camper." The lesson continues later, paradoxically at a time when Jack is attempting to raise Parry's confidence about women so that he will more actively pursue his courtly lady, Lydia. Jack explains that "women are great. They make homes and kill the livestock so the knights can go out there and get grails and slaughter villagers with a clear head." But Parry challenges Jack's analysis of male/female relationships: "Is that what your girlfriend does for you?" When Jack answers, "Sure," Parry just pulls on his own nose, a la Pinocchio. Continuing this effort to educate Jack on the value of human beings—specifically the woman who loves him but whom he treats quite badly—Parry facetiously seduces Anne in front of Jack, talking about what a great woman she is and how she is going to waste. At times, Jack slides back, reverting to his old ways after he has affected a meeting between Parry and Lydia: he returns to his former job (where his theme song is still "Hit the Road, Jack"), leaves Anne for a new flashy girlfriend, and denies (as Peter denied Christ) the homeless person he and Jack saved in Central Park. But even here his development into a real person is in process, as he no longer thanks God on-air that he is not like other people but identifies himself to his audience of the "bungled" as "one of the botched."

Consistent with the grail story, the most important aspect of what happens is indirect. Parry's direct efforts to teach Jack to connect in a meaningful way with others are ultimately less important than the subtle—but most powerful and successful—way in which Parry finally brings Jack to the point of self-sacrifice: simply by his woundedness— his need for help. When he first realizes his role in Parry's dementia, Jack's impulse is to deal with his guilt by making a sort of trade—a practical transaction, a quid pro quo that cancels the emotional debt. Just like the medieval grail hero, who believes erroneously that he can earn the grail by being a great warrior, so Jack wants to remain who he has been and simply work a deal. "I wish there was some way I could just pay the fine and go home," he tells Anne. Even as he goes off to seek Parry's grail, he still uses the language of exchange: payment of an I.O.U. in order to be free of debt. But the miracle that results comes about because of a transformation rather than a transaction. The lesson Jack eventually absorbs is that doing the right thing may well make one feel better (it may even be healing), but that cannot be the reason one does it.

Ultimately, Parry teaches Jack (as Jesus teaches his followers) by suffering for him and demonstrating that suffering for another is how we save ourselves. This selfless suffering is the essence of attunement—becoming sensitive enough to the experience of the other to suffer with and celebrate with that person—for attunement is made possible by atonement, the ability to become one with that other. In this film that connection is shown by the merging of Jack and Parry.

This convergence is brought home visually and acoustically when Jack scales the castle wall (Gilliam having discovered a mansion in downtown New York that looks just like a medieval castle, complete with stone tower, turrets, and circular staircase). Jack does this wearing Parry's clothes and, as he carries out Parry's quest, he has Parry's visions: he hears the neighing of the horse of Parry's Red Knight antagonist and vividly experiences Parry's nightmare of the massacre of his wife. His closeness to Parry is shown when he returns to Parry's bedside with the cup. In what may sound like the same old bargaining language, but is not (its conclusion is Parry's welfare rather than Jack's), Jack closes Parry's hands around the cup and says: "All right, I did my side of the bargain—here's your cup. You going to wake up now?" Jack's acting out of Parry's dream is supposed to result in Parry's awakening from his coma. The two men are now more than a team—they have virtually become the same person.

Throughout, Jack thinks Parry needs help, while Parry recognizes Jack as the truly needy person because he is a hollow man, someone without feelings. Parry's feelings may make him act crazy, but even this insanity is better than having no feelings at all. The turning point for the two men occurs when Parry is beaten the way Jack would have been beaten had Parry not intervened. Now it is Jack's turn to help Parry, and paradoxically, it is Parry's wounding that leads to Jack's healing. In the end, both have been healed, one from the disease of insanity, and the other from the far more insidious disease of inhumanity.

As a narcissist who is wounded by his inability to look beyond himself, Jack has been unable to feel. Psychologist James Masterson tells us that the "narcissistic wound" is healed only when the narcissist truly learns to care about someone else (Masterson and Klein 133). Unconditionally loved by Anne, Jack is incapable of returning that love for much of the film. By the end, however, he is able for the first time to express that love. Parry, at the beginning of the film, saves Jack, a stranger, for no reason—he is the Good Samaritan who describes himself as "the Janitor of God." Parry loves Lydia unconditionally but, spiritually wounded by the horror of what has happened to his wife and physically wounded by the Yuppie vigilantes, he becomes Jack—comatose, incapable of feeling anything. Yet he is loved by Lydia and saved by Jack, who has become attuned to him—a process mirrored also in the male/female relationships, as Lydia becomes attuned to Parry, who has always loved her, and Jack becomes attuned to Anne, who has always loved him. These relationships are described by Anne as a paradigm for what it will take to save society:

> I don't believe that God made man in his image, 'cause most of the shit that happens is 'cause of man. I think man was made in the devil's image and women were created out of God 'cause, after all, women can have babies, which is kinda like creating. . . . So the whole point of life . . . is for men and women to get married so that God and the devil can get together and work it out.

The narcissistic wound, natural or acquired, will be healed only by another human being who can fill the emptiness we have created by our inability to reach beyond ourselves on behalf of others.

At the beginning of the film, Jack is someone who intentionally humiliates his radio show callers by finishing their sentences for them, who whinnies the name "Ed" to humiliate the deranged killer-to-be caller by associating him with TV's "Mr. Ed," and who says that "people are garbage." By the end, he is so attuned with another that he actually sees that other person's nightmares—even as he endangers himself to save that other. The Pinocchio doll that the child gives Jack as he goes off to attempt suicide is the perfect symbol for all this: not only does it remind us about the necessity of trying to become human, but it also shows that the way to avoid being human is to lie—to others and to ourselves—about who or what we are and what our needs are. (One of the film's last shots silently tells us that the transformation of the characters into real people has been accomplished. It shows the hospital bed, which we last saw occupied by the comatose Parry. This time the bed is neatly made up. Lying down on it is the Pinocchio doll.) In the New Testament, evil incarnate is called the "father of lies" (John 8:44). Parry is brutally honest, and he is clear about his needs from the beginning, thus modeling for Jack two very important behaviors. The catch phrase of the sitcom Jack is being offered at the beginning of the film is

"Forgive me"—a lie, since it is spoken without sincerity—but its true meaning is what Jack assimilates by the film's end. By then, he has learned that "forgive me" is not simply something to say when we bump into people; spoken sincerely, this is the essence of contrition and of the indispensable atonement that can then follow.

The grail story is best known to us in the genre of romance. That may seem, at first, to trivialize it, to make it simply a love story, a fantasy, but the romance—with its idealistic perspective—reaffirms what is most important: the creation of hope. While *The Fisher King* keeps its myth-informed story realistic and does not shrink from the seedy details of life in modern New York, it unapologetically maintains the traditional romance context of the grail narrative. Thus Parry's relationship with Lydia embodies the basic rules of courtly love, as he worships her from afar and would gladly serve her forever, without reward. Lydia, who is anything but a medieval lady, expresses the unspoken deal assumed in the modern date at the end of Parry's first evening with her. She muses her way through its predictable, impersonal steps: she expects that he will come up to her apartment for a drink, they will engage in small talk, they will have sex; the next morning he will seem distant, he will say that he will call, but he won't, and she will find herself "ever so slowly . . . turn[ing] into a piece of dirt." But Parry rejects the dinner-for-sex bargain (another example of the quid-pro-quo mentality that Jack must overcome): "I don't want just one night . . . I'm in love with you." He describes in detail her daily routine, showing his attunement with her; he knows when she leaves for lunch, where she has lunch and what she eats, when she has a jawbreaker for a treat and, most importantly, he knows how she feels and accepts her as she is. "I know if it's a good day—and I know you hate your job and you don't have many friends and I know sometimes you feel a little uncoordinated and you don't feel as wonderful as everybody else . . . feeling as alone and separate as you feel you are." His interest in her is clearly not just for this night and (though he has sexual feelings for her), it is certainly not just about sex. In response to his declaration of love, she answers, "you're real," and they share a simple kiss, as they participate in the attunement process that leads to mutual healing. (This kiss is nicely juxtaposed with the passionate sex that ends the evening for Jack and Anne.)

If one of the hallmarks of courtly love is the knight's willingness to humiliate himself in the service of his lady (Lewis 12), Parry demonstrates this characteristic with gusto in the film's hilarious Chinese dinner sequence. Obviously attempting to make Lydia feel comfortable, he not only overlooks her atrocious table manners but joins in and imitates them—she slurps, he slurps; she belches, he belches; she drops dumplings, he drops dumplings—not to mock her but to make her inappropriateness normal. (We cannot help but agree with Anne, as she observes: "I think they were made for each other—scary but true.") Explaining the unlikely relationship of Parry and Lydia to Jack, Anne quotes the essential medieval romantic sentiment: *Amor vincit omnia*— "love conquers all." In an inspired two minute sequence, Gilliam shows us the essence of being in love—the way it changes everything—as we join in Parry's vision of his beloved lady and see Grand Central Station at rush hour transformed into a gigantic ballroom, filled with couples dancing in slow motion, merely because Lydia, Parry's beloved, has entered the room. Finally, Parry peels away the stigma of escape entertainment from romantic literature when he encourages Lydia not to be apologetic about her penchant for reading cheap romance novels: "There's nothing trashy about romance—in romance there's passion, there's imagination, there's beauty; besides, you find some pretty wonderful things in the trash."

Jack's capture of the loving cup is based on blind faith, and this is only the most obvious way in which the film tells us that hope arises from faith. Of course, what we believe in is crucial. Edward Malnick (the restaurant killer) believes in Jack's directives and becomes a murderer because of that faith. At the beginning of the film, Jack has faith only in himself—even his radio show theme song proclaims, "I've got the power." Parry's conversations with Jack are all about faith, whether he is responding to Jack's denial that there is a holy grail ("Oh, Jack, ye of little faith . . . you heathen, there's a grail"), or in describing the king in the grail story ("He had no faith in any man, not even himself"). Anne's assessment of the grail is not unsympathetic, just not tuned in. She knows the grail from her Catholic upbringing and thinks of it as "Jesus' juice glass." As she explains to Jack, the devil may be more interesting ("women are so attracted to men, cause let's face it: the devil is a whole lot more interesting. . . . I've slept with some saints in my day and, believe me, I know what I'm talking about—boring!"). Nevertheless, her belief in God is at once practical and unshakable, as shown by her analysis of human reality (above). For Parry, the grail is quite simply "God's symbol of divine grace," and belief in the grail story and in the grail itself is what gives meaning to his life. Ultimately, Jack must shift from belief in his degrading vision of life and of human beings to acceptance of Parry's idealized vision, something Gilliam shows through Jack's sunglasses. The powerful, self-assured, emotionally insulated Jack always wears sunglasses, while the injured, needy Jack does not. As if trying to teach him how to see, Parry takes Jack's sunglasses off when he shows him Lydia for the first time—inviting him to see another human being directly—without protective filters. The final outcome of Parry's vision is forgiveness, prepared for early in the film when we see Jack sitting in his luxurious bathtub, smearing cold cream on his face (covering up the real self), repeatedly saying "Forgive me" in various tones of voice, as he experiments with the tag line for a joke in the sitcom he has been offered. By the end of the film, Jack has learned the meaning of repentance, contrition, and forgiveness—a journey rooted in faith and leading to hope—and the derisive shout of "forgive me" by the cab driver who narrowly avoids running him down, ironically makes this point as clearly to Jack as it does to us.

It is no accident that *The Fisher King* (released in 1991) comes out of the late 1980s, in the wake of Reaganomics and a social policy that blurred the lines between the homeless and the mentally ill (Jencks 37). This brought to an unavoidable level of consciousness people like Parry and the Vietnam vet in the Grand Central Station sequence of the film (the vet calls himself a moral stoplight for a culture that assuages its guilt and copes with its anger by giving him charity). The Yuppie vigilantes who brutalize Jack and Parry serve as metaphors for the criminalization of the homeless, punished for denying us the luxury of pretending that all is well in Pleasantville and that such members of our culture do not exist. *The Fisher King* does not end with the social healing that occurs in traditional grail stories where selfless achievement brings the wasteland to fruitfulness. It does, however, tell the intensely hopeful story of mutual healing for two unlikely compatriots in a society whose injuries they exemplify. Unfortunately, the film also prophesies the smothering influence of the media in the twenty-first century, anticipating the kind of stranglehold talk radio now has on our airways and even on our national politics.

Above all, however, *The Fisher King* is a visual narrative that gives us hope—a most Christian virtue—by showing us how unconditional love (true Christian love, certainly the kind of love Jesus was trying to teach us) heals. The message is actually summed up nicely in the seemingly innocuous song "New York in June," sung repeatedly in the film and, quite poignantly, at its closing, when Parry, fully healed, has taught it to the other wounded and ill who fill up his hospital ward.

> I like New York in June—how about you?
> I like a Gershwin tune—how about you?
> I like a fireside when a storm is due;

I like potato chips, moonlight and motor trips—
How about you?

Appropriately the film's theme of attunement is encapsulated in a tune, reinforcing the idea of singing in tune, sharing a tune—being in tune. In keeping with the retelling of a medieval quest/love story, the lyrics of this tune even address the eternal power of romance:

Holding hands in a movie,
When all the lights are low,
May not be new . . .
But I like it—
How about you?

And finally, and most appropriately, the lyrics address the ways in which literature creates hope:

I'm mad about good books—
Can't get my fill.
How about you?

Chapter 15

The Gift of Grace
Isak Dinesen's Babette's Feast

Maire Mullins

He said to them, "Is a lamp brought in to be put under the bushel basket,
or under the bed, and not on the lampstand? For there is nothing hidden,
except to be disclosed; nor is anything secret, except to come to light. Let
anyone with ears to hear listen!"

—Mark 4:21-23

In his book *The Analogical Imagination*, David Tracy focuses on the "personal recognition of the presence of the uncanny as the presence of a power not one's own." This presence Tracy describes "as that power, gift, and command named grace" (374). The transforming power of grace is a central motif in Isak Dinesen's *Babette's Feast*. The presence of grace is evident throughout the story (originally published in 1950) and the film (directed by Gabriel Axel in 1987) and culminates in the transformation of the community during the feast scene. Dinesen constructs the tale so that smaller epiphanies lead to communal conversion and healing at the end of the story. Each character, even those who are minor, is affected by the workings of grace. The story is broken into twelve sections. All of the action takes place in the small Norwegian town of Berlevaag. The community has fallen away from its cohesion in faith. Its leader, the Dean, a gifted preacher and holy man, has died, and his two daughters have been left to try to sustain his vision. But they have been unsuccessful, and the community has drifted into discord. Their memories of past wrongs have displaced the message of Christ that the preacher had kept alive. The village is remote, yet three strangers from the outside world find their way to Berlevaag and contribute to the transformations that take place in the story.

Dinesen wrote *Babette's Feast* in 1950 for the *Ladies Home Journal*. *Babette's Feast* was later included in a collection of stories that Dinesen entitled *Anecdotes of Destiny* (1958). Robert Langbaum notes that this title "suggests that she had in mind stories which were to be both light and profound. The stories would, in the manner of anecdotes, make their witty points, but the points were to be about the strange ways in which destiny works out its own patterns" (246). The central mystery that the story explores is vocational choice. Each of the main characters faces a moment in which his or her life may change dramatically, and this moment, in turn, affects the small community of believers in Berlevaag. The two sisters, Martine and Philippa, choose not to leave Berlevaag so that they may stay and help their father with his ministry. Lorens Loewenhielm, a general, is haunted by the decision he made when he left Martine behind in order to pursue a successful career in the military. Achille Papin, a famous opera singer, cannot forget Philippa's beautiful voice and the choice she made to reject what he foresaw as a brilliant career. Babette, a renowned Parisian chef, comes to the community in exile because of the choices she, her husband, and her son made to be part of an unsuccessful revolutionary attempt in France. She also chooses to spend unexpected lottery winnings to recreate a sumptuous French feast in memory of those meals she used to prepare at the Café Anglais in Paris. Individual members of the community of Berlevaag continue to be torn apart by the memory of past choices, past hurts, past slights: as a group, they were "becoming somewhat querulous and quarrelsome, so that sad little schisms would arise in the congregation" (Dinesen 3–4). Hannah Arendt, in her foreword to a collection of Isak Dinesen's essays, writes "All her stories are actually 'Anecdotes of Destiny,' they tell again and again how at the end we shall be privileged to judge; or, to put it differently, how to pursue one of the 'two courses of thought at all seemly to a person of any intelligence'" (Arendt xix–xx).

By the end of the tale, the feelings of pain, difficulty, and regret about choosing or not choosing one path or another dissipate because of an event that brings the community together and that, in a moment of grace, heals and nurtures the collective body and soul of the small group through a restoration of hope.

The plot of the story is complicated, moving backwards and forwards in time; yet it retains a single setting: the small Norwegian town of Berlevaag (in the film, however, the story takes place in Denmark rather than Norway). In her introduction to *Norwegian Folk Tales*, Pat Shaw Iversen notes that "rural life in Norway has always been centered in family farms—small isolated communities, often surrounded by great forests and high mountains" (5). Berlevaag is such a place: small and isolated and, in the winter, even more isolated. Three outsiders come to this town, two to lay the groundwork for the third. A series of small coincidences and revelatory moments leads up to the feast at the end of the story. The first section of the story ends with a reference to Babette's presence in Berlevaag: "These two ladies had a French maid-of-all-work, Babette. It was a strange thing for a couple of Puritan women in a small Norwegian town; it might even seem to call for an explanation" (4). The rest of the story unfolds from this moment and explains the "true reason for Babette's presence in the two sisters' house," a reason that "was to be found further back in time and deeper down in the domain of human hearts" (4).

Bearing the sorrow of the choices that one makes in life and the uncertainty and confusion about whether those choices were good, Lorens Loewenhielm has for many years, but particularly of late, been unsure about the choice he made when he was a young man to leave Martine behind. For the general, Martine is linked to a side of his family history that is mysterious, uncanny, and inexplicable: "In the Loewenhielm family there existed a legend to the effect that long ago a gentleman of the name had married a Huldre, a female mountain spirit of Norway, who is so fair the air around her shines and quivers. Since then, from time to time, members of the family had been second-sighted" (5–6). For Lorens, Martine will come to represent the Huldre—"the air around her shines and quivers" in much the same way. The Huldre is more than just a "female mountain spirit," however. In Norwegian folklore, the Huldre is Adam's first wife and predates Eve. According to one version of the legend,

> That woman, who was created in the very beginning, was Adam's equal in every way, and would never be under him in anything. She

considered herself just as good a creation as he. But God said that
it wasn't good for man and woman to be equal, and so he sent her
and her offspring away, and put them into the hills to live. They are
without sin, and they stay there inside the hills, except when they
want to be seen. (Skar)

Marleen Barr sees Babette, not Martine, as the Huldre: "Babette is
analogous to this spirit in that she is a female alien, a French woman
who enters the home of two unmarried sisters residing in the Norwegian
town of Berlevaag. The sisters associate her with the marvelous. . . .
Babette is a magical alien who soon becomes an integral part of the sisters' familial female community" (23). Initially, Babette is looked upon
by the sisters and by the community as an exotic and fantastic presence
in the household of the two sisters. In the film, Babette soon proves her
worth to the sisters by bargaining shrewdly with the local fishermen and
the grocer, compelling one member of the community to observe that
"'She's a clever one.'" The sisters note that they have "more money than
before" Babette came because of Babette's skills and her keen sense of
housekeeping. Thus, the sisters are able to extend their humble ministry
of nurturing and tending to their deceased father's flock, and the whole
community benefits.

What the community, and the sisters, do not know is that Babette is
a renowned, extremely gifted French chef—the premier chef in Paris.
Like the Huldre, Babette is in exile. She practices her art every day,
transforming the dreary, ordinary meals of the sisters and the community they serve subtly but with an artist's touch. The extraordinary meal
she prepares at the end of the story is her way of revealing herself to the
sisters: her past self, her gifted self. She thus chooses to be seen in a new
way; yet ultimately she also chooses to retain her identity as servant and
remain with the sisters. In the film, the elaborate arrangements in anticipation of the feast serve to illustrate Babette's stoic grandeur: in one
scene, she is the regal leader of a group of followers carrying the feast
ingredients through the small town and back to the sisters' home. The
scenes in the kitchen represent some of the highlights of the film and
show Babette's culinary talents and mastery over her material as she
calmly orchestrates the cooking and serving of the food with firmness,
graciousness, and joy. Winning the lottery allows Babette to reveal her
true identity to the sisters yet also to share her good fortune with the
community. Her fortune, however, is not the amount of money she has
won, nor the meal she prepares; it is her artistry. What the sisters discover at the end of the tale is not that Babette can cook, but that she has

been cooking and providing for them and for the community all along. Her brief absence earlier to visit her nephew (and to order ingredients for the feast) allows the sisters and the community to realize how valuable Babette is to the town; without her, the sisters cannot perform their ministry as effectively; without Babette, the food that is served nourishes but does not satisfy those who are homebound in the same way. Babette is missed, and the sense of dread that grips the sisters—as Babette's seemingly inevitable longer absence looms before them—spreads through the small town. The extraordinary event of the feast serves as the yeast that allows the community to come to new life through a better understanding of themselves and the faith that sustains them as individuals and as a community. Hope and new life are restored.

For the young Lorens, Martine represents the Huldre: she lives "at the foot of the mountains," a place of transition between the world of the Huldre and the world of humans. Instead of viewing Martine as an ordinary woman, Lorens sees her as extraordinary and feels that she is calling him to a life that is infused with deep spirituality and piety. In her presence Lorens experiences "a sudden, mighty vision of a higher and purer life, with no creditors, dunning letters or parental lectures, with no secret, unpleasant pangs of conscience and with a gentle, golden-haired angel to guide and reward him" (6). But Lorens knows that if he were to embrace life with Martine, he would have to renounce his military career and stay in Berlevaag. Moreover, he cannot bring himself to speak in Martine's presence or in the presence of her father. Each time he visits he "seemed to himself to grow smaller and more insignificant and contemptible" (6). While he admires Martine's holy, gentle ways, he feels silenced and lost in her presence, and fears the loss of his voice, his agency, his being. Yet he also simultaneously feels great physical attraction to Martine. After he hears the Dean cite the following lines from Scripture, "Mercy and Truth, dear brethren, have met together. . . . Righteousness and Bliss have kissed one another," Lorens can only think of one thing: "the moment when Lorens and Martine should be kissing each other" (6). Unable to reconcile the spiritual and the physical in his own nature, Lorens becomes afraid and loses hope, so he leaves abruptly, telling Martine "I am going away forever! . . . I shall never, never see you again! For I have learned here that Fate is hard, and that in this world there are things which are impossible!" (7). Later, Lorens tells himself that he leaves Martine because he "did not want to be a dreamer; he wanted to be like his brother-officers" (7). In the story, however, Berlevaag is not the dream, it is the reality. The general's whole life outside of Berlevaag seems to have passed like a dream;

his return to this place represents a return to his best self, and it is a sliver of this self that he retains as he moves among the outside world. Before the feast, Lorens feels both haunted and mournful as he confronts his younger ambitious, restless self; he is unsettled by the possibility that he may have made the wrong choice in rejecting the life that Martine had to offer.

Soon after the young Lorens departs, Achille Papin, a famous French opera singer, also comes to Berlevaag. Unlike Lorens, he has already established himself as a successful figure. Yet, like the older Lorens, he feels "small in the sublime surroundings; with nobody to talk to he [falls] into that melancholy in which he [sees] himself as an old man, at the end of his career" (9). Then he, too, has a vision; he hears Philippa singing in church, and he dreams of taking her to Paris where he is sure she will be a "prima donna of the opera" (9). So he begins to give her voice lessons and regains his sense of hope. Because Achille is French, a famous singer, and "a handsome man of forty, with curly black hair and red mouth," he already powerfully represents otherness and sensuality to the Dean and to his daughters. But when the Dean learns that Achille is also a Roman Catholic, "the old clergyman, who had never seen a live Roman Catholic, grew a little pale" (10). Many critics focus on the humor present in the later feast scene, but Dinesen sets the groundwork for the comedy that follows in the understatement and restraint of these early parts of the story. The film effectively contrasts the sensuousness of Achille with the austerity of the Dean through clothing, mannerisms, hair, and voice. Achille dresses fashionably in capes and tall hats; the Dean's clothing is humble and mostly black. Achille uses dramatic gestures and flourishes; the Dean is constrained and controlled. Achille's hair is black, curly, and abundant; the Dean's is gray, straight, and slicked straight back from his forehead. Finally, Achille breaks spontaneously into songs as the mood strikes him; the Dean's voice is measured. These differences in the film help the viewer to understand the extent of the exotic nature of Achille's person for the villagers; he is remarkable, even more so than Lorens, for he is the epitome of the cultured citizen of the world.

Tracy writes that for some Christian thinkers "the ordinary itself in its full concreteness is the major locus of a manifestation-event. . . . These masters of the retrieval of the extraordinariness of the ordinary free their readers by their journey into the concreteness of particularity and through particularity to the whole as the concretely graced" (380). Like Lorens, Achille experiences the extraordinary in the ordinary. A visit to a small, isolated Norwegian town becomes a transformative event in both of these men's lives. Achille sees in Philippa great potential, a tremendous artistic talent, and a power to do good in the world. He tells her that "the common people would worship her, and she would bring consolation and strength to the wronged and oppressed" (10). But Achille goes one step further than Lorens; he attempts to fuse the physical with the spiritual. As Achille and Philippa sing from Mozart's opera *Don Giovanni*, he "drew her toward him and kissed her solemnly, as a bridegroom might kiss his bride before the altar" (11). Achille, in this instance, might be just acting out the opera, but there is a sacramental quality to his action. He kisses her not in a moment of passion or out of rote adherence to a script, but in a deliberate, serious, and heartfelt way, a way that suggests the potential for future union of a spiritual as well as a physical kind. This time, it is Philippa who responds to this possibility out of fear, "surprised and frightened by something in her own nature" (12). Consequently she flees, like Lorens, to what she knows. Philippa abruptly cancels the lessons, Achille is dismissed, and he leaves Berlevaag without her.

Langbaum describes the main tension in *Babette's Feast* as the contrast "between the ethical and esthetic life, with the ethical represented by the Puritan North and the esthetic by the Catholic, sensuous South" (248). This contrast can be more deeply understood in relation to what happens in the story by using Tracy's ideas about grace. Tracy writes: "Whenever that event [the event and person of Jesus Christ] is experienced in the present situation through some personal sense of the uncanny, the event-character itself moves to the forefront of Christian theological attention. The primary Christian word designed to emphasize that event-character is the word 'grace'" (371). Tracy divides the "locus of an experience of the event-character of manifestation" into "theologies of the ordinary" (381) and "theologies of the Word" (389). Practitioners of theologies of the ordinary free their readers "to re-experience the ordinary world of body, history, community, nature in all its concrete, shocking extraordinariness" (380). Babette represents this approach. She frees the sisters, and the community, to do their work. The sisters "soon found that from the day when Babette took over the housekeeping its cost was miraculously reduced, and the soup pails and baskets acquired a new, mysterious power to stimulate and strengthen their poor and sick" (16). The community, too, "felt a happy change in their little sisters' life, rejoiced at it and benefited by it" (17). Although Babette is a master chef—perhaps the greatest French culinary artist of her generation, in France—her work in this community seems ordinary and prosaic. Yet, Babette's "quiet countenance and her steady, deep glance had magnetic qualities; under her eyes things moved, noiselessly, into their proper places" (15). The feast represents the extraordinary moment of "event-character of manifestation," but what is just as extraordinary is Babette's steady transformative presence in this household. Her daily work reflects the "dignity and common humanity of the ordinary world of the every-day" (Tracy 381). Babette has humbled herself in order to become the servant/housekeeper/cook for the sisters, yet she is not humiliated. One scene in the film shows Babette scrubbing and washing the outside windows; here is one of the greatest Parisian chefs, with a cloth and a bucket of water, cleaning the windows of a small house in a small village. In Axel's film, there is always the sense in which the viewer can see both: the chef and the servant. The evidence of Babette's extraordinary strength and depth of character is that she can be both at once, and thus serve as an emblem of Christ.

In contrast to the "theologies of the ordinary," Tracy also describes "theologies of the Word." These traditions are "grounded in a profound religious sense of the power of the tensive subject matter revealed in the proclaimed word in the scriptures. . . . They recognize both judgment and grace in the preached word. They live by the memory of Luther's theological innovation when preaching became sacrament" (387). The community in *Babette's Feast* is grounded in the Word, especially the Word of God as preached by the founder of their "pious ecclesiastic party or sect," the Dean. Martine and Philippa are named after Martin Luther and "his friend Philip Melanchton" (3). The members of this sect "renounced the pleasures of this world, for the earth and all that it held to them was but a kind of illusion, and the true reality was the New Jerusalem toward which they were longing" (3). While he was alive, the Dean's ecclesiastic party "was known and looked up to in all the country of Norway" (3). Over the years, the hope that the community had felt as they looked toward the New Jerusalem has been obscured and forgotten in a tangle of memory, sinful behavior, jealousy, and petty quarrels. Despite their gentle and good ways that serve as models of Christian living, the sisters cannot keep the peace in the community now that the Dean has died.

In sections 2 and 3 of the story, the Dean, still alive, dominates the action. His daughters are beautiful and attract many suitors, but the Dean prevents their leaving him by emphasizing how trivial earthly love is: "the Dean had declared that to him in his calling his daughters were his right and left hand. Who could want to bereave him of them? And the fair girls had been brought up to an ideal of heavenly love; they were all filled with it and did not let themselves be touched by the flames of this world" (5). There is no mention of their mother; why she is absent, or what happened to her. The dutiful daughters have in some ways taken her place and serve as companions and helpmates to their father. When Lorens visits their house for dinner, the Dean declares "Mercy and Truth, dear brethren, have met together. . . . Righteousness and Bliss have kissed one another" (6), perhaps in an effort to keep the relationship between Martine and Lorens chaste. Later, when Achille arrives and requests permission to give Philippa lessons, the Dean says "God's paths run across the sea and the snowy mountains, where man's eye sees no track" (10). The Dean is referring to the great distance Achille has traveled and the lack of human understanding of God's ways. After Achille leaves, the Dean responds by saying "And God's paths run across the rivers, my child" (11). The sea, the mountains, and the rivers are all natural boundaries that separate one area or region from another. What connects them is the path of God that cuts across and through. This interconnectedness is reflected in the events of the story: Lorens leaves, but never forgets Martine; Achille leaves, but remembers Philippa. Both of their departures set the stage for the feast that occurs later in the story. The Dean's words emphasize connectedness and trust in God, but his inability to consider his daughters' agency provides the backdrop for the discord and unhappiness that later threaten to engulf his congregation.

Because the community under the leadership of the Dean focuses on, to use Tracy's words, "the empowering experience of God's decisive word of address in Jesus Christ," forgiveness and healing are possible "if God comes to disclose our true godforsakenness and our possible liberation" (386). "The theologies of the Word," Tracy writes, "recognize both judgment and grace in the preached word. . . . Those theologies communicate the forgiveness offered in the shocking and liberating message of justification by grace through faith" (387). In an effort to establish peace once again in the congregation and to return the brothers and sisters to the memory of their earlier, more pious selves, the two sisters plan to host a humble dinner in honor of the one hundredth anniversary of the Dean's birth. By coming together, eating a simple meal, and reflecting on the words of their founder, the sisters hope that the members of the congregation will finally be able to put aside past hurts and grudges. Memory, loss, regret, and silence play important roles in the narrative: memory brings Babette to the doorstep of the sisters as a supplicant. Exiled, homeless, and "deadly pale," Babette hands them a letter from Achille, who remembers the two sisters as "good people" who will help Babette. When he thinks of Philippa, he pictures her "no doubt surrounded by a gay and loving family, and of myself:

gray, lonely, forgotten by those who once applauded and adored me, I feel that you may have chosen the better part in life" (14). Philippa, of course, has chosen to follow the path that her father had laid out for her. Esther Rashkin writes that "the first five chapters of the twelve-chapter story recount a series of losses . . . each loss is associated with an inability or refusal to speak" (358). Rashkin traces the "silenced or suppressed voice" in these episodes, finding a "pattern of loss borne in silence," especially in the case of Babette.

What Rashkin overlooks in her analysis, however, is the reversal implied in the narrative, even early on, and especially in Babette's case. In his letter to the sisters, Achille mentions in a very casual way, "Babette can cook." Achille, of course, knows of Babette's stature as a chef and artist. Perhaps he does not wish to scare or overwhelm the sisters by telling them too much about Babette's background, or perhaps he is protecting Babette, who may have a price on her head for her revolutionary activities. Babette's arrival and early days in Berlevaag are described in language that has Biblical overtones:

> Babette had arrived haggard and wild-eyed like a hunted animal, but in her new, friendly surroundings she soon acquired all the appearance of a respectable and trusted servant. She had appeared to be a beggar; she turned out to be a conqueror. Her quiet countenance and her steady, deep glance had magnetic qualities; under her eyes things moved, noiselessly, into their proper places. . . .
>
> In the course of time not a few of the brotherhood included Babette's name in their prayers, and thanked God for the speechless stranger, the dark Martha in the house of their two fair Marys. The stone which the builders had almost refused had become the headstone of the corner. (15, 17)

Babette remains quiet and stoic until two events occur: she wins the French lottery, and she asks if she can prepare the Dean's celebration meal. Because she has won the lottery, she wishes to pay for the dinner herself. Of course, the sisters refuse: "Did she believe that they would allow her to spend her precious money on food and drink—or on them? No, Babette, indeed" (23).

For twelve years Babette has been cooking the simple cuisine ("split cod and an ale-and-bread soup") that the sisters had shown her how to prepare when she first arrived. A French meal would be an extraordinary event in this small town. For the meal to serve as a commemoration of the Dean's one-hundredth birthday, given his emphasis on the illusory nature of this world, seems extremely inappropriate to the sisters, and might be viewed negatively by the congregation as well. "Martine and Philippa looked at each other. They did not like the idea; they felt that they did not know what it might imply. But the very strangeness of the request disarmed them. They had no arguments wherewith to meet the proposition of cooking a real French dinner" (22). When they both strongly refuse to allow Babette to pay for the dinner, she takes a step toward them. As a servant, she would have been expected to keep a respectful distance from her employers. Nevertheless, "there was something formidable in the move, like a wave rising. Had she stepped forth like this, in 1871, to plant a red flag on a barricade? She spoke, in her queer Norwegian, with classical French eloquence. Her voice was like a song" (23). Babette's speech, her voice, now represents a mixing of the two cultures, a mélange. Her Norwegian might be "queer"—clearly nonnative—but it is inflected with the "eloquence" of French culture, and sounds like music, a precursor of the feast to come. The two Marys acquiesce, and Martha triumphs.

Their consent transforms Babette: "They saw that as a young woman she had been beautiful" (24). Their consent also transforms the sisters' understanding of themselves and the role they have played in Babette's life: "And they wondered whether in this hour they themselves had not, for the very first time, become to her the 'good people' of Achille Papin's letter" (24). It has taken twelve years for the two sisters to see themselves this way. Until Babette wins the French lottery, the two sisters had taken her presence in their lives for granted. Yet over the years, Babette has done tremendous good for the sisters and for the community in her silent, effective way: "They found that troubles and cares had been conjured away from their existence, and that now they had money to give away, time for the confidences and complaints of their old friends and peace for meditating on heavenly matters" (17). Their consent marks an important turning point in the story. By granting Babette's request, the sisters move closer to a "theology of the ordinary"—they now see the extraordinary in the ordinary. They remember the way in which Achille thought about them twelve years ago, and how he characterized them.

"They gave themselves into their cook's hands," Dinesen writes (25). The distrust that the sisters had felt for Babette's seemingly extravagant French ways when she first arrived has now, before the feast, become a mixture of trust and dread. As the ingredients arrive, the sisters increasingly feel a sense of foreboding and unease. Finally, after the arrival of a "monstrous" tortoise, Martine has terrible dreams: "[S]he thought of her father and felt that on his very birthday she and her sister were lending his house to a witches' Sabbath" (26). She goes to the members of the congregation and confesses her guilt. Just as Martine and Philippa had earlier begun to change because of their compassion for their servant, the congregation, too, begins to change because of their love for the two sisters. They resolve that "for their little sisters' sake they would, on the great day, be silent upon all matters of food and drink" (26). Even before the feast is begun, it has an effect on the congregation, bringing them together in unity for the first time in a long time.

The sisters' preparation for the feast and the guests' appreciation of their work are grounded in the everyday and the ordinary. Martine and Philippa "hung a garland of juniper round their father's portrait on the wall, and placed candlesticks on their mother's small working table beneath it; they burned juniper-twigs to make the room smell nice" (29). As the brothers and sisters arrive, they enter the room "slowly and solemnly. . . . Tonight the guests were met on the doorstep with warmth and sweet smell, and they were looking into the face of their beloved Master, wreathed with evergreen. Their hearts like their numb fingers thawed" (29). This scene foreshadows the later and more significant thawing of hearts that will take place during and after the meal. Tracy writes, "[T]he ordinary itself manifests itself in its true concreteness as extraordinary. The ordinary, the concrete, the everyday, not the 'unhappy consciousness' of the metaphysician is for some the surer, as the more home-ly route available in our situation of homelessness" (379). Indeed, this is the only time in the story that Martine and Philippa's mother is mentioned. The Dean's portrait represents his visage and his far-reaching sermons; he is a public figure and his likeness is meant to recall his continuing presence. There is no portrait of his wife, only her humble worktable, which suggests her ordinariness and her daily physical toil. She remains nameless and faceless. This small working table also serves as a reminder of Babette, who labors in the kitchen while the congregation, the sisters, and the general enjoy their meal and recall the Dean's sermons. Tracy asserts that "the ordinary, the concrete, the everyday" can be places where grace occurs. This simple room

> with its bare floor and scanty furniture was dear to the Dean's disciples. Outside its windows lay the great world. Seen from in here the great world in its winter-whiteness was ever prettily bordered in pink, blue and red by the row of hyacinths on the window-sills. And in summer, when the windows were open, the great world had a softly moving frame of white muslin curtains to it. (29)

The interior setting shows domestic order in its attention to small aesthetic concerns like flowers and the seasonal appearance of curtains. These small details provide a direct contrast to the "great world," which has already come to Berlevaag in the form of Lorens and Achille and which even now is represented by Babette, a famous French chef.

Prior to the feast, General Loewenhielm has found himself in a "strange mood" (31). He has not been in Berlevaag since his abrupt departure thirty years before. His military career has been successful; he is prosperous and well married; yet, even so, "something was wrong somewhere" (31). Lately, he has found himself "worrying about his immortal soul" (32). He considers himself "a moral person" but "there were moments when it seemed to him that the world was not a moral, but a mystic, concern" (32). He remembers his earlier refusal of Martine, and he associates that refusal with his fear of the Huldre of family legend. Had he made the right choice, all those years ago? He remembers, before he arrives at the sisters' home, how he had dined "at the finest restaurant" in Paris to celebrate a military achievement; it was at this dinner that he became engaged to his wife. Lorens will soon see Martine again, and the meal that he ate at that famous French restaurant, unbeknownst to him at this point in the story, will be replicated. He thinks, with satisfaction, about how this evening he would "come to dominate the conversation round that same table by which young Lorens Loewenhielm had sat mute" (34). Marlene Barr writes, "Babette and General Loewenhielm . . . experience new social worlds. Babette moves from the excessiveness of Paris to the austerity of Berlevaag; he moves from Berlevaag to Paris. They come together at the table, a particular artistic space where women and men can coexist" (26). Yet they do not really come together at the table; rather, their relationship is prefigured by the earlier vignette of the Dean's portrait and the mother's work table. The general, a public figure, looks forward to dominating the dinner table with talk of his accomplishments and career, in the hopes of erasing the memory of his earlier silence and, for him, defeat. Meanwhile, Babette labors in the kitchen, nameless and faceless to the general and the congregation, yet present though her work.

After the congregation has assembled in the dining room and they have "said grace in the Dean's own words," they remind themselves of the ordinariness of the meal, and how God can be present even in humble Berlevaag. "They were sitting down to a meal, well, so had people done at the Wedding of Cana. And grace [had] chosen to manifest itself there, in the very wine, as fully as anywhere" (35). What happens at Berlevaag mirrors, in some ways, what happened at Cana. Christ transforms water into an extraordinary, delicious wine, just as Babette transforms the ingredients she has assembled into an exquisite meal. The general is completely taken aback by the wine, the soup, the appetizers, and the famous "Cailles en Sarcophage" that are served; he thinks he remembers the chef who could prepare such a dish. Ironically, his earlier intent to dominate the dinner table has been superseded by yet another silence; he can only marvel to himself about the delicacies that are placed in front of him:

> General Loewenhielm, who was to dominate the conversation of the dinner table, related how the Dean's collection of sermons was a favorite of the Queen's. But as a new dish was served he was silenced. "Incredible!" he told himself. "It is Blinis Demidoff!" He looked around at his fellow-diners. They were all quietly eating their Blinis Demidoff, without any sign of either surprise or approval, as if they had been doing so every day for thirty years. (36)

His surprised delight at each dish or type of wine is met only with incomprehension or pliant agreement by his fellow diners; this adds to his incredulity. The Dean's followers, meanwhile, have begun to reminisce about the Dean's accomplishments. As Tracy describes in *The Analogical Imagination*, what happens simultaneously in this scene is "some personal recognition of the presence of the uncanny as the presence of a power not one's own. . . . The sense of the uncanny in the situation discloses a religious dimension to the situation itself" (374). The congregation, sworn to silence about matters of food and drink, and usually quiet at mealtime, this evening becomes unusually talkative. The subject of their talk is the "strange happenings which had taken place while the Dean was still among his children, and which one might venture to call miracles" (36). While the congregation dwells happily on the memories and accomplishments of the Dean, Babette quietly and capably presents to them course after course of sumptuous food and drink, consuming her lottery winnings as the evening passes in order to recreate the cuisine that she would have served at the Café Anglais. The congregation continues to be rooted in the preached word; yet, even as they tell stories about the Dean and his ministry, the extraordinariness of the food and the drink displaces this emphasis on the word.

The experience of grace, Tracy writes, "releases the interpreter to hear, to attempt some personal response. The recognition of the event-gift-happening reality of the response as not merely disclosive of, but elicited by the power of the whole, releases the interpreter to listen further" (375). While the congregation dwells on the memory of the Dean, the general, too, remembers "that dinner in Paris of which he had thought in the sledge" (36). Colonel Gallifet, his friend, tells the general that the chef was "a person known all over Paris as the greatest culinary genius of the age . . . 'And indeed,' said Colonel Gallifet, 'this woman is now turning a dinner at the Café Anglais into a kind of love affair—into a love affair of the noble and romantic category in which one no longer distinguishes between bodily and spiritual appetite or satiety!'" (38). As he speaks, the general comes to understand the meaning of his sudden decision to leave Martine and Berlevaag all those years ago. Instead of dominating the conversation at the dinner table, he "speaks in a manner so new to himself and so strangely moving that after his first sentence he had to make a pause. For he was in the habit of forming his speeches with care, conscious of his purpose, but here, in the midst of the Dean's simple congregation, it was as if the whole figure of General Loewenhielm, his breast covered with decoration, were but a mouthpiece for a message which was meant to be brought forth" (40). The general's message focuses on the meaning of grace and its presence in the lives of all who gather at the table. Mary Ann Fatula describes the general's experience in this way: "In returning to Fossum, Loewenhielm cannot escape the anguished question his soul asks. . . . In a moment of completely unexpected, exquisitely tender grace poured out at a festive meal, he finds the answer. The graciousness of God is infinitely more lavish than even his mistaken life choices" (166). Instead of dwelling on the past and on the heart wrenching difficulty of choice, the general gently asserts that "grace is infinite. . . . that which we have chosen is given us, and that which we have refused is, also and at the same time, granted us. Ay, that which we have rejected is poured upon us abundantly" (40). His words here echo the earlier scriptural passage used in reference to Babette: "[T]he stone which the builders had almost refused had become the headstone of the corner" (17). Babette's entry into the lives of the sisters represents the culmination of a long process of life choices and decisions on the part of the Dean, General Loewenhielm, Achille Papin, and the sisters them-selves. "Grace for the Lutheran," Mary Podles writes, "is an outpouring of unmerited, even unappreciated favor, of transcendent and supernatu-rally charged existence, raising those who correspond to it to an elevated, transfigured plane. Grace is poured out regardless of the right of the recipient to receive" (564). All who sit at the table, then, are blessed, regardless of their past sins, their flawed natures, their regrets, and lost hopes. The feast renews the group and allows General Loewenhielm to reconcile his past.

The tastes, the smells, and the physical fact of the feast have been repeatedly denied by the congregation even as they eat and drink their way through the courses. Nevertheless, the food and the drink have affected the humble group: "Most often the people in Berlevaag during the course of a good meal would come to feel a little heavy. Tonight it was not so. The *convives* grew lighter in weight and lighter of heart the more they ate and drank" (37–38). Tracy describes grace as a continuing, reverberating presence: "The power released by that event, gift, grace releases still other interpreters to a response of fundamental trust in the ultimate reality—a trust named faith" (375). The congregation, having listened to the General's speech, turn to one another in forgiveness and in hope. They cannot later remember clearly what happens: "[T]hey only knew that the rooms had been filled with a heavenly light, as if a number of small halos had blended into one glorious radiance" (41). Now they sing, laugh, and tease each other about the past. No longer bitter, they are affectionate and playful with each other, in a kind of "celestial second childhood. . . . bodily as well as spiritually hand in hand" (43).

When the two sisters have said good night to their guests, they suddenly remember Babette, the one responsible for the feast. "A little wave of tenderness and pity swept through them: Babette alone had had no share in the bliss of the evening" (44). The sisters have learned much this evening, especially Martine, but they are about to learn more. Babette, the exiled outcast, has now truly become the "headstone of the corner" (17). Even before her request to prepare the feast, Babette had made the decision to stay in Berlevaag with the two sisters. On the workings of grace, Tracy writes that "new possibilities of response occur through new experiences of recognition, response, reflection" (375). The sisters are simply stunned to learn that Babette has spent her entire lottery winnings on the meal that they have just consumed: "'What will you, Mesdames,' said Babette with great dignity. 'A dinner for twelve at the Café Anglais would cost ten thousand francs'" (46). They think that Babette's motive for spending all of her money on the feast is gratitude, but this is not the case. Babette has recreated the conditions under which she could practice her art. She presents the food to this humble and skeptical group as she would have done for French aristocrats and generals. The Dean's congregation has no knowledge of her artistry or her background as a famous French chef; only the general can really appreciate the exquisiteness of the meal from an educated viewpoint. Yet it is Philippa who has the best insight into Babette's decision. At the end of the story she tells Babette, in words that echo what Achille Papin had written to Philippa many years ago, "'In Paradise you will be the great artist that God meant you to be! Ah!' she adds, the tears streaming down her cheeks. 'Ah, how you will enchant the angels!'" (48).

What Philippa and Babette know, in their hearts, is that this evening represented the last opportunity that Babette would have to practice her art in the manner to which she has been trained. The simple daily fare of the congregation presents its own special challenges, but Babette will most likely never have the resources to replicate the meal that has just been served. Even if she were to return to Paris, she could not return to the Café Anglais, because the people for whom she has been trained to cook are all gone. And so, what Babette has left is what Philippa has left: the promise and hope of the afterlife, the "New Jerusalem" (3), the "millennium" (42). As Langbaum notes, "We are reminded that Christianity began with a Supper which it renews in its ritual" (252). The feast evokes the Last Supper in the number of guests invited, in its Eucharistic imagery, and in the effect it has on those gathered.

Babette's feast captures the moment when the "theologies of the concrete, the ordinary, the everyday" and the theology of the "proclaimed word" (Tracy 381) blend into each other. This moment is the moment of grace, gift, favor, the manifestation of God's presence. Distinctions between Berlevaag and Paris, the sisters and Babette, the past and the present, are erased. The feast brings the community together, allows the general to reconcile with his past, and cements the bond between the sisters and Babette. The general had thought that he had left Martine behind, all those years ago. When he left Berlevaag as a young man, he told Martine, "'I have learned here that Fate is hard, and that in this world there are things which are impossible!'" (7). Now, as he leaves Berlevaag, perhaps never to see Martine's living face again, he tells her, "[T]onight I have learned, dear sister, that in this world anything is possible" (42). Anything is possible because God's grace comes in unexpected moments to those who perhaps do not expect it or deserve its sudden transformative power. Whether through the ordinary, the extraordinary, or the Word, grace is present throughout the narrative of *Babette's Feast*, and manifests itself especially during the feast scenes. Babette has given all she has, not in terms of the French lottery but in terms of her talent, one last time. It does not matter that her audience (except for the general) cannot immediately identify the dishes that are served to them and do not possess educated palates; what matters is the effect the feast has on the community, the joy Babette experiences in preparing the meal, and the exquisite unity that takes place between the collective body and soul of those who partake of the feast. Having been touched by the extraordinariness of Babette's feast, Dinesen's characters return to the ordinariness of life in Berlevaag, but with renewed faith and hope.

Section Five

Hope and the Imagination

The capacity to construct futurity, . . . which is a central function of the imagination, is essential to our humanity and to its movement forward in the creative purposes of God.

—*Trevor Hart*

Clearly, the imagination plays a crucial role in envisioning and sustaining hope, whether we are talking about hope for individuals suffering from illness or death, or hope for nations seeking to recover from war and genocide. Commenting on the impoverishment that occurs when the imagination is impaired, George Steiner asks what human existence would be like without the capacity to think forward, to imagine a future better than the present—in other words, without the capacity to hope (*After Babel* 146), for hope resides, at least partly, in our ability to think, dream, and imagine. In his book *Images of Hope: Imagination as Healer of the Hopeless*, William Lynch puts it this way:

Imagination, if it is in prison and has tried every exit, does not panic or move into apathy but sits down to try to envision another way out. It is always slow to admit that all the facts are in, that all the doors have been tried, and that it is defeated. It is not so much that it has vision as that it is able to wait, to wait for a moment of vision which is not yet there, for a door that is not yet locked. It is not overcome by the absoluteness of the present moment. (35)

Yet true hope is not simply "an interior, self-sufficient absolute," Lynch says, but a deep awareness or faith that "there is help on the outside of us" (39–40). In the context of Christian faith, we might say hope is an "activity of imaginative faith" (Bauckham and Hart 53).

The essays in this collection view storytelling and story as imaginative acts with the potential to inspire hope. As Steiner says elsewhere, all hopeful imaginative acts involve a "wager on transcendence" that "quicken[s] into lit presence the continuum between temporality and eternity, between matter and spirit, between man and 'the other'" (*Real Presences* 4, 227). A Christian literary perspective that foregrounds eschatology makes this continuum more explicit. Works of literary art may anticipate or foreshadow the promised future, evoking hope for the unfolding of God's kingdom. The poet, the writer, the composer, and also, we would argue, the teacher, editor, and literary/film critic are involved in a labor of eschatological dimensions. For a "creative wager on transcendence" may occur in all these arenas that opens new "visions of reality (including its possible futures)" and thereby invents and extends what is or can be possible (Bauckham and Hart 64). The Creator, it seems, distributes the gift of imagination broadly, without regard to our state of belief or unbelief; at least that is the perspective at work in the first essay in this section, "The Redress of Imagination: Bernard MacLaverty's *Grace Notes*," by Barry Sloan in chapter 16. The power of the imagination to inspire hope is at the heart of Irish writer Bernard MacLaverty's novel *Grace Notes*. Not only is *Grace Notes* the title of the novel, it also embodies MacLaverty's view of the nature of art. Not incidentally, it is also the term used for notes in a musical composition added for embellishment or ornamentation, and in Christian doctrine, for the unmerited favor of God in providing redemption from a sinful past, restoration to wholeness, and inspiration and strength to live a creative and virtuous life.

MacLaverty's central character, Catherine McKenna, is a lapsed Catholic who presumably no longer seeks grace in traditional Christianity but instead through music as experienced by the novel's fictional composers Huang Xiao Gang, a Chinese Taoist, and Anatoli

Ivanovich Melnichuck from Kiev, a survivor of years of Communist oppression. These culturally diverse artists have a strong influence on Catherine's artistic development, and, as it turns out, on her spiritual development as well. When Melnichuck describes music as a way of praying, a way of receiving God's grace when religion was banned in his country, Catherine listens; what she can no longer receive from her Catholic heritage she is able to hear through her musical mentors. MacLaverty presents the development of Catherine's skills of musical composition against a background of complex domestic, religious, personal, and artistic tensions, and, through his own narrative art, she enables readers to experience her first major musical composition as a creative triumph of hope over depression. Sloan examines the hopeful and affirming power of art represented in *Grace Notes* in light of various writers' views on the connections between imagination and the generation of hope. Topics include Seamus Heaney's notion of the "redress of poetry," Don Cupitt's belief in the place of stories in enabling us to make sense of our lives, Moltmann's eschatological perspective, and Delbanco's concern for the loss of "sustaining narratives." The tensions are evident throughout the essay between the Romantic and humanistic view of the imagination, which looks largely within for creative expression and hope, and a more explicitly Christian view that looks with suspicion on the "unbaptized imagination," as C. S. Lewis might say, and reaches heavenward for inspiration. Interestingly, at the climax of the novel, Catherine's reflections on music and creativity are formulated increasingly in Christian, and often specifically Catholic, terms. At the climax of a performance of her music, she recalls how she had "reached down into the tabernacle of herself for this music and now feels something sacred in its performance" (270–71); we wonder if the author is trying to reconcile the more secular Romantic view of art with a more traditionally Christian view. For Catherine experiences an epiphany of sorts when she realizes "The same thing could be two things. Transubstantiation" (275). The reader is left to ponder the metaphor.

In chapter 17, Emily Griesinger looks at the imaginative hopefulness of the Harry Potter series in her essay "The Search for 'Deeper Magic': J. K. Rowling and C. S. Lewis." When Jesus spoke of entering the kingdom as a little child, it is easy to think he meant for all of us, adults and children, to let our imaginations soar. What we are able to imagine shapes what we believe, who we become, and how we spend our lives. Since the Harry Potter books have taken the world of children's literature by storm, Christian parents and educators have passionately debated the merits and perils of the series for young minds. Griesinger addresses some of the most difficult questions in her essay: What is the role of the imagination and fantasy in drawing readers to or away from God? Is there a way to read fantasy texts like J. K. Rowling's Harry Potter series that does not violate biblical prohibitions and cautions against things magical? She begins by establishing a relationship between the genre of fantasy and the concerns of Christian eschatology, or in terms derived from Moltmann, the "theology of hope." Combining insights from Christian eschatology with ideas found in two fantasy writers well-known in the Christian community, J. R. R. Tolkien and C. S. Lewis, Griesinger argues that Rowling's magic, like the magic in Tolkien and especially the "deeper magic" in Lewis, is best understood as a narrative device that articulates hope. According to Griesinger, rescue of the unloved from the unloving, and sacrifice as part of what it means to love and be loved are variations of deeper magic found in the Potter series. While deep magic in Harry Potter lacks the Incarnational element of Lewisian Christology in the Narnia series, and while Harry Potter draws on imagery and symbols associated with witchcraft and the occult, Rowling paradoxically incorporates and celebrates ideas that are decidedly Christian: friendship, courage, self-sacrifice, and love. Both Lewis and Tolkien believed in the creative use of the "baptized imagination" and acknowledged the capacity of children's fantasy to arouse desire for heaven and even lay the groundwork for presenting the gospel. Griesinger concludes that the magic in Harry Potter works similarly, arousing desire for a world where all of us, even geeks, athletes, and nerds, can experience the deepest magic of all, which is to know we are accepted and deeply loved. Rowling sets the stage for the Christian gospel and provides the reader, as Lewis says, a "real though unfocused gleam of divine truth."

Three different polls have named J. R. R. Tolkien's *Lord of the Rings* the most important book of the twentieth century. It seemed fitting, therefore, to end this collection with a thoughtful essay by Ralph C. Wood devoted to this triumph of the imagination, a truly sustaining narrative that nourishes and enables hope. Wood's essay "J. R. R. Tolkien: Postmodern Visionary of Hope" in chapter 18 argues that while Tolkien is often viewed as "a *pre*-modern antiquarian of despair," there are good reasons for reading his Lord of the Rings trilogy in "hope-filled postmodern terms." Tolkien's praise for cultural pluralism and particularity, his insistence that knowledge and truth be historically located, his critique of modernity as coercive in making false claims to universality, and his profound demonstration that modern evil can be combated only by communities of humble and seemingly weak "hobbits" who come together and stay together by refusing coercive power, are the carefully argued ways in which Wood sees Tolkien embodying a postmodern vision of hope. Toward the end of *The Two Towers*, Samwise Gamgee observes that some tales matter more than others, and the best tales, the ones that "stay in the mind," are not necessarily ones where the adventure or quest ends happily, where characters come to a good end. Stories that really matter have heroic characters, like Sam and Frodo, who have lots of chances to turn back but do not. Moreover, Tolkien has interwoven into his trilogy, implicitly if not directly, truths of the Christian gospel, the ultimate hope-giving story that subverts coercion with humble acts of pity, mercy, and reconciliation. Real heroes, like Sam and Frodo, must simply slog on, venturing forward in hope for a victory not yet seen. As Wood explains in "The Lasting Corrective," the fourth chapter of his book *The Gospel According to Tolkien*, "[I]t is given to none other than Samwise Gamgee to discover the necessity of living according to the right Story if we are to have real hope. . . . The tales that rivet the mind . . . involve a Quest that we do not choose for ourselves . . . What matters, Sam wisely concludes, is that we enact our proper role in an infinitely larger Story than our own little narrative" (146–47). To complete such a quest requires "the highest of all virtues: hope as well as faith working through *love* (Gal. 5:6)" (148).

Chapter 16

The Redress of Imagination
Bernard MacLaverty's Grace Notes

Barry Sloan

At the outset of his lectures given as Professor of Poetry at Oxford University, Seamus Heaney spent some time introducing the theme he had chosen as the keynote to the series and which is captured in the title of the published version of these talks: *The Redress of Poetry*. He points out that the *OED* definitions of the verb *redress* include "to set (a person or thing) upright again; to raise again to an erect position. Also fig. to set up again, restore, re-establish"; and he locates the "redressing effect of poetry" in "its being a glimpsed alternative, a revelation of potential that is denied or constantly threatened by circumstances" (15, 4). Thus, Heaney suggests, "the redress of poetry comes to represent something like an exercise of the virtue of hope as it is understood by Václav Havel"; he continues by quoting a passage from Havel's *Disturbing the Peace* which refers to hope as

> a state of mind, not a state of the world . . . a dimension of the soul
> . . . not essentially dependent on some particular observation of the

> world or estimate of the situation. . . . It is an orientation of the
> spirit, an orientation of the heart; it transcends the world that is
> immediately experienced and is anchored somewhere beyond its
> horizons. (4)

Heaney's passionate affirmation of the power of poetry not only to give
pleasure and to surprise, but also to enable release from the "labyrinth"
of experience through the strength and power of the imagination, may
not be entirely original, although it has seldom been uttered with greater
eloquence. However, his particular emphasis on the restorative (redressing) potential of poetry and its relationship to the nurturing of hope,
proposes a striking set of connections and invites comparison with the
perceptions of other artists and scholars on the same theme.

While Heaney's lectures are concerned with poetry, Gesa E.
Thiessen makes similar observations about modern painting in her book
Theology and Modern Irish Art:

> The imagination enables a person to free her/himself from their
> own confines; it can bring about a unified perspective arising from
> the depths of the human being, i.e., one's emotion and intellect. It
> is by its power to overcome constrictions of despair and fear that
> the imagination becomes an ally of hope, a way of coping with,
> rather than avoiding, reality, an instrument of healing. (265)

Thiessen offers detailed commentary on the beliefs, views, and
selected works of ten leading Irish painters, and she draws upon the
writings of theologians such as Jürgen Moltmann, Paul Tillich, Horst
Schwebel, and Karl Rahner to explore the relationship between art and
theology. She substitutes the word "theology" for "Christianity" in her
reformulation of Moltmann's claim that "Christianity is eschatology, is
hope, forward looking and forward moving, and therefore also revolutionizing and transforming the present" (*Theology of Hope* 16). Thus,
she writes, "Theology is eschatology and eschatology means hope—
hope, faith and redemption even in the midst of and despite despair"
(252). Thiessen further contends that "it is the gift of the imagination to
creatively transcend dualisms through its power to connect opposites, to
juxtapose and hold in creative unity light and darkness, to bring
together what otherwise may be regarded as disjointed or irreconcilable.
It is the imagination that makes possible and builds dialogue, including
that between theology and the arts" (265).

Thiessen's repeated references to theology rather than Christianity
reflect the diverse beliefs of her chosen artists, which range from the
Christian feminism of Mainie Jellett to Colin Middleton's humanism,

and from Patrick Graham's Catholicism to the "agnostic-atheist convictions" of Patrick Scott. Some of Scott's "highly spiritual-transcendent works of art . . . have been included in places of worship, which proves an important point in the whole dialogue of art and theology, namely that the spiritual or even the religious-Christian content in a work of art does not depend on an artist's religiosity" (121). The implicit point here is worth stressing: a work of art can possibly transcend the artist's own unbelief in conventional theology and communicate awareness of a different order of reality; it may offer, in effect, the kind of spiritual insight, intimately allied to the Christian understanding of hope, which has its origins in the materiality of the world and the contrariness of human experience, yet is not finally crippled or constrained by them. As the theologian Dermot A. Lane has written, hope "arises out of the experience of the negative. The reality of evil in the world therefore evokes hope and so we are thrown back once again on hope against hope in the face of evil" (165). Insofar as art—be it poetry, painting, fiction, or the musical composition imagined in the novel that is discussed below—enables us to realize the assimilation of the negative and its transformation through the resources of imagination (in creative alliance with the disciplines involved in doing so), it is a compelling witness to the endurance of human hope, even in a culture characterized by existential doubts, postmodern uncertainties of value and knowledge, and the decline of religious faith.

Indeed, one may go further. Andrew Delbanco has observed the fundamental human need "to organize the inchoate sensations amid which we pass our days—pain, desire, pleasure, fear—into a story." He has pointed out that "When that story leads somewhere and thereby helps us navigate through life to its inevitable terminus in death, it gives us hope" (1). But he has also identified a crisis: "[W]hile we have gotten very good at deconstructing old stories"—and here he alludes to his discussions of the stories of puritan Protestantism, and of nationalism in America—"when it comes to telling new ones, we are blocked" (106). Writing in a more general way than Delbanco, the theologian Don Cupitt makes very similar points:

> Stories are interpretative resources, models and scenarios through which we make sense of what is happening to us and frame our own action. Unlike the forms and concepts of philosophy, stories are stretched out in time, as melodies are. They shape the process of life. It is through stories that our social selves, which are our real selves, are actually produced. (ix)

Religion, according to Cupitt, "is the attempt so to live as to make life make sense, whatever happens." Religious stories encourage us to believe that such an attempt is possible: "The pleasure of stories . . . is the pleasure of the metaphors that make us intelligent and the metonymies that enable us to live meaningful lives in time" (15).

Like Delbanco, Cupitt recognizes that old stories, or, perhaps more accurately, stories in their old forms, may cease to be "interpretative resources" to which modern generations can relate in the same way as their forebears. He seems, however, more optimistic about the potential of humans to overcome this problem when he declares:

> Truth is no longer something out there: it is a way of words. The preacher, interpreter or artist is now making truth in the telling of the tale. Truth is no longer held firm and self-identical in eternity; instead, it lives and grows and changes in time. The interpreter's job becomes one of creating new truth, by letting the old signs move around and drop into new and fertile relationships. The interpreter is no longer just a servant of the Truth, but has become someone whose job is the endless production of truth. Truth is like music and love; it has to flow continually. Out of us, like living water. (23–24)

This description of the "interpreter's" job might serve equally well as an account of literary, artistic, or musical creativity, and, indeed, Cupitt illustrates his argument with references to the prose of James Joyce and the music of Igor Stravinsky. The truths which the most important stories communicate may be expressed and encountered in various forms—verbal, visual, musical. These constitute the kinds of "sustaining narrative[s]" upon which Delbanco claims that we depend; without "some such symbolic structure by which hope is expressed," we risk losing the ability to "imagine some end to life that transcends our own tiny allotment of days and hours" and may slip into a state of melancholy in which hope has diminished or is wholly absent (Delbanco 1–2).

The particular example of a "sustaining narrative" that is the subject of the rest of this essay is a novel, *Grace Notes*, by Bernard MacLaverty, first published in 1997, and nominated for the Booker Prize that year. MacLaverty, an Ulsterman, is the author of four collections of short stories: *Secrets* (1977); *A Time to Dance* (1982); *The Great Profundo* (1987); and *Walking the Dog* (1994). He has also written three other novels: *Lamb* (1980); *Cal* (1983); and *The Anatomy School* (2001), as well as film, radio, and television adaptations of his work. These include both a radio and a television script based on "My Dear Palestrina," a story from his 1982 collection that centers on the relationship between a young boy and his female music teacher set against the background of sectarian violence in Northern Ireland. This story may now be seen in some ways to have anticipated the much more ambitious exploration of the power of music in *Grace Notes*. This novel is especially interesting because it not only represents the struggle of the principal character, Catherine McKenna, to take control of forces which threaten to cause her life to disintegrate, but shows how her crisis is inseparable from her attempts to articulate herself—her story—through practicing her own art of musical composition.

A variety of factors, personal and social, contribute to the complexity of Catherine's situation: an only child, she has become estranged from her parents' provincial life in County Derry, Northern Ireland, and especially from their Catholicism; her musical ability, once a source of pride, and particularly her compositional imagination, further exacerbate the relationship because her family no longer understand what she is trying to do or the vision or story she is striving to express in her work. Furthermore, Catherine herself is highly conscious of her own unusualness as a composer within an art form which, historically, has been dominated by men. We learn that her parents only discovered retrospectively from neighbors about a broadcast of her first major commissioned composition (the event with which the novel concludes). When Catherine returns briefly from Scotland after her father's sudden death, her mother is further hurt and morally outraged to discover that her daughter is the unmarried mother of an eighteen-month-old child. Catherine's relationship with Dave, the child's English father, collapses because of his chronic drinking and violence against her. Accordingly, she leaves the island of Islay, on which they have been living when he is hospitalized for his alcoholism, and takes refuge with friends in Glasgow. Throughout the period after Anna's birth, Catherine also struggles with postpartum depression. Her mood fluctuates between fear of harming her child or blaming her for destroying her musical creativity and discovering in her baby the very source and inspiration of her newest and most important composition.

A more general point about Catherine's circumstances must also be noted: her Northern Irish Catholic background means that she is profoundly aware of a violently divided community. On her journey back to Ireland for her father's funeral, she senses that all the Irish travellers are treated as suspects by airport security staff, and she finds her hometown struggling to recover from the devastation caused by a terrorist bomb. One of her strongest childhood memories is of listening with her father to the thunderous sound of the huge Lambeg drums played by Protestant Orangemen around the Twelfth of July. The Lambeg drum is a very large, loud drum associated with Protestant Loyalist demonstrations and named after a village in County Antrim, Northern Ireland. Struck with canes, it can produce sound that carries for miles and may resemble the rattle of automatic gunfire. Understandably, Mr. McKenna dismisses such drumming exhibitions as racist bigotry, but Catherine intuitively recognizes the thrillingly inventive sound patterns and rhythms that, years later, she will incorporate into her own music.

However, MacLaverty not only sets up a complex personal and social narrative; he also structures it in a way that further enriches the story we are told. The novel is in two parts, but the first succeeds the second in chronological time. The earlier section opens with Catherine's arrival in Northern Ireland for her father's funeral after a prolonged absence from home, during which she has studied as a postgraduate in Scotland, travelled to Russia, moved to Islay to take a teaching job, begun and ended her relationship with Dave, given birth to Anna, and completed her commissioned work, *Vernicle*, which, we understand, was broadcast a few weeks earlier. In this part of the book, Catherine's revelations to her mother are painfully difficult, and their relationship remains antagonistic. She also pays a visit to her first piano teacher, Miss Bingham, who is dying of cancer, and who had listened appreciatively to the broadcast of *Vernicle*. Their conversation provides both Catherine and the reader with an alternative view of herself, of her work, and of the future directions it may take.

Throughout her stay, Catherine exhibits growing anxiety about Anna's well-being in the care of her friend in Glasgow. We are unable to understand the full significance of this anxiety until we read the second part of the novel, which furnishes us with much more insight into Catherine's musical education and development as well as the events that culminate in the composition and first performance of *Vernicle*. This performance, created for the reader in the words of the extraordinary closing pages of the book, is an immensely moving and life-affirming expression of hope. In it Catherine first confronts crucial episodes in her past experience and then passes beyond them to unforeseen resolutions and harmonies which are the product of her imagination and compositional skills. Because of the chronologically reversed two-part structure of the novel, MacLaverty resists an oversimplified ending in which the hope gained appears immune to future lapses into melancholy, loss of self-esteem, and pain. Hope must not only be achieved; it must also be won again and again, and the novel points to this process too.

From childhood, Catherine finds that the sounds and rhythms of music are integral to her sense of who she is. At an early piano lesson with Miss Bingham, she surprises her teacher by clapping the rhythm of her name with seven rather than six syllables, and when questioned about this replies: "My music name is my full name, Catherine Anne McKenna. Seven claps are better than six" (31). Remembering this incident as a troubled adult, she tells herself she must "hold on to a sense of herself, of who she was, and how it could be told in terms of sound" (31). The novel as a whole circumscribes Catherine's efforts to preserve her "sense of herself" and to tell her story "in terms of sound." She achieves this by drawing deeply upon diverse influences in her own work, using and synthesizing them in ways that are new and personal, and yet also capable of communicating with others. Since MacLaverty is writing a novel, not a piece of music, there is the danger that he will merely tell us how Catherine's music works without enabling us to believe that we have shared it and experienced it for ourselves. His resourcefulness in solving this problem is itself a testimony to the imaginative power of storytelling and story. Catherine is represented as thinking intuitively in terms of musical analogy, and some of the specifically named compositions which she recollects at moments of particular intensity may also be familiar to readers of the novel, thereby providing a further entry into her world of stories in sound.

For example, confronted with the grave of a former classmate who has been "killed on active service" for the Provisional IRA—"He gave his life for Ireland," declares the inscription on his gravestone—she immediately thinks of Janáček's piano sonata, *I, X:1905, From the Street,* written after the death of a youth at the hands of Austrian troops for demonstrating "in support of the idea of a Czech university" (84). Later, walking back from the graveyard through some woods, she remembers another of the same composer's works, *On the Overgrown Path,* which she thinks of as "bleak beyond words," a reflection which leads her to the realization that the essence of music is "emotion beyond words" (86). Elsewhere, when she learns the story of Shostakovich's *Babi Yar Symphony,* written in response to Yevthushenko's poem about the Nazi massacre of the Kiev Jews, Catherine is prompted to recite to herself "the geography of the places of death in her own country" (i.e., the sites of sectarian atrocities) and of IRA terrorist outrages in England (127). The duality of her reactions to these thoughts is symptomatic of her own fluctuations between despair and hope, unbelief and faith in the power of both music and motherhood:

> It was awful to think that if she wrote the most profound music in
> the history of the world it would have no effect on this litany [of
> the names of places where killings have occurred]—it would go on
> and on adding place names. . . . Yet somehow she knew that her act
> of creation, whether it was making another person or a symphonic
> work, defined her as human, defined her as an individual. And
> defined all individuals as important. (127–28)

This revelation is further illustrated when, at perhaps the lowest ebb
in her domestic situation and postpartum depression, feeling her "mind
. . . attacking itself," "flagellating itself," like "a crown of thorns worn on
the inside," and seeing her life reduced to endless nappy changing and
avoidance of her partner's drunken abuse, Erik Satie's piano piece
Vexations, which "was to be played 840 times," provides her with the
analogy for her mental state (199). It is a memory of more music.
Kathleen Ferrier singing Mahler's *Kindertotenlieder* ("a voice full of pure
music which broke the heart") drives her back into "thinking about what
she did *not want to think about*. She felt the darkness of the bright days
descending on her step by step. A cascade winking out hope" (201).
Because the readers, like the character, are reminded by these examples
of the affective power of music that they, too, have heard, accepting and
believing in the power of Catherine's own compositions becomes possible.

In addition to specific musical references, MacLaverty's countless
allusions to the sounds produced by objects, words, wordplay, and natural phenomena further persuade us of the strength and dominance of
Catherine McKenna's auditory responsiveness and imagination.
However, the two composers who influence her most are the novelist's
own creations—Huang Xiao Gang, a Chinese Taoist, and Anatoli
Ivanovich Melnichuck, a native of Kiev who has preserved his artistic
integrity throughout years of communist oppression. The former poses
questions about the very origins of music—"Do you compose the music
or does the music compose you? Where are the notes between the notes?
Graces, grace notes or, as the French would have it, *agréments*" (33). He
also speaks of "*pre-hearing*" music before anything is written down,
which is what Catherine herself later experiences. Like Huang Xiao
Gang, Melnichuck's cultural background is radically different from
Catherine's own, as she quickly realizes when she visits him: "The city of
Kiev was somewhere else. Other. Half-way between East and West"
(121). She is deeply moved by the singing and bell-ringing in the
Eastern Orthodox Church and understands that although "human pain
and suffering were evident everywhere . . . the people were getting some-

thing which satisfied a deep spiritual need," a striking contrast to the absence of spiritual sustenance she senses in her native Catholic tradition (122). Melnichuck tells her, "I can see music as the grace of God. Through all the communist times they did not allow religion. For us music was a way of praying, music was a way of receiving God's grace" (125). Even before this statement, we know that part of the original appeal of his own music to Catherine lay in her sense of its spirituality and of the paradox of this kind of music coming from "a country which had long ago dispensed with religion and the spirit" (62).

Significantly, both Huang Xiao Gang and Melnichuck employ the word *grace* in talking about music. *Grace Notes* is not only the title of the novel and, perhaps, an implicit declaration of the author's own view of the nature of art; it is also, of course, the musical term used for notes added as embellishment or ornamentation. In a theological context the word *grace* itself is specific to Christian doctrine, referring to the free gift of God's sustaining assistance, which enables the sinful individual to resist temptation and despair and to perform righteous acts, thereby leading to sanctification. Catherine McKenna is a lapsed Catholic for whom the concept of grace in the latter sense is presumably meaningless, but nevertheless she is in search of the wellsprings of spirituality, which she glimpses in the teaching of Huang Xiao Gang, the music of Melnichuck, the singing of the priests, and the tintinnabulation of the bells in the Orthodox Church. She also comes to discover a kind of sacramental grace both in the act of composition and in the sounds of her own work. Repeatedly, her reflections on music and on her creativity are formulated in Christian, and often specifically Catholic, terminology. Thus, when she fears her creative powers have died, she thinks, "The sanctuary lamp was out" (38); and, waiting for the broadcast performance of her work to begin, "The only equivalent, she thought, was sitting in church.—But this *was* church" (269): the concert venue is a deconsecrated church building. She even compares the red transmission light to "a BBC sacristy lamp" (267). During the concert itself, she senses that she has "reached down into the tabernacle of herself for this music and feels something sacred in its performance" (270–71). As it moves to its climax, resolving earlier dissonances in new harmonies, she realizes, "The same thing could be two things. Transubstantiation" (275). Catherine calls her work *Vernicle* after the badge worn by medieval pilgrims:

> Proof that you'd been there. In a land of devastation. At the bottom
> of the world. And come through it—just. She'd brought back

evidence in the shape of a piece of music. *Vernicle.* A feather in her cap—for full orchestra. From the shrine of desolation. (245)

Andrew Delbanco concludes *The Real American Dream* by quoting with approval Ralph Waldo Emerson's self-contradictory observations in the 1830s, in which he first declares little hope of a new faith emerging to replace his inherited version of Christianity. He then follows this declaration with an exhortation to "do what we can to rekindle the smouldering nigh quenched fire on the altar" (118). Bernard MacLaverty's representation of Catherine McKenna's imagined music might be regarded as just such an effort at rekindling, and a successful one at that. When Catherine visits her terminally ill former music teacher, Miss Bingham tells her:

> That night I listened to your concert—just before Christmas—the same week the doctor told me things were not as they should be. It was all just beginning to sink in. And when I sat down I was . . . a person can be too much locked up in their own mind—isolated even—then something happens to say no—someone else has been through this. You are not the only one. *I am where you have been.* Your music spoke to me that night. (112)

And she adds:

> It gave me hope. . . . I don't mean for a change in . . . what I have. . . . Our sort [Miss Bingham is a Protestant] doesn't go with that kind of thing, Lourdes and the like. No—listening to it gave me hope. And joy. The end gave me great joy. (112–13)

Thus, within the novel itself, one character acknowledges how the art of another has been for her, in Delbanco's phrase, a "sustaining narrative." Given, too, the Northern Irish context, it is notable that this musical narrative has transcended the denominational differences that have frequently alienated individuals and divided society, and which are deeply embedded in tunes and styles of music that have long-established sectarian associations. Nevertheless, Catherine is dismissive of the reductive interest of the press in "a Roman Catholic using Protestant drums, the Lambeg angle" (105), as Miss Bingham puts it. She insists that her motives in using them were musical, not political. Any reader who is alert to the cultural implications of what she has done will be struck by the unexpected hopefulness of her appropriation and incorporation of these particular rhythms and sounds.

Catherine is also shown to be aware of the truth that music has the power to provide a "sustaining narrative" for her own life: in the depths of depression, she knows that "Anybody who composes dark music, music without hope, is still a million miles better off than somebody like her. Sitting too tired, too dejected to even lift a pencil" (231). Paradoxically, the act of writing "music without hope" would itself be hopeful, as she understands even more clearly when she has composed *Vernicle*: "To write something really dark, despairing even, is so much better than being silent" (266). Bearing in mind Seamus Heaney's comments, this testimony, perhaps, hints at what might be called the "redress" of music.

Vernicle is represented as a creative synthesis of a multitude of memories and emotions, all of which MacLaverty, like a good composer, has carefully laid down earlier in the novel. It evokes domestic tasks, the intricate patterns of Celtic art, the Lambeg drum rhythms of her childhood; but also the mystery of reproduction, the blackness of postpartum depression, the despair that follows the brutalization of body and spirit. It echoes the monastery bells in Kiev and, above all, it expresses "the individuality and uniqueness of one human being . . . [a] joy that celebrates its own reflection, its own ability to make joy. To reproduce" (276). It is not only Catherine's most significant musical achievement, but it provides MacLaverty with a resonantly affirmative conclusion to his novel. Still, it is more than this. By a memorable paradox, the reader hears the performance of *Vernicle*, a piece of music that exists only in the novelist's words, and that lasts only for as long as it takes to read, just as a concert lasts only for the time it takes the musicians to play. Readers will hear their own music, but all will share in the reconciliations, both personal and cultural, which MacLaverty's words convince us that Catherine McKenna has reached in her composition and which he has achieved in his fiction.

Even this account is incomplete, however, because of the pointers we are given as to the direction in which Catherine's work is developing after *Vernicle*. These, too, are significant, particularly when we recall Cupitt's emphasis on the interpreter's role as the endless producer of truth. She is composing a suite of short piano pieces ("They're like *haiku* for piano," she tells Miss Bingham, reminding us again of the influence of Huang Xiao Gang) prompted by Vermeer's paintings of rooms and of the women in them (109). One of these pieces, *Woman Holding Balance*, seems a particularly apt symbol for Catherine herself, but Miss Bingham's comments on Vermeer—"He began by painting religious subjects. Then he turned to the ordinary—elevated it. Made saints of you, me and the likes of us"—also hint at the nature of what Catherine is attempting to achieve in her music (110).

Perhaps even more important, Catherine is beginning to realize that her next large composition will be a mass. She laughingly tells Miss Bingham that this will be her way of getting back at the patriarchal Catholic Church that would not allow her to serve at the altar, although this is only half a joke. More seriously, she is struck by the potential of the form and structure of the mass, despite her loss of faith in what it celebrates. Predictably, her proposal to appropriate the mass for her own purposes intrigues Miss Bingham but incenses Catherine's mother. In her state of rising agitation after she returns to Glasgow from her father's funeral—the climax to the first part of the novel—Catherine begins to prehear the music that will be "The *Credo*. Her *Credo*. The linchpin of the mass she is writing" (132). She equates the seven syllables of the words *Credo In Unum Deum* with the seven syllables of her own full name, thereby both subverting and making meaningful for herself the religious form from which she felt estranged. She begins to see once again how her music will both incorporate different influences and transcend them to become

> a rope of sound, a cincture which will girdle the earth so that there is neither East nor West. . . . She feels good about this. And suddenly she feels good about herself. Wellness was inside her, waiting, on the edge of its seat. Like the Rose of Jericho. Ready to flower however long it has been dormant. (133)

This, then, is Catherine McKenna's desacralized resurrection hope—the hope that must be repeatedly recreated in each new composition, and which is itself exemplified by Bernard MacLaverty in the fiction he has conceived in *Grace Notes*. At the close of *What Is a Story?* Don Cupitt writes: "our make belief will be a fictioned belief that, nevertheless, our life still matters, fragmentary and fictitious though it is. We'll have to produce from nowhere, and just by spinning stories, the conviction that our life is worth living" (154). Such "dogma-less faith will perpetually renew itself by retelling its own stories" and will, he suggests, be akin to what Paul Tillich calls "the courage to be" (Cupitt 154). It will give us "the experience of Grace, providing that we don't mind acknowledging that it is textually generated" rather than "something out there working to vindicate you and your beliefs" (94–95). This is both what we see happen to Catherine McKenna and is also an effective description of the experience produced by reading the novel.

Bernard MacLaverty's achievement is twofold, for not only is his writing of *Grace Notes* a powerful act of imaginative storytelling in itself, but its very subject is a dynamic revelation of the human need for the kind of narratives which make life bearable and, in Cupitt's phrase, *worth living*. "The one who still hopes still believes in the possibility of life, however faint or vulnerable such faith may be. Indeed hope is essential to believe in a tomorrow, to trust in a future," writes Thiessen, after commenting that eschatology "may be applied in a more specific christological sense or in a wider context connoting essentially the presence of and search for hope as a fundamental necessity to human living" (279). When we read *Grace Notes*, we are observers of this kind of search. We recognize its pains and difficulties, we share in its celebration of hope gained against the most difficult odds, and we are left to reflect upon the power of art to provide us with life-affirming, "sustaining narratives."

Chapter 17

The Search for "Deeper Magic"
J. K. Rowling and C. S. Lewis

Emily Griesinger

With the remarkable 3.5 million first printing of *The Goblet of Fire*, the fourth volume in the Harry Potter series, followed by the phenomenal 1,679,753 copies sold on the first day of publication for the fifth volume, *The Order of the Phoenix*, Joanna Kathleen Rowling has achieved the dream of every adult or children's author. People everywhere are buying, reading, writing, and talking about Harry Potter. Roger Sutton, however, editor of *The Hornbook Magazine*, one of the best known journals in the field of children's literature, judged Rowling's first book "critically insignificant" (500). Nonetheless, the sales of the first five novels—*Harry Potter and the Sorcerer's Stone* (1997), *Harry Potter and the Chamber of Secrets* (1999), *Harry Potter and the Prisoner of Azkaban* (1999), *Harry Potter and the Goblet of Fire* (2000), and *Harry Potter and the Order of the Phoenix* (2003)—have been significant enough to make their author, according to some estimates, wealthier than the Queen of England ("Rowling's Guilt). For those who value the creative imagination and who are at the same time concerned about raising children who know and fear God, Harry Potter raises some difficult issues. What is the role of the imagination and fantasy in drawing us to or away from God? Is there a way to read a fantasy like Harry Potter that does not violate biblical cautions and prohibitions against "things magical"? In the next few pages I want to answer these questions by establishing a relationship between the genre of fantasy and a Christian theology of hope. Combining insights from Christian theology with ideas found in two fantasy writers well known in the Christian community, C. S. Lewis and J. R. R. Tolkien, I will argue that despite potential problems associated with witchcraft, Rowling's magic, like the magic of Tolkien and especially the "deeper magic" of Lewis, is best understood as a narrative device that articulates hope. Paradoxically, while drawing on imagery and symbols associated with witchcraft and the occult, Rowling nevertheless incorporates into the magic of her vision ideas that are neither occultic nor pagan but decidedly Christian.

In the unlikely event that anyone is unfamiliar with the series, I should explain that Harry Potter is an ordinary ten-year-old boy whose hair pokes out in all directions and who wears nerdy glasses. His parents are dead, and he has to live with a boring aunt and uncle, the Dursleys, and their spoiled son, Dudley. Everything changes on his eleventh birthday when Harry discovers he is not ordinary but extraordinary. A huge giant named Hagrid is the messenger who calls our hero to adventure with the statement that changes his life forever: "Harry, yer a wizard" (*Sorcerer's Stone* 50). A magical train ride transports Harry and his friends Ron Weasley and Hermione Granger to Hogwarts School of Witchcraft and Wizardry where they have all sorts of magical adventures, including competing in Quidditch championships. Quidditch is the Hogwarts version of soccer, hockey, and baseball played while flying on a broomstick. Each book follows a similar pattern: Harry lives with the Dursleys in the nonmagical "Muggle" world during the summer, boards the magical train for Hogwarts every fall, has marvelous adventures all year, and returns to the Dursleys at the end of the term.

Scholarly criticism on the Harry Potter series has been slow in coming, perhaps because the series is not complete. One of the two remaining volumes, *Harry Potter and the Half-Blood Prince*, has recently been released; the other is promised by 2006. Fairy tale expert and German professor Jack Zipes votes against the series in his book *The Troublesome Success of Children's Literature From Slovenly Peter to Harry Potter*. Writing from a Marxist perspective, Zipes complains that Rowling does nothing to challenge and instead merely repeats "the same sexist and white patriarchal biases of classical fairy tales" (186). Feminist critic Deborah Thompson agrees: boys in the series solve mysteries and fight dragons, but girls are "studious, weepy, or simpering" (43). Harry and Ron pass their exams and still have time for adventure while Hermione spends all day and sometimes all night in the library. An emancipatory fairy tale like *The Stinky Cheese Man* or the popular film parody *Shrek,* and now *Shrek II,* would have shattered these stereotypes, but, as Nicholas Tucker notes in "The Rise and Rise of Harry Potter," Rowling's fantasy succeeds precisely because of its "determinedly old fashioned" and "backward-looking" qualities (221–22). Harry Potter is a British version of the all-American hero, "a classic Boy Scout, a little mischievous like Tom Sawyer or one of the Hardy boys" (Zipes 178).

Such criticism is not as troubling to thoughtful Potter fans as the material found on the World Wide Web or in popular Christian magazines and journals. For example, the article "Harry Potter Books Spark Rise in Satanism among Children" that appeared in the online satirical newspaper called the *Onion* claims that applications to the First Church of Satan in Salem, MA, have gone up from one hundred thousand to fourteen million because children are reading Harry Potter! Many adult readers who should know better continue to cite this article as confirming evidence that Rowling is a member of the occult. *The Reader's Digest* printed an editorial response to "countless people" taken in by the *Onion* article (Rice 18). Although Rowling has stated that she does not believe in magic the way it is portrayed in her novels and has claimed to be a Christian (Nelson 32), the use of witchcraft and wizardry in the series is still problematic. Harry Potter is a wizard. He goes to a wizard school to learn witchcraft and wizardry. He buys a cauldron, a magic wand, a black robe, a pointed hat. Traditionally, the witch is an evil figure whose defeat is never in question. In *Harry Potter* witchcraft is a desirable vocation; indeed, in this fairy-tale version of the bildungsroman, coming to maturity means coming of age as a wizard! Rowling may not believe in magic or witchcraft, but Christian parents and teachers worry about impressionable children who might read her novels and become curious, "discovering too late," in the words of Focus on the Family analyst Lindy Beam, "that witchcraft is neither harmless nor imaginary."

Connections between theology and the fantasy genre are not immediately obvious. One possible link that pertains specifically to science fiction, as well as fantasy more broadly, is the area of Christian eschatology. As indicated in the "Introduction" to this volume, in Christian tradition eschatology refers to the doctrine of the end of time when Christ returns and the kingdom of God is established forever. For my purposes in this essay, eschatology is simply that branch of theology having to do with the future. It seeks to answer the questions, what can I know about tomorrow, about the day after tomorrow, and on into eternity? What can I hope for? In his foundational work *Theology of Hope*, Jürgen Moltmann argues that Christianity is fundamentally and essentially a religion of hope: "From first to last, and not merely in the epilogue, Christianity is eschatology, is hope, forward looking and forward moving, and therefore also revolutionizing and transforming the present" (16). Richard Bauckham and Trevor Hart stress the eschatological work of the imagination, and specifically fantasy, in arousing and enabling hope for the future. "The quest for meaning, truth, goodness and beauty is closely bound up with hope as an activity of imagination in which we seek to transcend the boundaries of the present, to go beyond the given, outwards and forwards, in search of something more, something better, than the given affords us. . . . Imagination and hope, which are closely tied to our ability to speak the future, are capacities which fit us for survival" (52, 54). The role of the imagination in awakening and sustaining hope has profound implications for literature. Frequently quoted in this volume is the statement by Andrew Delbanco that "human beings need to organize the inchoate sensations amid which we pass our days—pain, desire, pleasure, fear—into a story," and "when that story leads somewhere and helps us navigate through life, it gives us hope" (1).

While Delbanco laments the disappearance of navigational stories in postmodern culture, by which he means overarching metanarratives that draw people together in pursuit of a common dream, I would argue that at least in children's literature, there are hopeful signs on the horizon, the recent popularity of the Harry Potter series and The Lord of the Rings trilogy being a case in point. Indeed, children's fantasy may be one of the few places readers may still look for and expect to find, if not the larger Story, then at least smaller stories that lead somewhere and inspire hope. Borrowing from Bauckham and Hart, children's fantasy literature allows children to "protest in the face of the given, to refuse to accept its limitations and lacks and unacceptable features, to reject the inevitability of the intolerable" (86). A special form of imaginative self-transcendence, children's fantasy and fairy tales equip children to transcend difficult circumstances in their present lives and to hope for something better in the future. Child psychologist Bruno Bettelheim argues in a similar fashion in *The Uses of Enchantment* when he says fairy tales help children deal therapeutically with the psychological problems of growing up. Through fairy tales children learn to cope with "narcissistic disappointments, oedipal dilemmas, [and] sibling rivalries"; they are enabled "to relinquish childhood dependencies, gaining a feeling of self-hood and of self-worth, and a sense of moral obligation" (6). Bettelheim agrees that the primary purpose of fantasy and fairy tales is to give children hope. John Goldthwaite, author of *The Natural History of Make-Believe*, locates the source of that hope in our hunger for the supernatural and the miraculous. "The reader lost in the right story at the right moment may be visited by a transcendent awareness that the world itself is in a condition we could only call a state of grace. . . . Every work of make-believe bears the same implicit message . . . [that] the world is possessed of a quality that is beyond empirical knowing" (351).

Thus, there is a close connection between the genre of fantasy and the "unslaked craving for transcendence" that is characteristic, according to Delbanco, of postmodern culture. Tracing that link further, Kath Filmer argues that fantasy may offer a skeptical age what religion once offered in an age of faith, which is a way of "looking at and explaining the human condition, and of seeing in it something for which to hope" (138). The skepticism of the postmodern, in Filmer's view, has actually provoked writers of fantasy, bringing them out of the closet to undermine or deconstruct the cynicism and materialism of this age and to offer in its place "consolation, healing, and hope." In its truest forms, "fantasy fulfills the deepest and most heartfelt of human needs, the hope that the future will be better, that, indeed, there will be a future" (21–22). While traditional religious discourse is alien to many postmodernists, there is still a psychological and spiritual need ""if not to believe, then at least to hope," and this need is met in fantasy literature, which operates in the same domain and uses the same literary devices—metaphor, image, symbol—as the discourse of religion and "does so largely to the same end: the articulation of hope" (iii).

For C. S. Lewis, the gift of story contained or embedded in children's fantasy includes this dimension. In his essay "On Three Ways of Writing for Children," Lewis contends that the best fairy tales arouse longing for ideal worlds, even as they enrich the real world with a new dimension (37–38). Tolkien believes similarly that fantasy offers recovery of imaginative vision, the ability to see our own world clearly, without "the drab blur of triteness and familiarity" ("On Fairy-Stories" 74). Fantasy provides escape from materialism and arouses a desire to transcend the "ancient limitations" of hunger, thirst, pain, poverty, sorrow, injustice, death (79). For these and other reasons, both Tolkien and Lewis were entirely comfortable using magic in the creation of secondary fantasy worlds, and, though differing and even disagreeing with each other on how these secondary worlds relate to the primary world, or to reality as we know it, both agreed that the craft and artistry involved in imagining such worlds was a God-given gift and could be used under His inspiration and guidance to communicate religious experience and truth. Both acknowledged as well the contrary position that unbridled imagining could do harm as well as good, that even morally good literature could be read poorly, and that morally bad literature could corrupt and lead astray. Nevertheless, for Lewis, all fantasy truly written, even when not Christian in intent, can baptize the imagination and impart a "real though unfocused gleam of divine truth" (*Miracles* 137–38). In Narnia this revelation is the function of "deeper magic," which is the equivalent of Christian grace and can be linked as well with Tolkien's concept of "eucatastrophe," the turning point in a fairy story that brings a "lift to the heart" and assures the happy ending ("On Fairy-Stories" 81). The greatest eucatastrophe of human history is the incarnation and resurrection of Christ (83–84).

There is an eschatological dimension in children's fantasy that both Lewis and Tolkien appreciated, though to my knowledge neither ever used this word. Both saw the making or glimpsing of otherworlds as a form of imaginative activity that nurtures hope, both for dealing with the present and taking hold of the future, which for Christian believers means eternity, heaven, and Christ. Of the *Chronicles of Narnia*, Lewis once told a friend, "I am aiming at a sort of pre-baptism of the imagination . . . [that would] make it easier for children to accept Christianity when they [meet] it later in life" (Sayer 192). Given eschatological longings for the "already" but "not yet" fully accomplished rule and reign of Christ, which is the essence of Christian hope, fantasy and fairy tales can express our desire to believe the promised future is coming. We glimpse the principles and values of the kingdom—bravery, loyalty, honesty, faith, hope, love—in the best fairy tales. In some we might even catch sight of the King, or at least his goodness and moral wisdom. As Cinderellas or Ugly Ducklings or tiny Tom Thumbs, we are ignorant or misinformed of our true identity as sons and daughters of the king. Through the magic of Christ's mercy and grace, we discover the good news that we are not orphans or beggars or slaves, after all, but beloved children. We enter a personal relationship with the king, inherit the treasures of the kingdom, and live happily ever after. My point is this: fairy tales and fantasy literature do not simply meet children's psychological needs, as Bruno Bettelheim and other child psychologists suppose, though they may in fact meet these needs. They also evoke and to some degree satisfy spiritual longings. That said, I want to take a closer look at the issue of fantasy in *Harry Potter*. In particular, I want to examine the way Rowling uses magic and especially "deeper magic" to awaken and sustain hope.

Rowling employs magic in two ways in the Potter series. The first has to do with setting—the artistic creation of a secondary ideal world. Some have argued that *Harry Potter* has little literary art, but I disagree. Children especially respond to the imaginative detail of Hogwarts School of Witchcraft and Wizardry. Who can resist owls that deliver the mail, stairways that lead somewhere on Monday and somewhere else on Friday, and doors that want to be tickled before they will open? Most children have not taken courses in Herbology, Transfiguration, Charms, Potions, and Defense Against the Dark Arts. They think it is hilarious that Harry has to read books like "Gadding with Ghouls," "Holidays with Hags," and "Break with a Banshee" (*Chamber of Secrets* 43). They wish they, too, could go on field trips to magical places like Honeydukes and Hogsmeade and eat the magical candy sold there, Fizzing Whizbees, Pepper Imps, Ice Mice, and Bertie Bott's Every Flavor Beans (*Prisoner of Azkaban* 197). Best of all, they imagine themselves playing soccer or baseball or whatever Harry plays in the air on his broomstick. Of course, they see themselves winning the Quidditch championship in every book, like Harry. This magic is neither occultic nor subversive, as some have alleged, but entirely appropriate to the conventions of fantasy. To make a secondary world inside which magical events and magical creatures will be credible, writes Tolkien, requires intensive labor and thought and a special skill, a kind of "elvish" craft. "Few attempt such difficult tasks," Tolkien says, "But when they are attempted and in any degree accomplished then we have a rare achievement of Art: indeed narrative art, story-making in its primary and most potent mode" ("On Fairy-Stories" 68). Besides being a lot of fun, the magic of the Hogwarts world awakens the desire for transcendence. It encourages children to imagine that the real world of boring homework and boring school is not the only world there is.

Magic is not just props and machinery, however. Rowling uses magic in a second way to develop the major theme of the series, which is Harry's transformation from neglected, unloved orphan to world-famous wizard. While he must learn how to use magical power, for example, in the fight against Lord Voldemort, it is not for his magical power alone that children want to be like Harry Potter. Children admire this "Cinderlad," as one critic calls him, not because he is a wizard but because in the battle between goodness and evil, he makes the right choices (Natov 316). Conservative Christians are concerned that the worldview in Harry Potter is morally confusing, without clear boundaries between evil and good (Abanes, Chambers, Fawcett, Lentini, Murray). I do not see this confusion. Both Harry and the reader are informed about legal and illegal uses of magic from the beginning. Young wizards are not allowed to use magic in the Muggle world during summer vacations, for example, and with one or two exceptions, Harry does not. When Harry and his friends break the rules during the school term, they face serious consequences. Helping the groundskeeper and loveable giant Hagrid get rid of a baby dragon costs them 50 points each, which puts their team 150 points behind in the Quidditch championship. As further punishment, they must spend the night in the Forbidden Forest. Adult wizards who break rules, like stealing property or killing people, end up in the Prison of Azkaban. Rowling's magical world is not morally neutral, and part of Harry's development as a wizard and as a human being involves learning and playing by the rules.

In their book on literature and moral values, William Kilpatrick and Gregory and Suzanne Wolfe assert that books that build character "not only capture the imagination, but cultivate the conscience" (18). In such books children form "an emotional attachment to goodness and the desire to do the right thing" by imaginative identification with a hero who is "on his way to but has not yet achieved moral perfection" (21). In the process of rooting for and suffering with a hero like Harry Potter, who in every novel so far desires and ultimately does the right thing, children find courage to believe they, too, can struggle and make right choices. The moral dimension of Harry's development is easily missed, though, if readers focus too rigidly on the fact that he is a wizard. To see wizardry and magic itself as metaphors for power is more helpful. What matters is how this power is used. Voldemort uses magic for the purpose of evil; Dumbledore, for the purpose of good. Obviously, parents hope Harry will identify and want to be like Dumbledore not Voldemort. But they should not expect it will be all clear sailing. Without conflict, there is no story. When it comes to right and wrong uses of magic, or more broadly, good versus evil, Harry must struggle and parents must let their children struggle with him.

Harry's difficulties during the Sorting Hat ritual are a case in point. All first-year students are assigned to dormitories by sitting on a stool and putting on a singing hat that reads their heartfelt desires. Bravery, loyalty, wisdom, and a willingness to work are some of the qualities that distinguish one school from another—Gryffindors are chivalrous, Hufflepuffs are just, Ravenclaws are studious, and so on. The fourth school belongs to cunning Slytherins who "use any means to achieve their ends" (*Sorcerer's Stone* 118). Harry has to decide which group to follow. Who will his role models be, honest Gryffindors or conniving Slytherins? This decision is important because the entire wizarding world believes Harry has a special destiny, though he does not always understand what it is. Whether he has the strength of character to fulfill that destiny is not clear, not even to Harry. Before Harry begins his training at Hogwarts, Hagrid tells him to relax, "Just be yerself" (*Sorcerer's Stone* 86), but Harry, like most eleven year olds, is not sure who that is. Days before entering Hogwarts, Hagrid informs him, "There's not a single witch or wizard who went bad who wasn't in Slytherin. You-Know-Who was one" (*Sorcerer's Stone* 80). Harry is confused, therefore, when the Sorting Hat seems to think he, Harry Potter, is a Slytherin: "Are you sure? You could be great, you know, it's all here in your head, and Slytherin will help you on the way to greatness, no doubt about that—no? Well, if you're sure—better be GRYFFINDOR!" (*Sorcerer's Stone* 121).

Interestingly, the virtues of selflessness and love, both of which figure prominently in Christian theology, are not mentioned by the Sorting Hat as characteristic of any of the Hogwarts schools. However, lenty of examples in this novel and the next four, suggest that selflessness and love, as well as forgiveness, mercy, and grace, are virtues in Rowling's fantasy world. Rowling has said on several occasions that she read and loved Lewis's Narnia tales as a child (Shapiro 25). There she encountered a "deeper magic," which is Lewis's metaphor for divine mercy, grace, and love. The key scene occurs in *The Lion, the Witch, and the Wardrobe*. Edmund Pevensie has betrayed his brother and sisters into the hands of the White Witch. In keeping with the law of deep magic, —something like Old Testament law or, as Lewis explains elsewhere, the Tao—the White Witch has the right to take Edmund's life. She is prevented from doing so only because Aslan, the King of Narnia, out of love and mercy offers himself in Edmund's place. "Though the Witch knew the Deep Magic, there is a magic deeper still which she did not know. . . . [I]f she could have looked into the stillness and the darkness before Time dawned . . . she would have known that when a willing victim who had committed no treachery was killed in a traitor's stead, the Table would crack and Death itself would start working backward" (178–79).

Lewis obviously means for this episode to suggest the Christian doctrine of the atonement. A fairy tale picture of the "self-sacrificing compassion" of Christ (Ford 131) and the magic of grace, Aslan's death recounts in images children can understand the good news of the gospel. The idea of "voluntary self-sacrifice on another's behalf," observes

Charles Huttar, "is one that is valid throughout the universe," an archetypal myth involving "descent into the underworld, a journey to danger and death, to perform a rescue" (131). Deeper magic is the triumph of voluntary sacrificial love on another's behalf. We see this theme throughout the Potter series beginning with *The Sorcerer's Stone*; here we learn that Lily Potter sacrificed her own life to save Harry from "He-Who-Must-Not-Be-Named," the dark Lord Voldemort. No greater love has anyone than this, Scripture tells us, than to lay down one's life for another (John 15:13). Like Aslan's sacrifice for Edmund in Narnia, Lily Potter's sacrifice for her son Harry is emblematic of grace and overwhelming love, and the result is the same. Goodness and love defeat or at least diminish hatred and evil. Voldemort disappears, and no one knows why. "[T]hey're saying that when he couldn't kill Harry Potter, Voldemort's power somehow broke—and that's why he's gone" (*Sorcerer's Stone* 12). Meanwhile, Harry has the lightning bolt scar on his forehead as a reminder that the Dark Lord wanted to kill him but could not.

Admittedly, the "mark of the beast," mentioned in Revelation 13:16, appears on the forehead (also the right hand) and the jagged letter "S" used by the heavy metal group AC/DC is thought by some to be a Satanic symbol. It does not follow, however, that the jagged scar on Harry's forehead is meant to suggest Satanic worship or the occult. Understandably, such associations, if intended, would cause problems for Christians, but do we find such associations in the story? Harry neither worships the Dark Lord nor is he drawn to the Dark Arts. The scar is a mark left by evil and a protection from evil. "That's what yeh get when a powerful, evil curse touches yeh," Hagrid tells him. "[It] took care of yer mum an' dad an' yer house, even—but it didn't work on you, an that's why yer famous, Harry" (*Sorcerer's Stone* 56). One of the lessons Harry learns throughout the series is that in the struggle between good and evil, sacrifice is necessary. The most difficult and costly sacrifices are motivated by goodness and unconditional love. "Your mother died to save you," Dumbledore tells him. "If there is one thing Voldemort cannot understand, it is love. He didn't realize that love as powerful as your mother's for you leaves its own mark. Not a scar, no visible sign . . . to have been loved so deeply, even though the person who loved us is gone, will give us some protection forever. . . . It was agony to touch a person marked by something so good" (299).

This passage comes from the end of the novel, but the theme of love and belonging is present from the start. The opening pages make it painfully clear that for the first ten years of his life Harry Potter is unloved. He sleeps in a cupboard with spiders, gets no presents on his birthdays, and never gets to eat hamburgers or ice cream. By contrast, his detestable cousin Dudley is indulged and pampered from morning until night. "Dinky Dudlydums," as his mother calls him, eats gallons of ice cream, which makes him four times larger than skinny Harry. Dudley has his own bedroom, or two bedrooms, since he needs extra storage for his thirty-nine birthday presents, nearly all of which, Harry is happy to report, are broken. Harry knows almost nothing about his own mom and dad. He has no photographs, and he is forbidden to ask questions. Even at school, he has no one: "Everybody knew that Dudley's gang hated that odd Harry Potter in his baggy old clothes and broken glasses, and nobody liked to disagree with Dudley's gang" (*Sorcerer's Stone* 30). All of this sets us up for the magical fantasy of Hogwarts School where Harry's need for love and belonging is met in marvelous ways. At Hogwarts he finds his own friends, Ron and Hermione, and begins to establish his own identity as a talented Seeker on the Quidditch field. And, finally, he gets enough to eat.

Rescue of the unloved from the unloving is one variation of the deeper magic theme; sacrifice as part of what it means to love and be loved is another. In the final pages Harry risks expulsion from Hogwarts in an effort to keep one of his professors, who he mistakenly thinks is in league with Voldemort, from stealing the Sorcerer's Stone, which ancient philosophers believed could produce the Elixir of Life. When Harry suggests breaking school rules to keep Voldemort from getting the stone, Hermione and Ron can only think about losing points for Gryffindor. Harry wisely grasps the bigger picture: "If Snape gets hold of the Stone, Voldemort's coming back! Haven't you heard what it was like when he was trying to take over? There won't be any Hogwarts to get expelled from! He'll flatten it, or turn it into a school for the Dark Arts!" (*Sorcerer's Stone* 270). Harry is willing to sacrifice his reputation as the best Seeker Gryffindor has ever had to keep Voldemort from getting the stone. Ron and Hermione are so impressed by Harry's determination and courage that they make sacrifices of their own: Hermione, by drinking a liquid potion that could be poison; Ron, by allowing himself to be bludgeoned and left for dead in a game of live chess.

If Aslan sacrifices his life to save the life of another, Voldemort sacrifices the lives of others to save himself. On the night before his final encounter with Voldemort, Harry finds evidence to suggest that the Dark Lord has killed an innocent unicorn in order to preserve his own dwindling life. "The blood of a unicorn will keep you alive," the centaur Firenze tells Harry, "even if you are an inch from death, but at a terrible price. You have slain something pure and defenseless to save yourself, and you will have but a half-life, a cursed life, from the moment the blood touches your lips" (*Sorcerer's Stone* 258). Thus Voldemort sacrifices others to save himself, which is the exact opposite of what Aslan does in Narnia. The blood of the unicorn is not nearly as potent or salvific as Aslan's blood in Narnia either. It cannot give Voldemort eternal life. He is still desperate to find the stone, which has fallen into Harry's pocket. At the last possible moment Dumbledore arrives, destroys the stone, and for Harry's courage and bravery, awards Gryffindor the points needed to win back the Quidditch Cup. Everyone but the Slytherins cheers Harry Potter, and the novel ends.

We find traces of deeper magic again in *The Chamber of Secrets* when Harry asks Dumbledore about his ability to speak Parseltongue, the language of snakes. Harry finds it useful to talk to snakes, since his task in this novel is to find and kill the Basilisk, a huge snake that has been slithering around the school endangering the students. Still, he cannot fathom why he should have the gift of Parseltongue. It is clearly one of the Dark Arts, more appropriate to the house of Slytherin, whose emblem is a snake, than the house of Gryffindor, whose emblem is a lion. According to Dumbledore, Harry is not a Slytherin because when given the option, he chose Gryffindor: "It is our choices, Harry, that show what we truly are, far more than our abilities" (*Chamber of Secrets* 333). Affirming that choice, Dumbledore gives Harry the sword of Godric Gryffindor, and at the end of the novel Harry uses this sword to kill the Basilisk. It stands to reason that "God"ric Gryffindor, whose emblem is the lion not the snake, is Rowling's image for ultimate goodness. At least in this scene Harry would appear to be watched over and protected by some kind of grace or supreme goodness, if not specifically by God.

The term "deeper magic" also occurs at the end of *The Prisoner of Azkaban* when Harry confronts Peter Pettigrew, the man who betrayed and murdered his parents. James Potter's friend Sirius Black, who has been falsely accused of the crime and has recently escaped from Azkaban Prison, is determined to kill Pettigrew: "YOU SHOULD HAVE DIED! . . . DIED RATHER THAN BETRAY YOUR FRIENDS" (375). Although Pettigrew clearly deserves to die, Harry refuses to let Black kill him. Showing mercy to one's enemies is an example of "magic at its deepest, its most impenetrable," Dumbledore tells Harry later. "When one wizard saves another wizard's life, it creates a certain bond between them . . . and I'm much mistaken if Voldemort wants his servant in the debt of Harry Potter" (427). Unlike Edmund Pevensie, who responds to deeper magic by becoming a better character, Pettigrew only disintegrates more than before. We meet him again as Wormtail in the opening pages of *The Goblet of Fire*. Readers of Lewis will recognize his name and his personality as an allusion to Wormwood in *The Screwtape Letters*. Like Wormwood, Wormtail works hard to please his master, Voldemort, and usually fails. In the horrible scene that ends the novel, he actually cuts off his own right hand to supply an ingredient for a potion that will rejuvenate the Dark Lord. Immersing himself in the cauldron that holds Wormtail's hand, a drop of Harry's blood, and a few other nasty things, Voldemort comes back to life.

This episode is difficult to unpack theologically. It could suggest a reversal or perversion of Christ's resurrection or possibly Christian baptism. What are we to make of the fact that Harry's blood in the cauldron aids the Dark Lord's recovery? Why does Harry's wand interact so mysteriously with Voldemort's in the wizard duel that follows? And how important is Voldemort's transformation? For the first half of the series, he has been weak, in hiding, and presumably near death. Now he and his supporters, the Deatheaters, are back in power. Whatever that means for the rest of the series, we know it cannot be good. Dumbledore's comment at the end of *The Goblet of Fire* about darker times ahead suggests a more serious confrontation than we have seen before between Harry and Voldemort, something on a global scale that will rock the wizarding world. Preparation for such an event is the focus of the fifth book in the series, *Harry Potter and the Order of the Phoenix*. In this 870-page volume, the longest so far, Harry and his friends join Dumbledore's army, the Order of the Phoenix, ultimately to battle the Deatheaters for possession of a glass sphere containing a prophecy. The prophecy mandates that Harry must kill or be killed by Voldemort because "neither can live while the other survives" (841). Whatever happens, Dumbledore reminds Harry that he has a "power the Dark Lord knows not," a force "more wonderful and more terrible than death, than human intelligence, than forces of nature" (843). This is the power of sacrificial love that saved Harry from Voldemort when he was a baby, the power Harry himself demonstrates in risking his life for Sirius Black toward the end of this volume, the power that ultimately saves Harry from possession by Voldemort "because he could not bear to reside in a body so full of the force he detests" (844). Based on the connections between these ideas and the Narnian themes discussed above, I would argue that this is Rowling's version of deeper magic.

According to Lewis, only when a person realizes he has broken the law of deep magic and deserves to pay the penalty, only then can the deeper magic of Christian atonement penetrate the heart to the point of conversion (*Mere Christianity* 38–39). Rowling does not go this far. (For that matter, neither does Lewis since in the scene already mentioned in Narnia, Edmund is not converted in this manner.) Thus far, Harry's encounters with Voldemort do not involve a choice to do evil the way Edmund's encounter with the White Witch does in Narnia. Deep magic, in the sense Lewis uses that term in the Narnia books, is implied, however, in the lessons Harry learns from Dumbledore and the choices he has to make to become a wise wizard. The most significant difference between Rowling and Lewis comes in their understanding and presentation of the deeper magic, that power that flies in the face of evil and ultimately defeats it, no matter what the cost. While Rowling uses the term "deep magic" to describe this power, thus far in the series this is not the deeper magic portrayed in Narnia, or not exactly. Rowling's deep magic lacks the incarnational element of Lewis's Christology, the idea of a Master Magician intentionally laying aside his magical powers in order to defeat evil once and for all and opening the way for good to reign. The series is not over. We can speculate that Dumbledore will make this sacrifice on Harry's behalf, or perhaps as suggested in the prophecy in *The Order of the Phoenix*, Harry will lay down his life in battle with Voldemort, perhaps to save Dumbledore, or more dramatically, to save the world.

Rowling is purposely vague about how the series will end. A member of the Church of Scotland who says she "believes in God, not magic," she is nevertheless reluctant to discuss her faith. Yet she once told a reporter "If I talk too freely about that, I think the intelligent reader—whether ten [years old] or sixty—will be able to guess what is coming in the books" (Nelson 32). We can speculate, then, that Harry will probably not be unmasked as the son of Lord Voldemort (as Luke Skywalker discovers he's the son of Darth Vader in *Star Wars*!) or go over to the dark side, at least not knowingly, not if he can help it. Will Harry Potter die to fulfill the prophecy, or will a deeper magic intervene? We will have to wait and see. In the meantime children and adults continue to read and reread what Rowling has created thus far, an outstanding fantasy that offers a truthful articulation of hope. Specifically, *Harry Potter* articulates the hope that goodness will triumph over evil, that wrongs done to the small and the weak will be righted, that courage, loyalty, and friendship will overcome hatred, bigotry, and fear. We gain hope from *Harry Potter*—hope that in an age where moral goodness does not seem that important and evil is on the rise—that one little nerdy person, not terribly smart or good-looking, can make a difference.

The extraordinary success of the Harry Potter series demonstrates that parents and educators, as well as book publishers and filmmakers, still want and need to believe that stories can have this kind of impact. *Harry Potter* proves children can be drawn to something other than Ninja Turtles and Pokemon. Parents and teachers should be careful, then, about stifling the energy and enthusiasm of Potter fans, some of whom have never read anything longer than *Peter Rabbit* or more complicated than *The Cat in the Hat*. Imagine the shock of discovering sons and daughters who cannot be pried away from television or video games long enough to eat dinner hunched over Rowling's 800-page *The Order of the Phoenix*, probably the longest novel they have ever seen let alone read.

If Christian parents and educators take it for what it is, a work of literary fantasy, *Harry Potter* should not hinder and could even help children embrace and receive the true magic of the gospel. With spiritual preparation, *Harry Potter* could at least call children's attention to the battle between good and evil, not in fantasy or fairy tales, but in the real world. As a literary device, the magic in *Harry Potter* should not and need not be linked with the occult at all. It can be read simply as a metaphor for power. We admire Dumbledore and Harry Potter because they use power wisely; we despise Voldemort and the Deatheaters because they abuse power and use it for evil. Children learn from *Harry Potter* that power is not morally neutral. The battle between goodness and evil is real; our choices are costly, to ourselves and others. Regardless of our size, age, appearance, or ability, we must recognize that our choices matter. Finally, the magic in *Harry Potter* offers the recovery of imaginative vision, arousing desire for a world where each of us—the strong, the beautiful, the weak, the athlete, the geek, the nerd—can experience the deepest magic of all, which is to know we are accepted and special and deeply loved. In this Rowling sets the stage for the Christian gospel and provides readers a "real though unfocused gleam of divine truth."

Chapter 18

J. R. R. Tolkien
Postmodern Visionary of Hope

Ralph C. Wood

It may seem manifest madness to describe J. R. R. Tolkien as a post-modern visionary of hope, especially when we recall the many reasons for describing him as a premodern antiquarian of despair. Truthfully Tolkien regarded nearly everything worthy of praise in English culture to have ended in 1066. He despised the imposition of Norman culture on a vibrant English tradition that had flourished for more than 500 years; he looked upon the Arthurian legends as an alien French import and thus no fit basis for a national mythology; he lamented Chaucer's introduction of Italian iambic meter into English poetry; he regarded Shakespeare as hopelessly modern, since so many of his characters remain so obsessively subjective in their quandaries. Tolkien also judged the Reformation to be a terrible error, insisting that the cathedrals of England were stolen Catholic property, the booty of what G. K. Chesterton called the sixteenth-century "revolution of the rich" (140). Nor was he happy that C. S. Lewis, his dear friend and companion, remained for the entirety of his life what Tolkien derisively called "an Ulster Protestant."

The litany of Tolkien's antimodernity could be extended almost endlessly. He was a confessed Luddite, for example, who lamented the Triumph of the Machine, as he described the Industrial Revolution. He refused, moreover, to drive a motorcar once he saw the damage that paved roads and automobiles had done to the English countryside. Tolkien also remained a lifelong Tory and an unapologetic monarchist in his politics, believing that hierarchical distinctions are necessary for the flourishing of any polity, whether academic or ecclesial or governmental. He longed, in fact, for the return of Roman Catholicism as the established state religion of England. In both his poetry and his prose, Tolkien demonstrated repeated recourse to decidedly premodern literary forms, especially to the conventions of epic and romance. As Kenneth Craven has recently written: "J. R. R. Tolkien was an 'Ancient' in the sense that he never wanted to live in the present time, but in saner ages and in eternity. . . . Tolkien [was] as ancient as Treebeard, a mossy poet who lived in the languages and poems of the Dark Ages" (145).

Yet I contend that, for all of his admitted troglodytic sentiments, Tolkien can also be read in hope-filled postmodern terms. To make this counterintuitive case, I will first seek to define what I mean by both "modernism" and "postmodernism." Then, in the central section of my essay, I will cite four of the many ways in which Tolkien's work embodies a postmodern vision of hope: (1) in his praise for cultural pluralism as a necessary good in order for particular peoples to prosper; (2) in his refusal of modernist and foundationalist accounts of reason, insisting instead that knowledge and truth are historically located and grounded; (3) in his critique of modern culture as wickedly coercive in its false claims to universality, especially in its resulting warfare; and (4) in his demonstration that the most hopeful means of combating modern evils is to be found in small communities of the weak and the emarginated who overcome modern self-aggrandizing individualism by refusing all coercive power. Finally, in a brief postlude, I will suggest how Tolkien's work remains radically relevant for the formation of a culture of hope amid the culture of death and the deceits of modernity—namely, by enabling Christians to enter the postmodern "tournament of narratives."

Modernism and the Right Refusal of It

Richard Rorty has suggested that we drop the term *postmodern*, so elusive has become its meaning, so crude has been its overuse. It is surely wrong to embrace Jean-François Lyotard's celebrated claim that to be postmodern is to be incredulous about metanarratives. Lyotard's assertion that no totalizing account of human existence is possible is rather like the declaration that there can be no truth. Just as the denial of truth must itself be true if it is to be credited, so does Lyotard unwittingly narrate what has become the chief metanarrative of postmodernity— namely, that no credible metanarratives exist ("Interview"). Far better, in my judgment, is to define postmodernism as a rejection of the chief modernist assumption: the notion that, from some allegedly neutral stance, we can deliberately distance ourselves from any particular past or received tradition that we now regard as naive. The irony of modernism, as Gustavo Benavides observes, is that the task of self-extrication proves to be perpetual. We must also distance ourselves from our own modern culture of scientific development and economic advance as being, at least in its recent manifestations, incredibly callow and simpleminded (186–87).

Admittedly, at least in this sense, postmodernism is an extension of modernism—a self-critical extrication from it. Nor can there be any return to a premodern world lacking any self-consciousness about the historical belatedness of our own age. Even so, the postmodern negation of modern negativity can operate in things cultural as well as mathematical, and thus make for something powerfully positive. Our task, therefore, is to determine which ancient and modern traditions we want to reclaim and which to reject—such retrievals and such repudiations being put to peculiarly postmodern uses. Among the modernist qualities that postmodernism rejects, Benavides names its endless self-reflexivity and cognitive instability, its domestication of ordinary life into separate domains (e.g., sacred and secular, public and private, work and play, the political and the individual), its creation of massive bureaucracies through centralized state power, its elevation of impersonal scientific experimentation and proof over religious ritual and sacrament, its enlargement of the conceptual realm over the narrative and storied world, and finally its inadvertent creation—by way of reaction and rebellion—of an inwardly subjective art and an inwardly experiential and private religion. In short, postmodernism of a hopeful kind seeks to reverse the essential tendencies of modernism: "from the organic to the mechanic; from the corporate to the individual; from hierarchy to equality; from an understanding in which everything resonates with everything else . . . to one built around precision and the increasing differentiation of domains" (190).

Rather than showing how Tolkien offers alternatives to nearly all of these modern proclivities, I will concentrate on but a single problem: the ahistorical individualism that lies at the heart of the modern project. The great Danish philosopher-poet-theologian Søren Kierkegaard, early in the nineteenth century, first discerned the chief modernist mistake. He saw that modernity was built on the attempt to determine truth from the viewpoint that he described as *sub specie aeternitatis*: ". . . that Archimedean point from which he could lift the whole world, the point which for that very reason must lie outside the world, outside the limitations of time and space" (Kierkegaard 4). At the heart of the Enlightenment project lay the notion that we can stand above the flux of history to view it from outside the universe, examining it "under the aspect of eternity"; i.e., from a timeless and placeless stance.

The great *philosophes* of the Enlightenment believed that they could occupy a neutral perch high above both the heavens and the earth. From this oxymoronic stance in midair—this supposedly neutral and godlike perspective—they proposed to inspect all morality and religion, the better to choose universal ethical norms and spiritual truths, those that redound to the good of humanity as a whole. Hence, Lord Herbert of Cherbury formulated five reasonable propositions concerning God and morality that, according to him, all people of all times have held, without regard to race or religion, except when obscured by the distortions and accretions of so-called revealed truth.[1] The seemingly salutary aim of Locke and Herbert, of Jefferson and the American founders, was to prevent a repetition of the sixteenth- and seventeenth-century "wars of religion" that required the state to intervene among battling Christians. The way to stop such internecine strife was to remove conflicting Christian doctrines and practices from the public realm, lest Europe, no less than the newly born American republic, be bathed in religious blood yet again. Thus did the modern notion of tolerance come to flower in the Treaty of Westphalia, in Locke's "Letter Concerning Toleration," in Jefferson's *Notes on Virginia*, and the like.

William Cavanaugh maintains that this standard account of the triumph of tolerance is deeply flawed, perhaps even wrongheaded. He demonstrates that the halting of the so-called "religious wars" was less a political necessity than a political convenience. According to Cavanaugh, these wars signal the birth pangs of the sovereign nation-state. Political power was centralized so as to provide "a monopoly on violence within a defined territory" (191). Public discourse was deliberately secularized during the Enlightenment, Cavanaugh argues, in order to save the state from the threat posed by the churches: "Christianity produces divisions within the state body precisely because it pretends to be a body which transcends state boundaries" (189). Once religion is safely confined to the private sphere, the law is no longer regarded as having been "disclosed" by its divine source through the workings of custom and tradition; instead, the law is a thing to be "made" or legislated by the state (192). Cavanaugh points up the terribly ironic consequence of this new birth of tolerance—namely, its intolerant disbarment of all publicly ordered religions and all historically nourished traditions. The Enlightenment ideal of tolerance thus excludes the communal body of the church, says Cavanaugh, "as a rival to the state body by redefining religion as a purely internal matter, an affair of the soul and not of the body" (190). In the name of an alleged inclusivity, therefore, a drastic exclusion was promulgated.

The rise of the modern nation-state is premised on an elevation of this isolated and autonomous individual who is defined by his accumulation of privately owned goods. As an essentially propertied creature, modern man has relation to other individuals largely by means of self-protecting contracts. These contracts have a temporal duration, moreover, even as they are contingent upon the agreement of the contracting parties. Contracts can also be dissolved by limiting clauses or by mutual consent. No longer does an unbreakable bond unite the entire body politic in devotion to common ends. The basis for such politics has also disappeared—namely, the indissoluble covenant between God and his people, as this bond is sealed through the sacraments. "It is not surprising," declares Benavides, "that . . . Descartes placed 'among the [antique] excesses all of the promises by which one curtails something of one's freedom,' that Milton wrote a treatise on divorce, and that Kant condemned the covenants that bind one's descendants" (190).

It follows that the state alone, not the church, can establish a true commonwealth, for religion now pertains chiefly to the individual: "The care of each man's soul belongs only to himself," wrote Locke ("A Letter Concerning Toleration"). "The legitimate powers of government," added Jefferson, "extend to such acts only as are injurious to others. But it does me no injury for my neighbor to say that there are twenty Gods, or no God. It neither picks my pocket nor breaks my leg" ("Notes on Virginia"). From such sentiments emerges the modern individualism that values freedom, negatively, as doing no harm to others and, positively, as constructing one's own life without let or hindrance. No longer is freedom construed as obedience to a telos radically transcending ourselves and thus wondrously delivering us from bondage to mere self-interest. Rather liberty comes to mean a life lived entirely according to one's own construal of reality.[2] At its extreme, such individualism holds that we can make up our identity entirely out of whole cloth, that we can strip away all bothersome particularities that locate us within concrete narrative traditions, and thus that we can be free only as we rid ourselves of the troublesome commitments and obligations that we have not chosen entirely for ourselves. In sum, we can become autonomous selves who are immunized from all moral and social obligations except those that we have independently elected.

As Alasdair MacIntyre has pointed out, traditional cultures take exactly the opposite tack. They regard the human self as irreducibly social and dependent, not individual and autonomous. For our premodern forebears, the self is formed by a synthesizing of communal roles and personal wills. The requirements of life in such societies are at once imposed from without and assumed from within. One becomes a person, therefore, to the extent that one finds and fulfills one's proper role. Character thus becomes a moral ideal legitimating certain modes of social existence. Wife, brother, cousin, household servant, village tribesman: these social roles are not accidental characteristics that must be sloughed off in order to disclose the real self. They provide the very framework for one's essential being:

> They are part of my substance, defining partially at least and some-
> times wholly my obligations and my duties. Individuals inherit a
> particular space within an interlocking set of social relationships;
> lacking that space, they are nobody, or at best a stranger or an out-
> cast. To know oneself as such a social person is however not to
> occupy a static and fixed position. It is to find oneself placed
> within a certain point on a journey with set goals [or a Quest, as
> Tolkien calls it]; to move through life is to make progress—or to
> fail to make progress—toward a given end. Thus a completed and
> fulfilled life is an achievement and death is the point at which one
> can be judged happy or unhappy. Hence the ancient Greek
> proverb: "Call no man happy until he is dead." (33–34)

Traditional cultures, whether Christian or pagan, hold that only in death is human life brought to its completion, whether for good or ill. Thus did Christians celebrate the witness of those who are supremely good—the saints—not on the day of their birth but of their death. In modernist cultures, by contrast, death is the dread enemy, since it ends our quest for self-satisfaction. Indeed, death becomes virtually a disease to be cured. For the aim of life is no longer to die faithfully and well in the fulfillment of one's communal and religious vocation; instead, the purpose of life is to stay alive as long as possible, the better to enjoy oneself.

Tolkien's Postmodern Vision of Hope

Tolkien can certainly be read in the traditionalist terms that MacIntyre sets forth. Yet I believe it important to show that his work is not entirely traditionalist. Thus we turn to four of the ways whereby Tolkien offers a postmodernist response to modernism.

Tolkien's Postmodern Embrace of Cultural Pluralism

In calling Tolkien a cultural pluralist, I do not mean to suggest that he is a cultural relativist. Unlike many postmodernists, Tolkien holds neither to the supposed equality of all cultures nor to the impossibility of making judgments among them. Neither seeking, like the allegedly objective modernists, some impossibly Archimedean stance outside the universe, nor claiming, like the radically subjective postmodernists, that Western culture has authority only for Westerners, Tolkien approaches other cultures as an unabashed Christian. He follows St. Augustine's injunction to his fellow Christians that they "take the spoils of the Egyptians"— making good Christian use of the many accomplishments of the Greco-Roman world (*On Christian Doctrine* 2:40:60). Thus does Tolkien retrieve from various ancient Northern cultures those virtues that serve his Christian project, just as he largely ignores their many vices: witchcraft, slavery, incest, polygamy, and human sacrifice. Tolkien's heroes do not employ any of the pungent four-letter epithets that serve to salt the Anglo-Saxon tongue. Some of Tolkien's critics have objected, in fact, to such sanitizing. Tom Shippey wittily complains, for instance, that Tolkien's noble characters "are so virtuous that one can hardly call them pagans at all" (202).

One of the most deleterious effects of modernism has been the eclipse of particular languages and cultures in favor of those forms of speech and social order that rely on unhistorical abstractions, on unnarrated concepts, on words unrooted in either time or place. In the name of such untraditioned political systems and ideas has much if not most of our modern mischief been done. From George Orwell to George Steiner, we have been reminded that the unprecedented bloodletting of the modern age is largely the work of omnicompetent governments acting on and legitimated by abstract slogans and deadly neologisms. When words are deracinated from their concrete origins and converted into empty abstractions, they can be put to wicked use. We need not look to modern political rhetoric as proof of this danger; Tolkien's Saruman illustrates it all too well. Knowing that he has earned Gandalf's respect, Saruman urges his fellow wizard to join with him in an alliance with

Sauron. Together they would use the power of the Ring to accomplish great good. Saruman is so nearly persuasive because his rhetoric so eloquently disguises the sinister quality of his Sauronic methods. He urges Gandalf to forgo his alliance with such weak creatures as men and hobbits, and thus to keep silent about the malevolent means necessary to accomplish such high-sounding ideals as Knowledge, Rule, and Order (1:272–73).

Tolkien understands that lovely words, like other kinds of beauty, can be put to evil purposes. He expresses alarm, in fact, that our world finds "it difficult to conceive of evil and beauty together. The fear of the beautiful fay [fairy] that ran through the elder ages almost eludes our grasp. Even more alarming: goodness is itself bereft of its proper beauty" (*"The Monsters and the Critics"* 151). Thus does the remarkable beauty of Galadriel, the elven-lady, expose her to unique temptation. If she were to accept the Ring of coercion, she confesses, her loveliness would become binding rather than inviting. Everyone would bow down and adore her beauty, hopelessly subjecting their wills to hers—thus putting an end to all true loveliness and liberty. Galadriel would come to preside over a despairing crowd of slaves, not a living community of souls. She would become a new and worse Sauron, a terrible Queen of Absolute Power.

Saruman is the master rhetorician in his ability to put beautiful words to bestial uses. When he later speaks from his tower called Orthanc ("Cunning Mind"), he addresses the Company with a voice that is suave and sweet in contrast to the seeming ineloquence of others. His enchanting words thus elicit easy agreement—until Gimli suddenly detects what is false in Saruman's mellifluous speech. Though dwarves often seem obtuse, this one acts like an early George Orwell writing *Animal Farm*. For Gimli penetrates Saruman's perverse attempt to give deceptively pleasant expression to sinister intentions, upending the obvious meaning of ordinary terms: "In the language of Orthanc help means ruin, and saving means slaying, that is plain" (2:184). Tolkien set his face like flint against such abominations. To preserve the humility implicit in things local and particular, he became the advocate of a cultural pluralism that has considerable postmodern resonance. As John Garth has recently demonstrated in *Tolkien and the Great War*, Tolkien's philological concerns were moral and historical from the start. His two forms of elvish—eventually they became known as Sindarin and Quenya—were based on the phonological principles he had learned from his study of Welsh and Finnish, respectively. These studies were premised, in turn, on Tolkien's conviction that Celtic and Northern cultures enshrined virtues that were largely absent, not only from the late modern world, but from the antique cultures of Greece and Rome as well.

Unlike both Victorian and contemporary enthusiasts for ancient Celtic life—naively believing that it was warmly feminine and spiritually comforting—Tolkien learned from the Celts that nature is teeming with *faery*—with elven creatures who, as ambassadors from the natural world, are rather like the angelic emissaries from the heavenly sphere who appear in Scripture: fierce, even frightening. In their close alliance with nature, they reveal it not to be as entirely rational and benignly ordered as Newtonian modernism once held, but rather as a living and dangerous realm, a raucous plentitude that invites Job-like awe and fearful participation, not a dead Cartesian domain that invites our bullying mastery. So, too, were ancient Northern languages and cultures also replete with a heroism that Tolkien found largely absent in both the ancient Mediterranean and the modern European world—namely, a dauntless human courage in the face of unremitting hostility, a heroic willingness to perish without any hope of postmortal reward.

Tolkien was convinced, moreover, that languages and cultures are inextricably rooted in time and place, that geography is hugely determinative of the way people think and act, that human variety is tied to the knotty particulars of culture, that a people's first products are its myths and stories, and that these narratives are the essential carriers of both religion and morality. He lamented, therefore, the ruthless monoculturalism of the Romans in failing to preserve the Northern European cultures that they had conquered. Not for Tolkien, it follows, was the Enlightenment-inspired desire to transcend locality for the sake of wooly universal values. He lived long enough, alas, to witness the slaughter of roughly 180 million souls in the name of such putatively timeless and placeless truths. As a Christian, Tolkien takes his stand on the terra firma of English language and soil, retrieving from other cultures and literatures those virtues that were congruent with his faith.

Tolkien also abominated the prospect that English would emerge as the new lingua franca of the modern commercial world. Such a commodifying of his native tongue would destroy the vitality of the many local languages that English would come to displace, Tolkien complained, while also ruining the rich local dialects of English itself. Such cultural and linguistic pluralism prevents Tolkien's imaginative metanarrative enterprise from becoming hegemonic or triumphalist. On the contrary, there is a postmodernist strain in Tolkien's celebration of other cultures and narratives than his own, his abjuring of abstract ideas and political programs as inherently coercive, and thus his ready confession that we inhabit a world of blessed linguistic particularity and saving cultural limitation. Tolkien's kind of postmodernism gladly and hopefully sets the various historical traditions in conversation and engagement with each other. Rather than being hermetically sealed off from communication and exchange, cultural traditions are meant to be mutually fructifying. Neither Israel nor the Church relies on a founding epic such as Homer and Virgil provided for their own cultures. Scripture is not an epic of triumphalism but a canon of failure and corruption and defeat: the prophets were slain and Christ was crucified. It is a narrative, instead, of a strange kind of hope, as victory and vindication come only to those who neither expect nor deserve it. Such antitriumphalism enables Tolkien, as we shall see, to envision true hope.

Tolkien's Postmodern Denial of Modern Foundationalism

In addition to his embrace of cultural pluralism, Tolkien remained implicitly postmodern in rejecting Enlightenment foundationalism—the notion, namely, that we can exercise our reason without presuppositions and apart from historical conditions. As Christopher Mitchell has observed, Tolkien's friend C. S. Lewis was devoted to the Socratic Club at Oxford—where he eagerly debated nonbelievers, attempting to flatten their arguments—for two reasons rather than one: not only to establish Christian truth against its opponents, but also to restore the Enlightenment ideal of free inquiry with its assurance that, if he and his interlocutors would fearlessly "follow the argument wherever it led," the truth would surely emerge (183, 193).[3] Thus would "the marketplace of ideas"—a revealing metaphor itself—produce a conclusion worthy of common consumption. It hardly needs observing that this foundationalist notion of free-thinking—thinking apart from tradition and without suppositions, and thus on the foundation of timeless rational categories—undergirds the Enlightenment quality of the American project, especially its political and educational enterprises. As no sort of foundationalist at all, Tolkien looked with considerable disdain on the apologetic work of his friend, calling Lewis "Everyman's theologian" (qtd. in Carpenter 232). This was far from a compliment, for only a Joe Blow sort of theologian, in Tolkien's estimate, would seek to defend Christianity by stepping outside it and proving its validity from some neutral point above the Church as well as above its cultured despisers and deniers.

The religious and fictional consequences for this divide between Lewis and Tolkien are enormous. For Lewis, unlike Tolkien, one must first hold to a worldview that admits the possibility of miracles before one can embrace the Christian gospel. Without such a metaphysical foundation, Christianity has nowhere to stand. In his fiction, therefore, Lewis creates a parallel universe that readers must first credit in order to enter imaginatively into it. Thus do we move from the natural and ordinary to the magical and supernatural realm as if they were essentially disjunct, even though they are finally knitted together. Lucy and Edmund, Susan and Peter, pass wondrously *through* the back of the wardrobe and *into* Narnia. Ransom travels *from* the earth *to* Malacandra and then Perelandra. In Lewis's fiction, the realm of Deep Magic always lies on the *other* side of the quotidian world.[4]

Not so for Tolkien. He seeks to lay no timeless and spaceless foundation on which his imaginative world might be erected. For him, transcendent reality is to be found in the depths of this world rather than in some arcane existence beyond it. Tolkien argues, for example, that fairy-stories "cannot tolerate any frame or machinery suggesting that the whole story in which they occur is a figment or illusion" ("On Fairy-Stories" 45). Such devices create a skepticism that undermines the truthfulness of the entire fictional enterprise: "The moment disbelief arises, the spell is broken" (60). Tolkien elects, therefore, to set his readers right down in the midst of Middle-earth. There is no time voyage or space travel in his fiction, no slipping through the back of a wardrobe into a magical realm. The Company of Nine receives its mandate from Gandalf, the wizard who has studied the history of the Ring ever so carefully, and they are bound by concrete ties of friendship and remembrance and trust rather than reliance on abstract principles. When they enter warfare, therefore, they do not shout such slogans as "Liberty, Equality, and Fraternity" but "The Shire!" Tolkien seeks, therefore, to convince his readers that his imaginative world is already and utterly real, having no other foundation than the consistency of its own laws and conventions—just as Israel and Christ and the Church are not erected on some prior culture or civilization but have their own inherent purposes and stand as drastic alternatives both to the best and worst qualities of their host cultures.

Tolkien's Postmodern Critique of Modern Coercions and Addictions

A third and even more important conjunction of Tolkien's work with postmodernism is to be found in his conviction that modern culture is coercive beyond all others, and that its worst coercions have resulted in the hideous wars of this the bloodiest of all ages. More people were killed by violent means—most of them by their own governments—in the twentieth century than in all preceding centuries combined: at least 180 million. As Tom Shippey has shown, Tolkien wrote directly in the face of unspeakable horrors—not only the evil regimes of Fascism and Nazism and Stalinism, but also "the routine bombardment of civilian populations, the use of famine as a political measure, the revival of judicial torture, the 'liquidation' of whole classes of political opponents, extermination camps, deliberate genocide and the continuing development of 'weapons of mass destruction' from chlorine gas to the hydrogen bomb" (324–25).

John Garth argues, in similar fashion, that Tolkien's grand legendarium was decisively shaped by his participation in the Great War. For while Tolkien began to construct his huge mythological system well before 1914, largely in response to his early immersion in the languages and literatures of the ancient North, he radically reshaped it because of the horrors he experienced at the Battle of the Somme. Like Karl Barth and many others, Tolkien came to discern that the Victorian age did not end nor did the twentieth century begin with the Queen's death in 1901. Something dreadfully new entered modern life in 1914—with this war that was supposed to end all wars. A fundamental cleavage in Western culture occurred at Verdun and Passchendaele, at Ypres and the Somme. These battles were conducted not with swords and catapults and rifles but with tanks and howitzers and airplanes. Here was revealed the essential modernist legacy: the murderous Machine. These new instruments of war were designed no longer to kill individual soldiers but to obliterate entire towns, to blast the countryside clean of forests and farms, and thus to lay waste to nearly every living thing. Thus Tolkien lived to witness the fulfillment of the dire prophecy that Nietzsche perversely celebrated in 1887: "we now confront a succession of a few warlike centuries that have no parallel in history; in short, . . . we have entered the *classical age of war*, of scientific and at the same time popular war on the largest scale (in weapons, talents, and discipline). All coming centuries will look back on it with envy and awe for its perfection" (V, Sect. 362:318).

Unlike Nietzsche, Tolkien did not respond to the nihilistic terrors of his time by recurring to the romantic idea of morally cleansing warfare. Rather did he set out to create a redemptive and antimilitaristic mythology for his native England. Convinced that the Arthurian legends were not only an inimical French import but also that their exclusively Christian character made them oblivious to the greatness of England's pagan past, how could Tolkien be faithfully English while not also becoming sinfully chauvinistic, even imperialistic? How, in short, could he retrieve the noblest virtues of his own land and people while avoiding any notion of "England, England, *über alles*"? The answer lay, in part, with his long immersion in *Beowulf* and the *Eddas* and the *Kalevala*. There he had discovered human heroes who face undefeatable enemies. Unlike their Greek and Roman counterparts, whom the gods either assist or frustrate, often for their own selfish ends, the deities of the aboriginal North do not intervene. On the contrary, they are themselves destroyed at Ragnarök. There, in that final battle, after all social and familial and cultural order has collapsed, everything returns to chaos and permanent night.

An implicit godlessness is inherent in the indigenous Nordic cultures. Tolkien saw a cosmic vacancy that eerily resembles our late-modern sense of divine absence and abandonment. As the Venerable Bede notes in his *Ecclesiastical History of the English People*, life in the pre-Christian world of the antique North could be best imaged in the flight of a sparrow into one end of a lighted mead hall and out the other (129): from the Void into a brief moment of light and warmth and merriment then back into the Void. The Nazis thus seized upon the dark traditions of the ancient North in order to create their own racist and imperialist myth of national greatness. In defense of a demonic *Blutbrüderschaft*, Hitler would slaughter seven million Jews—not to mention the millions of Gentiles who died either defending or defeating Hitlerism. As a lover of the antique Northern myths, how could Tolkien avoid the mythic nihilism that the Nazis had exploited? In a remarkable act of postmodern cultural and spiritual retrieval, Tolkien found his answer lying in a previously neglected quality of the heroism of the primeval North. The spirit that animates it, he remembered, is not preening victory so much as somber defeat.

At precisely this point, we discern why Tolkien is postmodern in his visionary hopefulness. If he were merely a reactionary antimodern, he would surely have opposed coercive power with its medieval counterpart—namely, by creating a warrior Christ such as we find in the Germanic recension of the four gospels called the *Heliand*. Instead, Tolkien made the radically antithetical and implicitly postmodern decision to enshrine loss rather than victory at the heart of his legendarium. Not only would he thus eschew any sort of English triumphalism; he would make his work thoroughly Christian as well. For the gospel is not a narrative of conquest but of defeat. The resurrection does not cancel so much as it vindicates the Cross as the essential instrument of Christian vocation. It summons Christ's disciples to live in the light of a strange sort of victory—to embody a heroism of submission rather than strength, to enflesh a triumph that comes not by seizing but by surrendering coercive power, even unto death.

By granting the Ring the power to coerce the will, Tolkien reveals what he regarded as the chief evil of the modern world—the various tyrannies that have trampled the human spirit. The most obvious examples are to be found in the assorted totalitarianisms of Germany and China and Russia. Quite apart from the multiplied millions who were slaughtered by their own governments, many more were made to live in constant fear of violating the oppressive state system and thus of bringing its terror upon them. Theirs was the daily dread that the Nine Walkers and their allies also confront. Never have fear and coercion been so pandemic, as millions were murdered for no reason at all, and as countless millions more were made to practice secret surveillance on their neighbors, lest they themselves be devoured by the gigantic bureaucracy of oppression and manipulation.

We who live in the so-called Free World—the nations of the democratic West—are hardly immune from this worst of modern legacies: mass death. This is not to deny the brutality of many premodern ages and cultures. In addition to practicing human sacrifice and cannibalism, our forebears often chopped heads and lopped hands for trivial offenses, and many of our ancestors lived in constant terror of various royal autocracies. Even so, our age is incomparably Sauronic. Our culture of comfort and convenience can be as subtly coercive as dictatorial regimes are obviously enslaving. In the United States, for instance, we have created a demonic drug culture and an enslaving eroticism that are hardly less addictive than the Ring itself. Perhaps we need reminding that, while Sauron is defeated at the Cracks of Mount Doom, readers are told that he will assume new and even more sinister guise. The Sorcerer is still subjecting the human spirit to hideously coercive pressures.

Almost everyone exposed to the Ring experiences its mesmerizing power, even the splendidly innocent Samwise Gamgee. Only Faramir, among our own human kind, remains so pure in spirit as to be totally immune to its magnetic attraction. Yet it is Frodo, the most valiant of the hobbits, whose will is most severely tested by the Ring. The closer he comes to the place where it was forged in the very heart of Sauron's evil empire, the greater its power over him. It has not only left Frodo physically emaciated; it has also drained his spirit, overwhelming him with hopelessness. The dread fear that he will not succeed in his mission, especially as the obstacles to his errand increase in fury and horror, afflicts Frodo with a paralyzing pessimism. The Ring takes control of him, both awake and asleep. "I begin to see it in my mind all the time," Frodo confesses, "like a great wheel of fire. . . . I am naked in the dark, Sam, and there is no veil between me and the wheel of fire. I begin to see it even with my waking eyes, and all else fails" (3:196, 215).

Having arrived at the Cracks of Mount Doom so weary that he cannot walk, Frodo seems incapable of self-defense, much less of self-will. But when Gollum leaps on his back in an attempt to seize the Ring, Frodo flicks him away as if he were an insect. Sam is rightly startled to find Frodo suddenly so strong and so merciless. In an act of seeming sanctity, Frodo is seeking to draw strength of will from the Ring in order to keep Sauron from getting it. So fully is he imbued with a kind of holy severity that Frodo undergoes a virtual transfiguration. Sam is given a sudden mystical vision of his friend. He sees Frodo as a stern and terrible figure, "untouchable now by pity, a figure robed in white" (3:221)—as if he were a new Saruman who has returned to replace Gandalf. Yet at the very apogee of his mistaken attempt to combat evil with evil, Frodo is overwhelmed by the Ring's bullying power, a force so strong that even Sauron can no longer command it. Frodo becomes, in fact, a virtual puppet for the ventriloquizing Ring. On all other occasions of true heroism, Frodo speaks in the passive voice, as Tolkien makes clear that he is being graciously acted upon no less than himself acting. But here he speaks in the active voice, loud and stentorian, since his will is no longer his own but belongs to an evil Other: "I have come," Frodo declares. "But I do not choose now to do what I came to do. I will not do this deed. The Ring is mine!" (3:223).

This is surely a great and terrible postmodern anticlimax to Tolkien's epic fantasy. After his year-long twilight struggle to take the Ring back to the Cracks of Mount Doom, Frodo fails at the very last—not because his will is weak but because the Ring finally overwhelms him. Thus the Quest culminates not in jubilant victory but in dispiriting defeat, as Tolkien deflates the reader's hope for a conventionally heroic ending— whether ancient or modern. It is a quintessentially postmodern moment, this failure of Frodo at the end of his Quest. It reveals the hobbit not to be a proverbial antihero who embodies a sort of upside-down goodness in his very insufficiency. Neither is he a tragic hero like Oedipus, who is ennobled even in his defeat. Rather is Frodo a postmodern hero, one who proves unable to resist the coercive force of the Ring, the Force that rules and finds and brings them all, and in the darkness binds them. His is a humbled and partial heroism, a goodness that remains terribly flawed, an achievement that is compromised—as we discover not only that much of the Shire had gone over to Sauron's side during their year-long absence, but also that Frodo himself is too wearied and worn by his Quest to enjoy the delights of victory. Instead, he departs for the Grey Havens amidst a tearful and enormously sad farewell.

Tolkien's Postmodern Answer to Modernist Individualism

What, then, is the nature of Tolkien's postmodern hope, especially in view of the novel's somber ending? The answer lies, at least in part, in his rejection of the modern view that all evils, being humanly generated, can be humanly overcome. What is broken can be fixed, so that even tragedy remains a problem to be solved rather than, as Flannery O'Connor said, a mystery to be endured. Against such modernist illusions, Tolkien demonstrates the postmodern truth that there are evils too great for human resistance, forces too powerful for human control, coercions that can be conquered only by the transcendent power of noncoercion. For while Tolkien is a multiculturalist, he is no religious pluralist. Without apology, he holds to the absolute finality of God's act of self-disclosure and self-definition in the Jews and Jesus and the Church. Yet Tolkien is ever so subtle in his depiction of divine authority and power, lest it appear hegemonic even in its silent and anonymous victory. Tolkien confesses, in fact, his desire to evoke a Presence that would be felt by its absence, and this is surely a postmodern tactic. The destruction of the Ring is accomplished, therefore, by the operation of secondary causes, not by supernatural intervention. The greed-maddened Gollum, having bitten the Ring off Frodo's finger, dances his jig of joy too near the brink of the volcanic fissure, thus tumbling into the infernal lava that alone can liquefy it. For the undiscerning reader, therefore, the Ring is destroyed by Gollum's hobbitic presumption and carelessness. For the discerning reader, however, the standard workings of natural causation and human willing are providentially guided. Just as Bilbo was meant to find the Ring, so was the Ring meant to be destroyed by the very evils that it has spawned. That so many millions of readers, whether Christian or not, have found the scene completely convincing demonstrates the wisdom of Tolkien's postmodern strategy. In a world driven by coercive power, only a modest, even a failed kind of heroism—failed because it is an uncoercive heroism—can yield lasting hope.

It is not difficult to discern what follows from Tolkien's account of Frodo's postmodern heroism: his insistence that the coercions plaguing late-modern life can best be combated by communities rather than individuals, yet not by strong and dominant communities, but rather by a seemingly weak and emarginated fellowship, by the little people of the world, the *populi minuti*. The Company of the Nine Walkers is a frail and often broken community. They are sustained throughout their seemingly hopeless struggle not by ties of self-interest, much less by contractual agreement. Their unbreakable bond—the covenant that undergirds their Quest—lies in their forgiving faith and their enduring trust in each other: in their friendship. Sauron, by contrast, can form no community. His orc-slaves serve him out of fear, not from devotion. Tolkien is convinced, in fact, that there can be no true company of vice, no fellowship of the wicked, however rigidly loyal its members may remain. Whether in the Taliban or the mafia, whether in Al Qaeda or street gangs, their common dedication to evil also makes their unity internecine from within and contemptible from without.

Over against all such aggregations of force, Tolkien poses the Nine Walkers. They are chosen by Elrond as Middle-earth's answer to the Nine Riders of Sauron—the nine mortal men who, wearing the rings that the Sorcerer made for them, have come totally under his power and thus have been turned into the fearsome Ringwraiths. But while the Nine Riders have been made into vaporous shadows of an evil sameness, the Nine Walkers are a remarkably diverse assemblage of the unlike. This surely is one of their most remarkably postmodern qualities. Yet Tolkien makes clear that diversity for its own sake is no virtue. The members of a polyglot group chosen only for their race and class and gender differences would, if lacking any commonailty of transcendent and self-surrendering purpose, merely take sides and fight, in a Hobbesian war of all against all—or else they would come to a contractual agreement about how best to preserve the self-interest of each individual—such contracts being inevitably broken when one person's or community's self-interest comes into radical conflict with another's. That many if not most educational institutions and business enterprises and nation-states manage to combine both of these unhappy modernist traits makes them notably unpleasant places.

Elrond chooses nine radically disparate travelers for a seemingly impossible journey by electing them according to the unique strengths they bring to their singular task. Gandalf is chosen for his wisdom, Aragorn for his royal link to the Ring, Boromir for his manly valor in battle, Legolas for his elvish mastery of the woods, Gimli for his dwarfish knowledge of mountains and mines, and Sam because he is Frodo's closest and most trustworthy companion. When Merry and Pippin also insist on accompanying Frodo, Elrond objects that such youngsters cannot imagine the terrors that lie ahead. Gandalf admits that if these two youngest hobbits could foresee the dangers that await them, they would surely hold back. Yet they would also be ashamed of their cowardice, and thus be made even unhappier at staying than going. Merry promises that they will hold hard to Frodo until the very end comes, no matter how bitter—maintaining their solidarity with him regardless of circumstances, and keeping confidences without fear of disclosure. They will not allow Frodo to go off and face danger and difficulty alone. Their deceptively simple reason for wanting to accompany Frodo is voiced by young Meriadoc Brandybuck himself: "We are your friends, Frodo" (1:116). With those four plain monosyllables, had Sauron heard and fathomed them, his mighty fortress at Barad-dûr would have been shaken to its foundations. For this little community of noncoercive weaklings, as we discover at the end, will help bring down the seemingly impregnable strongholds of the master Force-Wielder.

Not only does the Fellowship consist of friendly representatives of all the world's free peoples; it also includes two examples of historic enemies: the elf Legolas and the dwarf Gimli. Yet through their radically communal life of mutual devotion and sacrifice, they become the fastest of friends, even being allowed at the end to spend their lives together in Valinor. The Company also contains its own subverter and betrayer in the overly brave warrior Boromir. As is nearly always the case in Tolkien, community is broken by force. In a foolhardy desire to attack Sauron himself with the aid of the Ring, Boromir tries to seize it from Frodo. For such a heinous act of betrayal, he surely deserves to be ousted from the Fellowship. If his community were traditionally heroic or merely contractual, he would no doubt have been driven out, perhaps even executed. But as we have noticed briefly before, covenantal communities cannot be broken, even when egregious evils are committed by one of their own, since they are grounded in a redemptive and noncoercive source beyond themselves.

Here, then, is Tolkien's most radical postmodern move: not only to create a noncoercive community willing to suffer terrible loss but also to found it on a radical sense of forgiveness. The leitmotiv of the entire epic lies in Gandalf's crucial speech (though virtually ignored by film director Peter Jackson) explaining why Bilbo refused to kill the murderous Gollum, choosing to spare him in pity: "The pity of Bilbo may rule the fate of many" (1:58). It is important to note that Tolkien is at once unclassical and unmodern in this privileging of pity. In both ancient heroic societies as well as so-called modern meritocracies, pity is not a virtue but a vice. The Greeks, for example, extend pity only to the pathetic, the helpless, those who are able to do little or nothing for themselves. When Aristotle says that the function of tragic drama is to arouse fear and pity, he refers to the fate of a character such as Oedipus. We are made to fear that Oedipus's plight might tragically befall us, and thus do we pity him for his unjust fate. But whether in the ancient or the modern world, pity is never to be given to the egregiously unjust or undeserving, lest they be denied the justice that they surely merit. Yet *The Lord of the Rings* is a book imbued with such unmerited mercy and forgiveness. It is extended not only to the unworthy Gollum over and again, but also to the far unworthier Saruman, not once but thrice.

Perhaps knowing that his readers would not draw this historical distinction, and perhaps fearing that any overtly Christian allusions would meet with modernist incredulity, Tolkien offered his subtlest and least direct version of transcendent forgiveness in the death of Boromir. This exceedingly courageous warrior would seem to be the Judas of the story, for it is he who breaks the Fellowship by trying to seize the Ring from Frodo. Frodo in turn is forced to wear it in order to escape—not, alas, from orcs or Ringwraiths or even Saruman, but rather from his friend and fellow member of the Company. Yet as soon as Boromir has seen the horror that he has committed, he calls out to Frodo in shame at what he has done, pleading with him to return rather than to flee, explaining that a momentary madness had overtaken him. It is too late in the literal sense, because Frodo has already fled. But it is not too late in the spiritual sense, for in Boromir's death we are shown one truly binding tie that can knit a community of the weak and uncoercive into an unbreakable unity.

When Aragorn and Legolas and Gimli at last hear the horn of the desperate Boromir, they fly to him, only to find him dying from his orc-wounds, after he has slain many of the enemy in order that Sam and Frodo might go free. Yet Boromir does not boast of his valor, nor does Aragorn accuse him of betrayal. They perform, instead, the ultimately communal act, one that Tolkien conveys with supreme craft and tact—again proceeding with postmodern indirection rather than with overt Christian reference. Yet Tolkien allows the discerning reader to see that this reconciling act is also sacramental. For Aragorn, the future king with priestly powers, leads Boromir through the three steps of what was once called the sacrament of penance. First, the *confessio oris*, as Boromir admits that he tried to seize the Ring from Frodo. Yet Boromir's oral confession alone will not suffice unless he genuinely laments his evil deed, which he does, declaring, "I am sorry." Yet this *contritio cordis,* this sorrow of the heart, has validity only if it issues in *satisfactio operis*, works of satisfaction. And so Boromir poignantly concludes: "I have paid" (2:16).

Aragorn knows that these last words are not Boromir's vain boast that he has bravely recompensed for his community-rending sin; they are an admission, on the contrary, that he has paid the terrible price of breaking trust with Frodo and the Fellowship. Hence his last words: "I have failed" (2:16). Aragorn reads this final admission aright: it is Boromir's final penitential act, and thus a declaration that refutes itself, since it enables his pardon and thus his reconciliation with the Company he once betrayed. Aragorn absolves the dying hero by holding Boromir's hand and kissing his brow, assuring him that his life is not ending in the pain of absolute loss but in the confidence of permanent gain. "You have conquered," says the priest-king. "Few have gained such a victory. Be at peace! Minas Tirith shall not fall" (2:16).

Again, Tolkien offers an indirect affirmation. Boromir's last gesture, a silent smile, could be construed as his ironic doubtfulness, as if to say: "My people at Minas Tirith will hardly be saved by this rag-tag Company, on whom Sauron and his minions will feast like jackals." Boromir's smile may also be read as an expression of gratitude, a sign that he has received mercy and been restored to the community that he once had broken. On either reading, it is fair to say that Tolkien has placed a multicultural community at the center of his epic. It is not a company united either by high-minded ideals or private excellence. Rather is it a fellowship bound in unbreakable solidarity by the ultimate remedy to coercion: the act of pity and mercy and reconciliation. In a power-driven world characterized by community-denying coercions of all kinds, this noncoercive community, built on a willingness to lose and a willingness to forgive, is surely the key to Tolkien's postmodern appeal.

Tolkien and the Postmodern Tournament of Narratives

Our remaining task is to determine how such a community can make its witness to the postmodern world. Tolkien has made the answer plain though far from easy. It is not by adopting the tactics of modernism, especially not the modern enlargement of the technical and conceptual realm over the narrative and storied world. On the contrary, it will happen as we live and move and have our being in postmodern and hobbit-like fellowships. Among Christians, such companies will welcome others into the ever-widening circle called the "Church universal." Or else they will be contracted into an ever-shrinking circle by the persecution which truly noncoercive communities nearly always face. Even then, the tiny circles constituted by the blood of the martyrs will always remain the secret seed of the church.

Literarily, the postmodern task for Christians will consist in the indirect display of the Christian story by means of such carefully crafted works as *The Lord of the Rings*. The massively popular reception of Tolkien's epic demonstrates that Christians are able to enter what the late Baptist theologian James William McClendon called "the tournament of narratives" (Wood, "Alternative Vision" 16). McClendon discerned that the postmodern revolution, despite its potential relativism and even nihilism, enables Christians to set their tradition alongside its various competitors and companions. It also frees them to confess that theirs is fundamentally a narrative tradition, that they are sustained by the constant retelling and thus the repeated reenactment of the Christian story via the proclaimed Word and the dramatized sacraments. Even the creeds are but compressed plots, with their beginning, middle, and end.

So strong does story figure in Tolkien's work that he makes very few appeals to historical fact. Myth and history come to resemble each other, Tolkien notes, because, like story and truth, they are radically interdependent. Mythical pattern gives form to history, just as historical occurrence gives substance to myth. Story is not merely the vehicle of truth. Nor does Tolkien merely clothe Christian themes in the pleasant guise of fiction, as if the religious element were the kernel covered by the sweet coating of the mythology. Such a tactic would be a reversion to the old modernism. What we have in *The Lord of the Rings* is Tolkien's bold act of postmodern Christian confidence: a willingness to retell the gospel story in an indirect and mythological and anticipatory way, setting his metanarrative right alongside the many others—whether Joycean or Lawrentian, whether Nietzschean or Marxist, whether capitalist or socialist, liberal or conservative. Who wins and who loses this tournament is not Tolkien's primary concern; he desires only that his vision be seen and his voice heard. This, after all, is the chief Christian desire, since the metanarrative of the gospel is built upon a rejection and loss that constitute the ultimate victory.

Tolkien remained convinced that the first task of the Church is not to answer critics and to defeat enemies so much as to body forth its story in both word and deed. Nor can these be separated, for the right deed is nourished and enabled by the right word, the right story. This is the point that Samwise Gamgee, the least reflective of the hobbits, comes to discern. In the Tower of Cirith Ungol, as he and Frodo have begun to doubt whether their Quest will ever succeed—and thus to fear that they will die and be utterly forgotten—Sam seeks to distinguish between tales that really matter and those that do not. Many competing stories vie for our loyalty, and Sam is trying to distinguish among them, to locate the one hope-giving Story. Yet what is perhaps most notable is that Sam judges from a stance within his own story, not by seeking to transcend all narratives and assess them from a delusory eagle-eyrie perch above space and time. He declares that, if they themselves had known how hard was the road that lay ahead of them, they would never have come at all. Yet such is the way of stories, he adds, that rivet the mind and of songs that are sung for the ages. They are not about fellows who set out on adventures of their own choosing, Sam confesses, but about folks who found themselves traveling a path that they would have never elected to follow. But while they were chosen for the quest, they could have turned back. On the other hand, if they had turned back, no one would have ever sung their story, since those who defect from their calling are not celebrated. What counts, Sam wisely warns, is not that these heroes defeated their enemies and returned home safely to relish their triumph, but that they soldiered ahead and slogged forward to whatever end awaited them, whether good or ill.

If it is not a happy ending that matters, then what does? After all, each particular human story—and of course the stories of all fellowships and companies—will finally end and permanently disappear. Does this mean that all stories are equal—even perhaps equally futile and vain? Not at all, says Sam. What matters is whether our own little story forms part of an infinitely larger Story, and thus whether we rightly enact our own little roles within this grand saga. If we do, Sam adds, then when our own story is done, someone else will take the tale forward to either a better or worse moment in the ongoing drama. We cannot stand outside space and time to see the final outcome: we can only hope with a postmodern modesty. Yet we can also know what kind of story we are enacting: whether we are participants in one of the various modern stories of individualist coercion or statist domination, or whether we are actors in the only pre- and postmodern narrative that centers on those who, rather than coercing and killing their enemies, are willing to forgive them because they know themselves to have been forgiven. In this infinitely larger Story that encompasses all the smaller stories, nothing is lost—not even the story of modernity. For the shadow-side of every human story finds its surprising place in the one Story: "Why," says Sam, "even Gollum might be good in a tale" (2:322). No wonder, then, that so many readers of Tolkien have been converted, often unawares, from their hegemonic and triumphalist modernism to the humbly hopeful postmodernism of the hobbits and their friends.

Notes

1. Lord Herbert's five foundational principles were: (1) God exists; (2) he ought to be worshipped; (3) virtue and piety are the chief parts of worship; (4) there must be repentance for crimes and vices; (5) there are rewards and punishments in the life to come based on the ways we have acquitted ourselves in this earthly life (*De Veritate* 56).

2. In the Supreme Court case upholding *Roe v. Wade*, Justice Anthony Kennedy confirmed this Enlightenment assumption by declaring that every American has the right to construe reality for himself.

3. Yet, at least in *The Discarded Image*, Lewis rejected such a flight from history. There, rather than subjecting the medieval worldview to modernist terms, he demonstrates its own internal consistency and integrity, showing that it is as persuasive in its own way as the Darwinian naturalism that has replaced it. The English poet John Heath-Stubbs confessed to me, in a 1988 personal interview, that he became a Christian largely from hearing Lewis deliver *The Discarded Image* lectures at Oxford in the 1950s. They convinced him that the ancient Christian outlook was more cogent and persuasive than the materialist worldview of modernity.

4. In *Till We Have Faces*, Lewis locates his narrative in the ancient pagan kingdom of Glome, making its life-world marvelously and chillingly credible. Yet even there, Orual remains torn by the natural-supernatural distinction, as she is forced to decide whether Psyche's heavenly palace is objectively real or her own subjective illusion.

Works Cited

Abanes, Richard. *Harry Potter and the Bible: The Menace Behind the Magick*. Camp Hill, PA: Horizon, 2001.

Abrahamson, Irving, ed. *Against Silence: The Voice and Vision of Elie Wiesel*. Vol. 1. New York: Holocaust Library, 1985. 3 vols.

Alcoff, Linda M. "Phenomenology, Post-structuralism, and Feminist Theory on the Concept of Experience." *Feminist Phenomenology*. Ed. Linda Fisher and Lester Embree. Dordrecht: Kluwer, 2000. 39–56.

Allen, Pat B. *Art Is A Way of Knowing*. Boston: Shambala, 1995.

American Beauty. Dir. Sam Mendes. Perf. Kevin Spacey and Annette Bening. Universal Studios, 1999.

Anzaldúa, Gloria. *Borderlands/La Frontera*. San Francisco: Aunt Lute, 1997.

Arendt, Hannah. "Isak Dinesen 1885–1962." Foreword. *Daguerrotypes and Other Essays*. By Isak Dinesen. Chicago: U of Chicago P, 1979. vii–xxv.

Arnold, Matthew. *Prose and Poetry*. Ed. Archibald L. Bouton. New York: Scribner, 1927.

Auchincloss, Eve, and Nancy Lynch. "Disturber of the Peace: James Baldwin—An Interview." *Conversations with James Baldwin*. Ed.

Fred L. Standley and Louis H. Pratt. Jackson, MS: UP of Mississippi, 1989. 64–82.

Augustine. *Confessions*. Trans. Henry Chadwick. New York: Oxford UP, 1991.

———. *On Christian Doctrine*. New York : Liberal Arts, 1958.

———. "Sermon 87." *The Works of Saint Augustine: A Translation for the 21st Century*. Trans. Edmund Hill. Ed. John E. Rotelle. Vol. 3. New York: New City P, 1990. 397–418. 3 vols.

Babette's Feast. Dir. Gabriel Axel. Perf. Stéphane Audran, Bibi Anderson, Birgitte Federrspiel, Bodil Kjer, Jarl Kulle, Jean-Philippe LaFont, and Ebbe Rode, 1987. DVD. MGM Home Entertainment, 2001.

Baldwin, James. *The Amen Corner*. New York: Vintage, 1998.

———. *Another Country*. New York: Vintage, 1993.

———. *Blues for Mister Charlie*. New York: Dial, 1964.

———. *The Evidence of Things Not Seen*. New York: Holt, 1985.

———. *The Fire Next Time*. 1963. New York: Vintage, 1993.

———. *Giovanni's Room*. New York: Dell, 1964.

———. *Go Tell It on the Mountain*. New York: Dell, 1970.

———. *Going to Meet the Man*. New York: Dell, 1966.

———. *The Price of the Ticket: Collected Nonfiction 1948–1985*. New York: St. Martin's P, 1985.

———. *Tell Me How Long the Train's Been Gone*. New York: Dial, 1968.

Baldwin, James, and Margaret Mead. *A Rap on Race*. Philadelphia: J. B. Lippincott, 1971.

Ball, Alan. *American Beauty*. London: FilmFour, 2000.

Barnes, Hazel. *The Story I Tell Myself*. Chicago: U of Chicago P, 1997.

Barr, Marlene. "Food for Postmodern Thought: Isak Dinesen's Female Artists as Precursors to Contemporary Feminist Fabulators." *Feminism, Utopia, and Narrative*. Ed. Libby Falk Jones and Sarah Webster Goodwin. Knoxville: U of Tennessee P, 1990. 21–33.

Battleship Potemkin. Dir. Sergei M. Eisenstein, Grigori Aleksandrov. Perf. Aleksandr Antonov, Vladimir Barsky, and Grigori Aleksandrov. 1925. DVD. Delta Music, 2004.

Bauckham, Richard, and Trevor Hart. *Hope against Hope: Christian Eschatology at the Turn of the Millennium*. Grand Rapids: Eerdmans, 1999.

Bauman, Zygmunt. *Intimations of Postmodernity*. London: Routledge, 1991.

———. *Life in Fragments: Essays in Postmodern Morality*. Oxford: Blackwell, 1995.

Beam, Lindy. "Exploring Harry Potter's World." *Teachers in Focus on the Web* Dec. 1999. 14 Feb. 2000. <http://www. focusonthefamily.org>.

Beauvoir, Simone de. *The Second Sex.* New York: Vintage, 1989.

Becker, Ernest. *The Denial of Death.* New York: Free Press, 1973.

Becker, Jurek. *Jakob the Liar.* Trans. Leila Vennewitz. New York: Plume, 1999.

———. *Jacob the Liar.* Screenplay for 1974 East German film. Dir. Frank Beyer. Perf. Vlastimil Brodsky. Icestorm International, 1997.

Beckett, Samuel. *Three Novels: Molloy, Malone Dies, The Unnamable.* New York: Grove Press, 1955. 179–288.

Bede. *Ecclesiastical History of the English People.* Trans. Leo Sherley-Price. London: Penguin, 1955.

Begbie, Jeremy. "Through Music: Sound Mix." *Beholding the Glory.* Ed. Jeremy Begbie. Grand Rapids: Baker, 2000.

Beker, J. Christiaan. *Suffering and Hope: The Biblical Vision and the Human Predicament.* Philadelphia: Fortress, 1987.

Bell, Linda. "Friendship, Love, and Experience." *Feminist Phenomenology.* Ed. Linda Fisher and Lester Embree. Dordrecht: Kluwer, 2000. 195–211.

Benavides, Gustavo. "Modernity." *Critical Terms for Religious Studies.* Ed. Mark C. Taylor. Chicago: U of Chicago P, 1998. 186–204.

Berenbaum, Michael. *The Vision of the Void: Theological Reflections on the Works of Elie Wiesel.* Middletown, CT: Wesleyan UP, 1979.

Berger, Peter. *A Far Glory: The Quest for Faith in an Age of Credulity.* New York: Macmillan, 1992.

———. *A Rumor of Angels: Modern Society and the Rediscovery of the Supernatural.* 1969. New York: Doubleday, 1990.

———. *The Sacred Canopy: Elements of a Sociological Theory of Religion.* New York: Doubleday, 1967.

———, ed. *The Desecularization of the World: Resurgent Religion in World Politics.* Grand Rapids: Eerdmans, 1999.

Bergin, Lisa. "Gloria Anzaldúa's *Borderlands/La Frontera* and Rene Descartes' *Discourse on Method*: Moving beyond the Canon in Discussion of Philosophical Ideas." *Presenting Women Philosophers.* Ed. Cecile T. Tougas and Sara Ebenreck. Philadelphia: Temple UP, 2000. 139–46.

Bernstein, Susan David. "Confessing Feminist Theory: What's 'I' Got to Do with It?" *Hypatia* 7 (1992): 120–47.

Bettelheim, Bruno. *The Uses of Enchantment: The Meaning and Importance of Fairy Tales.* 1975. New York: Vintage, 1989.

Betts, Doris. *Souls Raised from the Dead.* New York: Scribner, 1994.

———. "Southern Writers and the Bible." *Friends of the Library Dinner Meeting.* Chapel Hill: U of North Carolina, 1984. *Bookmark* 53 (1985): 3–11.

———. "Whispering Hope." *Image* 7 (Fall 1994): 79–84. *Image.* 11 Sept. 2005. <http:// www.imagejournal.org/back/007/betts_essay.asp>.

Binder, Wolfgang. "James Baldwin, an Interview." *Conversations with James Baldwin.* Ed. Fred L. Standley and Louis H. Pratt. Jackson: UP of Mississippi, 1989. 190–209.

Blake, William. *Complete Poetry and Prose.* Ed. David V. Endman. Garden City, NY: Doubleday, 1965

Bloch, Ernst. *Philosophy of Hope.* Trans. Neville Plaice, Stephen Plaice, and Paul Knight. Oxford: Blackwell, 1986. 3 vols.

Bloom, Harold. *The American Religion: The Emergence of the Post-Christian Nation.* New York: Simon, 1992.

Bondi, Roberta. *Memories of God: Theological Reflections on a Life.* Nashville: Abingdon, 1995.

———. *Night on the Flint River. An Accidental Journey in Knowing God.* Nashville: Abingdon, 1999.

Braude, Claudia. "Elusive Truths." *Mail and Guardian Online.* 17 June 1998. 30 July 1999. <http://www.mg.co.za/articledirect.aspx?articleid=182212&area=%2farchives_print_edition%2f>.

Brody, Howard. *Stories of Sickness.* New Haven: Yale UP, 1987.

Brown, Robert McAfee. *Elie Wiesel: Messenger to All Humanity.* Notre Dame: U of Notre Dame P, 1983.

Bruner, Jerome. *On Knowing: Essays for the Left Hand.* Cambridge, MA: Belknap-Harvard UP, 1962.

Burke, Edmund. *On the Sublime and Beautiful.* Vol. 24, part 2 of 50. The *Harvard Classics.* New York: P. F. Collier, 1909–14. *Bartleby.com.* 2001. 9 Dec. 2004. <http://www. bartleby.com/24/2/>.

Burrell, David B., and Elena Malits. *Original Peace: Restoring God's Creation.* New York: Paulist P, 1997.

Cargas, Harry James, ed. *Harry James Cargas in Conversation with Elie Wiesel.* New York: Persea, 1978.

———, ed. *Responses to Elie Wiesel.* New York: Persea, 1978.

———. "What Is a Jew? Interview of Elie Wiesel." *Responses to Elie Wiesel.* Ed. Harry James Cargas. New York: Persea, 1978. 150–57.

Carpenter, Humphrey. *The Inklings: C.S. Lewis, J.R.R. Tolkien, Charles Williams and Their Friends.* Boston: Houghton Mifflin, 1979.

Cavanaugh, William T. "The City: Beyond Secular Parodies." *Radical Orthodoxy*. Ed. John Milbank, Catherine Pickstock, and Graham Ward. New York: Routledge, 1999. 182–200.

Census Data Center and South Dakota State Department of Rural Sociology. *South Dakota Population, Housing, and Farm Census Facts*. Brookings: South Dakota State U, 1993.

Chambers, Joseph. "Harry Potter and the Antichrist." *Paw Creek Ministries*. 14 June 2001. <http://www.pawcreek.org/articles/end-times/HarryPotterAndTheAntichrist.htm>.

Chatman, Seymour. *Story and Discourse: Narrative Structure in Fiction and Film*. Ithaca: Cornell UP, 1978.

Chesterton, G. K. *A Short History of England, 1917*. London: Chatto & Windus, 1930.

Cimino, Richard, and Don Lattin. *Shopping for Faith: American Religion in the New Millennium*. San Francisco: Jossey-Bass, 1998.

Coles, Robert. *The Secular Mind*. Princeton: Princeton UP, 1999.

Colson, Charles. "Can Anything Good Come out of Hollywood?" *Breakpoint Online*. 28 March 2000. 11 Sept. 2005. <http://www.pfmonline.net/transcripts.taf?_function=detali&ID=905&site=BPT&_UserReference=D16CE3CF47D481BA43238FF9>.

Cook, Hugh. *The Homecoming Man*. Oakville, Ontario: Mosaic, 1989.

Costello, Elvis, and the Attractions. "All This Useless Beauty." By Elvis Costello. *All This Useless Beauty*. Warner Brothers, 1996.

Craven, Kenneth. "A Catholic Poem in Time of War." *A Hidden Presence: The Catholic Imagination of J. R. R. Tolkien*. Ed. Ian Boyd, C.S.B., and Stratford Caldecott. South Orange, NJ: Chesterton P, 2003. 145–63.

Cupitt, Don. *What Is a Story?* London: SCM, 1991.

DailyConfession.com. D. O. U., Inc. 2000–2005. <http://www.dailyconfession.com>.

Dante Alighieri. *The Divine Comedy: Inferno*. Trans. Allen Mandelbaum. New York: Bantam, 1980.

Davidson, Osha Gray. *Broken Heartland: The Rise of America's Rural Ghetto*. New York: Free P, 1990.

Dawkins, Richard. *A Devil's Chaplain: Reflections on Hope, Lies, Science, and Love*. New York: Houghton Mifflin, 2003.

DeCurtis, Anthony. " 'An Outsider in this Society': An Interview with Don DeLillo." *South Atlantic Quarterly* 89.2 (1990): 281–304. Rpt. in *Introducing Don DeLillo*. Ed. Frank Lentricchia. Durham: Duke UP, 1996. 43–66.

Delbanco, Andrew. *The Real American Dream: A Meditation on Hope.* Cambridge, MA: Harvard UP, 1999.

DeLillo, Don. *Mao II.* New York: Penguin, 1991.

———. *The Names.* New York: Knopf, 1982.

———. *Underworld.* New York: Scribner's, 1997.

———. *White Noise: Text and Criticism.* Ed. Mark Osteen New York: Penguin, 1985.

Dewey, John. *A Common Faith.* New Haven: Yale UP, 1950.

Dinesen, Isak. *Babette's Feast and Other Anecdotes of Destiny.* New York: Vintage, 1988.

Doody, Terrence. *Confession and Community in the Novel.* Baton Rouge: Louisiana State UP, 1980.

Duncan, Marvin, Dennis Fisher, and Mark Drabenspott. "America's Heartland: Can It Survive?" *USA Today: The Magazine of the American Scene* 125.2614 (1996): 12–15.

Duvall, John. *Don DeLillo's* Underworld*: A Reader's Guide.* New York: Continuum, 2002.

Eagleton, Terry. *After Theory.* New York: Basic, 2003.

Eck, Diana. *A New Religious America: How a Christian Country Has Now Become the World's Most Religiously Diverse Nation.* San Francisco: Harper, 2001.

Egan, Timothy. "Along the Missouri, Life Ebbs and Flows." *The New York Times.* 1 June 2003, A1.

Eliot, Alexander. *The Universal Myths.* New York: Truman Talley-Meridian, 1976.

Eliot, T. S. *The Complete Poems and Plays, 1909–1950.* New York: Harcourt, 1971.

Ellul, Jacques. *Hope in Time of Abandonment.* Trans. C. Edward Hopkin. New York: Seabury, 1973.

Engels, Friedrich. *The Condition of the Working Class in England.* Ed. and trans. W. O. Henderson and W. H. Chaloner. Oxford: Blackwell, 1958.

Estes, Clarissa Pinkola. *Women Who Run with the Wolves.* New York: Ballantine, 1995.

Estes, David C. "An Interview with James Baldwin." *Conversations with James Baldwin.* Ed. Fred L. Standley and Louis H. Pratt. Jackson: UP of Mississippi, 1989. 270–80.

Estess, Ted L. *Elie Wiesel.* New York: F. Ungar, 1980.

Fatula, Mary Ann. "Current Trends: Feasts of Grace." *Spirituality Today* 41.2 (1989): 166–73.

Fawcett, John. "Harry Potter Review." *Leanne Payne Pastoral Care Ministries Newsletter* (Winter 2000/2001): 5–6.

Felman, Shoshana, and Dori Laub. *Testimony: Crises of Witnessing in Literature, Psycholoanalysis, and History.* New York: Routledge, 1992.

Fiddes, Paul. *The Promised End: Eschatology in Theology and Literature.* Challenges in Contemporary Theology. Oxford: Blackwell, 2000.

Fields, Don. *Nehemiah: The Courage to Face Opposition.* Downers Grove, IL: InterVarsity, 2002.

Filmer, Kath. *Scepticism and Hope in Twentieth Century Fantasy Literature.* Bowling Green, OH: Bowling Green State U Popular P, 1992.

Ford, Paul. *Companion to Narnia.* New York: HarperCollins, 1994.

Foucault, Michel. *The History of Sexuality.* Trans. Robert Hurley. 3 vols. New York: Vintage, 1978–1980. Trans. of *Histoire de la sexualité.* 1976–1978.

Frankel, Ellen, and Betsy Platkin Teutsch. *The Encyclopedia of Jewish Symbols.* Northvale, NJ: Jacob Aronson, 1992.

Frankl, Viktor. *Man's Search for Meaning: An Introduction to Logotherapy.* 3rd ed. New York: Touchstone, 1984.

Frye, Northrop. *The Critical Path: An Essay on the Social Context of Literary Criticism.* Bloomington: Indiana UP, 1971.

Gallagher, Susan VanZanten. *Truth and Reconciliation: The Confessional Mode in South African Literature.* Portsmouth, NH: Heinemann, 2002.

Gallup, George, Jr., and D. Michael Lindsey. *Surveying the Religious Landscape: Trends in U.S. Beliefs.* Harrisburg: Morehouse, 1999.

Garth, John. *Tolkien and the Great War: The Threshold of Middle-earth.* Boston: Houghton Mifflin, 2003.

Gilman, Sander L. *How I Became A German: Jurek Becker's Life in Five Worlds.* Washington, DC: German Historical Institute, 1999.

Gobodo-Madikizela, Pumla. *A Human Being Died That Night: A South African Story of Forgiveness.* Boston: Houghton Mifflin, 2003.

Goldberg, Jake. *The Disappearing American Farm.* New York: Franklin Watts, 1995.

Goldstone, Richard J. Foreword. *Between Vengeance and Forgiveness: Facing History after Genocide and Mass Violence.* By Martha Minow. Boston: Beacon Press, 1998. ix–xii.

Goldthwaite, John. *The Natural History of Make-Believe: A Guide to the Principal Works of Britain, Europe, and America.* Oxford: Oxford UP, 1996.

Good News Bible. New York: American Bible Society, 1976.

Grenz, Stanley, and John R. Franke. *Beyond Foundationalism: Shaping Theology in a Postmodern Context.* Louisville: Westminster John Knox P, 2001.

Griesinger, Emily. "The Shape of Things to Come: Toward an Eschatology of Literature." *Christianity and Literature* 53.2 (Winter 2004): 203–31.

Gunton, Colin E. *The Christian Faith: An Introduction to Christian Doctrine.* Oxford: Blackwell, 2002.

Hall, John. "James Baldwin Interviewed." *Conversations with James Baldwin.* Ed. Fred L. Standley and Louis H. Pratt. Jackson: UP of Mississippi, 1989. 98–107.

Hampton, Howard. "Lynch Mob." Rev. of *The Straight Story.* Dir. David Lynch. *Artforum* January 2000: 21–22.

Hardy, Thomas. *Collected Poems.* London: Macmillan, 1920.

Harmon, A. G. "Doris Betts: An Interview." *Image* 11 (Fall 1995): 51–68.

Harp, Lonnie. "The Bitter Harvest." *Education Week* 14.8 (1994): 24–29.

"Harry Potter Books Spark Rise in Satanism among Children." *The Onion on the Web.* 17 July 2000. 19 Dec. 2000. <http://www.theonion.com/onion3625/harry_potter.html>. Reprinted in Robert Siegel, ed. *Dispatches from the Tenth Circle: TheBest of the Onion.* New York: Three Rivers Press, 2001. 36.

Hart, Francis R. "Notes for an Anatomy of Modern Autobiography." *New Directions in Literary History.* Ed. Ralph Cohen. Baltimore: Johns Hopkins UP, 1974. 221–47.

Hart, Trevor. "Imagination for the Kingdom of God? Hope, Promise, and the Transformative Power of an Imagined Future." *God Will Be All in All: The Eschatology of Jürgen Moltmann.* Ed. Richard Bauckham. Edinburgh: T&T Clark, 1999. 49–76.

Hauerwas, Stanley. *A Community of Character.* Notre Dame: U of Notre Dame P, 1981.

———. *The Hauerwas Reader.* Ed. John Berkman and Michael Cartwright. Durham: Duke UP, 2001.

Havel, Václav. *Disturbing the Peace.* London: Faber & Faber, 1990.

Hawkins, Anne Hunsaker. *Reconstructing Illness.* West Lafayette, IN: Purdue UP, 1993.

Heaney, Seamus. *The Redress of Poetry.* London: Faber & Faber, 1995.

Heath-Stubbs, John. Personal Interview with Ralph Wood. 13 June 1988.

Hedley, Jane. "Nepantilist Poetics: Narrative and Cultural Identity in the Mixed-Language Writings of Irena Klepfisz and Gloria Anzaldúa." *Narrative* 4 (1996): 36–54.

Hegeman, David Bruce. *Plowing in Hope: Toward a Biblical Theology of Culture*. Moscow, ID: Canon P, 1999.

Hemingway, Ernest. *The Sun Also Rises*. New York: Scribner, 1926.

Herbert, Lord of Cherbury. *De Veritate*. 3rd ed. Trans. Meyrick H. Carré. Bristol: J. W. Arrowsmith, 1937. Trans. of *On Truth in Distinction from Revelation, Probability, Possibility, and Error*. 1645.

Herwitz, Daniel. *Race and Reconciliation: Essays from the New South Africa*. Public Worlds. Vol. 11. Minneapolis: U of Minnesota P, 2003.

Herzlich, Claudine, and Janine Pierret. *Illness and Self in Society*. 1984. Trans. Elborg Forster. Baltimore: Johns Hopkins UP, 1987.

Hibbs, Thomas. *Shows about Nothing: Nihilism in Popular Culture from the Exorcist to Seinfeld*. Dallas: Spence Publishing, 1999.

Hodgson, Bryan. "Tough Times on the Prairie." *National Geographic,* March 1987: 320–47.

hooks, bell. *All About Love: New Visions*. New York: Harper, 2000.

———. *Teaching to Transgress*. New York: Routledge, 1994.

———. *Where We Stand: Class Matters*. New York: Routledge, 2000.

———. *Wounds of Passion: A Writing Life*. New York: Henry Holt, 1997.

Hopkins, Gerard Manley. *God's Grandeur and Other Poems*. 1918. Repr. New York: Dover, 1995.

Horowitz, Sara R. *Voicing the Void: Muteness and Memory in Holocaust Fiction*. Albany: State U of New York P, 1997.

Huntley, E. D. *Amy Tan: A Critical Companion*. Westport, CT: Greenwood, 1998.

Huttar, Charles. "C. S. Lewis' Narnia and the 'Grand Design.'" *The Longing for a Form: Essays on the Fiction of C. S. Lewis*. Ed. Peter Schakel. Grand Rapids: Baker, 1977. 119–35.

Huxley, Thomas. *Christianity and Agnosticism: A Controversy*. New York: Humboldt, 1889.

Hyde, Harlow. "Slow Death in the Great Plains." *Atlantic Monthly* June 1997: 42–45.

Insdorf, Annette. *Indelible Shadows: Film and the Holocaust*. 1983. Rev. ed. Cambridge: Cambridge UP, 2003.

"Interview." In *Philosophy Now*. October/November 2003. One Good Move Website. <http://onegoodmove.org/1gm/1gmarchive/001171.html>.

Iversen, Pat Shaw. "The Norwegian Folk Tales and Their Illustrators." Introduction. *Norwegian Folk Tales*. By Peter Christen Asbjørnsen and Jørgen Moe. Trans. Pat Shaw Iversen and Carl Norman. New York: Pantheon Books, 1960. 5–8.

Jacoby, Russell. *The End of Utopia: Politics and Culture in an Age of Apathy.* New York: Basic, 1999.

Jakob the Liar. Dir. Peter Kassovitz. Perf. Robin Williams. DVD. Columbia Tristar, 2004.

Jefferson, Thomas. *Notes on the State of Virginia.* New York: Harper & Row, 1964.

Jencks, Christopher. *The Homeless.* Cambridge: Harvard UP, 1994.

Jenkins, Jerry B., and Tim LaHaye. Left Behind Series. Wheaton, IL: Tyndale, 1995–2005.

Jenkins, Philip. *The Next Christendom: The Coming of Global Christianity.* New York: Oxford UP, 2002.

Jenson, Robert W. "How the World Lost Its Story." *First Things* 36 (1993): 19–24.

Jewett, Robert. *St. Paul Returns to the Movies.* Grand Rapids: Eerdmans, 1999.

Johnson, Daniel. "Contrary Hopes: Evangelical Christianity and the Decline Narrative." *The Future of Hope: Christian Tradition amid Modernity and Postmodernity.* Ed. Mirâslôv Volf and William Katerberg. Grand Rapids: Eerdmans, 2004. 27–48.

Jones, Joe R. *A Grammar of Christian Faith.* Vol. 2. Blue Ride Summit, PA: Rowman & Littlefield, 2002.

Julian of Norwich. *Revelations of Divine Love.* Trans. Clifton Wolters. New York: Penguin, 1966.

Karabell, Zachary. *A Visionary Nation: Four Centuries of American Dreams and What Lies Ahead.* New York: HarperCollins, 2001.

Kassovitz, Peter, and Didier Decoin. *Jakob the Liar.* Dir. Peter Kassovitz. Perf. Robin Williams and Alan Arkin. Columbia Pictures, 1999.

Katerberg, William. "Redemptive Horizons, Redemptive Violence, and Hopeful History." *Fides et Historia* 36.1 (Winter/Spring 2004): 1–14.

Kaup, Monika. *Crossing Borders: An Aesthetic Practice in Writings by Gloria Anzaldúa.* Iowa City: U of Iowa P, 1996.

Keating, Ann Louise. "Myth Smashers, Myth Makers: (Re)Visionary Techniques in the Works of Paula Gunn Allen, Gloria Anzaldúa, and Audre Lorde." *Critical Essays: Gay and Lesbian Writers of Color.* Ed. Emmanuel S. Nelson. New York: Haworth, 1993. 73–93.

———. "Writing, Politics, and las Lesberadas: Platicando con Gloria Anzaldúa." *Frontiers* 14 (1993): 105–30.

Kermode, Frank. *The Sense of an Ending: Studies in the Theory of Fiction.* New York: Oxford, 2000.

Ketchin, Susan. "Doris Betts: Resting on the Bedrock of Original Sin." *The Christ-Haunted Landscape: Faith and Doubt in Southern Fiction.* Jackson: U of Mississippi P. 230–59.

Kierkegaard, Søren. *A Kierkegaard Anthology.* Ed. Robert Bretall. New York: Random House, 1946.

Kilpatrick, William, Gregory Wolfe, and Suzanne Wolfe. *Books That Build Character: A Guide to Teaching Your Child Moral Values.* New York: Simon & Schuster, 1994.

Koestler, Arthur. *The Yogi and the Commissar and Other Essays.* New York: Macmillan, 1945.

Kreider, Tim, and Rob Content. Rev. of *The Straight Story.* Dir. David Lynch. *Film Quarterly* (Fall 2000): 26–33.

Kreitzer, Larry. *Gospel Images in Fiction and Film: On Reversion the Hermeneutical Flow.* London: Sheffield Academic, 2002.

———. *The New Testament in Fiction and Film: On Reversing the Hermeneutical Flow.* Sheffield, England: JSOT, 1993.

———. *The Old Testament in Fiction and Film: On Reversing the Hermeneutical Flow.* London: Sheffield Academic, 1994.

———. *Pauline Images in Fiction and Film: On Reversing the Hermeneutical Flow.* London: Sheffield Academic, 1999.

Kren, George M., and Leon Rappoport. *The Holocaust and the Crisis of Human Behavior.* 1980. Rev. ed. New York: Holmes & Meier, 1994.

Krog, Antjie. *Country of My Skull: Guilt, Sorrow, and the Limits of Forgiveness in the New South Africa.* New York: Random, 1998.

Lane, Dermot A. *Keeping Hope Alive: Stirrings in Christian Theology.* Dublin: Gill & Macmillan, 1996.

Langbaum, Robert. *The Gayety of Vision: A Study of Isak Dinesen's Art.* New York: Random, 1964.

Lasch, Christopher. *The True and Only Heaven: Progress and Its Critics.* New York: Norton, 1991.

Leitch, Thomas M. *What Stories Are: Narrative Theory and Interpretation.* University Park: Pennsylvania State UP, 1986.

Leizman, Reva B. "The Road Towards Regeneration and Salvation in the Novels of Elie Wiesel." Diss. Case Western Reserve U, 1977.

Lentini, Alison. "Harry Potter: Occult Cosmology and the Corrupted Imagination." *Spiritual Counterfeits Project Journal* 23.4–24.1 (Spring/Summer 2000): 18–29.

Lester, Julius. "James Baldwin—Reflections of a Maverick." *Conversations with James Baldwin.* Ed. Fred L. Standley and Louis H. Pratt. Jackson: UP of Mississippi, 1989. 222–31.

Lewis, C. S. *The Allegory of Love.* Oxford: Oxford UP, 1936.

————. *The Discarded Image: An Introduction to Medieval and Renaissance Literature.* 1964. New York: Cambridge UP, 1971.

————. *The Lion, the Witch, and the Wardrobe.* New York: HarperCollins, 1950.

————. *Mere Christianity.* New York: Macmillan, 1943.

————. *Miracles: A Preliminary Study.* Glasgow: Collins Fount, 1960.

————. "On Three Ways of Writing for Children." *C. S. Lewis: On Stories and Other Essays on Literature.* Ed. Walter Hooper. 1966. New York: Harcourt, 1982. 31–43.

Lewis, Ida. "Conversation: Ida Lewis and James Baldwin." *Conversations with James Baldwin.* Ed. Fred L. Standley and Louis H. Pratt. Jackson: UP of Mississippi, 1989. 83–92.

Lincoln, Abraham. *Speeches and Writings, 1859–1865.* Ed. Don Fehrenbacher. New York: Library of America, 1988.

Lindvahl, Terry. Private correspondence with Robert K. Johnston. n.d.

Lloyd, Genevieve. *The Man of Reason: "Male" and "Female" in Western Philosophy.* Minneapolis: U of Minnesota P, 1984.

Locke, John. "A Letter Concerning Toleration." Trans. William Popple. 1689. Constitution Society Website. 31 Oct. 2005. <http://www.constitution.org/jl/tolerati.htm>.

Longino, Bob. "'Beauty' Maker." *Atlanta Journal-Constitution*, 26 March 2000: L4.

Lynch, Michael F. "A Glimpse of the Hidden God: Dialectical Visions in Baldwin's *Go Tell It on the Mountain*." *New Essays on* Go Tell It on the Mountain. Ed. Trudier Harris. Cambridge: Cambridge UP, 1996. 29–57.

————. "Just Above My Head: James Baldwin's Quest for Belief." *Literature and Theology* 11.3 (September 1997): 284–98.

————. "Staying Out of the Temple: Baldwin, the African American Church, and *The Amen Corner*." *Re-viewing James Baldwin: Things Not Seen.* Ed. D. Quentin Miller. Philadelphia: Temple UP, 2000. 33–71.

Lynch, William F., S.J. *Images of Hope: Imagination as Healer of the Hopeless.* Baltimore: Helicon, 1965.

Lyon, David. *Postmodernity.* 2nd ed. Minneapolis: U of Minnesota P, 1999.

Lyotard, Jean-François. *The Postmodern Condition: A Report on Knowledge.* Trans. G. Bennington and B. Massami. Minneapolis: U of Minnesota P, 1984.

MacIntyre, Alasdair. *After Virtue: A Study in Moral Theory.* 2nd ed. Notre Dame: U of Notre Dame P, 1984.

8

MacLaverty, Bernard. *Grace Notes*. 1997. London: Vintage, 1998.

Marx, Karl, and Friedrich Engels. *The Communist Manifesto*. 1848. New York: International, 1979.

Masterson, James, and Ralph Klein. *Psychotherapy of the Disorders of the Self: The Masterson Approach*. New York: Brunner-Mazel, 1989.

McAdams, Dan P. "Unity and Purpose in Human Lives: The Emergence of Identity as a Life Story." *Studying Persons and Lives*. Ed. A. I. Rabin, Robert A. Zucker, Robert A. Emmons, and Susan Frank. New York: Springer, 1990. 148–200.

McClure, John. "Postmodern/Post-Secular: Contemporary Fiction and Spirituality." *Modern Fiction Studies* 41 (1995): 141–63.

McGrath, Alister. *A Brief History of Heaven*. Oxford: Blackwell, 2003.

———. *Christian Theology: An Introduction*. 3rd ed. Oxford: Blackwell, 2001.

———. *The Foundations of Dialogue in Science and Religion*. Oxford: Blackwell, 1998.

———. *The Twilight of Atheism: The Rise and Fall of Disbelief in the Modern World*. New York: Random, 2004.

McKim, Donald. *Westminster Dictionary of Theological Terms*. Louisville: Westminster John Knox, 1996.

Memento. Dir. Christopher Nolan. Perf. Guy Pearce and Carrie-Anne Moss. Columbia Tristar, 2000.

Middleton, J. Richard, and Brian J. Walsh. *Truth Is Stranger Than It Used to Be: Biblical Faith in a Postmodern Age*. Downers Grove, IL: InterVarsity, 1995.

Milbank, John. *Theology and Social Theory: Beyond Secular Reason*. Cambridge: Blackwell, 1991.

Miller, Donald E. *Reinventing American Protestantism: Christianity in the New Millennium*. Berkeley: U of California P, 1997.

Miller, Joshua L. "The Discovery of What It Means to Be a Witness: James Baldwin's Dialectic of Difference." *James Baldwin Now*. Ed. Dwight A. McBride. New York: New York UP, 1999. 331–59.

Miller, Nancy. *Getting Personal*. New York: Routledge, 1991.

Minow, Martha. *Between Vengeance and Forgiveness: Facing History after Genocide and Mass Violence*. Boston: Beacon P, 1998.

Mitchell, Christopher. "Following the Argument Wherever It Leads." *Inklings-Jahrbuch* 17 (1999): 172–96.

Mizruchi, Susan L. "Introduction." *Religion and Cultural Studies*. Ed. Susan L. Mizruchi. Princeton: Princeton UP, 2001.

Moltmann, Jürgen. *The Coming of God: Christian Eschatology*. Trans. Margaret Kohl. Minneapolis: Fortress, 1996.

———. *The Experiment Hope.* Trans. M. Douglas Meeks. Philadelphia: Fortress, 1975.

———. *Theology of Hope: On the Grounds and the Implications of a Christian Eschatology.* Trans. James W. Leitch. 1967. Minneapolis: Fortress, 1993.

Moore, R. Laurence. *Selling God: American Religion in the Marketplace of Culture.* New York: Oxford UP, 1994.

Mossman, James. "Race, Hate, Sex, and Colour: A Conversation with James Baldwin and Colin MacInnes." *Conversations with James Baldwin.* Ed. Fred L. Standley and Louis H. Pratt. Jackson: UP of Mississippi, 1989. 46–58.

Muggeridge, Malcolm. *Something Beautiful for God.* San Francisco: Harper, 1971.

Murray, John Andrew. "The Trouble with Harry." *Focus on the Family Citizen Magazine.* 5 Feb. 2000. <http://www.family.org/cforum/citizenmag/index.cfm?ym=200002>.

Natov, Roni. "Harry Potter and the Extraordinariness of the Ordinary." *The Lion and the Unicorn* 25.2 (2001): 310–27.

Nelson, Michael. "The Gospel According to Lewis." *The American Prospect* 13.iv (2002): 29–32.

Nietzsche, Friedrich. *The Gay Science.* Trans. Walter Kaufmann. New York: Vintage, 1974.

Noll, Mark. "What Evangelical Media?" *Books and Culture* (May/June 2003): 6.

Norris, Kathleen. *Dakota: A Spiritual Geography.* Boston: Houghton Mifflin, 1993.

O'Connor, Flannery. "Revelation." *Everything That Rises Must Converge.* 1956. New York: Noonday, 1998. 191–218.

O'Doherty, Paul. "Becker's *Bronstein's Kinder* and the Question of Post-Shoah Jewish Assimilation in Germany." *Jurek Becker.* Contemporary German Writers. Ed. Colin Riordan. Cardiff: U of Wales P, 1998. 45–56.

O'Donovan, Oliver. "Keeping Body and Soul Together." *On Moral Medicine: Theological Perspectives in Medical Ethics.* Ed. Stephen Lammers and Allen Verhey. Grand Rapids: Eerdmans, 1998. 223–38.

Okada, John. *No-No Boy.* 1957. Seattle: U of Washington P, 1998.

Osteen, Mark. *American Magic and Dread: Don DeLillo's Dialogue With Culture.* Philadelphia: U of Pennsylvania P, 2000.

Pawley, Daniel. "Ecclesiastes—Reaching Out to the 20th Century." *Bible Review* 6 (October 1990): 34–36.

Payer, Lynn. *Medicine and Culture: Varieties of Treatment in the United States, England, West Germany, and France.* 1988. New York: Holt, 1996.

Phillips, Patrick. "The Film Spectator." *An Introduction to Film Studies.* Ed. Jill Nelmes. New York: Routledge, 1999. 129–60.

Pieper, Josef. *Faith, Hope, Love.* San Francisco: Ignatius, 1997.

———. *On Hope.* Trans. Mary Frances McCarthy. San Francisco: Ignatius, 1986.

Planned Parenthood of Southeastern Pennsylvania v. Robert P. Casey. Supreme Court of the United States. No. 91-744. 505 U.S. 833. 29 June 1992, Undecided.

Podles, Mary Elizabeth. "Babette's Feast: Feasting with Lutherans." *Antioch Review* 50 (1992): 551–66.

Polkinghorne, John. *The God of Hope and the End of the World.* New Haven: Yale UP, 2002.

Porter, Horace A. *Stealing the Fire: The Art and Protest of James Baldwin.* Middletown, CT: Wesleyan UP, 1989.

Price, Reynolds. *A Whole New Life.* New York: Scribner's, 2000.

Quantic, Diane D. "Women's Response to the Great Plains: Landscape as Spiritual Domain in Kathleen Norris and Sharon Butala." *Literature and Belief* 23.1 (2003): 57–79.

Rashkin, Esther. "A Recipe for Mourning: Isak Dinesen's *Babette's Feast.*" *Style* 29 (1995): 356–75.

Remnick, David. "Exile on Main Street: Don DeLillo's Undisclosed *Underworld.*" *The New Yorker,* 15 September 1997: 42–48.

Rice, Laurie. "Devil of a Tale." *Reader's Digest,* April 2001: 18.

Ricoeur, Paul. *The Conflict of Interpretations: Essays in Hermeneutics.* Evanston: Northwestern UP, 1974.

———. *Time and Narrative.* Vol. 1. Trans. Kathleen McLaughlin and David Pellauer. Chicago: U of Chicago P, 1984. 3 vols.

Roof, Wade Clark. *Spiritual Marketplace: Baby Boomers and the Remaking of American Religion.* Princeton: Princeton UP, 1999.

Rorty, Richard. *Achieving Our Country: Leftist Thought in Twentieth-Century America.* Cambridge: Harvard UP, 1998.

———. *Philosophy and Social Hope.* London: Penguin, 1999.

Rowling, J. K. *Harry Potter and the Chamber of Secrets.* New York: Scholastic, 1999.

———. *Harry Potter and the Goblet of Fire.* New York: Scholastic, 2000.

———. *Harry Potter and the Half-Blood Prince.* New York: Scholastic, 2005.

————. *Harry Potter and the Order of the Phoenix*. New York: Scholastic, 2003.

————. *Harry Potter and the Prisoner of Azkaban*. New York: Scholastic, 1999.

————. *Harry Potter and the Sorcerer's Stone*. New York: Scholastic, 1997.

"Rowling's 'Guilt' at Potter Wealth." *BBC News UK Edition Online*. 19 June 2003. 30 Jan. 2004. <http://news.bbc.co.uk/ 1/hi/entertainment/arts/3004760.stm>.

Sacks, Oliver. *The Man Who Mistook His Wife for a Hat*. 1970. New York: HarperCollins, 1985.

Sanders, John. *The God Who Risks: A Theology of Providence*. Downers Grove, IL: InterVarsity, 1998.

Saterlee, James, and Gary A. Goreham. *Changes in South Dakota Farms, 1935–1982*. Brookings, SD: Department of Rural Sociology and Agricultural Experiment Station, 1985.

Sayer, George. *Jack: C. S. Lewis and His Times*. San Francisco: Harper, 1988.

Schreiter, Robert J. *Reconciliation: Mission and Ministry in a Changing Social Order*. Boston Theological Institute Series. Vol. 3. Maryknoll, NY: Orbis, 1992. 3 vols.

Schuster, Ekkehard, and Reinhold Boschert-Kimmig. *Hope against Hope: Johann Baptist Metz and Elie Wiesel Speak Out on the Holocaust*. Mahwah, NJ: Paulist P, 1999.

Schwobel, Christopher. "The Church as a Cultural Space: Eschatology and Ecclesiology." *The End of the World and the Ends of God: Science and Theology on Eschatology*. Ed. John Polkinghorne and Michael Welker. Harrisburg: Trinity International, 2000. 107–24.

Scott, Joan. "Experience." *Feminists Theorize the Political*. Ed. Judith Butler and Joan Scott. New York: Routledge, 1992. 22–40.

Scott, Katherine Hutt. "South Dakotan: Rural Life in Jeopardy: Towns Struggling and Schools Closing." *Argus Leader*, 3 Febuary 2001: A1.

Seligman, Martin E. P. *Learned Optimism*. New York: A. A. Knopf, 1990.

Shade, Patrick. *Habits of Hope: A Pragmatic Theory*. Nashville: Vanderbilt UP, 2001.

Shapiro, Marc. *J. K. Rowling: The Wizard behind Harry Potter*. New York: Griffon-St. Martin's, 2000.

Shippey, Tom. *The Road to Middle-earth*. Rev. ed. Boston: Houghton Mifflin, 2003.

Sibelman, Simon P. *Silence in the Novels of Elie Wiesel.* New York: St. Martin's, 1995.

Silverwood, Brian. "Building Healthy Bones." *Pediatric Nursing* 15.5 (June 2003): 27–29.

Simms, Laura. *The Bone Man: A Native American Modoc Tale.* New York: Hyperion, 1997.

Sittler, Joseph. *Gravity and Grace: Reflections and Provocations.* Minneapolis: Augsburg, 1986.

Skar, J. "The Origin of the Huldre Folk: The Huldre Minister." *Gamalt fra Setesdal.* 1903. Trans. Pat Shaw Iversen. 8 Feb. 2003. <http://www.feri.com/dawn/huldrefolk.html>.

Smith, James K. A. "Determined Hope: A Phenomenology of Christian Expectation." *The Future of Hope: Christian Tradition amid Modernity and Postmodernity.* Ed. Mirâslôv Volf and William Katerberg. Grand Rapids: Eerdmans, 2004. 200–27.

———. *The Fall of Interpretation: Philosophical Foundations for a Creational Hermeneutic.* Downers Grove, IL: InterVarsity, 2000.

Snyder, C. R. *The Psychology of Hope: You Can Get There from Here.* New York: Free P, 1994.

Sobol, Joshua. Personal Interview with Eric Sterling. Catholic University, Washington DC. 22 Feb. 1995.

Stark, Rodney. *For the Glory of God: How Monotheism Led to Reformations, Science, Witch-Hunts, and the End of Slavery.* Princeton: Princeton UP, 2003.

———. *One True God: Historical Consequences of Monotheism.* Princeton, NJ: Princeton UP, 2001.

Steele, Michael R. *Christianity, Tragedy, and Holocaust Literature.* Westport, CT: Greenwood, 1995.

Steiner, George. *After Babel.* 2nd ed. Oxford: Oxford UP, 1992.

———. *Real Presences.* Chicago: U of Chicago P, 1989.

Stoeger, William. "Cultural Cosmology and the Impact of the Natural Sciences on Philosophy and Culture." *The End of the World and the Ends of God: Science and Theology on Eschatology.* Ed. John Polkinghorne and Michael Welker. Harrisburg: Trinity International, 2000. 65–77.

———. "Scientific Accounts of Ultimate Catastrophes in Our Life-Bearing Universe." *The End of the World and the Ends of God: Science and Theology on Eschatology.* Ed. John Polkinghorne and Michael Welker. Harrisburg: Trinity International, 2000. 19–28.

Sutton, Roger. "Potter's Field." *Hornbook Magazine.* Sept./Oct. 1999: 500–501.

Sydnor, Jr., Charles W. "The Inmate World: Life and Death in Auschwitz." *Art and Auschwitz: The Last Expression*. Ed. David Mickenberg, Corrine Granot, and Peter Hayes. Evanston, IL: Northwestern UP, 2003. 14–21.

Tan, Amy. Interview with Jami Edwards. *bookreporter.com*. 2003. 31 July 2003. <http://www.bookreporter.com/authors/au-tan-amy.asp>.

———. Interview with Sophia Ruiz. *Pages online*. March–April 2001. 31 July 2003. <http://www.ireadpages.com/archive/pdf/marapr01.pdf>.

Taylor, Charles. "Every Moment's a Gift." Rev. of *The Straight Story*. Dir. David Lynch. *Salon.com*. 15 Oct. 1999. 16 July 2003. <http://archive.salon.com/ent/movies/review/1999/10/15/straight/>.

———. *Varieties of Religion Today: William James Revisited*. Cambridge: Harvard UP, 2002.

Taylor, Daniel. *The Healing Power of Stories*. New York: Doubleday, 1996.

Taylor, Jane. *Ubu and the Truth Commission*. Cape Town: U of Cape Town P, 1998.

Taylor, Mark. *Erring: A Postmodern A/Theology*. Chicago: U of Chicago P, 1987.

The Fisher King. Dir. Terry Gilliam. Perf. Robin Williams, Jeff Bridges, Mercedes Ruehl, and Amanda Plummer. Screenplay Richard LaGravenese. Columbia Tristar, 1991.

The Lord of the Rings: The Fellowship of the Ring. Dir. Peter Jackson. Perf. Elijah Wood, Ian McKellen, and Cate Blanchett. New Line Cinema, 2002.

The Lord of the Rings: The Return of the King. Dir. Peter Jackson. Perf. Elijah Wood, Ian McKellen, and Cate Blanchett. New Line Cinema, 2003.

The Lord of the Rings: The Two Towers. Dir. Peter Jackson. Perf. Elijah Wood, Ian McKellen, and Cate Blanchett. New Line Cinema, 2002.

The Mabinogion. Trans. Charlotte E. Guest. Toronto: Dover, 1997.

The Sixth Sense. Dir. M. Night Shyamalan. Perf. Bruce Willis and Haley Joel Osment. Hollywood Pictures Spyglass Entertainment, 1999.

"The Skeletal System." 3 Feb. 2002. <http://www4. tpgi.com.au/users/amcgann/bod/skeletal.html>.

The Straight Story. Dir. David Lynch. Perf. Richard Farnsworth and Sissy Spacek. Disney, 1998.

Thiessen, Gesa E. *Theology and Modern Irish Art*. Dublin: Columba, 1999.

Thomas, Dylan. *Collected Poems*. New York: New Directions, 1953.

Thompson, Deborah. "Deconstructing Harry: Casting a Critical Eye on the Witches and Wizards of Hogwarts." *Beauty, Brains, and Brawn: The Construction of Gender in Children's Literature*. Ed. Susan Lehr. Portsmouth, NH: Heinemann, 2001. 42–50.

Thompson, Francis. *The Hound of Heaven*. Philadelphia: P. Reilly, 1916.

Tinder, Glenn. *The Fabric of Hope: An Essay*. 2nd ed. Grand Rapids: Eerdmans, 2001.

Todorov, Tzvetan. *Hope and Memory: Lessons from the Twentieth Century*. Trans. David Bellos. Princeton: Princeton UP, 2003.

Tolkien, J. R. R. "On Fairy-Stories." *Essays Presented to Charles Williams*. Ed. C. S. Lewis. 1947. Grand Rapids: Eerdmans, 1966. 38–89.

———. *The Fellowship of the Ring*. 2nd ed. Boston: Houghton Mifflin, 1967.

———. *"The Monsters and the Critics" and Other Essays*. Ed. Christopher Tolkien. Boston: Houghton Mifflin, 1984.

———. *The Return of the King*. 2nd ed. Boston: Houghton Mifflin, 1967.

———. *The Two Towers*. 2nd ed. Boston: Houghton Mifflin, 1965.

Tracy, David. *The Analogical Imagination: Christian Theology and the Culture of Pluralism*. New York: Crossroad, 1981.

Troyes, Chrétien de. "Le Conte de Gral." *Arthurian Romances*. Ed. William W. Kibler. New York: Penguin, 1991. 381–494.

Truth and Reconciliation Website. 23 Feb. 2005. <http://www.doj.gov.za/trc/legal/act9534.htm>.

Tucker, Nicholas. "The Rise and Rise of Harry Potter." *Children's Literature in Education* 30.4 (1999): 221–34.

Twelve Monkeys. Dir. Terry Gilliam. Perf. Bruce Willis and Madeleine Stowe. Universal Studios, 1996.

Understanding Osteoporosis. Chicago: American Medical Association and National Osteoporosis Foundation. n.d. In use by physicians, 2002.

Van Doren, Mark. "Sonnet 25." *Collected Poems, 1922–1938*. New York: Holt, 1939: 228.

Volf, Mirâslôv. *Exclusion and Embrace: A Theological Exploration of Identity, Otherness, and Reconciliation*. Nashville: Abingdon, 1996.

———. *Work in the Spirit: Toward a Theology of Work*. New York: Oxford UP, 1991.

Volf, Miroslav, and William Katerberg, eds. *The Future of Hope: Christian Tradition amid Modernity and Postmodernity*. Grand Rapids: Eerdmans, 2004.

Walker, Joe. "Exclusive Interview with James Baldwin." *Conversations with James Baldwin*. Ed. Fred L. Standley and Louis H. Pratt. Jackson: UP of Mississippi, 1989. 127–41.

Weber, Max. *The Protestant Ethic and the Spirit of Capitalism*. Trans. Talcott Parsons. New York: Scribner's, 1958.

———. "Science as a Vocation." *From Max Weber: Essays in Sociology*. Ed. and trans. H. H. Gerth and C. Wright Mills. New York: Oxford UP, 1946. 129–56.

Wiesel, Elie. *And the Sea Is Never Full: Memoirs, 1969–*. Trans. Marion Wiesel. New York: Knopf, 1999.

———. *Conversations*. Ed. Robert Franciosi. Jackson: U of Mississippi P, 2002.

———. *La Ville de la chance*. Paris: Ed. du Seuil, 1962.

———. *Memoirs: All Rivers Run to the Sea*. New York: Knopf, 1995.

———. Personal Interview with Carole Lambert. 6 October 1997.

———. *Tous les Fleuves Vont à la Mer*. Paris: Ed. du Seuil, 1994.

———. *The Town Beyond the Wall*. Trans. Stephen Becker. New York: Schocken, 1982.

———. *Twilight*. Trans. Marion Wiesel. New York: Schocken, 1988.

Williams, Rhys W. "German Literature and its Discontents: Jurek Becker's *Warnung vor dem Schriftsteller*." *Jurek Becker*. Ed. Colin Riordan. Cardiff: U of Wales P, 1998. 85–93.

Wood, Ralph. "An Alternative Vision for the Christian University." Address to the faculty of Campbell U, Buies Creek, NC. 30 March 2004.

———. *The Gospel According to Tolkien: Visions of the Kingdom in Middle-earth*. Louisville: Westminster John Knox, 2003.

Woodman, Marion. *Bone: Dying into Life*. New York: Viking-Penguin, 2000.

Woolf, Virginia. *A Room of One's Own*. San Diego: Harcourt, 1986.

Woster, Terry. "Sociologist Offers Idea to Preserve Rural South Dakota." *Argus Leader*, 18 January 2001: A1.

Wuthnow, Robert. *After Heaven: Spirituality in America Since the 1950s*. Berkeley: U of California P, 1998.

Yancey, Philip. *The Jesus I Never Knew*. Grand Rapids: Zondervan, 1995.

Zipes, Jack. *The Troublesome Success of Children's Literature from Slovenly Peter to Harry Potter*. New York: Routledge, 2001.

Zizek, Slavoj. *The Sublime Object of Ideology*. London: Verso, 1989.

List of Contributors

Kelvin Beliele is a Ph.D. student at the University of New Mexico, specializing in American literature. His dissertation explores genre subversion and nineteenth-century gender and sexuality in the travel writings of Bayard Taylor, Charles Warren Stoddard, and Herman Melville. He has published a recent article in *Literary Voices: American Literature in Historical Context, 1870–1920* (Twayne, 2006) and has two pieces forthcoming in *The Encyclopedia of Native American Literature,* and *Country Lyricists and Their Contribution to the American Literary Canon.*

Anne-Marie Bowery is associate professor of philosophy and director of graduate studies in philosophy at Baylor University. Her research interests include Plato, Augustine, and Friedrich Nietzsche, as well as pedagogy and technology. She has published articles in *Christian Scholar's Review, Teaching Philosophy, Analecta Husserliana,* and in a variety of edited collections. She is currently working on a book, *A Philosophic Muse: Plato's Socrates as Narrator.*

Harold K. Bush, Jr. is associate professor of English at Saint Louis University. He has published widely on a number of American authors. His first book, *American Declarations: Rebellion and Repentance in*

American Cultural History (U of Illinois, 1999), studies the development of American rhetoric and ideology within the context of religious and moral vocabularies. He has recently completed *Mark Twain and The Spiritual Crisis of the Gilded Age* (U of Alabama P, 2006), which focuses on Twain's engagement with the religion of the Gilded Age. His chapter here is a preview of his next book project, *The End of America*, which will theorize and analyze America as an eschatological project.

Kevin L. Cole is chair of humanities and associate professor of English at the University of Sioux Falls. He has published articles on many writers, including Jonathan Swift, Henry Fielding, John Milton, Cormac McCarthy, and Henry Carlisle. In 2002 he received a grant from the National Endowment for the Humanities to study regional literature, and in 2003, through the South Dakota Council for the Arts, he received a grant from the National Endowment for the Arts for his first collection of short stories.

Martha Greene Eads is associate professor and chair of the department of language and literature at Eastern Mennonite University in Harrisonburg, Virginia. She was a Lilly Fellow in Humanities and the Arts at Valparaiso University from 2001–2003 and has published essays in *Christianity and Literature, The Cresset, Modern Drama,* and *Theology.*

Mark Eaton is associate professor of English at Azusa Pacific University, where he teaches American literature and film studies. He has published articles and reviews in *The Boston Book Review, Modern Fiction Studies, Pedagogy, Prospects: An Annual of American Cultural Studies, Studies in American Fiction,* and *The Edith Wharton Review.* Other essays have appeared in *Henry James on Stage and Screen* (Palgrave, 2000), and *There She Is, Miss America; Pageants and the Politics of Sex, Beauty, and Race in America* (Palgrave, 2004).

Susan VanZanten Gallagher is director of the Center for Scholarship and Faculty Development and professor of English at Seattle Pacific University. She is coauthor with Roger Lundin of *Literature through the Eyes of Faith* (Harper and & Row, 1989), editor of *Postcolonial Literature and the Biblical Call for Justice* (UP of Mississippi, 1994), coeditor with Mark Walhout of *Literature and the Renewal of the Public Sphere* (St. Martin's, 1999), author of *A Story of South Africa: J. M. Coetzee's Fiction in Context* (Harvard UP, 1991), and *Truth and Reconciliation: The Confessional Mode in South African Literature* (Heinemann, 2002).

Emily Griesinger is professor of English at Azusa Pacific University, where she teaches courses in British literature, religion and literature, and children's literature. Her article on Toni Morrison's *Beloved* in *Christianity and Literature* received the 2003 Lionel Basney Award. A second article, "Your Daughters Shall Prophesy: The Charismatic Spirituality of Hildegard of Bingen," published in *Christian Scholar's Review* in 2000, won the Charles J. Miller Christian Scholar's Award. She has also published in *Books and Culture* and *Women's Studies: An Interdisciplinary Journal.*

Michael B. Herzog is pprofessor of English and senior faculty advisor to the academic vice-president at Gonzaga University. He specializes in medieval English and German literature and the poetry of Geoffrey Chaucer, as well as literature and film. His plays based on medieval poems have been produced in the United States and England, and he is currently writing a novel about Geoffrey Chaucer.

Robert K. Johnston is professor of theology and culture at Fuller Theological Seminary. President of the American Theological Society for 2003–2004, he also cochairs the Reel Spirituality Institute at Fuller, which seeks to engage Hollywood and the church in fruitful dialogue. His recent books include *Reel Spirituality: Theology and Film in Dialogue* (Baker, 2000), *Life Is Not Work / Work Is Not Life* (Wildcat Canyon, 2001, with J. Walker Smith), *Finding God in the Movies: 33 Films of Reel Faith* (Baker, 2004, with Catherine M. Barsotti), and *Useless Beauty: Ecclesiastes Through the Lens of Contemporary Film* (Baker, 2004).

Carole J. Lambert is professor of English and director of the Office of Research at Azusa Pacific University. She received a Fulbright scholarship to conduct research in Brussels, Belgium, plus four National Endowment for the Humanities grants. She is the author of *The Empty Cross: Medieval Hopes, Modern Futility in the Theater of Maurice Maeterlink, Paul Claudel, August Strindberg, and George Kaiser* (Garland, 1990), and coeditor with William D. Brewer of *Essays on the Modern Identity* (Peter Lang, 2000). She has recently published a book on Elie Wiesel, *Is God Man's Friend? Theodicy and Friendship in Elie Wiesel's Novels* (Peter Lang, 2005).

D. Brent Laytham is associate professor of theology and ethics at North Park Theological Seminary in Chicago. He is editor and coauthor of *God Is Not: Religious, Nice, One of Us, an American, a Capitalist* (Brazos

P, 2004). He is an ordained elder in the United Methodist Church. His teaching and research interests include Christian theology, worship, and ethics, and their intersections with the practices, life, and thought of the Christian community.

Elaine Lux is professor of English and deputy chair of the English department at Nyack College's Manhattan site. She is also a part-time mentor for SUNY Empire State College. She has done workshops on using writing and story to enhance healing, and she has presented papers at literary conferences on a variety of authors, including C. S. Lewis, Toni Morrison, and Amy Tan. Her essay "The Expanding 'I' in Absolute Truths" will appear in *Scandalous Truths: Essays By and About Susan Howatch,* edited by Bruce Arthur Johnson and Charles A. Huttar (Susquehanna P, 2006). Her current research focuses on intersections between the sacred and the secular in contemporary literature.

Marilyn Chandler McEntyre is professor of English at Westmont College, where she was teacher of the year in the humanities in 1999. She is author of *A Healing Art: Regeneration through Autobiography* (Garland P, 1990), *Dwelling in the Text: Houses in American Fiction* (U of California P, 1991), *In Quiet Light: Poems on Vermeer's Paintings* (Eerdmans, 2000), and *Drawn to the Light: Poems on Rembrandt's Biblical Paintings* (Eerdmans, 2003). She is also coeditor of *Approaches to Teaching Literature and Medicine* (Modern Language Association, 1999) and a contributing editor to *Literature and Medicine: An Online Annotated Bibliography*. Her essay "Institutional Impediments: Medical Bureaucracies in the Movies" appeared in *Sutured Words: Medicine and Film* (Duke, 2004).

Maire Mullins serves as coeditor of the journal *Christianity and Literature* and teaches as a visiting lecturer at Pepperdine University. Her articles on Walt Whitman have appeared in *Tulsa Studies in Women's Literature, The Walt Whitman Quarterly Review, The Walt Whitman Encyclopedia, The Tohoku Journal of American Studies* (Sendai, Japan), and *The American Transcendental Quarterly*. She has also written articles on Willa Cather, Hisaye Yamamoto, Isak Dinesen, and William Butler Yeats, and has published in the journal *Academic Leader*.

Barry Sloan is a lecturer in English at the University of Southampton, UK. He is the author of *Writers and Protestantism in the North of Ireland: Heirs to Adamnation?* (Irish Academic P, 2000), *The Pioneers of Anglo-*

Irish Fiction 1800–1850 (Barnes & Noble, 1986), and many articles on Irish writing, including a chapter on Protestant life-writing to be included in a collection of essays on twentieth-century Irish autobiography forthcoming from Palgrave/Macmillan.

Eric Sterling is distinguished research professor of English at Auburn University, Montgomery. He is the author of *Life in the Ghettos during the Holocaust* (Syracuse UP, 2005) and has published essays on bystanders during the Holocaust, Arthur Miller's *Incident at Vichy,* Shimon Wincelberg's *Resort 76,* Joshua Sobol's *Adam,* Martin Sherman's *Bent,* Peter Barnes's *Auschwitz, the kindertransports,* and the film *Schindler's List.*

Ralph C. Wood is professor of theology and literature at Baylor University. He is coeditor of *Civil Religion and Transcendent Experience: Studies in Theology and History, Psychology and Mysticism* (Mercer, 1988); and author of *The Comedy of Redemption: Christian Faith and Comic Vision in Four American Novelists* (U of Notre Dame P, 1988), *The Gospel According to Tolkien: Visions of the Kingdom in Middle-earth* (Westminster John Knox, 2003); *Contending for the Faith: The Church's Engagement with Culture* (Baylor UP, 2003), and *Flannery O'Connor and the Christ-Haunted South* (Eerdmans, 2004).

Index of Names